# THE TIME

# OF

# JACOB'S TROUBLE

## DR. LYLE P. MURPHY

*We acknowledge with gratitude the kind permission of Good News Publishers, Wheaton, Illinois, for permission to reprint the text of Tract #6A02,* **How to Recognize the Messiah.** *The tract is reproduced in its entirety in Chapter Nine. (Good News Publishers, 1300 Crescent Street, Wheaton, Il 60187. Copyright 1990, printed in USA).*

Copyright © 2004 by Lyle P. Murphy

For permission requests, write to the author at:
P.O. Box 1414
Lee's Summit MO 64063-7414

Printed in the United States of America

ISBN: 0-9742743-7-2

*For our daughters, Ruth and Kathy.*
*Godly wives and mothers.  Thanks!*

**Cover Design:  Jane Murphy**

*The author wishes to extend his sincere
appreciation to Mrs. Helen Axell, Carol Dillard,
Sr. Patricia Mulcahy, O.P., Mrs. Karen Potter,
David Schlotzhauer and Ralph Wagner, who read
the manuscript and offered helpful suggestions.*

# Contents

**Chapter**

# Chapter One
*Meet Sam Winston*

The green army sedan circled the manicured lawns of the Command and General Staff College on the Fort Leavenworth reservation, slowly passed the quaint, Nineteenth Century residence of Colonel George Armstrong Custer and headed out the main, tree-lined road. Turning east, they crossed the Missouri River bridge. The Army component of Team A-12, inspecting Reserve Officers Training Corps (ROTC) programs, was soon tooling down the interstate, cooled by the automobile air conditioner, a convenience almost unnecessary on an early fall morning.

Sergeant Major Rosie Carver was behind the wheel. Lieutenant Colonel Sam Winston slumped comfortably in the passenger seat. Winston was taller than Carver, but at least seventy pounds lighter. In service dress, Winston cut a commanding figure. The silver leaves of a Lieutenant Colonel on his epaulets were tarnished enough to reflect that he had been in grade longer than he expected. His Infantry crossed rifles and the initialed US on each lapel gleamed, carefully blitzed that morning.

Sam Winston was a non-observant Jew. Reform Jews, the Winston family - Weinstein originally - came to the United States in the early 1900's. The Weinsteins drifted into the junkyard business. The change of name to Winston took time. Business required a simple, American-sounding name that customers could remember. Business had its ups and downs. In time they prospered. Sam's parents, Irvin and Sylvia, made a move from the poorest district of north Saint Louis to Ladue, an exclusive suburb.

Sam, a late birth for Irvin and Sylvia, breezed through school. At thirteen he was bar mitzvah, a son of the commandment and for one night a celebrity in the temple. He enjoyed football, or more accurately, the circle of young women that surrounded him at every game. A running back at Clayton High School, he was above average in talent and ability, but he lacked the killer instinct to be a college prospect.

Choosing a college for Sam required study. Saint Louis' widely respected Washington University was too close to home and Saint Louis University was unacceptably Catholic. Winston chose Indiana University for no particular reason. His father, murmured over his choice. "Indiana in the twenties was a hotbed of Klan activities. Even the governor was a member! No place for a Jew." Sam pledged Zeta Beta Tau fraternity. Sam quickly found it was too Jewish for him. The other frat houses seemed to be for Gentiles. He turned in his beanie and found modest digs on Bloomington's Fourth Street.

Those were halcyon days. One of those students who rarely need to study, it was easy for Sam Winston to drink, flirt and cheat a little through his courses. He moved back into the dorm reluctantly. The ROTC made it worthwhile. The only thing he gave serious attention to was the Army Reserve Officers Training Corps. Winston was the top officer candidate at summer camp year after year. He graduated with a regular commission in the Infantry. The Winstons did not consider the profession of arms the best occupation for their son. In the normal run of things, Sam Winston should have followed in his father's footsteps. The money was attractive, but to remain at home meant marriage to a nice Jewish girl and to rust out in the junkyard business.

He took to Army life like a duck to water. Fort Benning was a challenge. The fledgling lieutenant passed the course with flying colors and was retained in a prestigious training assignment right there at the Infantry School.

That was eighteen years and a lifetime of experiences in the past. Korea, Germany, the Balkans, Panama, Iraq and a host of other assignments brought him to this cushy assignment, examining college ROTC programs to see if they were run according to Pentagon standards. It was a choice plum all right, but Winston was there because the Army did not know what to do with him. His career seemed to be on hold. Fort Leavenworth was a kind of Siberia for an officer with a questionable future.

Winston studied Carver closely. Sergeant Roosevelt Kennedy Carver, son of an Alabama cotton farmer, was the ideal American soldier. Just short of six feet, Carver's arms were as large as fire hoses. His shaved head and smooth skin were like burnished copper. It was surprising to discover Carver's soft blue eyes, a testimony to the 25% white blood in the African American gene pool. In a crisp service uniform, Winston eyed Carver's Ranger stripe, the chevrons and wreathed star of a Sergeant Major. Carver sported hash marks for twenty years of faithful service. The green beret rose at just the right angle. Yes, this was a soldier for anybody's army. Thank God it was ours.

Sergeant Carver pulled into the parking lot of the Morris Inn on the campus of the University of Notre Dame, the first assignment for Inspection Team A-12. Home of the fabled, "fighting Irish," Notre Dame has one of the largest ROTC program in the nation. The extremely high enrollment fees at Notre Dame, made the ROTC programs attractive. Even would-be pacifists found it hard to resist the free ride and the stipend. Tomorrow morning, A-12 would see how the program shakes out.

"Want to get a drink?" asked Winston as they walked to the hotel. "No, sir," replied Carver, "I don't drink." "How about dinner later - say seven?" proposed Winston. "That will be fine, Colonel." Carver effortlessly carried his baggage and over the Colonel's objections, Winston's as well.

Winston showered and shaved, and with obvious relief eased himself out of his service tunic into slacks, a sport shirt and a tennis sweater. The mirror-finish regulation low-quarters were exchanged for soft leather loafers. Studying his face carefully Winston noted how tired and drawn he looked around the eyes. He rubbed at the puffiness of his cheeks, but could not smooth it away. A confirmed bachelor, Sam Winston was considered a catch by scads of young women. His Mediterranean good looks made it difficult to tell if he was Italian, Greek or something else. Only Jews ever guessed he was Jewish. But he was 42 and looking the part. His straight black hair was thinning. "Male pattern baldness," he recalled from a TV ad.

Carver was a strange guy, thought Winston. He doesn't drink! Winston didn't know any "lifers," enlisted men or officers who didn't drink. Well, he certainly is a soldier. It was easy to recognize the Silver Star, three Bronze Stars and a handful of battle ribbons, under the paratroop wings, on Carver's chest. "He found a home," Winston laughed to himself, as he thought of the way soldiers brand men like Carver.

The dinner was excellent. The pair lingered over coffee discussing their duties on the morrow. "How would it be if I look at cadet progress reports and you check on the equipment inventory?" Winston suggested. "Sounds good to me," replied Carver, "we'll find out if the Irish can soldier as well as they play football." The conversation turned to past assignments, some brief references to battles, friends lost and made. They discovered they had been assigned to Fort Benning at roughly the same time. The two men had a great deal in common. A link was forged, each building respect for the other. Winston asked, "are you sure you won't join me across the street at the University Club for a, uh, Coke?" "No, thank you, Colonel, it's time for my Bible study and then the sack." With that, Carver said, "good night, sir" and walked away, every inch a soldier.

For an hour before retiring, Winston kept repeating, "Bible study." Sometimes it was a question, sometimes it was said with a sneer. Winston was incredulous. A lifer who does not drink is rare enough, but Sergeant Major Roosevelt Kennedy Carver, Winston guessed, was undoubtedly the only NCO in the Army who actually reads and studies the Bible.

In Rosie Carver's childhood home in Burnt Corn, Alabama, the Bible played an important part in family life. The Mose Carver family took their spiritual duties very seriously. Mose and Ruby and the six children prayed before every meal and sat through a Bible reading after supper every night. They were at the Fox Hollow Missionary Baptist Church every time the door opened.

Roosevelt Kennedy Carver was the eldest of six. As a boy, he outgrew clothes, shoes, everything. There was never as much on the table as he wanted to eat. Moses' favorite Bible passage was First Timothy 1:6-8, "but godliness with contentment is great gain. For we brought nothing into the world, and it is certain we can

3

carry nothing out. And having food and raiment let us therewith be content." Rosie learned early on that his hunger could not match Mose and Ruby's pain at being unable to spread a better table.

The Carver children grew up and left home, some for jobs in Birmingham, Atlanta, and Nashville. One remained at home. Rosie's favorite sister Eleanor, made it all the way to New York. She married badly and was the sole support for two small kids. Her husband passed through Rikers Island, and on to Attica. He was snared by the Rockefeller mandatory sentencing law for sale of a controlled substance. Rosie sent Eleanor money every month.

Rosie went off to Jackson State University. He was a fair student and an outstanding middle linebacker. A genuine NFL prospect, Rosie was named to several "all" teams. His career came to an end with an ACL injury to his right knee. His life at a crossroads, he met Lurene. A dark-skinned African American from Baton Rouge, Lurene did everything she could to discourage Rosie's attention. She was consumed with fabric print artistry. The big mills in the east were crying for people with Lurene Lott's talent.

Lurene was a Christian. Unwilling to get involved with Rosie romantically, she couldn't resist inviting him to a Campus Crusade meeting. Rosie had grown away from his Christian roots - he called it growing up. He was as far from the Bible as Burnt Corn is from Jackson State. But to be with Lurene, he would do anything. The Bible took on a renewed freshness for him. Had he been saved as a child? He wasn't sure. Lurene took him through the Gospel. He made sure of it one night on the steps of the campus library.

What would a slightly bruised middle linebacker do now? The MRI showed the knee was as good as surgery could make it, but pro scouts weren't interested. He had a degree in graduate studies and no job. Lurene was torn between her flowering love for Rosie and a big-city career. They parted for a time to pray about it. They met at crusade meetings and sometimes in the Student Union for cokes and popcorn. One evening, Rosie was more animated than usual. He blurted out, "honey, I joined the Army!"

Shocked, Lurene's eyes welled with tears. She had steeled herself to tell Rosie she was going to take a lucrative job offer as a print maker in a Carolina cotton mill. They could hardly bear to part, but they agreed to pray seriously about their future for a year.

Carver was made for the Army. He was the outstanding recruit in basic training at Fort Polk, Louisiana. It was the same at the Advanced Infantry Course at Fort Benning, Georgia. Airborne school at Fort Bragg allowed him to see Lurene occasionally and then it was off to the man-killing Ranger School at Eglin Field, Florida. Educationally qualified for an Officer Candidate School appointment, Carver turned it down in order to just plain soldier.

Lurene found that her career was as fulfilling as she expected, but the demands of office life ate into her creativity. In a year, she was ready to call it quits. Rosie and Lurene were married in the base chapel at Schofield Barracks, Hawaii.

Sam Winston hated to go to bed. He slept fitfully. It was always the same dream. Sometime in the wee, small hours, Winston rose from his bed and went to the window. The student body was bedded down for the night. The brilliantly lighted figure of Mary topped the golden dome of the main building. Mary seemed to be vigilantly guarding her sleeping students. "Well, one of our Jewish girls made good," Winston said aloud to himself with a smile.

The morning was cool. Sun-tipped campus buildings seemed to waken. Leaves painted in flaming colors gave promise of a beautiful mid-western autumn day. The Army component of A-12 strode in step to the ROTC building. A brief conference with the ROTC staff, a silent nod to the Navy and Air Force inspectors and it was right to work. The Pentagon did not need to worry. The ROTC program was in good hands. Winston and Carver were amused to learn that Notre Dame ROTC cadets had a special, spiritual guide. A priest, a retired Chief of Chaplains, hovered over the corps of cadets, assuring them that the profession of arms was, like cleanliness, next to godliness.

Conversation over lunch was as thin as the soup. Winston proposed, "since we must travel together Sergeant, how about calling me Sam?" "That won't be easy for me, Colonel," Carver replied." Softening, he added, "please call me Rosie, uh, Sam."

Winston wanted to talk, but the words came hard. Finally, he looked up from a half-eaten sandwich and said, "Rosie, you mentioned last night that you study the Bible. Are you, a Christian?" "Yessir, I am," said Carver, with evident pride. "Are you a Notre Dame kind of Christian?" asked Winston, with a wave of his hand toward the golden dome. Carver leaned forward and said, "No, I'm not that kind of Christian. Catholicism has some truth, but the Bible is not the main focus of Catholic faith. Let me show you something Sam, that I discovered when I was jogging this morning."

It was a short walk to a grungy statue of Jesus, the center point of the Notre Dame campus. Jesus, with outstretched arms had a heart emblazoned on his breast. Carver pointed to the Latin legend on the base of the statue. "Venite ad me Omnes," "Come unto me everyone." Do you know where these words are found, Colonel?" Sam shrugged. "They don't mean anything to me." "Well," continued the Sergeant, "they are the opening words of Matthew Chapter 11 and verses 28-30. From memory, Carver quoted the passage, "Come unto me, all ye that labor and are heavy laden, and I will give you rest. Take my yoke upon you, and learn of me, for I am meek and lowly in heart, and ye shall find rest unto your souls. For my yoke is easy and my burden is light." "Roman Catholicism has some truth, but the most

5

gracious invitation ever given to man is reproduced here in fragmentary form and in a language no one knows! What does that say about their commitment to reach a lost and dying world?"

"Wait a minute. Who said the world is lost and dying?" Winston shot back, tartly. "You've had eighteen years to take the world's pulse," exclaimed Carver, "do you see it as a better place than when you joined the Army?" "No, I don't," said Winston's with evident reluctance. "Sam, the Bible leads to the inevitable conclusion that these are the last days for this old world of violence and wickedness. God is about to bring mankind into judgment. He is about to ring down the curtain."

Carver paused, looked down at the ground and asked, "Sam, you are Jewish aren't you?" "Yeah, but I don't work very hard at it," was the curt reply. "Sam, I don't know more than a handful of Jews, but I owe a tremendous debt to the Jewish people. They gave us the Bible and the good news that Jesus Christ, the Savior-Messiah of Israel, came into the world to save sinners. A few years ago, I gave my life to Jesus the Christ. Jewish believers call Him Y'shuah. He saved me. I am on my way to the heaven, I believe Orthodox Jews call Gan Eden, the Garden of Eden."

"C'mon Rosie, it's all right to have a personal faith in something, to go to church or synagogue, to live a decent life and pay your bills, but let me tell you Jesus can't do anything for anyone. He is dead, a good example in a failing cause. When I die, Jesus will be the least successful Jew of all time," said Winston, feeling good about what he considered a brilliant rejoinder.

"Sam, have you weighed the evidence for a living Jesus? He died on the cross right enough, but He rose from the dead and He is alive right now. I talked to Him this morning." "Pardon me," said Winston, waving his arms like a referee, "you can't prove anything about Jesus. The evidence isn't there."

Lowering his voice for effect, Carver replied, "Colonel, you were trained to gather information carefully from every available source and then make your judgment about the findings. Unless, you have done some research you haven't mentioned in this conversation, you really know nothing about Jesus, do you?" Carver did not wait for an answer. "In this man's army you receive situation reports, technical information from many sources, the orders of superiors, the opinion and advise of specialists. Most of it you rarely question. Why? because you have faith in the system. You consider the facts, weigh the sources, and follow your instincts. Why not apply that kind of research and thinking before you pop off about Jesus Christ? For your information, Colonel, the bodily resurrection of Jesus is the best attested fact in ancient history."

Stunned by Carver's bold defense and his own stupid remarks, Winston turned to leave. "Before you go, Sam, one more thing you need to know. When God blows the whistle on this old world, the fur is going to fly and your people, the children of Israel, will be the main target of a very evil organization that is coming together as we speak." Winston stalked off for the hotel. "See ya, tomorrow," he tossed over his shoulder.

# Chapter Two
## *General Jean-Luc Armand Roy*

Since that night in Jordan, sound sleep had eluded Sam Winston. Throughout his military career he had been conditioned to fall off to sleep quickly and soundly in any situation. He had managed it under fire in a score of places. Now the short sleep periods were filled with the same frightening dream of a figure lying in a pool of blood. Big brass floated around demanding to know "Why, Winston? Why?" Dream sequences of Pentagon offices that opened freely to others were barred to Colonel Winston.

The dream, more a nightmare, was all too real to Winston. The nightmare was real. The man in the pool of blood was General Jean-Luc Armand Roy, of the Army of the Republic of France. Why would sinister forces gun down a peace emissary in the Jordanian desert? The Middle East was a dangerous place at the best of times, but no one was angry with France.

Roy was a rising military figure in the European Union. The general was not French, well, strictly speaking he was not French. Roy was a French Canadian. Like Winston, he was a grunt, an Infantry Lieutenant Colonel commanding a battalion of Canada's famous Royal Twenty-Second Regiment, the "Van Doos." Winston and Roy met as staff officers at the Canadian Forces Base at Petawawa, Ontario. In joint training exercises, they hit if off immediately. They joked together, lied shamelessly and drank too much. Six years later, in an incredible chain of events, Roy was propelled to the general staff of the French army.

The EU had no army of its own. Many held an army was not needed. Most of the EU partners were committed to the North Atlantic Treaty Organization. For more than half a century, NATO had been the bulwark of defense in Western Europe, first against the Communist eastern bloc countries and more recently in checking the unsettled Balkans. The real strength of the coalition was built around the U S missile capability. NATO now included nations in its fold, not in the EU geographically, an unacceptable situation for every partner in the EU. The United States was excluded from membership. The European Union began as a trade and commercial cartel. American trade and tariff interests dictated an attitude of vigilance toward the new world rival. The United States found it politically correct to have good relations with the EU, but only to protect America's baby, the NATO alliance. An EU army would spell an end to NATO.

Some brass hats committed to the EU, had looked around for a charismatic military figure to be the Trojan horse in a scheme to steal an army rather than build one. None of the EU partners had a leader acceptable to all. It needed a man the inner cabal could control. The goal was to force a shotgun wedding of the EU and NATO, and then to gut the NATO organization.

Staff planners sold the idea of looking outside the European Union for the figurehead leader the plot required. They hit on the idea of transferring a Canadian officer to the French army. Canada was a perfect fit for the plan. A NATO partner, Canada was for generations, the most respected nation on earth. It was an advantage that Canada could not be in the EU. France had cultivated a French - Canadian relationship on historical, cultural and linguistic grounds, clear back to the visit of Charles DeGaulle to Canada in the 1950's. Staff functionaries dug up the history of the French army sent to Canada four centuries before. No unit ever returned to Europe. They had wasted away in the inhospitable, frozen north. It was a portent of the end of the French foothold on the American continent. If the Canadians could be induced to fall in with this public relations coup, a French Canadian would represent the symbolic return to France of her long over-due expeditionary forces. They looked around for just the right Canadian and Roy was the unanimous choice. To the public, it was a Cinderella story that would play well all over the western world. Taking a dashing young French Canadian officer from Montreal to Paris was a coup worthy of Steven Spielberg. Roy was a Roman Catholic, a non-negotiable requirement for the powerful Catholic interests in the European Union.

That was four years ago, or was it five? Winston couldn't be sure. The tabloids and the media followed Roy's meteoric rise. He was a general the day they swore him in at the Quai D'Orsai. He was sure to have a marshal's baton soon. He spoke peerless French and seemed at home in the highest circles of the movers and shakers in European affairs. He did almost nothing of a military nature except take the salute of another full-dress parade or place a wreath at the monument of a long-forgotten war. Would Winston ever meet his Canadian opposite number again?

Winston had been comfortable in a new assignment at Fort Benning, Georgia, the Infantry School. The G-3 section, Plans and Training, was an important berth for a field-grade officer to step up to an O-6 assignment, a full colonelcy. It was a Monday to Friday job, with only a few weekends. The Army was definitely committed to field operations, so there were more nights on the cold, hard ground than he liked, but it went with the territory. That's when he got the word.

USAREUR (U. S. Army Europe) was walking the floor over a request from General Roy to have Winston as his liaison officer during the general's visit to the Middle East. Was it the long-standing friendship of Sam Winston and the Canadian or was there some other reason for the request? They could not decide. It was the kind of request an ally could hardly refuse. But the USAREUR was struggling with the growing certainty of an EU army. Reluctantly, army brass said "go for it."

Charged with security arrangements for Roy's official visit to Israel, Syria, Jordan, Iraq and Saudi Arabia, Winston had taken every precaution possible in a highly volatile region. If the United States Army wondered about Roy's mission, it was an even more puzzling question in Middle East capitals. Damascus said, "why here?" Cairo said, "why not here?" Roy was an engaging plenipotentiary, whatever his mission. He could talk learnedly with the Syrian Foreign Minister of the decisive battle of Kuchuk Kharnaji, a battle known only to graduate students in Middle Eastern studies. He could weep with the Jews at Yad Vashem and deplore the massacre of Palestinians at Deir Yassin. Roy didn't miss the religious photo-ops either. He visited the Dome of the Rock in Jerusalem, prayed before the painting of the black Madonna in Joppa and endured the Samaritans on Mount Gerizim. In Riyadh, Roy won the attention of the Saudis. The United Arab Emirates and the Kuwaitis were polite, but distant.

Canadian good will and native Gallic charm, carried Roy through some diplomatically sensitive discussions. Sam felt a prickly sensation at the nape of his neck on more than one occasion. Discussions over ancient battles, the visits to shrines and memorials and polite talk over tea in a host of capitals was mere window dressing for the meetings with trade officials, OPEC policy wonks and Middle Eastern movers and shakers. The blackout was total. No communiqués were issued by the Roy party, officially or unofficially. Winston was not privy to any of these talks. He simply had to worry about Roy's safety.   What was going on behind closed doors? Oil was always the easy answer, but maybe there was more.

The lone change in plans came in Iraq. The Iraqis denied entrance to Winston, an expression of Iraqi hostility to America. He sat it out in Amman, Jordan, awaiting the Roy motorcade from Baghdad. In Iraq, Roy toured the restored city of ancient Babylon. Winston's briefing notes indicated that while under construction it was used as a revetment to hide Iraqi aircraft in the Gulf War.  Now complete, it was the deposed Saddam Hussein's symbol of the return to the power of Nebuchadnezzar's day.

For some reason, aircraft were ruled out for Roy's return to the west. A secret message informed Winston the Roy motorcade had left Baghdad, nearly one thousand kilometers to the East. The long tiring drive through the Syrian desert, into the Jordanian panhandle and on to Amman was a grueling trip. On arrival, Winston reviewed the security procedures with the march units, sent a signal to Tel Aviv and they were off. On the dusty road between Amman and the Allenby Bridge, three men dressed as Bedouins came out of nowhere and sprayed Roy's limo with hundreds of rounds of AK-47. Roy's driver, an armed guard and a major in Jordan's Desert Legion, were dead. Riding in the land rover immediately in front of the limo, Winston sprinted to Roy's car in time to cut down two of the assailants but missed the third who made his escape. Roy was on the rear floor of the vehicle, blood streaming from multiple wounds to the chest and neck. Two medics in the convoy tried to give what first-aid they could. Both experienced EMT's shook their heads. Sam radioed for an Israeli army helicopter, that had to be cleared to enter Jordanian airspace. Forty-five minutes later, General Jean-Luc Armand Roy was in a hospital in Tel Aviv, Israel. Winston expected to learn the general was DOA.

The days following the shooting were a blur to Winston. He had written his report on the incident a dozen times. He had been interrogated by Israelis, French, Jordanians, European Union officials, NATO brass and platoons of U S Army and State Department big-wigs, in a crazy-quilt itinerary that took him to EU and NATO headquarters in Brussels, U S Army headquarters in Germany and to London and Washington. No one really blamed Winston for the bollix, but the U S Army is unforgiving of officers who are caught in the middle of an embarrassing situation for the Pentagon. Winston fully expected the word was out on him and he would be dropped from sight, never again to command, never to see that promotion to O-6, just one of a legion of officers who like Major Reno at the Little Big Horn, simply could not explain what happened.

The intelligence services of a dozen countries were charged with finding the assailants. No group claimed responsibility. Satellites were re-tasked to cover the usual suspects, Fatah, PFLP, Hamas, the Hezbollah, al Qaeda, Muslim extremist groups in Algeria, Syria, and Iraq. There were 52 known terrorist camps in Jordan, the work of the infamous Palestinian, Wadi Haddad. France maintained such a low profile in the Middle East, suspicion turned on a Corsican liberation movement, but there were no leads. The CIA theorized the attack site and the Bedouin costumes were cover for plotters closer to the European Union

After exhausting rounds of what the Pentagon whimsically calls a de-briefing, Winston was given orders for Fort Leavenworth, Kansas. "What happened to my G-3 slot at Fort Benning?" "Sorry, I have no information on that, Colonel. You are going to an ROTC inspection team that is temporarily headquartered with the Command and General Staff College. You'll love the duty," the AG officer said with a smile.

It was ludicrous for Winston and Carver to be stationed at Fort Leavenworth. The A-12 team kept the roads hot, covering ROTC units up to five hundred miles to the east. Big Ten universities, Minneapolis, Racine, Columbus, Chicago, West Lafayette, Champaign-Urbana, Bloomington; and others were on the Fifth Army schedule. The exchange on the campus at Notre Dame made it awkward for the Army two-some. It was back to Colonel, and Sergeant, in stilted conversations that were strictly business. Winston gave a lot of thought to asking Fifth Army head-quarters for a replacement for Carver. Questions would be asked for which no answers could be supplied. Carver was a top-rated soldier. Asking that he be replaced would be a slap in the face to an NCO, especially a long-service veteran. Winston was torn in his feelings. On the one hand, he felt that his Jewish heritage had been violated. Another part of him said, Carver knows so much about the Bible and its future for mankind, why not, pick his brains and leave the Jesus stuff alone?

Winston heard nothing further about General Roy's condition. He was nagged by the fear that after 18 years of service. Lt. Col. Samuel Winston, USA, was on some kind of watch list. Sam had a capacity for putting things out of his mind in respect to the need of the hour. He had to get along with Sergeant Carver. Wisdom dictated do your work and let Carver do his. Carver held up his end so well. As the saying goes, "if it ain't broke, don't fix it."

The break came for the duo, cooped up in a motel in Lafayette, Indiana. In town to inspect the Purdue University ROTC unit, bitter winter weather held them over for two and half days. Team reports had been written, corrected and re-written. Efforts at conversation with their opposite numbers in the Navy and Air Force got old and Winston found himself mostly sticking to the motel room and the 12-channel TV. Carver was busy all of the time with Bible studies. Winston tried to read the night-table Gideon Bible. The Book of Revelation made no sense to him. Most references to the Jews in the rest of the New Testament, he decided were negative. Did they blame his people for the death of Jesus?

Winston found a number of passages that branded men as sinners. He refused to believe he could be a heathen. The case the Apostle Paul made against his own people, the Jews, made Sam angry. He threw the Bible against the door. He stepped over and around it, but disdained picking it up. Longing for something to do, he reluctantly knocked on Carver's door. He stammered around, and finally got out, "Sergeant, if you have a little time while we are here, would you explain some things from the Bible for me, please? I've been reading it some and ...well, I've got tons of questions." Carver brightened. "Sure I will Sam" (He called me "Sam!" Winston noted with satisfaction). "What are you doing right now? Come on in, and we'll talk."

"My questions are mostly about future predictions, Sergeant," said Winston, hesitant to call him Rosie. Carver fixed a steady gaze on Winston and said slowly, "Sam, we got off on the wrong foot at Notre Dame and I am sorry for it. I ask that you forgive me, please. I get so excited about introducing people to Jesus Christ, I lose my objectivity at times."

Rosie got right to the point. "I know how absorbing prophecy can be, but I really believe you need to study the person and work of Jesus Christ first, then prophecy will make a lot more sense to you." "No, Sergeant, I do not want to talk about Jesus right now. The last thing you said to me was that the Jews are going to take it in the neck. Why or when, you didn't say. I know, I know," Winston, continued, "I bugged out just as you were about to answer."

Carver flipped through the pages of his Bible and turned to Winston solemnly. "Sam, you want to study prophecy, but not Jesus. Would you read a verse of scripture for me?" Carver passed the book over to Winston and pointed out the closing words of verse 10 of Chapter 19 in the Book of Revelation. Winston read,

"Worship God: For the testimony of Jesus is the spirit of prophecy."

(Revelation 19:10).

"You see Sam," Carver explained, "Jesus and prophecy go together. Having said that, while I firmly believe that you are not really ready for prophecy, I will give you an overlay sketch of God's plan for the last days for the world. I will begin that sketch, by telling you the very next event in prophecy involves the Messiah Jesus you do not want to hear about. There is no way of telling you anything about the events of the last days without explaining this event first. Are you game to listen?"

"Uhhh," said Winston, "yeah, I'll hear you out on that." Carver placed the room's nightstand copy of the Bible in Sam's hand, turned to the Gospel of John and had Sam read the first three verses of chapter 14. "Let not your hearts be troubled ye believe in God; believe also in me. In my Father's house are many mansions; if it were not so, I would have told you. I go to prepare a place for you, And if I go and prepare a place for you, I will come again and receive you unto myself that where I am there you may be also."

Assuming an Army instructor's demeanor, Carver pointed out three features of the passage. "Note, the speaker is Jesus. The listeners, we might call his Bible class, were devout Jews. If we had time to read the passages surrounding these words we would discover the lesson took place the evening before the arrest of Jesus and His crucifixion. In verse two, He tells them He is going to His Father's house, that is heaven. Then, he tells them the most important feature of the passage: 'I will come and receive you unto myself that where I am you might be also.' Sam, Jesus did return to the Father God, and He is coming again!" Carver said with evident enthusiasm.

Winston stirred, ill at ease, his eyes riveted on the text. Rosie deftly turned the pages for Winston and had him read the letter to Titus Chapter 2 and verses 11 through 14. "For the grace of God that bringeth salvation hath appeared to all men, teaching us that, denying ungodliness and worldly lusts, we should live soberly, righteously, and godly, in this present world; Looking for that blessed hope, and the glorious appearing of the great God and our Savior Jesus Christ; Who gave himself for us, that he might redeem us from all iniquity, and purify unto himself a peculiar people, zealous of good works." Carver explained, "these words were penned by a Jew, Saul of Tarsus, a former member of the ruling council of Israel. He was later known as Paul. You will notice that he talks about "looking for the blessed hope - the glorious appearing of Jesus Christ." This Jewish scholar took Jesus at His word, that Jesus would return to earth."

Turning again in the Gideon Bible, Carver turned up the Epistle to the Thessalonians and read Chapter four and verses 16-18. "For the Lord himself shall descend from heaven with a shout, with the voice of the archangel, and with the trump of God, and the dead in Christ shall rise first: Then we which are alive and remain shall be caught up together with them in the clouds, to meet the Lord in the air: and so shall we ever be with the Lord. Wherefore comfort one another with these words."

Winston closed one eye as though sighting a rifle, "Sergeant, I think I just got blind-sided. I didn't want to talk about Jesus and that is all I got." "I made it clear, Sam, that Jesus is the key to the last days." It was hard for Carver to determine if Winston was angry or merely stating a point. Had Sam noted the fact that each passage he read assumed the deity of Jesus Christ? Carver pressed on. "I know what you think, Sam, but I began with the statement that this event is the very first and the very next event in God's plan for the last days. You would have no point of reference for anything the Bible has to say about the end-times without knowing of Jesus' return. But, I will give you this, on a personal level I had to bring you to this passage because I live in the firm expectation that Jesus could return this very day! The passage says that after the "shout," "the voice of the archangel" and the trumpet call, "the dead in Christ shall rise first." Sam, that includes my dear mother and father and millions of other believers who gave their lives to the Messiah Jesus before they went to their graves. Their souls went to be with the Lord and He will bring them back when He returns. Then the text says, "we who are alive and remain," and by that he refers to those of us who are saved and alive at the time, trusting in Him for salvation, "shall be caught up together with them in the clouds, to meet the Lord in the air." "Sam," said the Sergeant with an excitement Winston had never seen before, "you could walk down here and knock on my door and I would not be around to answer. I'm outta here, when the Lord returns. I'm going to heaven, perhaps today." Carver paused and said, "had enough for today, Colonel?"

It took a while for Winston to answer. "Yeah," he said slowly, "could you write down those verses for me? I would like to read them over again for myself." Back in his room, Winston looked hard at the Bible lying face open on the motel room floor. He picked it up slowly and fumbled his way from the index to each passage on the slip Carver provided. "Hmm," he muttered to himself, "if the return of Jesus takes away all the Rosie Carver's living and dead, where does that leave the rest of us? Probably that is lesson number two and beyond," he reasoned.

The telephone interrupted his reverie. A crisp, female voice said, "Colonel Winston? This is Sergeant Elliott, Fifth Army Information Center, please stand by for a non-secured conversation with Colonel James Baxter, Fifth Army Adjutant General's Office." "Hello, Sam," the caller greeted cheerily, "how are you making it down there? Sitting on the radiator, I'll bet. We are too. Man the snow is knee deep to a tall Indian, here in Chicago." Faintly annoyed at the small talk, Winston remembered Baxter as a very spit and polish West Point officer. They had served together at Fort Irwin, California in the desert training center. Baxter was a decent guy, but it was hard to get him on any topic for long except the school for boys on the Hudson River. Baxter lived and breathed the U.S. Military Academy.

"Sam, I've got news that I'm sure will interest you. It came over the secure wire this afternoon. General Roy of the French Army is alive and well and has returned to limited duty in the new Brussels EU command center." "What?" Sam cried, "that's incredible." "Yes," said Baxter, "no mistake." Winston paced to the length of

14

his phone cord. "How could this be, Jim? I saw the man with multiple wounds. I was sure he bought the farm. Medics could barely find a pulse. I've waited for days expecting to hear of his death." "Well," Baxter continued, "I know it has been hard for you, security officer for that operation and all," said Baxter, carefully choosing his words," you are out of the woods now I would say, Sam. Get yourself a couple of stiff drinks and lift a cup in honor of whomever performed the miracle that saved the General's life." With that, Baxter clicked off.

A miracle, hmm, maybe, Sam thought, but I doubt it. It had to be those Israeli doctors and nurses that received him. He thought carefully over the painful incident and concluded it was twenty to thirty minutes before an Israeli evac helicopter made it to the scene of the shooting. Surely, Roy was DOA at Tel Aviv. And then what medical facility received Roy after surgery in Tel Aviv? In the hectic days of the investigation, Winston had asked officially and unofficially where Roy was treated and how he was doing. Information was on "a need to know," basis and Winston was not in the loop. At the time, he thought he was kept in the dark because of his involvement in the case. Well, it was a relief to learn he was no longer under a cloud.

The weather was due to break on the morrow. Winston and Carver met over breakfast and mostly talked shop. Winton finally brought up the subject of the return of Christ. "Rosie, this idea is so hard to get hold of, that I really must ask, is there any voice or voices in the world that say, 'I just don't believe this story?'" "Indeed, Sam, indeed." Retrieving a small testament from a back pocket, Carver rapidly turned to the Second Epistle of Peter, Chapter 3 and read verses 3 to 7: "Knowing this first, that there shall come in the last days, scoffers, walking after their own lusts and saying where is the promise of his coming? For since the fathers fell asleep all things continue as they were from the beginning of the creation for this they willingly are ignorant of, that by the word of God the heavens were of old, and the earth standing out of the water and in the water whereby the world that then was, being overflowed with water perished: but the heavens and the earth, which are now by the same word are kept in store, reserved unto fire against the day of judgment and perdition of ungodly men."

Carver made no comment on the passage, waiting for Winston to digest what he had heard. Quietly reflective for a couple of minutes, Winston said slowly, "so there are those who say there is no evidence for a return." "Yes," replied Carver, "if you noticed, the scoffing is said to be "in the last days." Winston took the New Testament from Carver's hands and re-examined the passage for himself. "What's this business about the "earth standing out of water and in the water? "and "whereby the world that then was, being overflowed with water perished?" "Good questions, Sam," commented Rosie, "the earth standing out of the water" speaks of God's creation of the world, information related to us in the first book of the Bible, Genesis and Chapter one. Then in the sixth verse, before us, water destroyed the world. This history is found in Genesis chapters six and seven. "Wait a minute,"

Winston protested, "who believes in a sequence of events like that? Did Carl Sagan or Isaac Asimov go for this story?" "No," replied Carver, calmly, "they were Uniformitarians and by the words you read in this passage, they were scoffers of the last days. God wrote only one book Sam. He tells us flatly that He created the heavens and the earth. He does not offer proof, the creator or inventor, never needs to do that. His handiwork proves that. When men fell into sin, God destroyed it by water."

Tempted to throw the Testament aside and never speak of biblical things with Carver again, Sam said nothing for what seemed like an eternity. "Do you really believe this stuff, Rosie?" he asked at last. "I believe every word of it, Sam. This Lord who saved me simply cannot lie and I have not a scintilla of doubt that He lived by His Word in the past, does so in the present and shall do so in the future." Sam, obviously confused, said, "I just don't know, I just don't know what to think." "I can understand that," Carver said, resting his hand on his friend's shoulder "Give it some time. God has infinite patience with those seeking the truth."

Winston rose to leave. Carver gently pressed him back into his seat. "There is more in this passage you need to get hold of, Sam. Let me read it to you. Second Peter 3:7-9: "But, the heavens and the earth, which are now, by the same word are kept in store, reserved unto fire against the day of judgment and perdition of ungodly men. But beloved, be not ignorant of this one thing, that one day is with the Lord as a thousand years, and a thousand years as one day. The Lord is not slack concerning his promise, as some men count slackness, but is long-suffering to us-ward, not willing that any should perish, but that all should come to repentance." Closing the book Carver leveled his gaze at his friend and said, "Sam, you need Jesus Christ as personal Savior. If the end is as near as the Bible seems to indicate it is, it will be the fire next time. Sam, God destroyed all living things in a worldwide flood. The fire will consume the world in the same way. Turn to Christ today Sam."

Shoulders bowed, struggling with his thoughts, Winston wordlessly picked up his check and made his way to the cashier. Better leave him alone, Rosie thought, it is time for the Holy Spirit to work on a very tough case.

# Chapter Three
## *Winston meets the Bible*

Insiders at Fifth Army Headquarters in Chicago offered no additional information on the astounding recovery of General Roy. The media reported it was business as usual for the rising star in the Western defense network. The pope congratulated Roy on his speedy recovery and promised the continued prayers of the church. The BBC reported unprecedented efforts to locate the terrorist cell that carried out the attack on Roy. No European Union official had ever been the target of an assassin. Would this failed attempt lead to other initiatives against key figures in the movement? Winston, euphoric over the rehabilitation of his own career, was kept busy answering questions about the meteoric rise of a little known Canadian officer and his miracle recovery.

Winston and Carver and the A-12 team were de-briefed on the first round of ROTC inspections and received a well done for their work. They were held over at headquarters for three additional days to review Madison Avenue's latest ROTC recruitment advertising. The Army estimated their needs at 600 to 700 new lieutenants each year. Appealing literature was a must. "Which do you like best?" the advertising pitchmen asked over and over again as TV ads rolled and magazine ads were passed from hand to hand. Carver quipped that the team was the Pentagon's equivalent of Siskel and Ebert. He and Winston gave a thumbs-up to the ads they liked and a thumbs down to those that lacked the punch the program needed.

The delay offered Carver additional time to continue Bible study with Sam Winston. Room service dishes and coffee cups, remnants of toast and donuts vied with pizza boxes and pop cans for space in their suite. They repulsed every effort of the housekeeping staff to make the beds and clean up the mess. Carver was convinced the testimony of Jesus Christ would finally pierce the Colonel's will to resist.

It was the testimony about Jesus Christ that Rosie Carver had to deal with first. Next, it would be Jewish issues. Winston had come to the firm conclusion that the New Testament teaches hatred of the Jews. From the internet, Sam learned Jules Isaac, a French concentration camp survivor, approached Pope John XXIII in the early 1960's and pressed his conviction that the New Testament, particularly the Gospel of John, was loaded with antisemitic sentiment. Isaac claimed that the New Testament charged the Jews with the death of Christ. He held the New Testament text gave a kind of tacit approval to carry out repressive measures against innocent Jews. These measures, he concluded, led to the "Final Solution," the murder of six million of the children of Israel.

Pope John XXIII was sympathetic. He began to set in motion initiatives that would declare the Jews free of the guilt of the crime of deicide. Pope John died and the initiatives were blunted by the more conservative Vatican coterie, some with explicit links to the Nazis. The murder of Christ was declared to be the shared responsibility of certain elements in the Israel of Jesus' day. The murder of the Jews was merely deplored, the Church said, claiming they had no power to condemn anything or anybody. The condemn/deplore issue came to the fore in an unusual way. A German play opened on Broadway in New York City. "The Deputy," by Rolf Hochhuth pointed a finger at the role of Pope Pius XII in the roundup and deportation of Italian Jews to the death camps in World War II. American Jews, in the forefront of the demand for a strong statement on antisemitism, were ready to flock to the stage production. Two Jewish-born Catholic priests, Oesterreicher and Baum, were sent to New York to warn that the Jewish community had to boycott the Hochhuth play or there would be no statement of any kind on antisemitism in the findings of the Second Vatican Council. A finding that the church deplored antisemitism was better than nothing. The Jews reluctantly caved in.

Arms folded, Winston turned to Carver and said grimly, "what do you say to that, Rosie?" "All the world is guilty of the murder of Jesus Christ," the Sergeant replied. "The Bible lays the blame squarely on two men and two groups of people. Turning in his Bible, Carver read from a prayer of Jesus' followers,

"For of a truth against thy holy child Jesus, whom thou hast anointed, both Herod, and Pontius Pilate, with the Gentiles, and the people of Israel, were gathered together, for to do whatsoever thy hand and thy counsel determined before to be done."
(Acts 4:27-28)

"You see, Sam, the on-site testimony is that sinful men slew Jesus Christ. Yes, some Jews, some Gentiles and the hated leaders at the time were co-conspirators. But note they were only able to do what God's plan allowed." For emphasis, Carver read, "to do whatsoever thy hand and thy counsel determined before to be done." Carver continued, "men can only do what God permits. In another place, Jesus said, no man takes my life from me. I lay down my life and I take it again. Satan, the enemy of man's soul, was determined to stop the sinless Son of God from carrying out God's plan of salvation by having Jesus killed. But Satan was foiled by his own plot. The blood of Jesus Christ provided cleansing for the sins of men. The very worst that the Devil could do is the very means by which salvation was made possible," Carver explained. "On the issue of Jewish responsibility, they had a share in the murder as did everyone who has ever lived. Sam, if you had been alive then you would have slain Jesus Christ, not because you are a Jew, but because you are a member of Adam's race, a sinner by nature and by choice. And you know what? I would have been right there with you, nailing Jesus to that cross."

"I miss the connection, Rosie, what does the death of Christ and His blood have to do with God's plan of salvation?" "Another good question from the Colonel. Most of the colonels I know don't ask good questions" Carver quipped. "The death of Christ was the culmination of a principle that holds throughout the Bible. The innocent must suffer for the guilty. In the Old Testament, your people the Jews, understood that rams and lambs, and bullocks, were to be offered in sacrifice to God as a covering for sin. The Bible says "it is the blood that maketh an atonement for the soul," Leviticus 17:11. In God's plan, the blood of an innocent sacrifice assures a dismissal of charges against the sinful man. All of these sacrifices were interim provisions for man's basic sin nature and his sinful choices. What God was looking for was not alone the sacrifice, but the heart that was right with God, a heart that recognized the sinner's dreadful offense to God. In the first coming of Jesus Christ, it was said, "behold the lamb of God which taketh away the sin of the world" John 1:29. Everyone in Israel understood this was a reference to the whole sacrificial system; the ultimate and only perfect sacrifice ever made. His once-for-all sin offering for men is the only sacrifice God will now accept. You see, Sam, to miss God's provision of His only Son for your sins and mine, is to miss it all. There is no "Plan B;" no drop-back position. It is Christ or nothing."

A subdued Winston, thoughtfully stroked his chin. "All right, can we get back to the Jews in prophecy again?" he asked. Carver brightened, "you just can't get away from that subject can you? Sorry for the delay. While Jesus was here on earth," Carver continued, " He visited the grand re-dedication of the temple at Jerusalem. It had taken years for Herod to refurbish the temple. Herod enlarged it and made it the show place of the Middle East. On the day that it was reopened, Jesus told His disciples "I say unto you, there shall not be left here one stone upon another; that shall not be thrown down" (Matthew 24:2). Startled, His disciples couldn't wait to hear how this could take place and when it would occur. The prophecy of the fulfillment of the destruction of the temple can be found in the twenty-first chapter of the Gospel According to Luke," Carver explained. "The city and the temple were utterly destroyed by the Romans in 70 A.D. Not one stone was left upon another."

"The answers you are looking for about the Jews follow in that same conversation with the disciples. It is found in Matthew Chapter 24. This message from the lips of Jesus Himself, provides the information in a kind of outline of the earth-shaking events after the Rapture. First of all," Carver explained, "you need to know that a period of seven years is the focus of prophecy concerning the Jews in particular and the world in general. The seven years begin immediately following the Rapture." Carver paused. "Sam, have I used the term Rapture before? This is a non-biblical term we use to describe the event I'm looking for, the return of Christ to earth.

The seven years begin with three and one-half years of a very uneasy peace. The last three years and a half, are marked by natural disasters and violence worldwide. The entire seven year period is a period of tribulation. But the Bible relates that the last half of the period will be horrendous:"

"for then shall be great tribulation, such as was not since the beginning of the world to this time, no, nor ever shall be."

(Matthew 24:21)

"Wait a minute," protested Sam, "I don't call it tribulation, but don't we have conditions today that are every bit as troubling as this so-called "great tribulation?" "I'll let one of your own prophets of the old covenant, Jeremiah, testify on that one, Sam," Rosie exclaimed. "Jeremiah describes it this way,

"Ask ye now, and see whether a man doth travail with child? wherefore do I see every man with his hands on his loins, as a woman in travail, and all faces are turned into paleness? Alas! for that day is great, so that none is like it: it is even the time of Jacob's trouble; but he shall be saved out of it"

(Jeremiah 30:6-7)

"Do you get the picture, Sam?" Rosie said with excitement. It will be unlike anything ever seen before. Notice the picture of a man about to give birth. Men don't give birth. In addition, childbirth is always something for which we are unprepared. For months we know it is coming and then we're surprised when the hour arrives. Men are fully aware that judgment is overdue. When it arrives, it arrives suddenly and no one is prepared. Let me re-emphasize Jeremiah's words,

"that day is great, so that none is like it."

Sam shook his head ruefully, "I'm still not convinced," he said slowly. "Maybe the Bible is talking about some future event rather than some violent episode, say in Jeremiah's day or at some other period in history." "O.K". said Rosie, "try these statistics on for size. The Apostle John prophesied of the Great Tribulation. He wrote, "And I looked and behold a pale horse: and his name that sat on him was Death, and Hades followed with him. And power was given unto them over the fourth part of the earth, to kill with sword, and with hunger, and with death, and with the beasts of the earth" (Revelation 6:8). "What is the population of the earth right now?" Rosie asked. "Let me see," said Sam, looking at the ceiling and stroking his chin reflectively, "I believe there is an eyelash under six billion people in the world." Rosie pointed at the words in the text, "the fourth part of the earth. That means, something on the order of a billion and a half people will die of the sword, that's war; hunger, that's famine; and with other exquisite ways to die, including man-eating animals! I ask you Sam, is there anything in history of man with anywhere near that casualty rate?"

Before Sam could answer, Rosie was quickly turning the pages of the Bible exclaiming, "there is a parallel passage that describes the casualties in Israel in the tribulation. Listen to this,

"And it shall come to pass, that in all the land, saith the Lord, two parts therein shall be cut off and die; but the third shall be left therein."

(Zechariah 13:8)

20

"That is from the Old Testament prophet Zechariah. Think of it, if the seven years of tribulation began today, how many Israelis would die?" "Hmm, two-thirds? About two million," Sam replied. "That's a lot of people." Rosie looked squarely at Winston and said slowly, "Sam, in a country roughly 60 miles wide by 180 miles long, that would mean Israel will be a cemetery. Has this ever happened before Sam? Don't forget," Rosie continued, "that your people, the Jews in the diaspora, would have to be figured in among the billion or more people that die in the rest of the world. Sam, I rest my case. There has never been anything like this at any time in human history. And it is coming soon. "But before we leave Zechariah's prophecy," Rosie continued, "let me read for you the great promise made to the Jews of Israel who survive the great tribulation. Listen:

"And I will bring the third part through the fire, and will refine them as silver is refined, and will try them as gold is tried: they shall call on my name, and I will hear them: I will say, it is my people: and they shall say, The Lord is my God."
(Zechariah 13:9)

Winston, weighing each word, asked, "who is in charge in this period of tribulation?" "Another good question, Colonel," Rosie replied, "you get the feeling that some malevolent power is in control and wreaking vengeance on the Jews and a hapless world, don't you, but that is not the Bible's answer to your question. Let's read in Revelation 6. That is the same chapter that told us of the horrendous loss of life in the tribulation. In Revelation 6:15-17 we read: "And the kings of the earth, and the great men, and the rich men, and the chief captains, and the mighty men and every bondman, and every free man, hid themselves in the dens and in the rocks of the mountains; and said to the mountains and rocks, fall on us and hide us from the face of him that sitteth on the throne, and from the wrath of the Lamb: for the great day of his wrath is come and who shall be able to stand? Sam, I read earlier to you, that Jesus is called 'the Lamb of God who takes away the sin of the world' (John 1:29). Jesus is the Lamb and He is in control during the great tribulation."

Carver, directed his friend's attention back to Matthew 24. "The outline of tribulation events begins in verse four," Carver continued. "Jesus' initial warning is that there would be a great number of false Christs at the beginning of the tribulation." Carver laid aside his Bible and fished through his briefcase for a sheet of yellowed newspaper. He unfolded it and handed it to Winston. It was page 7A of the USA Today for Monday, January 12, 1987. It was a full-page ad for the Tara Center, North Hollywood, California. The 40-point caption read, "THE CHRIST IS IN THE WORLD." Described as a great world teacher, a practical man with solutions, the ad went on to say, "It is My intention to reveal Myself at the earliest possible moment, and to come before the world as your Friend and Teacher." "Hmm," exclaimed Winston, "way back then there was a false Christ!" "Yes," agreed Carver, "and I have read estimates that as many as 2,000 false Christ's are in the world at any one time."

"The second warning is of wars and rumors of wars (verse seven). Colonel, you and I know about that. Historians say there are only 200 total years of peace in all of recorded history. United Nations statistics reflect that there are normally ten wars going on every single day."

"The same seventh verse," Carver pointed out, "tells of famines and earthquakes in various places. Some Bible versions add the information that it will be a time of increased pestilence. Webster defines that as 'virulent or fatal contagious disease.' These are fearful, natural catastrophes. From scientific and media reports, we have more of these calamities now than ever before." Carver closed the book and asked, "what do you think, Sam?"

Sam formed his hands into a "T," time-out. "I can see the four or five things that Jesus enumerated as the cause of such enormous casualties throughout the world, but I have not heard why a God of love would allow this dreadful stuff to hit mostly innocent people? Haven't my Jews suffered enough? Good heavens, Rosie, we lost six million in the Holocaust. Now you tell me that a million plus Israelis are going down and a quarter of all the people in the world? I tell you my friend, I hope you are wrong about this whole scene. I sincerely hope it is ancient history or someone's bad dream. I wouldn't wish this on my worst enemy," Winston said with conviction.

"Thank you, my friend," said Rosie solemnly, "you are saying what everyone has said who ever came to grips with Bible prophecy. The answer is that God decided to save men from their sins, by providing the dearest person to Himself, His own son, to die for miserable sinners. The record says,

"He [Jesus] came unto his own, and his own received him not. But as many as received him, to them gave he power to become the sons, [or the children], of God, even to them that believe on his name."

(John 1:11-12)

"Men rejected that Savior. Most still reject him today. It is in the nature of man to want to live by his own sinful choices and to refuse to be bound by God's laws. God has decided to allow men to choose their own gods, to follow the dictates of their own hearts and minds. We read about the result. God will continue His efforts to save men in that dreadful period and believe it or not, many will be saved. But unbridled sin and lust will produce not the self-made peace and contentment that man envisions for himself, but misery, woe and death."

"I just don't know what I think, Rosie," Winston said with resignation, "I've got to let this stuff simmer for a while and then I'll formulate some kind of impression of it. I don't want to anger you, my friend, but I am suspicious of picking verses out here and there and building a doctrine out of them." "You are wise to look at it that way," said Carver nodding in agreement. "The Bible, particularly the Jewish Old Testament is written with nuggets of truth buried in other important texts. In addition, many prophecies have both a near-and-far application, that is they had application to Old Testament events and at the same time looked far into the future to the periods like the one we have studied, the great tribulation."

"How did my old rabbi back in Saint Louis, may he rest in peace, look at these passages?" said Winston. In answer Rosie said, "I am sorry to say, Sam, that I understand most Jewish authorities simply ignore the prophetic scriptures that point to the Messiah. I doubt that your rabbi really studied this matter and arrived at the same conclusions, but that begs the question, how reliable was the testimony of a religious elite of Jesus' day, that ignored the hundreds of messianic prophecies that Jesus fulfilled to the letter? He was the long-sought Messiah of Israel. I love the Jewish people. They gave spiritual riches to Gentile Christians, but their resistance to the evident truth of Jesus' life and mission is hard to understand. Some Jews have studied messianic prophecy and trusted in the Messiah. I read the thrilling story of Joseph Cohn, a Hungarian rabbi, who read and believed the end-time calculations of the Book of Daniel. The Orthodox Jews called down curses on anyone who computed the time of the end, but Cohn's studies convinced him the Messiah had already come and would return as He promised.

Without knowing a word of English, Cohn landed in New York. He wandered into a church. On a blackboard, he saw the same mathematical calculations he knew from the Bible book of Daniel. The church was studying that book. Cohn was saved and became a missionary to his own people.

"That's a good story," said Winston, rising to go. "I've got a lot of study to do. I do believe you have convinced me that we must look again at Bible prophecy." Carver, eyes riveted on Winston, said finally, "Colonel, don't forget that I won't be here for the final revelation of any of the things we read about. As I told you before, I'm outta here when Jesus returns for me along with the millions of people who have trusted Him as Savior. The day I don't respond to your knock on the door, the day I am not there to drive you to Siwash U, or to Fifth Army Headquarters, just remember what I am telling you. I'm outta here, to live with Jesus Christ my Savior forever!" "I'll remember," Winston said wistfully, "I'll remember."

# Chapter Four
*Home Revisited*

The late afternoon sun danced along the apex of the great arch on the Saint Louis waterfront. The brown ribbon of the Mississippi and the city's downtown slid beneath the wing of the airliner. Sam Winston squirmed in his seat, checked his watch for the fifth time and scowled. Touchdown at Lambert Airport was scheduled for 4:30 PM. They wouldn't make it. Drive time gridlock was the grim prospect.

The message had simply said, "come home Sammy, Uncle Leopold dying. Love, Sophie." A trip to Saint Louis was as welcome to Sam as a root canal. It meant a legion of relatives, small talk on the downturn in the junk business, and the inevitable "why did you go in the Army, Sammy? You could have made something of yourself."

Sophie's son Derek, silently drove Sam to the suburban Ladue home he knew so well. It was a substantial sixteen-room, grey stone edifice dominating the cul-de-sac in the upscale suburban community. Sophie Bernstein, his sister, met him at the door. Derek carried his luggage to the second floor. Sophie was in great shape the direct benefit of a considerable investment in step aerobics and near starvation. Frankly fifty, Sophie showed her age in a face drawn down at the corners of the eyes and in the wrinkles of her throat. Her black hair, graying evenly, was neatly coiffed. She looked good in a figure-flattering black dress, Sam surmised was the creation of a west-end couturiere. Sophie displayed a small fortune in jewelry on long, tapered fingers and tanning-bed brown arms. Sophie was the quintessential Jewish princess.

Sophie brushed Sam's cheek with scarlet lips. "Welcome home," she said, adding the name he hated, "Sammy." "You look great, Sis. It's good to be home," he lied. Over an aperitif Sophie explained that Uncle Leopold was in the Jewish hospital. "He's worn out," she explained, "he has congestive heart failure. The doctor says it is only a matter of time."

Sam thought back over his years in this home. It was a great place. Sophie kept if up to west county standards. The furniture was new, or nearly new. The fixtures were the best money could buy. Every room was an interior decorator's dream and the grounds were immaculate. Sophie was kind of a family archivist. She kept the den as a Weinstein/Winston shrine. His discussion with Rosie of the Jews in the New Testament pressed Sam to look carefully at the wall of pictures of three generations of the family. Any Christ-killers here? Sam asked himself. Two small boys in sailor suits, Sam's father Irvin and Uncle Leopold, sat stiffly on Great-Grandfather's lap, in an oval, sepia-toned portrait. Apparently smiling was out in Nineteenth Century Germany. In another vintage photo an erect rabbi, a small tarnished plate identified as Rabbi Josef Glassman, posed in a black gown with white wing collars. Sophie explained that Glassman belonged to the Berlin Reform Society of the early 1900's. Glassman espoused a Judaism subordinate to the German State. Society members called themselves, "Germans of the Mosaic persuasion."

Carefully scanning a host of old-world Weinsteins, Sam reflected on how hard these people worked for full acceptance in German society. One uniformed figure proudly wore an Iron Cross for heroism in the service of the Kaiser. Like other German Jews, the Weinsteins had tried acculturation and assimilation, only to have it end in annihilation for those who did not make it to America. The Weinsteins were merchants. It was embedded in the Jewish psyche that you bought, sold and traded items that never lost their value. Diamonds for example. Antisemitism was endemic. Life for Jews could change suddenly. Jews secure today, could be fleeing for their lives tomorrow.

The Weinsteins were under no pressure to leave Germany, but most professions, most universities were closed to their children. At great sacrifice, the Weinsteins made the move to the United States. Runaway inflation left them with just enough money to make a start in the new world.

In this country, German Jews failed at first to find an accommodation with Yiddish-speaking Orthodox Jews, who fled the *shtetls* and villages of Russia and Poland. All were sons of Abraham, but sorely divided in religious interpretations, language, culture and social structures. Sam Winston, like other late generation American Jews, grew up with traditional values; love of home and family and respect for elders. Grandparents were important people, deferred to and obeyed. Jewish survival skills are taught mainly at the dinner table, where childish and youthful attitudes and opinions are freely indulged. Sam Winston loved his home in the years that home is important.

Uncle Leopold and Sam's father Irvin had a love-hate relationship. Leopold cared little for work. He loved cigars and wine. He lived alone. Irvin Weinstein worked seven days a week eking out a living in the metal salvage business. On paper, Leopold was his partner. It was a different life from the soft-hands merchandising of the family in the old country. It was difficult to give up the Sabbath, even for Reform Jews, but they had to in order to make a living. There was a climate of anti-semitism in America that ran high, sometimes to the level of violence. Saint Louis was an ethnic stronghold of immigrants from countries of central and eastern Europe where hatred of the Jews was bred in the bone. Thefts from the newly renamed Winston Metal Salvage was a fact of life. Irish and Polish cops on Saint Louis' north side dutifully recorded details of burglaries and vandalism, but nothing ever came of it.

The economic recovery of the late 1930's and early '40's, gave a lift to the junk-yard trade. Sales to Japan boomed and then World War II translated a slow recovery into a bottom-line bonanza. The family was large enough to hold all the key positions in the company. They employed good numbers of African Americans and true to Jewish tradition, treated them well.

Leopold Weinstein never married. He formalized his dissent from his Americanized brother by joining a Conservative synagogue. It gave Leopold a sense of religious one-upmanship over the Reform Winstons. Leopold said that he was more *frum*, observant, than the rest of the family. Leopold was careful to observe the feast days and said he never touched *treyf*, what Reform Jews euphemistically call "American food." Beyond prying eyes, Uncle enjoyed platters of eggs and bacon, ham or sausage. His mid-town apartment was a typical bachelor pad heavy with cigar smoke, newspapers and back issues of magazines.

Sam's parents, Irvin and Sylvia Winston followed Abraham's Reform Judaism. They avoided Uncle Leopold like the plague. On the high holy days they had to put up with their obnoxious relative. He was always dressed in the same seedy-looking suit, spotted by Manischewitz wine, gefilte fish and reeking of cigar smoke. Leopold knew more than anyone on any subject. His weakest arguments were always defended at the top of his voice.

For Sam, the drive to Jewish hospital was a return to his youth. He drove slowly through Clayton where he had played high school football. In University City, he recalled that Gentiles knew it as "*Jew*niversity City," a smear on its one-time Jewish majority. Sam had experienced nothing of antisemitism in spite of the ever-present hostility in the area. In the Army, theoretically color-blind on race, tolerant on religious and ethnic origin, a senior Jewish officer warned Sam early in his career, that Jews had to soldier harder than Gentiles in order to have even modest acceptance.

Jewish hospital in Saint Louis is a front rank institution, a credit to Jewish philanthropy and the best staff money can buy. Uncle Leopold was in a semi-coma. His labored breathing and the wavy line on his heart monitor the only evidence that he was alive. Sam was surprised to find his niece, Simone, seated next to Leopold's bed. She rose smiling to greet Sam. "Uncle Sammy," she said delightedly, "it's been a long time." Simone, in a denim skirt and jacket had grown into a beautiful young woman. Twenty-five now, Sam guessed, appraising the once gawky youngster he thought would never win the battle against acne. Sam grasped her at arms length, admiring the attractive young woman. "Simone Winston," Sam said slowly, "I'm sorry I'm twenty years older and a near relative for I would marry you in a heartbeat." "Uncle Sammy," she blushed, "you have always kidded me. You're kidding me now."

Uncle Leopold was an inert lump of flesh anchored to this veil of tears by tubes, bags that dripped nourishment and bags that carried waste away. Sam felt he had to speak to his dying relative. Was that a momentary blink of recognition? Probably not. Sam shook his head.

"You're a warm breath of spring, Simone," he brightened. "Say, let's go down to the food court and get a cup of coffee. I've got to get caught up on my favorite niece and the most beautiful woman in the Winston family." "I'm for it," Simone replied, "but the most beautiful woman in the family is Aunt Sophie."

Sam secured a table for them near a coffee dispenser. Simone listened carefully as Sam sketched his military career. She gasped in awe of his sensational desert exploit and urged him to take fewer chances in the future. Simone, her eyes fixed on her coffee cup said softly, "Uncle Sammy, you don't know about me, do you?" She looked up to measure his reaction. "No," said Sam, "I just know my finely-honed skills as an appraiser of women tells me you are the creme-de-la-creme of young ladies in their twenties." "Seriously, Uncle Sammy," said Simone impatiently, "you may not want to talk to me. No one else in the family does." "Why? What did you do, Simone, sell some junk to a competitor?" laughed Sam. "Uncle Sammy, I am a completed Jew. I believe in the Messiah Jesus." Eyes popping, Sam stammered, "you're a what?" "See, I knew that is what you would say. I'm a Christian Jew," she said evenly.

Sam, recovering from the shock, said, "Christian? as in born again, Bible-quoting and waiting for the Rapture?" Clearly amazed, Simone said "yes, that's where I am, but how do you know about those things, Uncle Sammy?" "Well," Sam replied, "my partner Master Sergeant Rosie Carver is your kind of Christian. He has taught me a lot about his faith." "Do you share his faith, Uncle Sammy?" Simone asked. "No," Sam continued, "I'm just an observer of unusual philosophies and belief systems. I respect Rosie because I know his faith is genuine and I'll bet the faith of my favorite niece is twenty-four karat, too." "Thanks, Uncle Sammy, but does it make a difference to you - is there a barrier between us now?" "Not at all," he said firmly, "you might learn a deep, dark secret about me. I am a card-carrying Republican, a political party no self-respecting Jew would join. But tell me how did you become a believer in the Messiah?"

"That is a story," she said brightly. "I was in the LA chapter of Meir Kahane's Jewish Defense League. I was a bonafide Jewish activist. "Never Again," was more than a T-shirt slogan for me. My principal target were the missionaries of Jews for Jesus. I hated them. At LAX one afternoon, I confronted a young girl wearing a "Jesus Made Me Kosher," shirt. I hit her, Uncle Sammy, as hard as I could. She took it. Tears streaming down her face, she told me "Y'shuah HaMuschiach, Jesus the Messiah, loves you and has a great plan for your life." I was so stunned by her sweet response to my attack, I stood there paralyzed as she pressed a broadside into my hands. I hid the broadside and when I got home I read it over and over again. It told how Jesus came into the world to be the once-for-all-time kipporah for Jews and Goyim. The broadside challenged the reader to pick up a New Testament and read about Adonai's salvation. I did, Uncle Sammy, and I found myself wanting to believe it."

"Uncle Sammy," she continued, "I was so ashamed of my assault on that girl. I thought, we can't win the war of ideas with our fists. Anyway, the broadside told of meetings for those interested and gave a date, place and time. I went. I met Jews for Jesus from every kind of Jewish background including the young girl that I had clobbered. I went again and then I went back again. They answered all my questions from the Jewish Bible, a book I did not know. It didn't take long, Uncle Sammy. I gave my heart to Jesus. Now I spend most of my time learning all I can about the Messiah in order to help other people to know him, too."

Sam, reflecting on all that Simone had to say, finally suggested "so now you are no longer a Jew." "No, no, no," Simone shot back, "I am a Jew and I will die a Jew." I've reached back in the history of our people and I have touched Abraham, Isaac, Jacob, David and all of our people of faith. I'm a fully completed Jew," she said in triumph, "and incidentally, I am no longer a Winston. I'm a Weinstein, like Uncle Leopold. I want to be identified with our people who suffered so much in Europe." Sam smiled and said, "I'm proud of you kid. Count on me to be cheering you on."

At an informal gathering in Sophie's home that evening, Sam looked around for Simone. He sidled up to her father Julius and asked if she would be there. "No, she is *geshmat*," Julius replied, using the Yiddish term for a Jew who converts to the Christian faith. "I won't permit her to come here. She is a disgrace to our family." Sam said nothing, but asked himself, where is the legendary Jewish laissez-faire attitude toward our people with divergent views?

Uncle Leopold stubbornly clung to life. At Sophie's request, Sam used up some of his accumulated leave to remain in Saint Louis. It gave him time to review Rosie's notes and to try and organize his thinking about the Jewish life he had not considered for so many years. The troubling thought was, if Carver is right and the Jews face dark days ahead, are we prepared to deal with it? His grim conclusion was that they were not.

Friday evening at the Temple was a pleasant experience for Sam. The modern edifice of Temple B'Nai El stood on the very ground his grandfather had given for the first synagogue. The Weinstein family built the original house of worship virtually alone. Sam was a little surprised that the presiding rabbi was a woman. Rabbi Rona Kravitz was mid-thirties, a little overweight, some would say *zaftig*, but with cherubic good looks. Her tiny kippeh pinned to short brown hair, and colorful doctoral robes did little to relieve Sam's surprise at finding a woman in a man's traditional domain.

Before the service began there was a ripple in the congregation. Heads turned to follow the Parnas, the president of the temple, as he left his seat in the eastern wall to deal with some kind of confusion at the door. Sam was startled to see it was Simone, at the center of the controversy. He heard the Parnas say, "no *meshumad* is welcome here. You must leave." Simone said nothing, turned and walked away.

The service went well for Sam Winston, the rare attendee. Rabbi Kravitz was a good speaker. She scored her congregation for a lackluster Judaism. She laid the blame to mini-faith. Mini-faith resulted in mini-commitment and mini-involvement. She urged a return to the faith of the fathers as the only way to build a viable Judaism for the future. The message was well received, mainly because it was mercifully short.

The *Oneg Shabbat* following the service, that marvelous custom of sharing refreshments and conversation, allowed Sam time to visit with old friends and a host of relatives he could barely recall by name. Sam worked the crowd carefully in order to corner the rabbi. Balancing a cup of coffee and a cream puff, Sam introduced himself and shortly identified himself as a non-observant Jew. The rabbi with a sardonic smile, said "*Nu*, to each his own." Sam pointed out that his cousin Louie, loudly talking across the room, claimed he was into Buddhism. Sam indicated a businessman nearby, with whom he had shared the bimah at his Bar Mitzvah years ago, who claimed to be a Socialist. He contended that religion is the opiate of the people. "Those facts seem to say, rabbi, that a Jew can espouse just about any cause or philosophy he chooses and still remain a Jew. Is that correct, rabbi?" Rabbi Kravitz shrugged resignedly, "yes, that is the liberal tradition in our faith."

"Well, then," said Sam, in a prosecutorial tone, "how is that there is no such liberty extended to Messianic Jews? Good heavens, rabbi, the parnas put my niece Simone out of the temple and she is more of a Jew than I am, or for that matter my cousin and the businessman. I didn't darken the door of a synagogue, temple or shul for twenty years and you welcomed me. She reads the Tenach all day long and you keep her out!" Desperate to flee, Rabbi Kravitz exclaimed, "I'm sorry Mr. Winston, from Jerusalem to Ladue, our people will not accept Messianists as Jews. That's just the way it is." She gathered her robes around her and headed for her office.

Uncle Leopold gave up the ghost and passed to his own place. Sam strained to remember the appropriate words - *Baruch Dayan Emet*, "Blessed be the True Judge." The *Chevra Kadesha*, the Holy Society, prepared the body in accordance with Jewish law. Leopold was robed in a simple white *tachrichin*. A bag of Israeli soil was placed under his head and he was laid to rest in a Jewish cemetery according to the *Din*, the burial regulations.

Sophie managed the *shivah* arrangement for her own home. "*Sitting shivah*," the Jewish mourning rites for the home, were technically for immediate family members. Sophie was determined to do it up right for Uncle Leopold. Pictures were carefully laid away for the period of mourning. Mirrors were draped. Sam fingered the button that spared him the traditional tear in the garment, and dutifully pinned it to his lapel. Like the other mourners, he sat on the floor and said nothing. He needed to think. He couldn't get over Simone and the synagogue that would not receive her and Jewish rejection of - what did Simone call them? "completed Jews."

Looking around the room, the mourners were typically Jewish, decent, good people. They had made something of themselves in this country, but it was the Torah and Tradition that gave these people a leg up on life. In 1954, American Jews celebrated "three hundred years without tears." The Jews are people with an amazing capacity to rise from obscurity to prominence in many fields.

The Jewish odyssey did not begin here in America. It began in the slave markets after the destructions of Israel in 70 A.D. and again in 135 A.D. The Jewish survivors of those bloody sieges were sold into slavery. They made good slaves. A highly literate people, they were too valuable to allow to die in Sicilian salt mines. They found their way into home service, medicine, even royal drawing rooms, and centers of art, music and culture. Self-imposed rules for survival were as closely woven as they had been for the temple sacrifices and life in Israel. The people in the Weinstein/Winston family proved that it worked.

Sam felt alternately proud of his Jewish heritage and alarmed at the Jewish lack of cohesion in the face of what Rosie and Simone called the impending Great Tribulation. Where do I fit in? he asked himself. Am I to die with the people in this room or will I find the truth my niece has found; the truth Rosie lives by? Time will tell, he concluded.

# Chapter Five
*Meet Hadassah Weizmann*

Winston flew back to Chicago to Fifth Army Headquarters in Chicago. It was good to be back. Life in the Army wasn't easy, but it was simple. You understood the rules and for the most part, the Army made your decisions for you. Civilian life on the other hand, Sam concluded, was tough. He had spent ten days in Saint Louis trying to figure out how to fit into a family he had outgrown and a Judaism from which he had long been estranged. He felt guilty. Sophie was, well, Sophie. The rest of the family was made up of nice people, but their lifestyles were unappealing. Simone was something special, but even she had added a troubling dimension to his already crowded considerations. He fingered the bronze *mizrach*, his only heirloom from Uncle Leopold's apartment. The plate told the visitor the direction for prayer to Jerusalem.

Saint Louis had not helped his search for meaning in religious life. He gave money from time to time, to this Jewish appeal and that *Yeshiva*, Israel bonds and a local temple. He felt it made him a kind of "alimony Jew," willing to pay some of Judaism's bills, but not willing to live with her. It was a relief to see things in the here and now once again. It was Army olive drab and green.

The Army's ROTC inspection teams were off the road. Planning was under way for the cadets' arduous six-week summer field training program. Sam and Rosie lounged in the headquarters' amphitheater awaiting the camp briefing. At headquarters, they were careful to observe military address. It was colonel and sergeant. It was said to be written in stone somewhere that "familiarity breeds contempt." The modern, professional Army had pretty well laid that maxim to rest, but the principle was observed in the breach. If an officer's efficiency rating was marginal, an added remark about familiarity with subordinates might be all that it takes to finish his career.

"How was the trip home, Colonel?" Rosie asked quietly. Fishing for words, Sam replied, "I don't know what to say. We buried a relative, I really didn't like. My sister Sophie and her family made me comfortable, which made me uncomfortable. The one bright spot in it all, was an unexpected visit with my niece Simone." Lowering his voice to a whisper, Winston exclaimed, "she is one of you, Rosie, a believer in the Messiah Jesus! Our family treated her coarsely and our synagogue would not allow her to worship. Rosie turned slightly toward Winston and said, "I would love to hear your reaction to Simone's faith." Winston savored the question and answered softly, "I saw genuine - what shall I call it? conviction? belief? faith?, maybe all of the above, that I see in you Rosie. I loved her for her sweet, winsome expression of faith."

The conversation ended abruptly as the briefing officer stepped to the podium. Lights dimmed, and the film rolled of armored vehicles maneuvering in the rough terrain of the Desert Warfare School, Fort Irwin, California. "So that is where our wannabe Pattons and Powells will spend the bulk of their summer," someone said with obvious satisfaction. That should weed out the pretenders and the faint-of-heart, Winston mused.

Strolling back to the two by four office they shared, Rosie, eager to learn if Sam was still interested in the Bible study they had dropped while on leave, explained that he had prepared a pretty comprehensive guide to end-time prophecy. "Interested?" he queried. "Yeah, sure," Winston shot back, with just enough vigor to excite Carver. Winston went on to say, "I am by turns confused and concerned. I thought I knew what makes our people tick, but now I'm not sure. I just hope these aren't the last days or the end-times as you call them. The tiny micro-image of Jewish life that I had for ten days, did not encourage me to believe our people are ready for anything like a great tribulation. Where would my family be, Rosie?" "Some Jews will survive," Rosie said gravely. He quoted Matthew 24:3, "But he that shall endure to the end, the same shall be saved." The way for the Jewish people to avoid the Great Tribulation is to turn to the Messiah Jesus now."

The telephone buzzed. Carver answered and handed the phone over to Winston. "Colonel Winston?" the operator queried, "Sir, there is a call for you from DA on 226." "Department of the Army?" Sam said, puzzled. "What did I do now?" "Lieutenant Colonel Winston, here" he answered. "Colonel," was the reply, "this is DA Personnel Section, Captain Lang on the line, sir. We have a TWX from US Army Section, NATO, Brussels. The message reads: LTC Samuel R Winston WP 1600 hours zulu, Wednesday next, Chicago to Brussels International Airport arriving NLT 1000 hours Thursday. Meet CPT Rita Brown, NATO section protocol officer on arrival. Complete travel arrangement at the Lufthansa desk, O'Hare International. Captain Lang added, "Colonel, pack your blues, sir." Winston knew better than to ask the purpose of the assignment, but he asked anyway. "Sorry, Colonel," Lang replied, faintly irked by the question," I'm just the messenger boy around here. Good luck, sir."

The long flight, O'Hare, then layover at Heathrow, London, on to Brussels, was an ordeal for Winston. Flying usually triggered mild panic attacks, a dark room in his psyche, Winston had managed to conceal from the Army. It simply meant no window seat, no looking down at the angry waves of the Atlantic and of course, no sleeping. It was a help to peruse Carver's prophetic notebook.

Captain Rita Brown, a plain, Government-Issue, staff officer, greeted the haggard-looking colonel in the crumpled green uniform. Brown drove him through Brussels. The capital is a city of broad boulevards, beautiful parks and squares. Handsome buildings, like those in the Grand Place in the lower city, are the show place of the Low Countries.

On the way to the Hotel Westburg, Brown briefed him on the purpose of the trip. A reception was laid on for the next day, in which the French government, with the kind permission of the King of Belgium, the European Union, and the approval of the several governments concerned, General Roy would confer French decorations on an Italian, an Israeli, a British and an American officer for distinguished conduct in the rescue of General Roy. Brown added that certain posthumous decorations would be awarded to those of the entourage KIA in the operation. "There will be a formal luncheon at 1300 in the Westburg ballroom and the investiture will follow. Questions, sir?"

Winston stared wide-eyed. For more than a year he had expected his part in the assassination attempt would somehow terminate his career. Now he was to be decorated for it. Something didn't add up. If he didn't deserve to be cashiered for the incident, he certainly didn't deserve to be decorated for it either. Brown seemed to read his mind. "Colonel, you will have to file DD Form 2268, "Request to Wear or Display Foreign Decorations." In triplicate of course," she added. She handed Winston his hotel room smartcard and dropped him at the ornate main entrance of the Westburg.

Winston napped, read and ruminated through the rest of Thursday. The incessant ringing of the telephone roused him the next morning. Captain Brown was on the line urging him to meet her in the hotel coffee shop. Over very strong Turkish coffee, Brown conveyed the real feelings of the U S Amy NATO section about the afternoon's investiture. The American staff didn't like the idea at all, but were powerless to do anything about it. They had never gotten over their reticence at having a U S officer in the Roy entourage to begin with. When the operation went south it confirmed their worst fears for it. Now it was to be a sideshow of ruffles and flourishes inappropriate to an incident that was best forgotten. Brown went on to say, that no one in diplomatic, military or media circles could ever remember so much honor bestowed on so many for so little. Winston groaned audibly. Now, he would be under a cloud for a medal he really didn't want.

About one hundred guests, about equally divided among military brass and swallow-tail, coated NATO and European Union functionaries, milled around in the ballroom waiting on General Roy. The honorees were herded into a corner and given instructions on where to stand, how to address the general, how to remain motionless when the medal was pinned on and to be prepared for the inevitable buss on both cheeks.

General Roy strode into the room, followed by his staff and accompanied by the black robed papal nuncio for Belgium. After a loud rendition of La Marseillaise, Luigi Cardinal Giancarlo muttered a short prayer, crossed himself and plunged into the tomato aspic. The honorees were seated at Roy's table. British Brigadier Desmond Carruthers, M.D., Royal Army Medical Corps, the thoracic surgeon credited with saving Roy's life in the four-hour long surgery in Tel Aviv, was seated on

33

Roy's right. Carruthers was uniformed in walking out dress. Four rows of ribbons testified of a long and distinguished military medical career. The papal nuncio was seated to Roy's left. He was totally absorbed in his wine and entree and spoke to no one.

Winston, in U S Army blues, was seated between the prelate and Lieutenant Hadassah Weizmann, of the Israeli Defense Forces. She wore a soft green uniform. Lieutenant Weizmann was the evac helicopter pilot who had plucked the general out of the desert. Winston kept up a light, but lively conversation with her all through lunch. Sam chuckled to himself that the table arrangements had created a kind of Jewish ghetto with Winston and Weizmann sandwiched between the papal nuncio and Major Pietro De Luca of the crack Italian Bersaglieri. De Luca had been Winston's deputy security officer in the run from Amman.

A civilian at the table, was introduced as M'sieu Dupin, a French embassy official. He looked and acted like a security agent. The surprise guest was Mother Maria Joseph Castaldi, the superior of a convent of the Sisters of the Common Life, the religious order that nursed Roy back to health in their remote, cloistered home on the Adriatic. Not the hospital setting, mused Winston, you would expect for one so grievously wounded.

Winston studied Roy carefully. He was amazed at the man he had given up for dead holding court as though three bullet wounds in vital organs was no more serious than a cold. Winston looked for diminished strength, any weakness in speech or hand-eye coordination. He found none. Roy was immaculate in French Army horizon blue with general's stars on the cuffs. He said little, but when he spoke it was warm and animated, displaying the strength he was at great pains to showcase. He addressed Winston in English as a familiar friend and then gave himself to deep conversation with Doctor Carruthers. In a table where everyone seemed to be at home in French, fortunately for Winston Lieutenant Weizmann spoke peerless English.

General Roy opened the investiture with a statement of gratitude to God and to Holy Mother Mary for his healing and for the surgical skills of Brigadier Carruthers, the healing arts of Israeli and Italian medics and for Mother Castaldi, and the religious of her Order. Then he thanked the armed forces of the United States, Italy, Israel and Jordan for officers who performed so valiantly under fire. Each of the officers received France's coveted Medaille Militaire. Mother Castaldi received another ribboned medal, but no kiss. The investiture was brief and impressive. As he bussed Winston, Roy whispered, "get your money down on the Canadiens to take the Stanley Cup, Sam." Amid ruffles and flourishes from the Belgian Army band, Roy was whisked out of the room through a service entrance, surrounded by a cloud of security officers. Heavy security for a mere French Brigadier General, Winston thought, but then Belgium is host to thousands of foreign nationals some hostile to everything in the West.

The shank of the afternoon Winston spent hanging around the hotel lobby. He was hailed by Major De Luca, with a loud "*Mio Colonello,*" and an open palm salute. De Luca looked good in the black-feathered Stetson of the Italian Bersaglieri. The only thing De Luca wanted to talk about was the one that got away. He had chased the assailant Winston missed, for a couple of miles down a long, deep wadi that bisected the route of the Roy motorcade. The wadi was deep enough to hide an armored division, with maddening twists and turns every hundred feet or so. Winston had noted the larger Wadi al Arabah skirting the Jordan River south of the route, but the depression at the attack site was not shown on his situation map. Winston cursed for failing to take special steps to handle the unexpected.

Winston longed to get some additional information on Roy's condition when the chopper delivered him to the hospital in Tel Aviv. It was time to talk to Lieutenant Weizmann. He went to the lobby house phone, lifted it from the cradle and then quickly replaced it. Would the young junior officer, far from home, think this old Yankee colonel was hitting on her? He decided it was worth the risk and had the operator ring her room. Giddy as a schoolboy fumbling over his words, Winston asked, "Lieutenant, how about dinner? Those who know me say I am relatively harmless and I know Brussels fairly well. Perhaps we can find a steak and gefilte fish combo somewhere." Weizmann giggled and stammered, "uniform or civvies, Colonel?" "Civvies of course, Miss Weitzmann, I have a pink polyester suit left over from the nineteen seventies, that will make me feel as young as you are. Say, seven?"

Sam Winston cut a fine figure in his dark blue Brooks Brothers suit. A tailored oxford button-down shirt and Countess Mara tie, turned the head of more than one woman in the hotel elevator and lobby. Hadassah Weizmann was lovely. Her dress was Middle Eastern fashionable of some fabric Sam could only guess at. It fit her tall, willowy figure to a T. Her hair, no longer imprisoned under a military cap, was black and sleek, parted on the side and falling to her shoulders. It was a perfect match for her black eyes and olive skin. A simple shoulder strap purse matched her sandals. Winston was struck.

They walked for what seemed like miles, his date barefoot, past the King's Palace, the parliament, the Palais de Justice, the Stock Exchange and the Opera House. They agreed it would be Hadassah and Sam. They had dinner at a delightful off-square restaurant, dimly lit with a strolling violinist. Hadassah described her life as a sabra, a native-born Israeli. The family home was on Kibbutz Kfar Halutz, a satellite of the mammoth twin farms of Degania. Degania designated Alef and Bet, A and B, is at the south end of the Sea of Galilee. The Weizmanns came from Poland before World War I, she explained, in the second Aliyah, a term Winston remembered means "going up." From everywhere in the world, to journey to Israel and particularly to Jerusalem, is said to be going up. They were hard-working farmers, doctrinaire Socialists and passionately dedicated to making a new life in a hard land. It meant a return to the days of Nehemiah, carrying a spade in one hand and a sword in the other.

Hadassah smiled coyly and said, "you may have heard of my Great-Grandfather,

Haim Weizmann. "Yes, I know about him," Winston responded, "let me see, it was Haim Weizmann, ha-nasi, ha-rishon. Haim Weizmann," he translated, "first president of Israel." Hadassah clapped in approval of Sam's lone, modern Hebrew sentence.

"You really want to talk to me about the extraction of General Roy, don't you Sam?" fixing her gaze on Winston. "Yeah, I would like that, if you are free to talk about it," he responded. "Well, she began, I was in the dispersal hut when the call came in. We had laid on six helicopters on stand-by, four attack and two rescue in support of the Jordanian crossing. The slogan of the IDF is *konnenut*, preparedness. I had responsibility for the rescue craft, an MH-53, your "Jolly Green Giant," - "yes," Winston interjected, "we now call it the Pave Low III," "Right," Hadassah continued, "and MH-60G, the Pave Hawk, smaller, but a great low-level chopper. No less a person than Rav-Aluf Galin ordered the Hawk because it was faster and all but Roy were expendable. The 53 would not hold everyone anyway. He reasoned you would not want to leave your transport in the dessert in any event.

I pushed the Hawk at 320/kmh and was there in minutes. You brought me in on flares and radio-telephone, but we had an ORION spy-plane overhead that pinpointed your position for me on take-off. Your medics had done what they could to stabilize the general, but he had lost so much blood. We pumped plasma into him and were off. I was directed to the heliport at the Tel Aviv hospital. The staff, surrounded by security people, rushed him into surgery. I reported in at the dispersal hut and was debriefed by Galin." "I can't believe Roy was not DOA at Tel Aviv?" Winston said. Hadassah explained, "all through the flight I asked the nurse and medic on board about his condition and every time it was a shrug."

Winston related his side of the story. "I cleared the bodies of the driver and the guard and moved my gear from the Land Rover into the limousine. Our Arab Legion escort came to me and said it was time for them to return to Amman. I questioned their timing. We had about an hour of open country to cross and a handful of guns. Were we being set up? No one in our entourage was important enough to be worth another assault, unless some group was out to embarrass the armed forces of the West."

"I drove to the Allenby Bridge, wind whistling through the shattered windows all the way. When we passed under IDF control, I turned over the limousine to an Israeli transportation officer. I was picked up by a Hummer and driven to the hospital. The place was crawling with agents of the SDECE, the French intelligence agency that I understand those in the cloak-and-dagger business call *La Piscine*, the "Swimming Pool." That's after their Paris headquarters near a public pool. They hassled me as though I was a Bedouin terrorist. Do you understand the term hassle, Lieutenant?" Winston asked. "Sure I do, and my name is Hadassah, remember?" "Pardon me," blushed Winston. "They treated me as roughly as they did the paparazzi that was there in good numbers." "Sam, do you know Israel went to Def-

Con 3 that night," Hadassah said soberly. "Defense Condition Three," Sam said with a whistle. "I bet France talked about some pre-emptive strike, but against whom?"

The dinner was more than adequate, the price exorbitant. Hadassah laughed as she offered to throw in a few Israeli Lirot, as her part of the check. Winston declined her offer with the declaration, "Uncle Sugar pays a heavy piece of change to O-5's, Lieutenant Colonels, Miss Weizmann, but if you would feel better about it I could submit a request through channels that the U S aid package for Israel be reduced a few dollars." "Don't do that Sam, we need all the help we can get. Israel has survived for most of a century on American aid and the free-will gifts of Jews the world over. We are the only country in the world that exits on donations from friends." Her mood changed to somber as she continued, "But funding is not the biggest problem confronting Israel and the Middle East." "What's that," Sam inquired. "Water," she said with emphasis. "For years, Turkey has planned to build twenty-one dams on the Euphrates. Downstream, Syria and Iraq stand to lose two-thirds of their water supply. Israel faces a water shortage of thirty percent. Add to that grim statistic forty percent of our water comes from two aquifers between the Gaza Strip and the West Bank. Contested territory." Winston could only shake his head.

On the walk back to the hotel, Sam felt like a schoolboy on his first date. The confirmed bachelor was clearly smitten by the young Israeli sabra, who he ruefully recalled was about seventeen years his junior. He tried to gauge Hadassah's feelings. Were those stars in her eyes? Was she a good junior officer dutifully attentive to a senior officer with whom she had shared an adventure? Was this just an evening to while away in a foreign city? Hadassah broke the spell. She had to fly out at 0600 for London's Heathrow Airport to connect with an El Al Israel flight. It's back to - what do you yanks call them, "the whirly birds?"

At her hotel room door Sam was seriously tempted to kiss her upturned face and scarlet lips. Instead he clasped her right hand in his and said, "this is your cyclic pitch, stick hand, isn't it, Lieutenant? Don't let go." With that he turned to leave. "Shalom, shalom," Hadassah called after him. Over his shoulder Winston promised, "we'll meet again, Lieutenant."

In his room, Sam Winston relaxed for a few minutes and then remembered Captain Brown's envelope. He found DD Form 2268, "Request to Wear or Display Foreign Decorations." But there was something else, a single, folded sheet of paper. It was a top-secret intelligence report.

Roy, Jean-Luc Armand
LTC, Canadian Forces [Royal 22nd Regiment]
Brevet, BG, Army of the Republic of France
Born: Kamouraska, PQ, Canada
Age, this report 43

Roy is a highly regarded Infantry officer with no combat experience. He partici-
pated in and led several UN peace-keeping missions with distinction.

Subject is a devout Roman Catholic, associated with extreme conservative figures
and movements within the Church. He has been identified with elements in the
Vatican opposed to Liberation Theology in the Third World and to the Progressive
Catholic movement in the United States, Austria and the Netherlands. He is also a
clandestine member of the separatist Parti Quebecois of French Canada, but has
never demonstrated any disloyalty to the Crown or to the Canadian government.

The transfer of Roy from the Canadian Army to the French establishment was
engineered by conservative Catholic authorities in the Vatican, in Paris and Quebec,
according to a confidential report from SISMI, the Italian intelligence agency. The
report holds that the transfer was effected in order to carve a European Union (EU)
military organization out of the present NATO structure.

Roy's visit to the Middle East was billed as a EU good-will tour, but unconfirmed
reports persist that he was there to sound-out Islamic leaders on a possible move of
Eurodollar interests to a new base somewhere in the area, possibly Iraq.

Roy was seriously wounded in an attack in the Jordanian desert. He was treated
and his life was spared. It is not known why he was flown to an obscure Catholic
convent on the Adriatic Coast for recuperation. He seems well at present. Some
ultra-conservative Catholic elements have been quoted as saying, Roy actually died
and was miraculously healed. The purpose, if any, for this claim is obscure.
NEED TO KNOW BASIS ONLY

What has Roy gotten into? Winston asked himself. If he is smart, he will go back
to Petawawa to Canadian Army garrison life. It will take months, maybe years, to
get over three slugs in the chest and neck. The wine and banquet circuit will com-
plicate recovery, but it seems that somebody wants Roy to go to the top in
European politics. That's tough.

# Chapter Six
### *Roy's miracle recovery*

Groggy, Winston reached for the telephone with its peculiar European ring. The digital clock showed 0430. "Rita Brown here Colonel. Did I waken you?" "Captain," Winston grumbled, "you are the Army's replacement for the bugle. Not even reveille goes at 0430." Brown ignored the barb. "Sorry, sir, but you have an 0900 de-briefing at NATO section." Brown drove Winston to NATO headquarters, skillfully threading her way through traffic gridlock. Brussels was a beautiful city. Last night it had taken on a special charm with Hadassah Weizmann.

The staff drones moved in and out of NATO headquarters, some in uniform, some in the nondescript suits of civilian functionaries. Winston placed a hand on the sensor plate beside the door of the U S Section. After a few seconds, the high-tech palm reader identified him and the door buzzed open. The section resembled a war room with a wall-size, computerized situation map of Europe, North Africa and the Middle East. Here a small contingent of military personnel seemed to bob and weave before a wall dedicated to Mars, the God of War. Winston immediately thought of the faithful at the Wailing Wall.

Winston was de-briefed by four field-grade officers. He was tempted to ask how many officers it takes to de-brief a luncheon? He smiled to himself as he thought, "hmm, maybe they want to see my medal." After some stiff pleasantries, a stuffy little intelligence officer, his eyes fixed on the ceiling said, "Colonel, what did General Roy say to you, before, during or after the luncheon?" I never had a conversation with the General at all, oh, yeah," he suddenly recalled," in the medal ceremony he bussed me on the cheek and told me to get my money down on the Canadiens to win the Stanley Cup." The grim de-briefers didn't appreciate the humor of it, but said nothing. Winston had held staff positions and hated every one. He was a field officer. Some men fit right into staff positions comfortably. Winston theorized professional staff people were seconded to their choice positions because someone held, "this officer has exhibited exemplary pusillanimous pussyfooting in a number of choice assignments."

You must be aware, Colonel, that Roy has requested through channels for you to be assigned to the staff of a shadow EU group," commented a bored major with arms folded. "Never heard of it," replied Winston. "I know they have tried for years to put together some kind of outfit, to show the EU flag, but no, no one has said anything to me about signing on." "Well, the major continued, "it is a only a paper organization right now."

The stuffy little intelligence officer, his eyes off the ceiling and directly on Winston, asked, "what would you think about an assignment to that unit?" "I dunno," Winston said, "what's required? Will it get me a promotion to O-6? I thought we didn't really like the EU." "We don't," was the sharp retort. "Unofficially, that is. Colonel," the officer with his eyes back on the ceiling said, "Colonel, we need an ear in the EU military establishment, but we are unsure if we ought to recommend approval of Roy's request for your services. What do you think?" "It's a new idea," Winston reflected, "but maybe it would work. I'm a little too old now for a good many assignments, but if it only exists on paper, perhaps I could do it. I'm a bachelor." The de-briefing was over and the foursome trooped out. Winston yawned, then thought of the distasteful flight home.

Packing mechanically, Winston was taken up with the English edition of television news. Film and commentary rolled on General Roy. He was in the south of France at the Church of the Holy Mother. In a ceremony the Catholic Church does so well, the papal nuncio for Spain conferred the Grand Cross of Isabel the Catholic on the general. The general was cited as "the defender of the one, true, church of Jesus Christ and the champion of liberty-loving peoples everywhere." Hmm, Winston thought, he has certainly come a long way for a mere Canadian lieutenant colonel. If Captain Brown's intelligence report is correct, the plotters are pulling out all the stops to make Roy the number one boy in the European Union. Is this something I need to be around to watch?

The news story on Roy segued to an interview with Brigadier Carruthers, the British Army surgeon who saved Roy's life. Carruthers, interviewed at his home near Aldershot, England, related that he was lecturing at Hebrew University in Givat Ram, Israel, when he was summoned by the medical staff at the Montefiore Hospital in Tel Aviv and asked to consult on an undisclosed emergency. "I was told later," Carruthers continued, "that it was General Roy of the European Union. He had been flown in from the attack site in Jordan. I found him bleeding from a gunshot wound mere centimeters from the carotid artery, a second wound through the left shoulder and a third serious wound three centimeters from the right ventricle of the heart. I was only there for consultation, but they asked me to operate." "Doctor," a reporter asked, "have you heard the report that General Roy died at some point and was somehow miraculously revived?" "No," Carruthers answered, "that's news to me. I am glad to say he was alive when we finished the nearly four hour surgical procedure." Carruthers continued, "I remained at the hospital through the first night and I popped in on him several times. I continued to monitor his condition through the next three or four days that I was in Israel. The hospital staff did an absolutely smashing job and I felt sure he would make it."

Television news went to a split-screen interview in Paris with Mother Maria-Joseph Castaldi, the prioress of the convent on the Italian Adriatic coast where Roy recuperated. Doctor Carruthers listened. Castaldi related that the Holy Father, the pope, asked her to take Roy in for security reasons. Mother Castaldi explained that the Sisters of the Common Life is a contemplative community, but when the Holy Father asked for the favor, she was delighted to comply. She went on to say, that Roy was in the convent for four months. Italian physicians and nurses were on the premises throughout his recovery. The nuns held round the clock vigils, she said, praying that the general's life might be spared. He did very well, but early in the second week of recuperation, he had a seizure and died. "He was gone for just seconds." Mother Castaldi crossed herself. "Perhaps it was a minute of two, and then he miraculously revived and from that moment on his recovery was simply amazing." "Do you believe the general's death and recovery is a miracle, Mother Castaldi," a reporter asked, "say on the order of other church miracles." "Oh," the nun exclaimed," that is for the church to say, not a poor nun. We believe in the power of prayer. The dear sisters enlisted the intercession of our Buddhist brothers. They pray wondrously. They invoked Tibetan spirit-guides on the general's behalf."

Pressing for answers, the news anchor asked, "Mother Castaldi, were any of the attending medical staff present when General Roy died and revived?" "No," she replied, "the sisters had surrounded the general's bed just before compline and prayed the Rosary. The nurses usually left his room when we came to pray. We prayed for three or four minutes then the general gasped. I looked up from my Rosary and felt for a pulse. He was gone! Then he breathed deeply and was with us again. I summoned the nurse and she examined his heart monitor, took his pulse and pronounced him stable."

"How do you respond to Mother Castaldi's account of the general's death and return to life, Doctor?" a news anchor asked Carruthers. "Dear boy, I am only an Army doctor. Miracles are out of my line." "Well, Doctor, is the report credible?" the newsman asked impatiently." "This dear lady certifies it to be true. Who could doubt such a vigilant nurse?" responded the unctuous Carruthers.

Winston used the flight home to get back into Carver's outline of prophetic events. It had been a long time. Winston closed his eyes and ticked off Carver's presentation of the first five events of the Great Tribulation. Let's see, False Messiahs (Matthew 24:4-5), wars and rumors of wars (verse 6), and famine, disease and earthquakes (verse 7). The review led Winston to a section Rosie called:

The Trigger. It began with a quotation from Daniel 9:27:
   "And he shall confirm the covenant with many
   for one week: and in the midst of the week
   he shall cause the sacrifice and the oblation to cease..."

Carver's commentary on the notes, began:

"he" refers to a leader out of Western Europe, the old Holy Roman Empire. This man receives power from Satan (2 Thessalonians 2:3-10). He is called the "Man of Sin" by the Apostle Paul and the Antichrist and the Beast in the writings of the Apostle John (See 1 John 2:18; Rev 13:2; 17:3,8-18).

"confirms the covenant" Bible scholars believe that the Antichrist will somehow procure the Jerusalem Temple Mount, presently the Muslim Dome of the Rock, through negotiation, threat, some means of purchase or trade. He will present the Temple Mount to the Jewish people, enabling them to rebuild a new temple for Judaism.


  "covenant with many" The guarantee of worship in the new temple is for Israeli Jews. It is thought that a great number of Jews and Gentiles outside of Israel would be forced into some kind of religious connection with pseudochristians, false religionists and cultists in a sole, legal, "one world religion."

  "for one week" This cryptic time period was familiar to Jews as a week of years, or seven years. This is the whole period of the Great Tribulation.


  "in the midst of the week he shall cause the sacrifice and oblation to cease" Sacrifice and oblation refers to the Old Testament animal offerings in prescribed ceremonials, rituals and on specific days. The restoration of these offerings, including priests of the family of Aaron and the Levites, lost since the temple was destroyed in 70 A.D., has been the cherished dreams of Jews, particularly Orthodox Jews.

  To have the covenant broken in the "midst of the week" means that after 3 1/2 years or 42 months, the Antichrist will abruptly end the Old Testament sacrifices.

## HOW WILL THIS HAPPEN?

  "...for the overspreading of abominations he shall make it desolate."

### (Daniel 9:27)

  The Antichrist sets himself up as the object of worship in the Holy of Holies in the Temple! No sin is as abhorrent to the Jews as worship of a man or an idol. Jesus cited Daniel 92:7 in Matthew 24:15, confirming the shocking nature of this discovery.

## WHAT HAPPENS NEXT?

  The breach of the covenant is the opening of the Great Tribulation, particularly as it falls on the Jews (see Jeremiah 30:4-7). Jesus wrote an extended warning about this period in prophecy:

  "When ye therefore shall see the abomination of desolation, spoken of by Daniel the prophet, stand in the holy place, (whoso readeth let him understand:) Then let them which be in Judea flee into the mountains: Let him which is on the housetop not come down to take any thing out of his house: Neither let him which is in the field return back to take his clothes. And woe unto them with child and to them that give suck in those days! But pray ye that your flight be not in the winter, neither on the Sabbath day: For then shall be great tribulation, such as was not since the beginning of the world to this time, no, nor ever shall be. And except those days should be shortened, there should no flesh be saved: but for the elect's sake those days shall be shortened."

(Matthew 24:15-22)

Winston was clearly shaken. But, he thought, perhaps this is not future, but rather a description of what took place in the Roman siege of 70 A.D. That idea was quickly dispelled as he read again, Matthew 24:21: "for then shall be great tribulation, such as was not since the beginning of the world, to this time, no, nor ever shall be." Carver's concluding remark for this section was: "the focus of end-time prophecy is on Israel, the Jews and the Temple Mount."

Sam thought back over the recent history of the Temple Mount. Israeli paratroopers burst through the St. Stephen's or Lion gate into the old, walled city of Jerusalem on Sunday, June 7, 1967, during the Six-Day War. Israeli soldiers were in the holy city for the first time in centuries. They had to hire a guide to show them to the Western or Wailing Wall of the remains of Herod's Temple. At the wall, Army Chief Rabbi Shlomo Goren prayed and there began a modern vision of a rebuilt Temple on the grounds of Mount Moriah, where Abraham offered Isaac. Solomon erected his magnificent Temple on these very grounds. At the close of the Babylonian Captivity, Zerubabel rebuilt the temple and later Herod spent years refurbishing it. It stood until a Roman torch destroyed it in 70 A.D. Winston recalled that before the guns fell silent in the Six-Day War there was a clamor to rebuild the Temple NOW! The Winston family was indifferent to the rebuilding of the Temple, like most Reform Jews, but secretly proud of the Israeli victory. They quietly gave liberally to the rebuilding project.

The problem for fifteen centuries is that the Dome of the Rock and the Al Aksa Mosque is the site of the third most holy place in Islam. The prophet Mohammed went to paradise from that spot. Golda Meir, the strong, resolute leader of Israel in 1967 ruled against any attempt on the Temple Mount on the likelihood that it would invite a UN takeover. For decades the Jews were only able to look on the Mount with great longing and the inextinguishable hope that has sustained them through hundreds of years.

Golda Meir and her successors in the Knesset were not able to suppress the Temple zealots for long. A group known as the Temple Mount Faithful, prayed at the holy place and even exchanged gunfire with the *Wakf*. They kept alive the dream of a restored Temple worship. If Carver's interpretation is correct, Winston thought, the Jews are going to build their Temple, but not with the happy ending they expect.

It was good to be back home. Carver greeted Winston warmly in the Student Union of the University of Minnesota, their next ROTC inspection site in Saint Paul. Over coffee, Carver examined the ribbon of Winston's new decoration. "Wow," he loudly exclaimed, "not many in this Army have that beauty. Congratulations, Colonel." "Oh, don't," Winston pleaded, "I would rather have the Good Conduct Medal. This decoration was no more deserved than a Triple-A, safe-driving award for a blind man. On the other hand, my conduct has never been good enough to rate a medal either."

Winston sketched the events of the Brussels assignment. Carver noted that he had more to say about Hadassah Weizmann than anyone else. "Will you see her again, Sam?" "I plan to," he said with some excitement. "We keep in touch by E-Mail." "Should I line up an arch of sabers for the Fort Leavenworth chapel," Carver laughed. "Cut it out, Rosie" Sam responded, "I'm not the marryin' kind."

Carver got serious. "Tell me about General Roy." "Well, he is really moving up in the European Union," Winston said, thoughtfully. I received an under-the-table intelligence report from somewhere that says his move from Canada to France was part of a plan to gut the NATO alliance and move the bulk of those forces into a new European Union army. And here is the kicker, Rosie, Roy has asked for me to be assigned to the EU army. The problem is the good old USA would be dumped in moving the NATO forces to the new formations. We are not in the EU; not even friendly toward it. Where would that leave me?" "Are you thinking of following that cockamamie plan? Carver asked, incredulous." "I told the US NATO section I was willing" Winston said with a shrug.

"How about the general's recovery?" Rosie asked. "That's interesting," said Winston, "he looks real good and all the reports say he has resumed a full schedule of activities. The night before I left Brussels a television news program carried an interview with the British Army surgeon who saved Roy's life. In a simulcast, the Catholic nun who took him into her convent for recuperation said Roy actually died and was miraculously revived. The doctor said he was alive when he had charge of his case, but the nun said he died in the second week of recovery. This miracle story has swept Western Europe."

"That's very interesting," Carver said slowly, as he reached for his pocket New Testament. He turned quickly to the book of Revelation. Winston smiled and thought to himself, Rosie has a text for every occasion. Carver read Revelation 13:3:

"And I saw one of his heads as it were wounded to death; and his deadly wound was healed and all the world wondered after the beast."

Carver closed the New Testament and said, "if you read The Trigger in my outline, you know about the Antichrist or the Beast as John calls him." "Are you trying to say General Roy is the Beast?" Sam said with evident annoyance. I've known him for years and he flatly does not fit into Bible prophecy. He is a soldier, a very good one and has nothing whatsoever to do with Bible prophecy."

"Sam, I'm not drawing any conclusions, here, but there are some interesting coincidences, if we can call them that," Carver continued. "You just related the nun's tale of the general's recovery and the public sensation it caused in Europe. Roy is moving up in what amounts to the revived Roman Empire of Old and New Testament prophecy, that will be the Antichrist's power base." "Not so fast, Rosie, your verse also says "one of his heads was wounded. Roy has only one, I don't know about your Beast." "Very perceptive," Colonel Winston," Carver replied, "most of our Bible scholars feel that there could be a double fulfillment of the wounded head. Listen to this footnote in my Bible: "Fragments of the Roman empire have never ceased to exist as separate kingdoms. It was the imperial form of government which ceased; the one head wounded to death. What we have prophetically in Rev.13:3 is the restoration of the imperial form as such, though over a federated empire of ten kingdoms; the "head" is "healed," i.e. restored; there is an emperor again - the Beast." (Scofield Reference Bible, Pg 1342). That could account for one of the heads," Rosie commented.

"Now, stay with me, Sam. This quote, from a respected scholar of many years ago, might provide clues to a second head. Listen: "John tells us that he beheld one of the Beast's head as having been slain to death. The expression is so strong, definite, and intensified, that nothing less can be grammatically made of it than that real death is meant here. A man who has undergone physical death is therefore in contemplation. Whether he comes up again in literal bodily resurrection, or only by means of an obsession of some living man, we may not be able to decide." This was written by J. A Seiss, in "The Apocalypse or the Revelation of Jesus Christ," VOL II, Pg 399.

"I have one last remark on the subject, my friend," Carver continued, "most Bible scholars believe that God alone has the power to give life. Therefore, scholars conclude that the confederation will be "healed," but that the reviving of the Antichrist from the dead is an hoax intended to trick an impressionable public."

The conversation was so unsettling to Winston, he suggested they walk around the university campus and talk of other things. It was easier said than done. They could talk about the Army, sports, favorite foods and entertainment, but Winston was at a serious crossroads in his thinking. Do I take the job in Europe with a man Rosie believes may be the Antichrist? Well, he didn't call him the Antichrist, but he seems to feel there are too many coincidences to ignore.

At dinner, Carver was reluctant to bring up anything spiritual, but he decided to cast all caution to the winds and said, "I think it is time for you to make a decision for Christ, Sam." Winston, anxious to avoid the subject, simply said, "I am not ready for that." Rosie fixed a strong, level gaze at his friend and quoted, "behold now is the accepted time, behold, now is the day of salvation." That's Second Corinthians 6:2." Ashamed of his dissembling, Winston laughed and said, "Rosie you are a case. You have a scripture for everything. All right, what's your pitch?"

Elated, Rosie replied, "Sam, since you are Jewish, I propose that we consider only Old Testament passages teaching salvation. Ready?" Without waiting for an answer, Carver began, "the first element in saving faith is the awful truth that every single human being - you included Sam - is a sinner, hell-bound, deserving only the wrath of God. Listen to the prophet Isaiah:

"But we are all as an unclean thing, and all our righteousnesses are as filthy rags; and we all do fade as a leaf; and our iniquities, like the wind, have taken us away."
> (Isaiah 64:6)

"Pretty strong language," Carver suggested. "Next, please note Sam, the righteous God must judge the sinner."

"Therefore I will judge you, O house of Israel, every one according to his ways, saith the Lord God. Repent, and turn yourselves from all your transgressions; so iniquity shall not be your ruin. Cast away from you all your transgressions, whereby ye have transgressed; and make you a new heart and a new spirit: for why will you die O house of Israel? For I have no pleasure in the death of him that dieth, saith the Lord God: wherefore turn yourselves, and live ye."

> (Ezekiel 18:30-32)

"Sam, you have seen God has passed judgment on the sins of men. Finally God has provided the answer to our sin problem:"

"All we like sheep have gone astray; we have turned every one to his own way; and the Lord hath laid on him the iniquity of us all."

> (Isaiah 53:6)

" Of whom is Isaiah speaking? Who is the "him" in that verse? " Sam asked. "Good question. Notice the verses just before Isaiah 53:6.

"He is despised and rejected of men; a man of sorrows, and acquainted with grief: and we hid as it were our faces from him; he was despised, and we esteemed him not. Surely he hath borne our griefs, and carried our sorrows: yet we did esteem him stricken, smitten of God, and afflicted. But he was wounded for our transgressions, he was bruised for our iniquities: the chastisement of our peace was upon him; and with his stripes we are healed"

(Isaiah 53:3-5)

Rosie bowed his head reverently. "This is Jesus of Nazareth, the King of the Jews, the Savior of all mankind."

Winston said nothing for two or three minutes and then, "I take it I am to see myself as a transgressor, on my way to hell, unless I agree that Jesus took my sins upon himself on the cross. Is that right?" "You got it," Rosie nodded. "Then it is merely a matter of verbal assent and I'm one of you, right?" Winston concluded.

"No," Carver responded, "you've got the facts right, but it is much bigger than merely a nodding assent to Jesus Christ. Jesus expressed it this way:

"No man can come to me, except the Father which hath sent me draw him: and I will raise him up at the last day."

(John 6:44)

"You are not asked to join a club. The sinner must cast himself upon the Lord for His mercy. You have mortally offended God by your nature, your life and your deeds. You must repent of your sins, cast yourself upon the Lord as an undeserving sinner and appropriate the grace of God in justifying you by faith alone."

Rubbing his temples in fatigue, Winston said, "Rosie, I'm a Jew. Not a very good one, but a Jew nonetheless. I've got to think about this. I appreciate your concern for me, but - if I am to be drawn by the Father - it will take time." "I understand," Rosie said with resignation, "let's get some sleep."

# Chapter Seven
*Sam Winston, the Army of the EU*

Special Order No. 27      Extract

Par 39. WINSTON, SAMUEL R. LTC, Infantry, USA, 472556109, is hereby reld of duty, Command and General Staff College, Ft Leavenworth KS and asgd HQ, Army of the European Union, (A-EU), Brussels, BG, at the convenience of asgd org. Subject officer is auth to receive full pay and alws under AR 45-2168, Payt in Eurodollars auth.

Ordinarily, Winston would have said, "the deal is done." This time he felt it had a more ominous ring, something like, "the die is cast." It had taken an endless round of conferences in high places. The US Army NATO Section, Brussels, recommended to USAREUR, Stuttgart, that Roy's request be turned down. Stuttgart agreed and passed on their worst fears to the Pentagon. USAREUR contended asking for Winston was designed to make it difficult for the US to object to gutting NATO when one of our own officers had a role in crafting the new EU force.

The Joint Chiefs of Staff discussed it and were divided. The Secretary of the Army was indifferent to the whole thing and Secretary of Defense Henry Koslow was all for it. Koslow found an ally at the cabinet level in Secretary of State Louise Campbell. Campbell argued it was time to warm to the EU. The president's economic adviser, Jaime Martinez, commented vehemently, "I'm for it if this guy Winston can somehow cause the EU some exquisite pain and discomfort." The president yawned and said, "what's next on our agenda."

It was hard to part with Rosie Carver. They spent most of two days together. Rosie tried to turn the conversation to spiritual things, but found himself locked out by a man with a mission. Winston was going back to troop leadership and command and he could talk of nothing else.

An almost tearful Carver said, "I've got a gift for you Sam. You won't have to use hotel room Bibles from now on." He produced a beautiful maroon. leather-bound Bible of the Old and New Testament edged and embossed in gold, "Lt Col Samuel R Winston, USA." "That's beautiful, Rosie, many thanks, "responded a choked Winston. The Bible even smelled new.

"And I've got a gift for you," Winston exclaimed. He fished through a paste board box filled with Styrofoam chips. He produced a long, blonde, olivewood chest. Rosie opened it to find a *shofar*, a double-curled ram's horn, the ancient instrument for summoning the Jews to worship. A gold plate was inscribed, "Sgt Major R. K. Carver -The Trump of God - Sam" An obviously delighted Carver said, "Oh, Sam, it's too much, but many thanks. Do you suppose I could ever learn to blow it?" "Rosie, I must tell you, the shofar is an ill wind nobody blows good." They dissolved in laughter. "Hadassah found it for me. I knew exactly what I wanted and my Israeli connection made a special trip to Safat to get the real McCoy. Rosie, it comes with my thanks for a truly great partnership. I won't forget you, friend. Incidentally, I tried to get you transferred to the EU with me, but the Pentagon said you were too valuable. I am the dude who is expendable."

Both men were used to parting with friends met along the way in military careers. You meet new associates, make friends of some and then just as quickly as you were thrown together you part. "Exigencies of the military service," was the official reason for these short, but meaningful encounters. Comrades swear they will meet again somewhere down the line. It rarely happens. Roosevelt Kennedy Carver was relieved of ROTC inspection duty and returned to a new assignment at Fort Leavenworth, to Lurene and their white picket fence.

Sam Winston had long ago given up on second-guessing a service assignment. Somehow, there was a nagging sense that this would be something less than a sparkling career move. It may have been the mistake of his life to join Roy, but so what? The one warm, recurrent thought was that he was getting closer to Hadassah Weizmann. Since their idyllic meeting following the medal ceremony, he had E-mailed her nearly every day. She usually responded within thirty-six hours. Once it had taken five days before she could answer. The media told of a serious firefight on the Israeli-Lebanese border. He figured she must have been involved in that operation.

It was hard for Sam to say what was in his heart. He cared for Hadassah more than he had ever cared for anyone. Their few hours together made it seem that this was middle-age puppy love, but the feelings just wouldn't go away. In a surface mail letter, Winston penned Hadassah the closest thing to a marriage proposal he had ever given to any woman. Her reply was guarded. She had a lot to say about her family, Israel and the Army, as factors a young sabra must weigh carefully. He breathlessly read through it, delighted to see she didn't turn him down flat. She made no mention of their age difference. He hugged her letter to his heart and said with soldierly determination, "I must have that girl!"

This time, it was no Hotel Westburg in Brussels. It was much more modest digs called the King Leopold in the old town. The elevators creaked. The estaminet was decorated in early mess hall, but the food was adequate.

The same brass were on duty at US Army NATO Section. Winston had privately dubbed them "the usual suspects," borrowing lines from Claude Rains, the police chief in the film Casablanca. They were more than cool to the officer who volunteered for an assignment they had openly opposed. Winston was treated like a mercenary in the army of some not-so-friendly foreign nation. The NATO section made it clear they expected regular intelligence reports on the formation of the EU army. Winston read it as get the dirt on the principal players. It sounded like an absurd order for a field grade officer that everyone in the EU command was sure to treat with suspicion. Everything Winston knew about the new assignment he had learned from the unofficial intelligence report Rita Brown handed to him. He had been around long enough to know the heart of conspiracy is for the spy to spy on the spies.

A rear door opened and out strode a tall, athletic two-star with four rows of ribbons. "Sam," he greeted warmly, "man, it's good to see ya again!" Major General Matt Cherry pumped Winston's hand forcefully, passed an arm around his shoulders and led him off to his office. Alone, Cherry congratulated Winston on his decoration. Plainly embarrassed, Winston shook his head, looked down and mumbled unintelligibly. "Look, Sam, that medal saved your career. Don't forget it. You performed up to the standard specs in the desert. Don't sell yourself short." "Thanks, General," Winston said sheepishly, "the whole incident has changed my career, in fact everything about me. The part I have not been prepared to face, sir, is that the medal and the kiss on the cheek did not put an end to this change in direction. I'm not the same man, General, and I do not expect to be the old Lieutenant Colonel Winston ever again." "Nonsense, Sam, your star is rising. I don't know if this assignment to Roy's staff is the way to go, but you'll land on your feet. You're that kind of soldier. Keep in touch, Sam. I'll be watching your career." Cherry's remarks and his handshake lifted Winston as nothing had for a long time.

The frosted glass office of the EU army, too new to even merit a name on the door, opened to a number of desks juxtaposed in good military style, attended by a few uniformed functionaries and a few civilians. Winston immediately thought of the cross-town NATO headquarters that looked like it was on a war footing in contrast to the easy, bureaucratic appearance here. They were not used to strange American officers wandering in. It took several minutes before he could get a Dutch corporal to listen to his plea for directions. Winston was escorted into a small room occupied only by frozen-faced civilians, obviously the security element of the new army. Winston recognized Dupin, the civilian table guest at the medal ceremony. Has France taken over the EU, Winston asked himself? They are everywhere. You could forget that Belgium is the host country here! Dupin motioned him to a seat and introduced himself as Maurice Dupin, of SDECE, the French intelligence bureau. Dupin was fiftyish, black hair, pasted down over a face that could mask courage or cruelty. His mouth was a red slash held in by a rather bulbous nose and ample cheeks. His breath was heavy with garlic. He wore a black suit that looked like he had slept in it. A starched white shirt was in at least its third day of wear pulled together by a figureless black tie. Dupin was not your James Bond kind of secret agent.

Winston turned over his 201-file, record jacket. Dupin perused it quickly and handed back his U S Army vehicle license, shot record and his World Health

Organization immunization card. Winston was asked a lot of questions about his political, social and religious memberships if any. Without comment Dupin seemed to take special note of the fact he was Jewish. Winston was given a long questionnaire in English and French. Dupin carelessly tossed the completed papers aside and then directed him to the next room for official induction into the EU military service. "A cold fish," Winston concluded.

Winston was photographed, finger-printed and over his protest, his U S Army I.D. card was photocopied. He was given a new EU identity card, showing no address, not even his blood type. Major La Farge, a French officer who identified himself as Roy's adjutant, gave Winston a pay card to sign, all in French. "Just a formality, mon Colonel," he suggested. Winston could read enough of it to know it called for payment in Eurodollars. He was ready to ask for assurances that he was still covered by U S Department of Defense pay, allowance and retirement credits, but thought better of it and signed. He was instructed to be at General Roy's office at 1600 hours the next day.

The only evidence that Winston belonged to a new army was the white beret he was given with a badge of twelve stars, bisected by two swords on a swatch of blue cloth. It was a good-looking beret as berets go, Winston thought, but white? The U S Army wears black. The Special Forces, Carver's outfit, wear green. British paratroopers seemed to own red and UN peacekeepers wore powder blue. I guess that only leaves white, Winston reasoned. Anyway, he would still be seen as an American officer from the U S on his lapels, metallic badges of rank and the distinctive green uniform.

Winston got through to Captain Rita Brown at NATO headquarters. Somehow, he didn't consider her to be "one of the usual suspects." She agreed to meet him at the estaminet of the King Leopold for dinner. They ate heartily on Potage St Germain and Coquilles St Jacques. They pronounced the meal passably good. A promising young officer in the Adjutant General's Department, Rita Brown was single, a graduate of the U S Military Academy. She was short, of slight figure, perhaps 120 pounds soaking wet, Winston guessed. She was not pretty, but her hair was neatly trimmed and bobbed off her shoulder. Twinkling brown eyes and a warm smile gave her a girl-next-door appearance.

Winston knew scores of young female officers just like Rita Brown. They are an asset to the service. All they lacked was upper body strength. Otherwise, they could hold their own with men in any phase of military life. At one time, Winston had headed up a team in the Seventh Army in Germany, tasked with investigating how male soldiers would respond to their female comrades in emergencies. Sadly, the team discovered that one of the first considerations for the men was the protection of the women. It took Army-wide re-training to stress that the mission comes first not the safety of female soldiers.

51

"I like your natty white beret, Colonel," Brown said with a smile. "Glad you like it, Captain," he responded. "I didn't like the Army's switch to black and I'm not crazy about white. Most important, I don't like any headgear you need a mirror to put on squarely." Winston fingered the cap badge. "Do you know anything about the twelve stars and the swords, Brown?" "Let me see," she said thoughtfully, "the stars are from a Bible story. Revelation eleven?" she proposed, "no, I think chapter 12. There is a woman pictured there with a crown of stars circling her head. For us Catholics, the woman with a crown of stars is Mary, the mother of Jesus. God crowned her queen for bringing Jesus into the world." "What's the story on the swords? I would think they would have crossed swords like our infantry crossed rifles, but these are side-by-side." Rita Brown closed here eyes in concentration. "Pope Boniface the Eighth claimed the church had both spiritual and temporal power. The pope spoke of each realm in terms of a sword. The church had both swords. Temporal power because Jesus told Peter to put his sword away. Don't lop off any more ears." "O.K.," queried Winston, "how did the European Union wind up with this as the emblem of the confederation's army?" "From the very beginning, the EU has had strong connections with the Catholic Church. Makes sense, doesn't it? The initial strength came from Catholic countries. There is a very powerful, conservative movement in the Catholic Church called *Opus Dei*. It is virtually a church within a church. It is a militant, "two swords" outfit. It was founded about fifty years ago by a Spanish priest, who is now a Saint, Joachim Escriva de Balaguer. I believe they are in the background on this EU military movement. There are about 80,000 of Balaguer's hard-core Roman Catholics disciples in the movement. Some are priests, bishops and cardinals. Many are important laymen in government, the media, the arts and the military." Winston, deep in interest, commented, "I remember the intelligence report you gave me, suggested General Roy was thick with the ultra-conservative Catholic crowd." Brown bristled. "I gave you no intelligence report, Colonel," she insisted. "O.K., O.K.," Winston replied "someone gave me a report to that effect." Brown confirmed that Roy was widely considered to be under the influence and patronage of Opus Del. "He is certainly a member," she related.

Winston's gaze narrowed as he asked, "whom do I need to watch in this new assignment?" "It is new territory, Colonel," the young woman replied. "I would not have taken the job if I were you, but right now your major opposition is right here – US Army NATO section. If that isn't difficult enough you will have trouble handling the politics of a socialist experiment in a confederation under the dominion of a religious organization. That would be a challenge for anyone. This is painful to say to you, but I believe it will be impossible for a non-Catholic, non-European, American Jew, to salvage a career in this environment."

"You mentioned you are Catholic, Miss Brown, do you share the conservative views of Opus Dei? Winston asked. "My, no," she said determinedly, "I'm what is called a Progressive Catholic. I am into a post-Second Vatican Council kind of Catholicism. I was influenced by women like Edwina Gately and Joan Chittister,

52

the real thinking women in our church. I believe in women as priests and married priests. I read everything Father Richard McBrien of Notre Dame wrote and I love the works of Gutierrez and Boff of the Liberation Theology movement. We are a big church and we have gotta be trendy and open to ideas that were anathema to our church a century ago. I am in sympathy with Dignity, the gay and lesbian movement and most radical of all, I support Catholics for Choice, the pro-abortion people in our church."

"Hmm, I never knew there were Catholics like you, Captain, but tell me, do you believe in Jesus as your personal Savior? Are you going to heaven in the Rapture?" Winston probed. "Personal Savior?" Brown savored the question. "Jesus died to save everybody. I don't know what the Rapture is, but if there is a heaven, I expect I will eventually get there." Winston said nothing, convinced Rita Brown was not a Rosie Carver or Simone Weinstein kind of believer.

The meeting with Roy the next afternoon turned out to be a cocktail party. Two-dozen or so officers from a dozen West European military services milled about, drinks in hand, in the convocation center of the Belgian parliament building. Just for fun, Winston decided to play the Rosie Carver role of the teetotaler, just to see the affect on others. The frowns on many faces, proved it was noted. Americans were notorious for being unable to hold their liquor. Here was one who defied convention. Winston was dismissed as insolently uncouth.

General Roy moved effortlessly among the guests, chatting amiably with this foursome, that trio and the occasional high-ranking officer alone. He was not the senior officer present, but he easily commanded the most attention. The general spent more time with Winston than any other guest. That too was noted. Roy pumped his hand vigorously and expressed his satisfaction at having Winston on his staff. "You are in for big things, mon ami," Roy exclaimed. "I'm anxious to get going. Will it be an infantry outfit, General?" asked Winston. "Mais non," Roy shrugged, "Winston, I have you penciled in for better things than that. In fact, I have a mission for you right now. Check with my adjutant, La Farge, in the morning." With that Roy was off to share a drink and a laugh in another circle of obsequious admirers. The crowd slowly melted away. When no one seemed to care, the teetotaler Winston vanished.

In the taxi ride to the King Leopold, Winston tried to place something troubling about his brief chat with General Roy. Was it his speech? No. Did he seem nervous? Ill at ease? No. Had he been drinking more than he should? No. Winston decided Roy was detached, almost vacuous. That was followed by the alarming question - drugs? Shocked at his own suggestion, Winston said, surely not.

In a morning briefing, Major La Farge informed Winston he was needed in the Irish Republic to inspect an APC, an Army Personnel Carrier the EU was considering for its new strike force. Dublin, via Aer Lingus, was Winston's destination that afternoon. Dublin contacts and other pertinent data were contained in a leather day planner. A large sheaf of Eurodollars were passed to Winston on his signature. A locked diplomatic pouch was passed around his waist and secured with a single handcuff on his left wrist. Diplomatic immunity was explained. He was instructed to hand the pouch over to a priest named Monsignor Cormac O'Brien in Dublin, the only person with a key to unlock the handcuff.

The Hidden Ireland Hotel on Lower Baggott Street, Dublin, was a step up from the King Leopold. It was an eye-opener to have his bags carried to his room and the proffered tip declined. My kind of hotel, Winston said to himself. Cormac O'Brien, a Catholic priest with a wide Roman collar, and the typical black suit, was at Winston's door almost as soon as his bags were dropped. *"Failte isteach,"* the priest greeted him, his eyes twinkling. O'Brien quickly unlocked the handcuff and the chain. He eagerly delved into the diplomatic pouch. There were papers and a large sum of money in U.S. dollars.

Monsignor Cormac O'Brien was portly with a matching pumpkin-shaped face, marked by a wide smile and lots of teeth. He had unkempt, thick white hair, typical enough to make him a principal in an Irish travelogue. O'Brien was the archetypical Irish priest. His speech was larded with all of the begorras and other vanilla expletives that make the Irish such delightful people.

Delivering funds to a priest underlined the fact that there was an alliance at work of church and state. O'Brien was clearly a trusted agent of the Catholic Church, probably under Opus Dei discipline and a stooge for the European Union. Is this a great army or what? Winston said to himself. Even a Dublin priest knows more about what's going on than any one in Brussels.

The U S dollars could be used for anything from payoffs, influence peddling, to Mafia laundering, he reasoned. Has any U S officer ever gotten into a labyrinth like this one? Winston did not have to mention the money. O'Brien explained that he had been an agent of the Irish Republican Army, the IRA. For years, O'Brien handled funds to continue the struggle for Irish independence. "Britain is a full member of the EU." Winston said. "Surely, the EU wouldn't conspire against one of its constituencies today, would they?" "Bless your heart, Colonel, the cause of the Church, the European Union and the struggle for Irish independence are all of a piece," O'Brien explained. He grew serious. "Holy Mother Church has struggled for the British Isles for too long. We tried the Spanish Armada. We flooded England with Jesuit agents. We produced the Douai-Rheims Bible in hopes of displacing the accursed King James Version. Those efforts failed. We thought that backing the IRA would at last do the job. Well, it worked only marginally well. Happily, Holy Mother Church discovered that Britain had fallen to her own spiritual apathy. Nine of ten thousand Anglican parishes are pastored by rank unbelievers. What we couldn't take by violence is falling to us through their own impotence. This money, placed in the right hands, will help bring Britain back to Rome!"

"I can't imagine how a cleric, like yourself, could support the Provisional IRA," a suddenly acerbic Winston countered. His countenance clouded, O'Brien said, "Colonel, I worked for the Provisionals." "I know your group, Father, I met them in South America in coin ops." "Coin?" what's that?" asked the priest. "Coin is counter-insurgency operations. The US Army provided training and intelligence for the government forces in several South American countries. We fought the Shining Path guerillas, the Tupac Amaru and FARC, the narcoterrorists of Colombia. Your IRA buddies trained in Libya along with terrorists from all over the globe. Your friends taught the so-called South American liberation movements everything from how to make car bombs to political assassination. The funds you passed around were probably the sacrifices of Irish Americans who were mislead about your cause which was no cause but murder."

Anxious to change the subject, O'Brien said, "Tomorrow, you visit our friends at the armament works, Colonel," the subdued cleric said. "You will enjoy those fellas. They understand military hardware. You'll find kindred spirits there." Winston nodded. Irish designers and engineers produced a very fine fighting vehicle, an armored personnel carrier. In a country usually identified with shamrocks and corn beef and cabbage, the Irish APC's were already in the military inventories of Argentina and Belgium. The APC looks like a tank to the uninitiated, but it is a prime mover of combat infantry. Up to twelve men are carried in addition to the crew. The vehicle has a thin armored skin and is vulnerable to all kinds of ordnance. The infantrymen are at risk for they are seated on the reserve fuel tanks. The riflemen are disgorged from the vehicle through a rear door. This facilitates rapid, battlefield deployment.

Security at the Dublin plant was relaxed, but the senior security officer asked for Winton's EU identity card. The officer read the front of the card, compared Winston with his picture and then turned it over. He passed the card over an identity sensor, listened for the clearance beep and said, "Aye, you've got the mark right enough, "Key Ky Sigma," and passed it back. The Irish engineers gave their visitor a full opportunity to test the APC. Winston was familiar with the Irish vehicle. He had inspected it as well as a number of allied and former Soviet-bloc vehicles at the Army's Aberdeen Proving Ground. He appreciated the speedier Irish carrier, but thought it inferior overall to the standard US Army vehicle. He was given the engineering specs, an estimate of their production capabilities and a suggested schedule of delivery dates. Winston was asked to convey to General Roy and the new EU army, the best wishes of the Irish manufacturing complex.

Sam wandered the Liffey for blocks, the rippling ribbon that ties Dublin to the sea. Sam walked over Half-Penny Bridge, visited the General Post Office and the other sites of the 1916 Easter Rebellion. A cab ride to Maynooth and the famous seminary reminded Sam of something he read years before. The Catholic Church learned that if they had trouble anywhere in the world it was smart to send an Irish priest and a nun from Quebec. They would take care of the problem in short order.

Saint Magdalene's convent looked grim and forbidding. Winston racked his brain to remember something about the institution. "Oh, yeah." The good nuns took in fallen women. They were held in virtual slavery. The girls, some held for years, worked in the convent laundry which did a land office business in washing the soiled garments of the city. When it was closed in 1996, convent authorities were charged under criminal laws. An estimated 30,000 women were held in physical and mental incarceration during the laundry's most productive years.

There was no flight to Brussels that afternoon. Winston stretched out on his king-sized hotel room bed and just thought. I have a lot to think about, Winston reasoned. The Irish personnel carrier people were hand-in-glove with the web of West European military planners, EU intelligence agents and Catholic clergy. I'm probably getting in deep doo-doo, here, he told himself with disgust. He shook his head vigorously, thinking, we Americans aren't in the same league with these Old World movers and shakers. Why, oh why, didn't I stick it out with Rosie Carver and the ROTC? Carver? Winston reached for the prophetic study he had just received from his friend, carelessly thrust into his overnight bag on the day he left for Dublin. Winston smoothed it out and read:


**666**


"Here is wisdom. Let him that hath understanding count the number of the beast; for it is the number of a man; and his number is Six hundred three score and six" (Rev 13:18).

Carver commented:

"The identity of the Antichrist or the Beast is obscure today. It has been shrouded in mystery for nearly two thousand years. The words "him that hath understanding," intimates that there will be a generation that is able to identify the monster by the number **666**. Greek letters have numerical equivalents. For centuries, men have added up the letters in the names of world figures attempting to identify the Antichrist. Nero was the first to yield 666 from the value of his name. He was a Beast but not the Beast. Napoleon made the list as did Lyndon B. Johnson and Henry Kissinger. None was the dreaded Antichrist. Someday it will be easy to make the identification."

Winston returned to Brussels. The diplomatic pouch took him speedily through customs. Asked for his EU army I.D., a customs officer passed it over the scanner. From the monitor on his side of the desk the officer quickly said, "your credentials are impeccable, Colonel. Welcome, once again to Belgium." The scanner had converted the Greek letters, Key Ky Sigma, into numerals. After Winston was out of earshot, the customs agent called to a co-worker. "Rudy, that is the only American, I have ever passed with the mark." The agent pointed to the numerals **666**.

56

# Chapter Eight
*The Rapture!*

In the most unusual assignment of his military career, Winston buried himself in his work. He fought with bureaucrats over the Army Personnel Carrier. Disinterested EU officers listened to his presentation of the pros and cons of the vehicle. Winston felt he clearly demonstrated the superiority of the American entry in the competition, but the bureaucrats shrugged off the invidious comparison, opting for the Irish model, simply because it was marketed by a confederation partner. Quality was not a consideration. Why did they send me to Ireland? Sam said to himself. It reminded him of the odd fact that all US arms and space contracts go to the lowest bidder. The final decision to buy the Irish APC required two more trips to Dublin. Winston also argued unsuccessfully for the purchase of the Israeli Tow anti-tank ordnance. The Israeli engineers came to Brussels for that competition, robbing Winston of a possible visit with Hadassah. Frustrated, Winston drove to Brno in the Czech Republic to look over an assault rifle. The Czechs have always made quality rapid-fire weapons.

Winston was graying rapidly on his EU duties. He wasn't built for negotiations, especially deals that were consummated elsewhere behind closed doors. It looked very much like Lt. Colonel Winston was only a symbol of American submission to a European military complex.

Toying with the idea of a visit to Mother Castaldi's convent on the Adriatic where the general had convalesced, Winston skirted the Alps and drove down the seam of the Italian boot. Winston found the convent of the Sisters of the Common Life between Ancona and Pescara. He had expected siege-blackened, turreted walls with gargoyles and hideous sculptures looming over dank, miasmal grounds. The palatial chateau on the highest of a number of rolling hills, was breathtakingly beautiful in the warm Italian sun. The gift of a devout Italian prince, the house was easily a hundred or more rooms, Winston guessed, under gabled roofs. Flowerbeds surrounded the chateau, a riot of colors blended with the rich green lawns. The inevitable high wrought iron fence surrounded the grounds. Winston rang the bell on the ornate, two-leaved gate. Over an intercom a thin female voice in Italian asked his business. Winston identified himself and asked for Mother Castaldi. In English, the woman asked him to wait while she summoned Mother.

Inside, the floors, rooms and furnishing were as immaculate as the exterior had promised. Nuns in ones and two seemed to glide about silently, never raising an eye to the man in uniform. One nun labored with wax over the floor of the entryway. She is probably on report, Winston guessed.

Mother Castaldi and her charges effected the long black habit of pre-Vatican II Catholicism. A cord belt at her waist and a large, valuable pectoral cross on her breast, Mother Castaldi was an ageless example of the perpetually professed religious. Courageous women like her had been the strength of the Roman Church for centuries. Mother Castaldi ensconced behind a beautiful oak desk easily eight feet wide, sat primly and looked straight at Winston. "You've come Mr. Winston to see the place where the general was healed." "That's right, Mother," Winston replied. "But you don't really believe it was a miracle do you," she challenged. "Mother Castaldi, I am a soldier. I don't know anything about miracles. I was responsible for the general's safety and I failed that duty. The fact that he is alive today is a miracle for my career." The aging nun softened a little under Winston's declaration. "Mr. Winston, we are women of prayer. We believe God heals in response to faith. We are also allied with others in the world who share our faith. Some are not in the one, true church, but they have some of the light and we join hands with them in intercessory prayer. When the Holy Father asked us to take in General Roy we enlisted the aid of our brothers in Tibet who share our constant devotion. They sent emissaries to join us in our vigil.

"Come here to the window, please." Mother Castaldi pointed out three conical huts just beyond a lagoon in rear of the chateau. The huts seemed to be about eight feet in height and covered with felt. "Those huts are called yurts, aren't they Mother Castaldi? I saw them while on a mission in Nepal." "Yes, Colonel, I am surprised that you would know the name. These are Tibetan yurts and they were the temporary lodging for a community of eight Tibetan holy men. They were here throughout the general's convalescence. They prayed and worked with him every day. They taught us yoga and other esoteric mysteries and disciplines. They returned to Tibet after the general was well enough to travel." Returning to her desk, Mother Castaldi said, "I would like you to meet their leader." She reached for a bell cord and in a few minutes a nun admitted a tall, slender oriental with shaven head and a Fu Manchu moustache. He was tastefully dressed in a gray Saville Row morning suit, soft rose-colored shirt and a blue tie. "Colonel Winston, may I present Lord Ten Sing, the Seventh Emanation of Gao Dai." The oriental bowed elegantly and offered his hand to Winston. The hand was cold and oily. Looking anything but Winston's image of a Tibetan holy man, the oriental spoke in a polished English accent Winston guessed was Oxford or Cambridge. Mother Castaldi informed Lord Ten Sing that Winston was on General Roy's staff and was here to see the place of healing for the general. "Ah yes, Colonel, I know of you. Congratulations on bringing our friend, General Roy through that dreadful experience in the desert." Winston blushed. "I failed in that mission, your lordship, good medical care in Israel, the tender ministrations of Mother Castaldi and her community and, from what she tells me, the unique contribution of you and your men, have given us back the leader for the hour."

"Lord Ten Sing," Mother Castaldi directed, "please tell Colonel Winston about the healing ministry of your community." "Ah, dear Mother Castaldi, you graciously do us more honor than we deserve. We were not in the general's room for that time when his heart stopped. It was the Sisters of the Common Life who were in prayer at that critical point. We were in prayer as well, but in our own circle. Nevertheless, as you request, I will say to you, Colonel, that we patronize spirit guides that freely move between the living, the dead and the disembodied spirits of the air. We harmonize with these forces and beings and procure these pure energies for many services of which healing human bodies is but one." The oriental's eyes seemed to dance with a magnetism that was palpable. Mother Castaldi shared the same kind of dancing senses. From a side board, Ten Sing moved two unlighted candles to Mother Castaldi's desk. He stroked a wick and it burst into flame. He seemed to lift that flame with his fingers and move it to the other wick. It flamed into life. Ten Sing bowed from the waist and was gone. Mother Castaldi seemed to awaken from whatever had gripped her. "You will see more of Lord Ten Sing, Colonel," she exclaimed, "he will soon be seconded to a very important post on the general's staff." She brightened and added, "you'll be colleagues. That will be good for both of you." These people are super-weird, Winston thought to himself.

Winston, anxious to go, had to endure a tour of a portion of the chateau. They showed him the room where the general spent four painful months. It was a typical nun's quarters, plain, showing no sign of having served as a hospital room. It had the inevitable crucifix on the wall above a bed that reminded him of his pad in office's candidate school. Winston extended his hand and expressed his gratitude to the provincial and showed himself out. Winston had a pounding headache as he retraced his route north through Italy. There was something definitely spooky about the convent, Mother Castaldi and especially Lord Ten Sing. I don't know what they were on, but it was powerful stuff. Strangely, they could turn it off and on. Why would Roy have an oriental holy man on his staff? The prospect of having Ten Sing as a colleague was anything but appealing to Winston.

A brief trip to Aubagne, in the south of France, gave Winston an opportunity to get acquainted with the French Foreign Legion company, the first element in the EU rapid response force. The company was drawn from the famous 13th Demi-Brigade. This unit had a long, distinguished history. The company was one hundred and fifty well-trained, hardened soldiers from a score of nations. It was redesignated as Number One Company, Sixth Brigade.

Winston was received with the same cold indifference every non-Legion officer received. It was indeed a foreign legion. The CO, Major Rolf Krueger a German, was powerfully built, a long horizontal scar across the forehead, mute testimony to a firefight or an indiscretion. The French love their legion, but prefer to have it fight on other soil, rather than garrisoned at home.

Winston endured an evening with Krueger in an Augabne bistro. Krueger consumed enough Sazarac to float a battleship. Winston steadfastly remained a teetotaler. Liquor loosened Krueger's tongue. He laughed and sneered at the U S Army. "You lost in Viet Nam, Colonel," he slobbered. "So did the French, Major. Do you remember Dien Bien Phu?" "Touché," Krueger conceded. Krueger loosed his tunic collar. "Professional officers like us are victims of the international bankers, Colonel. They make money off the wars and we do the fighting and dying. We've got to stop the Jewish internationalists before it is too late. Don't you agree?" "No, Major, I do not agree. That old international Jewish conspiracy story died generations ago. Sadly, men like you who should know better, pump life into one of the most atrocious lies ever invented." Krueger had no response. He had gone through the drinker's stages, jocose, bellicose and was very close to comatose. "Incidentally, I am Jewish," Winston said with feeling. He tossed some francs on the table and walked out.

It was difficult to track General Roy's activities. A French bullet train had nothing on the speed and velocity of the ubiquitous General Jean-Luc Armand Roy. He was all over the map. Breakfast with Arab oil magnates was followed by a visit to the Shrine of Lourdes. Dinner with the papal nuncio was abbreviated to allow for an hour-long personal interview with an American television commentator. Roy shouldered a basket of grapes in Tuscany, opened a mammoth new shopping center in Amsterdam and cut the ribbon on a new bridge over the Rhone.

Roy was not only the subject of puff pieces, he was steadily moving up in EU parliamentary circles. He was called in to help settle a eurodollar dispute in Wales. He consulted on wine parity in Languedoc. The European Central Bank was the Achilles heel of the European Union. Losing 25% of its value in the first two years of the euro, it had never become sound enough to settle the jitters in world financial centers. Roy vowed to change that.

King Juan Carlos of Spain entertained Roy over a weekend, a cover for a meeting of the European Center of Documentation and Information (CEDI), a blue-ribbon, aristocratic cabal whose objective was a modern resurrection of the Holy Roman Empire, around the Spanish Bourbons. The group brought together at the height of the cold war, was the creation of the Archduke Otto von Habsburg.

Sam Winston, back in his office in Brussels, was out of touch with everything. He was inundated with armament specs, troop requisitions and movement orders. NATO was disintegrating as the intelligence reports had predicted. Whole units of West European armies were quietly moved to the new EU army on almost a daily basis. Winston saw very little of Roy. The umbilical cord of the nascent EU army was in the person of Major Jacques La Farge, Roy's adjutant. Slowly, a staff was forming. Winston felt lost in this emerging staff element. More and more NATO officers were quietly reassigned to the EU. The Legion's entire 13th Demi-Brigade became the showcased unit in the new army. Rita Brown predicted it was just a matter of time before NATO would be KIA and the U S Army would go home.

It was a bad time for a vacuum in world military leadership. There were wars and rumors of wars. Rogue states were showing their muscle. Well-organized subversive groups were carrying out operations against civilian targets on what seemed to be a daily basis. South American narcoterrorists spread their tentacles as far north as Mexico. The most ominous signs of world unrest, as usual, were in the Middle East. Five predominantly Muslim republics born out of the break-up of the Soviet Union were under systematic radicalization by Islamic fundamentalists of Algeria and Pakistan. One of the republics, Kazakhstan, was home to more than eight million non-Muslims. The twenty-first century had dawned with a Muslim problem the West had not fully settled. It took no prophet to see that soon the West would have to deal with the burgeoning Islamic world once and for all.

Natural disasters, disease and famine took an increasing toll of human life and consumed staggering sums of aid funds. The World Court in The Hague, under pressure from the "have" nations, agreed to a quarantine of most of the Third World, sentencing more than a billion people to death by starvation and disease. Years of arms sales to the impoverished nations of the world, exhausted their meager resources. It was reaping a grim harvest of the innocent.

Winston spent a great deal of time thinking about Hadassah. E-mails, letters and a rare phone call had brought them closer together. It was a serious infatuation for Sam. Hadassah was interested, but with a reserve that agonized her impetuous suitor. Sam had applied for leave again and again, but La Farge always had another top priority mission. Winston began to consider himself a "gopher," the guy who has to "go for," this and that. Was he achieving anything? He concluded that he was not. He was truly just a mercenary in a causeless venture. Tempted to return to the United States, only the possibility of a life with Hadassah made it seem worthwhile.

La Farge summoned Winston to a briefing at Roy's headquarters. The army was really on the grow. You could tell by the expanded staff, rushing about with folders and maps. What was the purpose? General Roy, warm and expansive at times, other times with a vacant, hunted look, unveiled a plan to lead a mission to Jerusalem, a junket that he promised would shake the world and usher in an era of peace in the Middle East. There were few details. The news did not seem to excite anyone except Roy. He placed the staff on alert for movement to Israel within 72 hours. Staff reaction was cool. Let the Middle East stew in its own juice, seemed to be the general view. Winston raised the caveat of another Jordanian adventure, but it was waved aside.

La Farge informed Winston that he would be Chef-de-Mission, leading the staff element with Krueger's legionnaire company as an honor guard for Roy. The legion would also provide a modest show of strength in a region where power is carefully measured. "Just present your I.D. and you will have everything you need." Winston was ecstatic over the prospect of making it to Israel. He telephoned Hadassah that night, pleading with her to apply for leave. "On one condition," she demanded, "that you come to Galilee if you can get away from Jerusalem." "I Promise!" he exclaimed.

**61**

Winston buckled into a seat on the giant C-5A air transport, next to Major Krueger. The headquarters section of the legion company was on this aircraft and the main body of the troops were on a second plane. Both aircraft were provided courtesy of the U S Air Force. Stops were made at the Aviano Air Force Base in Italy and at Athens, Greece with one in-flight refueling over the Mediterranean. Every mile took Winston closer to the girl of his dreams.

One of the most significant events in world history occurred that night. In the twinkling of an eye, millions of earth's inhabitants vanished. China and South Korea sustained the greatest drops in population, upwards of fifty million people. Twenty-five percent of sub-Saharan Africa was gone. Brazil, Ecuador and war-torn Colombia reported unexplained absence of people in many towns and villages. Russia had surprisingly high losses of citizens.

New Zealand had the greatest number of the vanished, per capita, in the English-speaking world, followed by the United States, Australia and Canada. The British Isles trailed far behind their former colonies.

The world's vast middle, North Africa, through Central Asia, India, Pakistan, much of mainland China and Japan, the Muslim, Hindu and Buddhist world, officially closed to Christianity, were seriously underrepresented in the Rapture, but, there were more than anyone would have guessed. Years of radio, television, movies and tapes, the Internet and satellite transmissions had produced a harvest of silent believers. Israel, long closed to the Christian message, had an overnight drop of more than 5,000 citizens.

The problems arising from the Rapture were under-reported. Since the mass disappearance took place on a Sunday, in the western world, many churches and missions were deserted. People showed up, only to find Bibles and hymnals open, but unused. Pulpits had announcements of coming events that would never take place. Sermons rehearsed for the faithful, were never preached. On the other hand, many churches were full, with only a few parishioners missing. Absentees were considered ill or away on trips.

Vatican insiders, always abuzz with rumors and gossip, consumed copious amounts of wine and innumerable cigars discussing the Rapture reports. It was held to be fairly certain that Roman Catholic losses were infinitesimal. The comment invariably turned to the subject of how to make capital out of this curious event.

It received little or no immediate notice in a few countries. It was a mild sensation in more. It resulted in near panic in a few localities. The European Union took scant notice of the event, claiming that relatively few reports were received from confederation partners. It caused no end of trouble for spin doctors the world over as the reports came in from every quarter of the globe. A number of church historians said, "this sounds like the Rapture that the Fundamentalists and Evangelicals have discussed as fact for a couple of hundred years. The historians pointed out that Billy Graham, Jerry Falwell, professional athletes, a few public figures, and thousands of so-called born again believers, people in all walks of life, passionately believed in this return of Christ to take out His Church. Liberal apologists said, "Of course, we don't believe that Jesus has actually returned. Science and common sense will solve the mystery of this mass disappearance." Months after the event, secretly circulated memos placed the population losses at between 60 and 80 million.

The World Court in The Hague, in an emergency session awarded the assets and properties of all abandoned churches and organizations to the care of the confessional churches, the Roman Catholic, the Anglican and Episcopal and the churches of the several Eastern Orthodox rites. The pope was asked to head up the commission until a full study of the issue was complete. The pope promised the united churches would hold the properties and assets in trust, until the rightful owners came forward and reclaimed their prefectures. He noted that reports were coming in of churches looted, vandalized and many burned. Insurance companies feared staggering losses. The pope made an impassioned plea for calm.

The day after the Rapture, it was business as usual in most commercial centers. A few people were missing from governments, the courts and the world of the arts and entertainment. The agricultural industry was hit particularly hard in the US South, Middle West and West. Medical professionals were missing in substantial numbers. Many classrooms were untended. Some technically trained workers were reported missing. As a result there were insufficient hands to push buttons, turn handles and oversee the means of production. The financial houses, worldwide, after a few anxious hours, reported with relief that although they had lost many of their best clients and customers, the missing, left assets far greater than their debts.

Landing at Tel Aviv, there were snippets of conversation about the reports of disappearances worldwide. After he got settled, Winston placed a call to Rita Brown in Brussels. She told him what she knew of the Rapture story. In the NATO section a couple of officers and a handful of enlisted personnel had simply turned up missing. She guessed they vanished with the rest of the people all over the world. "How many people worldwide?" Winston asked with some alarm. "No one really knows Sam. There is almost nothing said about it here, but I take it the Pentagon is going crazy over defections in all of the services. Our NATO section Sergeant Major is pulling his hair out. Where do you place a man on the morning report who is missing and has a top-secret clearance? We have KIA and MIA classifications. Maybe this is VIA, vanished in action."

It was a sensational story. China clamped total censorship on reports of the vanished in the most populous nation on earth. The President of the United States couldn't be reached for comment. The House and Senate appointed select committees to study the matter. Both bodies had lost a few members. Some media sources speculated that this might be another Heavens Gate. The Heavens Gate cult in the

1990's had committed suicide in a body, leaving word they were going out to board an alien craft in space. That story didn't match the Rapture reports, for the Heavens Gate group included fewer than a hundred people.

Conspiracy advocates lost no time in constructing incredible theories to account for the disappearances. It was hard to make the case that you could spirit away an estimated several million Americans. Area 51, Roswell, New Mexico, the black hole of the conspiracy advocates, would hold the people, but the weight of numbers required something out of this world.

Not surprisingly, people quickly lost interest in what happened to the religious right. It was merely a joke. It was time for looting and vandalizing the homes of the missing and stealing their automobiles. The media blamed the departed for everything bad that had happened in the world from AIDS to the state of the economy. But they were gone, good riddance. Now the world could get on with the business of a one-world religion, a one-world government and a one- world economic order. Happy days were here again!

Sam Winston had to think. Was this the Rapture Rosie Carver anticipated? It matched everything he had to say about it. Then he hit on the answer. Call Sophie and ask nonchalantly about Simone. That's it. It wasn't easy to get through to the United States. Lines were swamped. Sam waited and watched the phone for hours. When he got through he did not have to mention Simone. Her anger unconcealed, Sophie shouted, "Simone's gone, Sam. Your family is fit to be tied. I knew that those Jews for Jesus freaks would do something to her. We're charging them with kidnapping." "Uh, Sophie," Sam said quietly, "who are you going to charge? Aren't the others in that movement gone too?" Sophie ignored the question. "You encouraged her Sam. When you were here you patronized that girl and her newfound Jesus. I hope you're satisfied. She followed them, probably to her death." With that, Sophie slammed the phone down.

So Simone was gone. Certainly Rosie and Lurene and the kids were gone, too. For a moment, Winston felt the same panic he experienced on transatlantic flights. "Get a grip on yourself," he said, "it is time to think clearly about where you are and where you are going. You have wasted a lot of time you could be using to get in touch with Hadassah. Things will work out."

An Israeli officer and a Palestine Authority policeman were tasked with support for Winston and the Legionnaires. There was a good deal of criticism in the Arab and Israeli press over a military presence for what was billed as a peace offensive. Winston took the advise of the IDF advisor and quartered the Legion company a long way up the coast, south of Akko between kibbutz Kfar Masaryk and kibbutz Ein Hamifratz. This gave the legion a large cantonment area well away from expected Arab demonstrations. Winston maintained an office there, but spent the majority of his time in shared quarters on the Jaffa Road outside the new section of

Jerusalem. He had a room in a modest hotel on King George the Fifth Street, but with the help of his Israeli aide, he wrestled a couch, Early Army Barracks styling, into one corner of his office as a place to crash when time permitted.

Dressed in civilian clothes, Winston walked through the old walled city, through the souks on narrow streets, the bazaars of the Muslim section, redolent with a thousand tantalizing odors. Oh, if these streets could talk. In the Jewish quarter he toured the Hurva Synagogue and the Ben-Zakai Synagogue, where tradition said Elijah would sound the shofar announcing the people's freedom. He entered the Church of the Holy Sepulcher and walked the Via Dolorosa. He passed through St.Stephen's Gate, the portal through which Christianity's first martyr was dragged to his death. Jerusalem was the Bible's burdensome stone. Many peoples had tried to possess it, none could. One day it would truly be "the foundation of peace."

Try as he might, Sam could not reach Hadassah. He had been in Israel for nearly forty-eight hours and there was no answer to telephone or E-Mail. His Israeli liaison, Captain Ari Avigdor promised to do what he could to locate her. Winston managed to stay busy. There were food requisitions to fill out. Arrangements for medical support had to be made. Electronic communications with Brussels were adequate, but invariably short on useful information. For local support it was a pay phone and a credit card. Is this any way to run an army? Winston grumbled. There was a knock on the door behind him. Expecting Avigdor, he tossed a "come in" and followed with "*shev b'vakehshah,* please be seated." "Well," a soft, feminine voice replied, "your courtesy lacks something, but your Hebrew is getting better." "Hadassah!" Winston turned with a shout, and swept her up in his arms. "Unhand me you cad," she protested, feigning a slap to his shoulder. "You are a guest in this country. Don't you forget it. You can't run around manhandling Israeli officers. We've got five wars behind us. We know how to take care of people bigger and heavier than we are!" Winston blushed. "I'm sorry. It's, just that...it's just that...you are a sight for sore eyes," he stammered.

Hadassah had four hours. They walked to a sidewalk cafe she knew on Ben Yehuda Street where the Turkish coffee was so strong it could wire you for hours. "Where are you stationed?" Winston asked. "You don't ask that question in Israel, Colonel. Everything is a military secret here. I'll tell you that I'm not too far away and I'll be around." Winston was absorbed with just looking at her. She was even more beautiful than his technicolor dreams had painted her. She wore no makeup and her army tunic did little for her, but to the career bachelor she was a dream walking. Instinctively, he reached out to hold her hand across the small round table. She withdrew hers, looking furtively to left and right. "You never know when the chief rabbi of the Army is watching," she said with a laugh. How he longed to take her in his arms and tell her how much he loved her. He was quite sure he looked like a sick cow at that very moment, but this was love.

65

It was over all too soon. Hadassah was gone, but with a promise they could get together next weekend at her home in Kfar Halutz. Neither of them could guarantee that they would have the time off, but it was worth planning. Winston was so determined to get there he feared he would go over the hill if his duties got in the way.

But where was General Roy? La Farge, back in Brussels, had no information. Roy had left for an undisclosed location within a few hours of the troop deployment. The English edition of the Jerusalem Post contained not a single article about Roy, but the letters to the editor were filled with caustic comments about the presence of the Foreign Legion. Several foreign news agencies sought to interview Winston. He refused, tempted to tell his questioners that he knew less about Roy's plans for Israel than any man on the street.

Winston used what little time he could spare to explore the Bible. Carver's outline urged a careful reading of Matthew Chapter 24, Daniel Chapters 2,7, and 9, Second Thessalonians Chapters 1 and 2, Second Peter Chapter 3 and the entire Book of Revelation. Two or three sleepless nights, reading and re-reading, and Winston confirmed the awful truth. All of those who were saved before the Rapture were with Jesus Christ in heaven. Those left behind were lost sinners, at indescribable risk to war, disease and natural disasters of every kind. Their greatest hazard was from the Antichrist who was a man of peace at first, the benefactor of the Jews and then clearly seen to be the Beast. Winston faced the truth about himself. He was lost, an enemy of God and bound for hell. It was even more sobering to realize Hadassah was lost as well. But who is the Beast? Winston recalled that when people are forced to take his mark, he will be known. What are his numbers? Oh,yeah,**666.**

Winston couldn't get the disclosures about the mark out of his mind. He recalled the security officer at the Dublin APC plant said that he had the mark, when he passed Winston's I.D. over the sensor. The Brussels customs officer hadn't mentioned a mark, but he said that his credentials were impeccable. La Farge said the he had everything he needed, when he briefed him on the Israel trip. It must be that I have the mark, he said with alarm. The next day, packing a bag and his attaché case, he asked Avigdor if he had access to a security sensor. "Sure," the Israeli aide said, "would you like to run over there with me?" "I certainly would," Winston replied, "I'll leave for Galilee from there. I'll be back on Monday. I will call and leave you a telephone number." "Don't bother, Colonel, if you are at Kfar Halutz or Degania Alef and Bet, I can find you in a hurry. Go and have a good time."

It was a few short blocks to an unofficial Shin Bet post, to all appearances a bookstore open for business. The Shin Bet was organized to combat terrorists. It was known to change headquarters on some irregular basis. In a backroom command center, Winston asked permission to pass his EU I.D. card over their sensor. "Of course, Colonel, help yourself," was the courteous response. Winston looked carefully at both sides of his laminated card and then purposely passed the card, face down over the Greek letters Key Ky Sigma. Immediately, the monitor flashed,

"**666**." Trying to conceal the shaking he felt inside, Winston, in a borrowed jeep, quickly left the office and drove north to Galilee.

Time was when you could drive due north out of Jerusalem through Nablus and then on to the Galilee area. Decades of volatile situations made that route impossible. Winston drove to Tel Aviv on the coast, Haifa and then east to the lake region. The trip gave him time to think, but it was hard to think clearly. He was madly in love. He longed to ask Hadassah to marry him. He wanted to spend his life with her, but from what he learned today, that life could be very brief. To add to the mix, Hadassah has no idea that we are living in a prophetic timewarp. She will pronounce me crazy when I tell her my commanding officer, General Roy, might be Satan's man to terrorize the world and particularly her beloved Israel. She will say, "I can't marry a *meshuggener*, a madman. You need professional help, Sam!"

It looked hopeless. Winston decided to focus on what he believed to be true. First of all, he felt very sure that there was a Rapture and true to God's Word and Rosie and Simone's expectations, they were taken to heaven. That is heavy stuff, Sam concluded, but the evidence is there. Secondly, Samuel R. Winston is not saved. He didn't go with the rest, so there must have been a time period in which to be saved, a time now expired. Next, the fact of the Rapture tends to verify the existence of an Antichrist and his all out assault on everything that is God's. Is General Roy that man? That required thinking on another level. We have the European Union which seems to match the prophecy of a revived Roman Empire. Roy fits the pattern so he could be **666**, the Beast. We are here in Israel for undisclosed reasons. If it turns out that the general is here to somehow give Temple worship back to the Jews that will be "the trigger," as Rosie called it, taken from Daniel Chapter 9. We will be into the "time of Jacob's trouble," the Great Tribulation!

The thought was disturbing. The only plus Winston could find for himself was that when all is said and done, I really believe the Bible is God's Word and that He means what He says. But does knowing the truths save you? Rosie often repeated John 8:32, "And ye shall know the truth, and the truth shall make you free." Just believing there is a God and that He wrote a book is not salvation. Everything I have read, everything Rosie had to say on the subject, even the cover page of every Gideon Bible, emphasizes that you must have saving faith. Faith, not in a collection of facts, but faith in a person, Jesus Christ. Yes, that's it, Winston concluded, you must rest your faith in Jesus Christ alone. How did that verse go? "Oh, yeah, "no man can come unto me, except the Father which hath sent me draw him: and I will raise him up at the last day" (John 6:44). Is it time to ask Jesus to save you, Sam? he asked himself. Yes, was the answer, but not right now. I've got to work things out with Hadassah first.

Degania A and B, the 1910 beginnings of the kibbutz system, just south of the Galilee bridges, was lush with orchards and gardens, vegetables and corn in the warm autumn sun. Winston drove in, past the rusted-out, Syrian Renault tank that was the high-water mark of the Syrian advance on the farms in the 1948 war. The embattled farmers and the gallant men of the Golani Brigade had repulsed a professional army, equipped with artillery and armored vehicles. Winston realized he was in the wrong place, drove out and circled Degania to the southwest to Hadassah's home in Kfar Halutz. Halutz is Hebrew for pioneer. Hadassah had a difficult time getting Sam to pronounce the H correctly. "It is like the "H" in Hanukah," she insisted. "I think American Jewish authorities vainly tried to get your people used to it by spelling it "Channukah.""

Hadassah was there. She held out her hand to him, obviously to keep him from embracing her. That was hard for Sam, for she looked lovely in a figured blouse and skirt. Winston could hardly speak. He was overcome with emotion, but his ruminations on the road north cast a cloud over what should have been a glorious reunion. Hadassah sensed there was something troubling Sam. She warned that it was Shabbat and they would have to be at the table for the lighting of the candles. Hadassah turned him over to Lev, an olive-skinned kibbutznik, who showed him to the men's dormitory. Winston freshened up and decided he better put on a better face.

Dov and Miriam Weizmann greeted Sam warmly. The home was simple, meticulously neat and bright with flowers. The best Sabbath dinnerware and utensils were on the table. Miriam lit the candles in the traditional way and dinner was served. The Weizmanns took their Judaism in easy doses. They were more earnest about traditional faith than Sam was, but it was mainly a Sabbath and holy days kind of religion. The dinner was delicious. Sam had not eaten a home cooked meal like it since he left the States. Seated next to Hadassah, he could not gauge her expression. She averted her eyes, even when passing dishes.

Sam sought for a sign that he was going over well with the Weizmanns. Miriam said little, her eyes always on the table. Dov, a sinewy man with bronzed hands and arms, was little more communicative than his wife. He was difficult to penetrate. The table talk first was of Sam and his American family, his views of Israel and the expected visit of the European, "what's his name, oh, yes, Roy." Winston had a thousand questions about Halutz and Degania. "Degania means 'cornflower 'I think, in English, Mr. Winston. Warming to what they guessed was another suitor for their daughter's hand, the Weizmanns spun yarns about the great Israeli philosopher, A. D. Gordon, memorialized in an agricultural and scientific museum on the Degania grounds. The hero of the struggle for the nation, Mosheh Dayan, was born at Degania and in young manhood, he fought in her defense.

After dinner, Sam and Hadassah watched the moon rise over the Sea of Galilee. Clouds gauzed the sky and then slowly drifted by. Starlight coruscated over the water. A gentle breeze flowing down over the Golan Heights to the east, played with Hadassah's tresses. Sam ached to tell her how much he loved her. Should he do that, now that they had the end of the world to contend with? Hadassah tried to make light conversation about General Roy's visit and something of her flight duties. She carefully sanitized her accounts of life in the air of any sensitive information. Sam could take it no longer. He turned her to face him. "Hadassah Weizmann, you know that I love you more than anything or anyone in the world and I want you to be my wife. So there!" "Sam, Sam," she clucked, "let's not talk of love. We hardly know each other. We're good friends, can't we leave it at that?" she pleaded. "We're from two different worlds, Sam. We are from two vastly different cultures. You were born to a capitalist home. I am from a frankly, Socialist tradition. We don't even speak the same language. Yes, we are both Jews, but even at that your German Jewish grandparents would not have spoken to my Polish Orthodox family." "Hadassah Weizmann, do you love me?" Sam said firmly. "Do I love you? Do I love you?" Hadassah mused, in no hurry to answer. Sam impatiently jibed, "you sound like Golda in 'The Fiddler on the Roof." Hadassah ignored the barb and repeated, "do I love you? Lieutenant Colonel Samuel R. Winston, I do not want to love you, but...but... I do love you, darn it!" Sam, broke into paroxysms of laughter and tears. He swept his love into his arms so tightly she fought for breath. Sam fell to his knees and clutching her feet poured out a pledge of undying love for this woman of his dreams. Hadassah stroked his hair and shed a tear. He tried to talk of marriage, but she pressed a finger to his lips. It wasn't time for that, he concluded. For now, it was enough to know she loved him.

Sam found it hard to sleep. By turns, he experienced transports of joy and then panic at the prospects that lay before him and his chosen one. What to do? If only God would speak. The kibbutz wakened early. After a leisurely breakfast, Hadassah walked Sam around the farm. He had to be introduced to scores of workers. They drove around to Degania A. Degania is the showplace of the kibbutz system. Everyone works and shares. No one owns Degania. Profits are communal, shared equally including goods and services. The remainder is invested in the farm.

Hadassah took him through Beit Gordon, the great philosopher's memorial. They visited the nearby Arab town of Samakh. Hadassah described the fighting around the village in the war of independence. Later, she drove him around the west end of Galilee. They had a sumptuous dinner at the Galei Kinneret Hotel. Sam wasn't interested in eating. It was enough to sit and look into her eyes. There was an unspoken agreement to avoid talking about their future.

# Chapter Nine
*Sam and "How to Recognize the Messiah"*

"Present arms!" Major Krueger cried in a deep command voice. Number One Company, 6th Brigade, The French Foreign Legion, snapped to as one man, to the opening strains of *La Marseillaise* followed by *O Canada*. General Jean-Luc Armand Roy, on the top step of the deplaning stairway, returned the salute and slowly walked down to the applause of the dignitaries carefully rounded up for the occasion. He was all smiles, an imposing figure in his horizon blue uniform and French Army kepi. Cardinal Durant of the Vatican Congregation for Defense of the Faith, followed him from the plane, and then to Winston's surprise, Monsignor Cormac O'Brien, his Dublin contact. He was followed by Mother Maria-Joseph Castaldi, the Catholic nun who nursed Roy back to health. Last off the plane was an Arab, dressed in the robes of the Saudis. Maurice Dupin, Roy's security officer, plainly bored sauntered down the stairway. Roy spoke into a clutch of microphones for a few minutes, offering the expected appreciation to the Israeli government, the rabbinical authorities and the great peoples of the Jewish and Arab world, for their gracious invitation. He gave no hint of the purpose of his visit. In short order, the limousines standing by on Winston's orders, whisked the official party off to a five-star Jerusalem hotel.

The next morning, Roy held a special briefing at the hotel to unveil a plan he called Operation Shalom. With the mayor of Jerusalem presiding, Roy revealed that secret protocols had been reached with Arab and Israeli leaders and Muslim and Jewish religious leaders to permit the Jews to rebuild their Temple near the Dome of the Rock, on the Temple Mount! The assent of every Arab government was secured, Roy said, rubbing his hands with satisfaction. The plan called for the immediate building of the Temple and the speedy resumption of Old Testament sacrificial worship as soon as practicable. Roy himself offered the traditional *Shekianu*, a prayer of thanksgiving for the new initiative, in very bad Hebrew.

Journalists from all over the world pressed the big question: "Is this the end of the Al Aksa Mosque and the Dome of the Rock?" "No," replied Roy's press secretary. "The Temple and the Islamic holy places will co-exist, side by side, in the spirit of Shalom and Salaam, Peace!" "Sounds like an architect's nightmare," one American news anchor, opined. "No, the press secretary replied, "the engineers have approved the plan. No further questions, thank you."

The announcement raised questions for the Gentiles present, but the Israelis cheered and danced around until the mayor gaveled them back to order. The Saudi prince, flown in for the announcement, pronounced Operation Shalom/Salaam as a significant step toward peace in the area. His sullen attitude seemed to cast doubts on his words. A Palestinian functionary spoke guardedly of the project. The Palestinians were obviously stunned by the end-run made on their own plans to make Jerusalem, Jewish-free, the capitol of a Palestinian state. The Chief Sephardic Rabbi and his Ashkenazic counterpart, spoke rapturously of this long awaited fulfillment of the Jewish dream. They noted the dream has been acted out in every Jewish wedding for centuries. The groom crushes a wine glass under his heel, a testimony that the faithful await the rebuilding of the Temple.

Operation Shalom? Winston said over and over again to himself. Peace? No, this is Rosie Carver's "trigger." The exact fulfillment of Daniel 9:27, the opening of the Great Tribulation! All the pieces were in place. Roy is the Antichrist! You had to marvel at the scope of the plan. The question remained, "what did Roy give to secure the Temple for the Jews? Did Roy get it by military coercion? Not likely. The European Union Army was still largely a paper outfit. Did he buy it or trade for it?" Winston had no clue.

Word spread quickly outside the hotel briefing. The Jewish Temple Mount Faithful were ready to march on the holy mount. It took Israeli Army muscle to restrain them. At the western or wailing wall, the ultra-orthodox Hasidim danced with non-observant Jews, their long-standing enmity forgotten in the euphoria of the hour. Visitors from all over the world, caught up in the excitement, danced and sang all over the city. Embittered Palestinians watched from cover, weapons cocked and ready.

Well, now the work begins, Winston muttered to himself. Krueger's legionnaires went back to Akko and Winston returned to his dingy Jerusalem office. He discovered he had to turn over a room to make office space for Dupin. The security officer wore the same seedy black suit, soiled tie and a shirt collar, edged with grime. Winston sized up Dupin as a latter-day inquisitor who collects obscure items of gossip and innuendo about everyone he meets. I'll bet you a nickel, Winston predicted, he knows all about Hadassah already. He may be assigned to spy on me, but he would do that with or without orders, Winston concluded. Corporal Pieter DeRuyter, a Belgian Army clerk, who spoke peerless English, was a welcome addition for some light office work. Winston liked the young man at once.

The English language edition of the Jerusalem Post, filled with Operation Shalom news, also carried reports that Winston noted were tune-ups to the Great Tribulation. The reports told of a 7.5 Richter scale earthquake in Turkey, a temblor felt that morning in Jerusalem. International response to the disaster was slow, but much better than the total absence of aid for a quake in India. The Indian quake rivaled the disaster around the city of Brujh in 2001. Earthquakes were commonplace now. The San Andreas fault line in California kept residents on edge. A quake on the New Madrid fault line in southeastern Missouri caused damage in Winston's hometown of Saint Louis.

World hunger was a fact of life, but there was news of growing famine in areas normally well endowed with crops. It was so bad in Central Asia, according to the report, that hunger-maddened animals were attacking humans. Every news program was filled with horror stories, punctuated by officials powerless to act on behalf of the victims. No government promised aid to those outside their own sphere of influence.

The back page of the Post told of an ultra-Orthodox demonstration in front of the Jerusalem Barclay Bank. The Hasidim were protesting the opening of four caches of Christian New Testaments in modern Hebrew, held in the bank's trust since 1938. The story related that the American Bible scholar, Dr. David L. Cooper of California had given $2 million American dollars to the Barclay Bank to distribute four large caches of the Testaments, warehoused under tight security in Tel Aviv, Tiberias, the new section of Jerusalem and in Haifa. In a press interview, trust officer Dov Eshcol, said that the bank was paid to hold the books until reports of great numbers of people vanishing from the earth seemed to be true. Then the bank was to open the caches and permit the books to be distributed without cost. Eshcol denied knowing the books were Christian literature and maintained that the bank could do no other than follow the legal requirement of the trust. The Israeli minister of domestic affairs promised to investigate and the protesters were dispersed.

There was E-Mail from Hadassah. "Darling, missed you today. Don't try to reach me for a couple of days. Love, Cornflower." Since their joining of hearts in the moonlight, Winston walked on air much of the time, and then crashed to the depths as he pondered their future together. Dejectedly, Winston walked down to the sidewalk cafe with the strong Turkish coffee and sat at a small round table. Lost in thought, he was startled at the figure sliding into a seat opposite him. "Excuse me, Colonel, but I must talk to you," the intruder said. "I know what you are going through. Mr. Winston, there is help for you." With a conspiratorial look around, he slid a paper across to Winston and he was gone. "What next?" Winston said audibly, and then to himself, "do I wear a sign saying,' dump problems here?" He unfolded the paper. It was entitled **How to Recognize the Messiah.** In a hasty examination of the paper, Winston found it had a listing of prophecies of the Old Testament and their fulfillment in the New. That might be worth looking at later, he thought, but why pass Gospel literature like a spy-thriller? He remembered that Israel had been as hard on Christian believers as his family had been on Simone.

Captain Avigdor knew a lot about the plans for building the Temple. Rumors of the construction were underway within a few days of the capture of the old city in 1967. There were early rumors of casting the twin pillars, Jachin and Boaz in Italy. Everyone knew someone in authority who spoke of importing Bedford limestone from Indiana. Avigdor related the reports of the training of priests persisted for years. "On the whole," Avigdor said, "there were kernels of truth in all of the reports. But come with me and I will show you just how far along we are in the program."

They began their tour at the Temple Mount museum dedicated to the dream of a Third Temple. A model was strategically placed in view of the mount where the Temple must stand. Winston carefully examined the seven-branched lampstand. When finished it would cost an estimated ten million dollars. Robes for the priests and the "Holiness unto the Lord" headdress for the chief priest were on display, along with a model of the Ark of the Covenant. Avigdor explained that the last Chief Rabbi of the Holy Places, believed that the Ark was hidden below the Temple Mount. A visit to the Yeshiva, the seminary where Jews of priestly descent were being trained topped off the tour. "Our people have scooped tomorrow's headlines, haven't they?" Winston opined. "We are a prophetic people, Colonel," Avigdor continued. "For example, during your Gulf War of 1990, huge numbers of mollusks washed up on our Mediterranean beaches. These were no ordinary snails, these were *Segulit* snails. Each snail yields a pin-drop of very blue color that the rabbis say was used to dye temple robes and the robe of the king. They were said to return to Israel every seventy-five years. The Jerusalem Post carried the story from the Talmud that relates when the snails return it is a portent of the coming of the Messiah."

"Ari," Winston said, "I don't see how General Roy got the Muslims to agree to the rebuilding of the Temple. The way I get it, the Muslims regard the places where the Prophet Mohammed stood too important to cede to anyone. How can they give up the Temple Mount?" "That is the big question," Avigdor replied, "some scholars have thought *Ha-Miqdash*, our Temple and the existing Muslim structures could be in the same general area, but the purists say emphatically, "No!" "Our renowned scholar A. S. Kaufmann and a number of others sought for the exact location of Solomon's Temple as the desirable site. There are those who say, that the red heifer offerings were stored on the Mount of Olives and that from that location one could look directly into the holy of holies. They contend that settles the location of the Temple. Line of sight calculations have been made as an aid to locating the exact spot. Well that's academic now," Avigdor continued, "The Temple will have to share space with the Muslim holy places and it means trouble."

It was time for Sam Winston to get out of Israel. The evidence was all in. The Temple Mount project proved that Roy was the Antichrist. Somehow, he must spirit Hadassah out of the country with him. But would she go! Besides, what place is safe in the Great Tribulation? The pressure was starting to wear on the usually clear-minded, physically-sound Colonel Winston. Exercise always helped when he had nagging problems, but he could not remember when last he had jogged. The spare tire around his middle was gradually inflating.

Sam was not ready for Cormac O'Brien. The jolly Irish priest turned up at Sam's office, "just to talk," he explained. He had been drinking. He had little to do it seemed. He was staying with the priests in the prestigious Ecole Biblique, the Catholic center for biblical research. The mirthful O'Brien with his thick Irish brogue, made it difficult to follow much of what he had to say. The gist of it was the untold story of Roy's coup in getting the Temple Mount for the Jews. Piecing the story together, Winston learned Roy had been back in Iraq before his arrival at Ben Gurion airport. The story got interesting. According to Father O'Brien, Roy met a Muslim group in Baghdad, a follow-up to his visit of a couple of years before, the visit that ended in the shooting in the desert. The meeting was to buy the Temple Mount or at least obtain the right to build there! "What did he have to give?" Winston asked. "The question was ignored at first. Winston asked again. "Well," said O'Brien, "something on the order of one trillion in gold and securities, but that was not the big item. Now, there is the real story," continued O'Brien, tantalizing Winston. "Come on, Father, give," Winston said impatiently. O'Brien got serious. "Iraq or Ancient Babylon is the goal of advocates of the One World Economic Order, within the European Union. They see it as the future capital of the world. They argue that it is near the center of the earth, for whatever that means. They also say it is an ideal location for a world trade center and an international banking combine. It is at the crossroads of Europe, Asia and Africa. Oil-dependent nations would love it. Those who know say the Gulf could be the busiest port in the world. Well, you see my boy," O'Brien continued, "the Arabs want that capital in their orbit and they are willing to coerce the most militant of Islamic groups to give up this little piece of Jerusalem to get it."

"How will this fly in Brussels, Father?" Winston asked. "The EU is weak as you know, Colonel," replied the priest. "They don't like it, but money talks and the power Roy now enjoys makes it difficult for them to do much about it. The real question under debate, is the attitude of Holy Mother Church." "Explain that," Winston pressed. "Well son, the Holy See must always be the Holy See. The Holy Father is so sure Roy is the future of a worldwide return to Rome that he will back anything the general has to say. The pope backed the plan. He put up the trillion dollars!" "What's in it for him, for the church, I mean?" replied Winston sardonically. "Well, the Holy Father got what he wanted. There is a secret accord in the Operation Shalom treaty that conveys spiritual authority over the whole world, except for Israel, to a new unified Church over which Rome would naturally hold sway. No other irregular churches or forms of worship will be tolerated within the signatory nations. We expect that with one billion communicants and 3,000 dioceses, or regional entities, authority will rest with us. We would finally realize our goal of world hegemony."

Frankly tired of the recital of Roman prestige, Winston asked, "What does an old IRA bagman like yourself have to do with this treaty?" With a twinkle, O'Brien responded, "for years, Opus Dei had what is called the "cloak and crucifix" squad of priests who entered Saudi Arabia as engineers, bankers and businessmen. Avoiding the watchful eyes of the Muslim religious police, they celebrated mass for Catholics where there is no church. They exerted influence over Muslims in key places. In addition our boys in the IRA made friends with the Arabs. IRA men trained in North Africa, Syria, Iraq, Iran and Afghanistan. Arab oil and Americans of Irish descent, bankrolled the movement. It was IRA influence, and the Vatican

Bank, that made the deal work." Winston was impressed with Cormac's knowledge of the inner-workings of the Islamic world. Deciding to test O'Brien's sources, he asked, "tell me then who gunned down Roy in the desert?" Without hesitation, O'Brien replied "some EU people who thought that killing the general would put an end to the Babylonian proposal. It was a desperately foolish act that almost succeeded. Roy knows who they are. They are on his short list for later." "Oh, one further question, Father. "Why is Mother Castaldi here?" "Just a photo-op, really, Colonel. Nothing else. You can't imagine what a bore she is. I get stuck with her at every meal!" said O'Brien mournfully. The general's miracle recovery was still unexplained.

The time away from Hadassah was hard on Sam. It was a good time to study. He went over the **How to Recognize the Messiah** tract, again and again. It was an attractive leaflet with a full color view of the old walled city of Jerusalem with the eastern gate in the foreground. Sam turned it over and read, #6A02 Good News Publishers/ a nonprofit corporation 1300 Crescent Street, Wheaton, Illinois 60187. c. 1990 Good News Publishers Printed in USA. This piece of literature had come half-way round the world. It began:

**Who is the Messiah?**
**How can we recognize him?**
**When will he come?**

Centuries ago prophets spoke of the coming of a great leader. He would be sent by God and would be called God's Anointed One, the Messiah. The current interest in the State of Israel awakens renewed interest in the Messiah. Here are six descriptions that identify him.

1. He must be of the seed of Abraham. Moses recorded the promise of God to Abraham in the following way: "In thy seed shall all the nations of the earth be blessed" (Genesis 22:18).

2. He must be of the tribe of Judah. When Jacob was dying, he said to his son Judah: "The scepter shall not depart from Judah, nor a lawgiver from between his feet, until Shiloh come; and unto him shall the gathering of the people be" (Genesis 49:10).

3. He must be of the house of David. In Isaiah's prophesy of the Messiah we read: "Of the increase of his government and peace there shall be no end, upon the throne of David, and upon his kingdom, to order it, and to establish it with justice and with righteousness" (Isaiah 9:7).

4. He must be born of a virgin. The prophet Isaiah wrote: "Therefore the Lord himself shall give you a sign; Behold the virgin shall conceive, and bear a son, and shall call his name Immanuel (Isaiah 7:14).

5. He must be born in Bethlehem as foretold by the prophet Micah: "But thou, Bethlehem Ephratah, though thou be little among the thousands of Judah, yet out of thee shall he come forth unto me that is to be ruler in Israel" (Micah 5:2).

6. He must be God. Isaiah clearly stated that when he wrote: "His name shall be

called...The Mighty God, The everlasting Father, The Prince of Peace" (Isaiah 9:6).

More than nineteen hundred years ago, a child was born in a stable in the town of Bethlehem. He was of the seed of Abraham. He was of the tribe of Judah and the House of David. His mother was virgin. The Messiah has come!

Who is the Messiah? The only one who meets all the requirements is Jesus. As a devout Jew, Jesus lived a remarkable life. He restored sight to the blind, healed crippled limbs and even raised the dead. He astounded the Jewish leaders of that time by his insight, wisdom and teaching of the Scriptures. By his words and works he proved himself to be God's Anointed One.

Then, according to the predetermined plan of God, Jesus gave himself as God's Passover Lamb - he died for the atonement of his people's sins. As the Prophet Isaiah predicted:

"He is despised and rejected of men, a man of sorrows, and acquainted with grief, and we hid as it were our faces from him; he was despised and we esteemed him not...But he was wounded for our transgressions, he was bruised for our iniquities; the chastisement for our peace was upon him, and with his stripes we are healed. All we like sheep have gone astray; we have turned every one to his own way, and the Lord hath laid on him the iniquity of us all" (Isaiah 53:3-6).

Jesus, the Redeemer, the Suffering Servant of God, died on the cross of Calvary and was buried. On the third day He rose from the dead and appeared to hundreds of eyewitnesses.

By the resurrection, God clearly demonstrated that Jesus is the Messiah. If you have not received Jesus as your Messiah, he invites you:

"If thou shalt confess with thy mouth the Lord Jesus, and shalt believe in thine heart that God hath raised him from the dead, thou shalt be saved?" (Romans 10:9).

Winston carefully studied every verse. It was good stuff; vintage Rosie Carver. He asked himself the question that had been on his mind for months: "If this is true, why do I hesitate to ask Jesus to save me? Maybe its not for Jews like me," he reasoned. Get real, was his answer. You know better than that. He slowly folded the tract and placed it in his Bible.

Hadassah made it back to the city with a bandage tightly wound around the palm of her left hand. Winston knew at once what had happened. "Caught a hot shell casing, didn't you?" She blushed. "On an extraction, my bow gunner tossed it in my lap. I picked it up. You know the rest." Sam gave her a long, lingering kiss on the lips and then kissed the injured palm. They drove to Tel Aviv for dinner. Over a good steak, Sam got right down to the business. "You said you love me, but you really don't want to. Explain that to me, please." "Sam, you really don't know anything about me," she pleaded. "Do you know my occupation?" she asked. "Sure, you're a chopper driver and a darn good one, and before that you played around with farming, I think." Hadassah, plainly annoyed, "played around with farming? I am an agronomist who has never been able to practice agronomy. As soon as I got out of the Technion I was on my way to the Army. You, a big city American, want

to take me away from Israel, from Kfar Halutz and my chosen profession."
Hadassah's hands went to her face, in a mock display of tears.

Sam, ill at ease, stupidly asked, "what does an agronomist do?" Hadassah brightened. "Did you know that Israel is the world leader in dew research?" "What kind of research?" Winston asked sardonically. "Dew research," she replied, "you know, ground moisture. The Bible says the Negev, our southern desert, will blossom like a rose. Well, it really does, because of dew research. I long to be part of that, not catching hot rounds in a chopper. That's why I said I don't want to love you. You are a professional soldier, what do you know or care about dew?" "Darling," Sam replied, in a voice husky with emotion, "I would give up the army, everything, in a nanosecond, to collect dew with you in the Negev, Halutz or on the moon." Hadassah silently studied Sam for a few minutes. She knew with a woman's intuition that Sam's declaration was well meant but meaningless. She looked at him steadily and said, "like Ruth, I will follow you and be with you forever, Sam." Winston laughed and cheered.

Hadassah's mood changed instantly. "Okay," she said," let's talk. If I am to be your wife, I want the *Kidushin* at Degania. I will be out of the army in 120 days. Is that time schedule alright with you?" Ignoring her question and the stares of other diners, Sam slipped to his knees. He held her hand and cooed, "Hadassah, you have made me the happiest man in the world. I love you and 120 days can't come too soon for me." Winston jumped to his feet, looked at Hadassah and ordered, "You translate. Ladies and Gentlemen, this is Hadassah Weizmann of Kfar Halutz and I am Samuel Winston of the United States and I want you to know this lady just agreed to marry me." From his pocket, Winston produced an inexpensive gold ring set with an Eilat stone, and slipped it on Hadassah's finger. "There my darling, that will have to do until we pick out the real thing," said the glowing Sam. Hadassah flew into his arms. Locked together, they were the only people in the world. Applause broke out all over the restaurant, amid cries of "mazal tov." The owner was so touched he tore up the check.

It was hard to part. Sam was mildly vexed that he could not know where Hadassah was stationed. Winston knew it was a secret it would be easy to probe, but both were committed to observing military discipline to the letter. They clung to each other until Hadassah was in danger of failing to report at the fixed time and place, a serious matter for an officer. One hundred and twenty days would hang on them like lead, but then they would be joined together forever. As Hadassah drove off, Winston felt that icy feeling once again. How long is forever in today's world?

Intending to crash on his couch for the night, Winston returned to his Jerusalem office. He slipped off his shoes, poured a cup of Corporal De Ruyter's cold, bitter tea and settled down to read **How to Recognize the Messiah** for the umpteenth time. He was not quite through the paper when he felt an overwhelming compulsion to go to his knees and pour out his heart to a God he did not know. In an audible voice, he cried, "O Lord, I know you are real and what little I know about you I really believe. First of all, I believe your Son Jesus is God, as you are. I believe that you sent your Son to save wretched, undeserving sinners like me. I believe he rose from the dead, proving he is God. I cannot think of one, single reason why you should save me, but O God, I cast myself upon you, here and now, and I ask you to save me for Jesus' sake. Then Lord, I ask that you would please save Hadassah Weizmann, too. She is a fine girl, Lord, and I just know you would be proud of her in your family. But Lord, she isn't going to believe anything I have to say about you because she has seen nothing of God in me. So Lord, I'm just asking for both of us, somehow save us in Jesus name." Sam remained on his knees for a long time, waiting for he knew not what. In the darkened adjacent office, Maurice Dupin heard every word. He slipped out quietly into the night.

# Chapter Ten
## *Meet Ben-Zion*

The Third Temple, a dream for nearly two thousand years, was at last underway. The problems were unimaginable. Winston in his U S Army BDU's, found himself on the job site from morning 'til night, the chef-de-mission indeed. His lazy days of requisitions and telephone conferencing gave way to general oversight of the work force, arbitrating disputes large and small and the endless haggling that is the staple of Middle Eastern life.

In a compromise agreement, the Temple would share the Temple Mount. The Dome of the Rock and the Al-Aqsa Mosque would remain standing. "For the present," Roy said privately. Building within the narrow confines of the Temple Mount, moved engineers to tears. Some threatened to quit on a daily basis. Only the distinction of being in on the most important construction event in modern history kept them going. Getting materials to the site was a monstrous problem that largely fell on Winston's shoulders.

Old hatred and bitterness did not die with the treaty. The Muslim Wakf, guardians of the Islamic holy places, prowled the Temple Mount looking for any insult to the Prophet or the sacred precincts. On the other side, the Jewish Temple Mount Faithful, feeling their oats over the realization of their dream, provoked confrontation on a daily basis, much to the irritation of Winston and the Israeli Defense Forces. The Muslim citizenry, inflamed with the rhetoric of their Imams, were sullen and resentful. They stole what they could, sabotaged equipment and made known their real feelings. Winston could only think, "what am I doing here?"

As a new believer in Jesus Christ, Sam Winston was assiduous in his spiritual growth. In fact, he concluded that he had never been so serious about anything since his ROTC cadet days and his first year of commissioned service. He had really worked at being an officer. He was determined to put that kind of effort into being a disciple of Jesus Christ. He rose before dawn every morning for prayer and Bible study. He could only guess at the proper language for prayer, but he knew what to pray for. His plate was full. This was the Great Tribulation. He was responsible for the great trigger mechanism of the Tribulation, the building of the Temple. He was actively in the pay and employ of the Antichrist himself. And he wanted to marry a young woman who knew nothing of any of this. It was certainly a time to pray. Sam devoured whole passages of the Bible. He felt it was important to get to know more about Jesus Christ. Matthew, Mark, Luke and John took on special importance. He re-read the Book of Revelation and the Book of Daniel to gain perspective on the events that now encircled him.

Security agent, Maurice Dupin tapped the receiver impatiently until the Paris operator signaled he was through to General Roy. "Mon General, Dupin here. I must report sir, that I believe Colonel Winston is a serious security risk." "What is it Dupin?" the General replied. "Sir, I believe Winston has become a Christian." "You mean a Catholic?" Roy asked. "No sir, you know one of those Christians who read the Bible and pray. I don't know about such things, but I believe Winston is now one of them." "That's preposterous Dupin, only peasants and old people do that anymore and soon we will deal with them harshly. But Winston? No, impossible." "General, I am an intelligence officer. I believe the man is a risk to your Middle East operations. He should be brought in for questioning. What are your orders? There was silence for a few minutes. Roy spoke slowly, "No, we will turn this matter over to Ten Sing. With his powers, he will quickly learn if Winston is a believer in – *That One*. You keep him under surveillance. I am bringing Winston to Brussels for a briefing. Ten Sing will deal with him at my headquarters."

A few days after his decision for Christ, Winston was alarmed to find himself questioning the truth of his salvation. The doubts lingered for a time, but it hit Winston that the fact that he had doubts was probably a proof that his salvation was real. I've joined groups, movements and activities in the past, he reasoned, and in no time at all I lost interest and I dropped most of them. I never staked my life on those groups, but I sure have staked everything on Jesus Christ. To doubt seems natural for anything as earth-shaking as salvation. Doubting must be a good sign. Sam Winston never doubted again.

Standing on the Temple Mount Sam pondered the question, "how do I get out of here?" A warm feeling stole over him. "I'm in charge," Jesus seemed to say to him. "I'll see you through this situation." Sam turned to watch a file of Arab porters, hired to carry materials to the project site. Bent beneath heavy loads, they plodded across the lot, trampling the red poppies. The poppies offered their beauty, mocking the efforts of mere men. One of the porters paused to adjust his load. He stepped out of line before Winston and said softly, "Tonight, midnight, Rehov Gemul 67" and passed on. Winston recognized the porter as the mystery man of the sidewalk cafe.

Winston knew "rehov," was Hebrew for street. Avigdor informed him "Gemul," means border. On a map, Avigdor pointed out Border Street. Just before midnight, Winston, dressed in civilian clothes, took a round-about way to 67 Border Street, careful to see that he was not followed. At number 67 Border Street, he knocked on the plain, dun-colored, single-story house. A shadowy figure within, opened the door part way and silently beckoned him in. Winston was invited to be seated in a small living room, with two over-stuffed couches, an easy chair of doubtful vintage and a coffee table. His host was the mystery man of the cafe and the Temple Mount. The man was clearly Middle Eastern Jewish, with no trouble passing as an Arab porter. He was frightfully thin with skin like leather. He slowly pumped Winston's hand in a surprisingly vise-like grip. It was hard to estimate his age. His face, once finely chiseled, sagged at the jowls under rheumy eyes, suggesting long periods without sleep.

"I am Ben-Zion," he said softly in English, "and I know who you are, Samuel Winston, the new believer in Y'shua HaMushiach." Shocked, Winston stammered, "how could you know this about me?" Ben-Zion answered, "known unto God are all his works from the beginning." My dear friend," Ben-Zion continued, "I am here to encourage you in your faith and to tell you something of God's great plan and purpose for your life." Winston paced the floor. Suddenly he stopped and whirled to face his host. "I know who you are! You are one of the 144,000 witnesses of Revelation Chapter seven, aren't you." Ben-Zion said nothing, but there was agreement in his eyes. Winston took his seat and leaned forward to catch every word from this messenger from God.

"Samuel, do you truly believe in Jesus as your Savior?" Ben-Zion asked. "I do, believe me I do," Winston insisted, "but I know so little about Jesus that I am not really his disciple at this point." "Rest easy, dear friend," Ben-Zion replied, "in due time, that will come. Tonight, you have the opportunity to take the first steps in discipleship. Samuel Winston are you prepared to follow Jesus? Are you prepared to share His reproach, even if it means your life?" "Yes, yes, I will," Winston said eagerly. "Arise," Ben-Zion ordered, "and be baptized." "You know," Sam said hesitatingly, I have read God's plan of salvation again and again and I did not see one word about baptism as a requirement in order to be saved." "You are right, Brother Winston, no ritual is part of salvation. Baptism is simply the first step in discipleship. It marks the believer as a follower of the Lamb. Will you take that step?

Sam's smile was assent. Ben Zion handed him a loose robe and motioned him to a room nearby. The robe suggested to Winston that he had stepped back two thousand years to meet Jesus himself. In an atrium at the center of the house, open to the stars, there was a small pool. Sam followed Ben-Zion into the waters and was there immersed in the name of the Father, the Son and the Holy Spirit. "Arise, Brother Samuel," Ben-Zion said triumphantly.

Certain he must be glowing, Winston dried himself, dressed and took his seat in the living room. Ben-Zion suggested the second step for the new believer is to receive communion, the Lord's table. Ben-Zion took a matzo, broke it into two parts and handed one to Winston. "Brother Samuel, the same night in which Jesus was betrayed, he took bread, blessed it, broke it and gave it to his disciples. He told them, take, eat, this is my body which is broken for you. Do this in memory of me." Ben-Zion and Winston ate together. Then Ben-Zion continued, "after supper, he took the cup and said this is the new covenant in my blood which is shed for the remission of sins. All of you drink of it." Ben-Zion sipped from the cup of wine and passed it to Winston.

"Brother Samuel, "we are baptized but once. Baptism signifies our union with Jesus the Messiah, a union which can never be broken. Sadly, believers sin, by which our communion with Jesus is broken. Therefore, we repeat the Lord's table observance throughout the believer's lifetime. Jesus' servant Paul the Apostle, said "for as often as you eat this bread and drink this cup you do show the Lord's death 'til he comes."

"Now, these are troubled times," Ben-Zion continued. "You should have listened to your army friend and your niece, now with the Lord, when they urged you to trust in Jesus the Messiah. But, now at last you have cast yourself upon the Lord and He has saved you. And now you have the privilege of sharing in His service. Are you sure you are prepared for that?" "Yes," Winston said slowly, "right now, I know just enough to be dangerous to the Lord's cause, but I am willing to learn."

Ben-Zion seemed to ignore the remark and went on to say, "Brother Samuel, your mother's maiden name was Katz. Is that correct?" Winston marveled, "yes, she was the daughter of Hyman Katz, a jeweler." "Good," Ben-Zion nodded, "Katz, I should tell you, is a contraction of the Hebrew words, Kahn and Tzedakah, priest and holy. It gives us the title "holy priest." Your mother came from the priestly family of Aaron, Ha-Kohen, Aaron the High Priest of Israel." Winston knew from his visit to the Yeshiva where priests are trained that people named Cohen are prohibited from entering cemeteries because they are supposed descendants of the high priest. Suddenly it dawned on Winston, "are you saying that I am of the priestly class?" "Yes, my brother, you are Samuel Ha-Kohen!" Winston recoiled in confusion. "What does that mean?" queried Sam. "It may mean a big job for you in the king-dom reign of the Messiah. You will share in the duties in the Fourth Temple." "You mean the Third Temple," Winston countered. "No," countered Ben-Zion, "as you will see, the edifice you are building now is not the Temple that will be the center of spiritual activities in the Thousand Year Reign of the Messiah. You should read about it in Ezekiel Chapters 40-48," Ben-Zion instructed.

"Brother Samuel, many will be saved in this time of Great Tribulation", Ben-Zion said with gravity, "but most will die for their faith. You must preach the Gospel of the grace of God, especially to our people the Jews. There are two points to our message, a message first preached by John the Baptist, who was the forerunner of the Messiah." Winston interrupted eagerly, "I know, he preached to Israel in the wilderness." Ben-Zion continued, "John said, "Repent ye, for the Kingdom of Heaven is at hand." (Matthew 3:2). The kingdom was offered then and it must be offered now. Secondly, John saw Jesus and preached "Behold the Lamb of God, which taketh away the sin of the world" (John 1:29). That is your message: repent for the kingdom of heaven is at hand and behold the Lamb of God who takes away the sin of the world. Brother Samuel, some will listen, some will not. Preach this message without fear or favor.

82

Ben Zion continued, "you are already in grave danger. Move with great care. The wicked one will have his agents looking for you everywhere. You are concerned about your involvement in the building of this false Temple. Events are shaping up to purge you from the Antichrist's inner circle. I do not know that you will survive the Tribulation, but in any event, you will be with the Lord Jesus when He returns to rule and reign."

"Brother Ben-Zion," Winston said with deep feeling, "I have this lady friend, Hadassah Weizmann. We are engaged. She knows nothing of Jesus and she does not know that I am a believer. Will she come to faith in Jesus?" "That is in the hands of the Lord, my Brother" he replied, "pray earnestly for the Holy Spirit to convince her of the spiritual need in her life and then fully explain the finished work of the Messiah on the cross for her sins. And then pray without ceasing."

"Brother Winston you must go. There is great danger. Ben-Zion wordlessly beck-oned to Winston to follow him. The older man glided out of the room through the atrium and into a veritable labyrinth of narrow passages. They moved quickly for ten minutes, Winston estimated, before Ben-Zion paused and pointed Winston toward a dimly lit street. Winston brushed at his clothes and then sauntered out on the route he had used to get to Border Street. There were a few vehicles on the road and fewer pedestrians. Winston had to steel himself not to look back over his shoul-der. I'll have to get use to this cloak-and-dagger stuff, he concluded.

Within twenty minutes Winston was back at his office. Turning his key in the lock, he was conscious of a figure at De Ruyter's desk. "Out on the town, tonight, Colonel?" Maurice Dupin questioned in his best inquisitor's voice. "Yes," Winston replied, "I got a little night air." "It's after one-thirty," Dupin countered," you need your rest, Colonel. Your nocturnal habits could reduce your efficiency at the Temple." "Good night, M'sieu," Winston said curtly and headed for his couch.

The Temple Mount was all work and no play. Winston managed to keep operations running smoothly. He was grateful there were enough engineers, archi-tects and artisans of all kinds to do the hands-on stuff. Slowly, but surely, the edi-fice rose. It was no Herod's Temple in terms of appearance. Herod the king had taken decades to refurbish the temple Zerubabel erected at the close of the Babylonian Captivity. This Third Temple would have rich appointments when com-plete, without some of Herod's ginger bread effects. Winston smiled to himself as he thought, "what would they say if I told them there will be another Temple after this one?" The most difficult parts of the project were the immense stones for the foundation. Herod's had foundation stones of incredible size. In the interest of speedy completion, the Third Temple incorporated more modest building stones. A second major problem was the 180-foot porch, a virtual tower. There was said to be good evidence that Herod's Temple had a porch of that size, but some project engi-neers were skeptical of the size because it would be disproportionate to the building proper.

Winston felt a momentary urge to sabotage the project. He then decided that God had determined that without divine authorization the Temple should be built. Arabs of all ages pilfered what they could, young men threw rocks at the Israeli soldiers and Palestinian rage grew right along with the Temple. Strangely, nothing was heard from the Muslim Hamas faction and the Syrian-sponsored Hezbollah guerrillas, usually active in car and bus bombings and other terrorist acts against Israeli civilians. Internationally, Muslim silence was deafening. Groups like the Algerian Islamic Group, the Islamic Jihad and other Muslim fundamentalist groups, took no position on the temple construction. Had they been bought off, too?

General Roy was on a whirlwind tour pressing the flesh in the Western world. He received a ticker tape parade in Montreal and was eulogized at the Oratorio of Saint Joseph. French Canadians were ecstatic with joy over the meteoric rise of their favorite son. He was wined and dined at the White House and walked away with a king's ransom in military weapons. The pope seated him in a place of honor in the Sistine Chapel, an unheard of honor for a public figure. Roy was now a full general in the French Army and rumors had it that he would receive his field marshal's baton when the European Army was fully manned. Roy spoke well and was quoted widely. Winston tried to analyze every statement the general made. When you know that he fronts for the father of lies, Winston reasoned, you know that every move he makes, every word he utters, is camouflage for a death-dealing monster. The Pentagon had opened up the opportunity for any American serviceman to transfer in grade to the EU army. It was recognition of an American force in the service of foreign powers for the first time in U.S. history. Winston asked La Farge in Brussels when he and Krueger's legionnaires would be free to return to Europe. La Farge ignored the question.

Hadassah managed to get a three-day pass. Avigdor agreed to stand in for Winston on the Temple Mount. It was a serious breach of construction regulations for Avigdor to ramrod the operation. The agreement with the Wakf, was that only a Roy staff member would referee the work of the laborers and porters. Avigdor felt he could get away with it for a short time. He wished Sam well on his drive up to Galilee.

Winston's lady was into the whirl of preparation for marriage with all of the verve she gave to piloting her chopper. Winston was consulted and gave wooden approval to fabrics for dresses, colors for the reception, and the ground where the kidushin would take place. The conversation was one-sided. "Will Sophie come?" "Uh, she's not speaking to me right now." "Who will be there from the Winston family?" "Hmm, probably no one." Sam decided, privately, that the work of being domestic was probably the reason he remained a bachelor for so many years. He smiled with satisfaction that at the end of it all, he would have Hadassah forever. But he thought, how long is forever?

Sabbath at the farm was taken up with wandering the shoreline of Galilee. Hadassah reluctantly agreed to a short recess from her wedding plans. Sam ached to talk to her about Jesus, but he found it hard to begin. "Darling, there was a man who lived around here, years ago, who has influenced my life in some very interesting ways." Hadassah wrinkled her brow, at Sam's obtuse opening. She did not interrupt and Sam resumed. "I knew almost nothing about this man, He was just a man from another day and time, who lived and died without touching my life in any way, that is until I became convinced that He was not some ordinary man. I now know that he was a man come from God, in fact was God in the flesh! Hadassah startled, turned and said, "what on earth are you talking about?" Winston smiled, and placed a protective arm around his love and said softly, "Hadassah, darling, I am a believer in Jesus the Messiah." Hadassah recoiled as though pole-axed. "*The mamzer*?" she cried incredulously, "the illegitimate one the Christians claim is the anointed one of Israel? Surely not, Sam, you couldn't believe in that *bobbe-myseh* of a story." Sam felt as though an air bag had just deployed against his chest. He decided Rosie Carver's tactic was his only ploy at this juncture and that was to say, "darling, you were scientifically trained to make a full study of the evidence in a case, before making some wild, ill-informed judgment. Will you give me a chance to tell you about Jesus the Messiah and what he means to me?" Hadassah heaved a sigh of resignation, and shrugged her assent.

"Hadassah, Jesus of Nazareth was born to a peasant family, but a family in the royal line of David the King. You grew up singing *David, Melech Yisrael*, David King of Israel. But Jesus' was no ordinary birth. The Bible says,

"But when the fullness of the time was come, God sent forth his Son, made of a woman, made under the law, to redeem them that were under the law, that we might receive the adoption of sons."

(Galatians 4:4-5)

The rulers of Israel and most of the people of our land refused to have Him, although He proved over and over again that He filled to the letter the resume of the Messiah contained in the *Tenach*. Details of the place of his birth, His sinless life, His goodness to the people of our land, His healing of their sufferings, proved to any honest investigator that this was the Son of God, the Messiah of Israel. God's Word, Hadassah, renders this judgment on our people,

"He came unto his own, and his own received him not. But as many as received, him to them gave he power to become the sons of God, even to them that believe on his name."
(John 1:11-12)

Jesus offered himself to the children of Israel as the promised Messiah. They said, "no." It was then that he took up the difficult role that has touched me to the depths of my soul. The absolute pure, sinless Jesus died on the cross for me as my *kippo-rah*, my sacrifice for sins. While the Temple stood, on Yom Kippur, the Day of Atonement, our people afflicted their souls and offered the animal sacrifices the Torah required. The blood of the innocent animal answered for the sins of the faithful Jew, for another year. When the Temple was destroyed, Yom Kippur became another day of atonement, but with no atonement! For you see, God was finished with that system. Now, His Son Jesus made one sacrifice for sins forever. The truly contrite Jew or Gentile who accepts Jesus' sacrifice for his sins, is fully justified. God is satisfied with His Son's sacrifice."

"You know very well that in the very first Passover, the children of Israel slew a lamb without blemish on the fourteenth of Nissan. They were told to paint the lintels of their doors with the blood of the lamb. Our forefathers ate that lamb that night. That night those who had the blood covering were spared. The first-born of the Egyptians died. Centuries later, a man named John, son of a priest, was sent by God to prepare our people for the coming of Messiah. He said,

"Behold the lamb of God, which taketh away the sin of the world."

(John 1:29).

Isaiah the prophet, 750 years before the coming of the Messiah said,

"All we like sheep have gone astray; we have turned everyone to his own way; and the Lord hath laid on him the iniquity [the sin], of us all."

(Isaiah 53:6)

"Hadassah, Jesus is the Lamb sacrificed for us and by His blood we are set free from the slavery of sin. God freed our fathers from bondage in Egypt. Men groan under the bondage of sin, a bondage with fatal consequences. Hadassah, a believing Gentile told me of this Jesus the Messiah. A believing Jew, my own dear niece Simone, was also a believer. Now they are in heaven - what do the Orthodox call it? Oh, yes, *Gan Eden* – the Garden of Eden, with Jesus.

"A couple of weeks ago, a man gave me a paper entitled **How to Recognize the Messiah.** I read it over and over again. It faithfully presents the teachings of our Tenach, about the Messiah point-by-point. The Bible tells where He would be born, the nature of His life, His offer of Himself to Israel, the record of our rejection and His atoning death for sinners. Then the *Bris HaChodosho*, the New Testament of the Christians, shows how He fulfilled those Old Testament prophecies to the letter."

Hadassah paced up and down, arms laced together. Protecting her heart, Winston reasoned. Slowly, she said, "Sam, I don't know much about the Bible, but I do know that our people have resisted the message of *That One* for centuries. Our people have suffered and died by the millions at the hands of Christians. The pioneers of Kfar Halutz and Degania left a Poland of cross-bearing, cross-wearing people who hated the Jews and slaughtered them at every opportunity. It was the same bloody story in Russia, France, Spain, Portugal and England. The crowning achievement of Christian love for the Jews was the Holocaust. Do you know Sam, three years after World War II, just three years after the war, the Jews of Kielce, Poland were assaulted by Christians on the ridiculous blood-libel charge. For centuries that false charge claimed our people murdered Gentile children and mixed their blood with the meal of the Passover matzo! In Massena, New York, in your own country, the same charge was laid against innocent Jews in the land of the free. No, Sam, I cannot be a Christian. You are asking me to be the very first in my family to turn from the traditions of our people."

"My dear, you argue powerfully and persuasively," Sam said softly, "but you are arguing from secular sources, ignoring spiritual history. Our people were given the Bible. No one else in the world had the spiritual riches of the Jewish people. The world around us was filled with blood, lust and idolatry so abhorrent we do not speak of it. The Jews were given the law from the hand of a loving God who taught us everything from washing our bodies to how to cleanse our souls. We were alone the people who could live to a ripe old age, as long as we obeyed the law. Now the law was imperfect because no one could obey it completely. God saw the problem and He had the answer. He sent His sinless Son born under the law to show first of all, His Son could fulfill the law to the letter, but most of all to die for sinners condemned under the law. God built a bridge between where He is and where we are. That bridge was the cross of Jesus. The blood that Jesus shed was an exact picture of what our forefathers saw in the sacrifice of animals. They were obedient to God. Many faithful Jews were ready for the fulfillment of the sacrificial ministry. Hadassah, all of those who first believed in Jesus were Jews. They were good Jews, but Jews who knew they could not please God by the keeping of the law. They trusted in the sacrifice of Jesus and received Him as Savior and Lord of their lives. Jews have been trusting Jesus in every age. I had little or no loyalty to the law of Moses, but I saw the awful truth that I was a sinner and I simply asked Jesus to save me and He did! The best part of the story of Jesus is that three days after His death he rose from the grave, proved to His followers that He was alive and then went back to heaven. He is coming again Hadassah and soon."

Sam continued, "Of course you are right, about the so-called Christians that have murdered, raped and plundered our people over the centuries. But I firmly believe they were not followers of Jesus. They were religious people fraudulently claiming to be Christians. They wore crosses and claimed to speak for Jesus, but their lives proved that they never belonged to Jesus Christ. Every Christmas season at home in America, counterfeit $20, $50 and $100 bills are in circulation during the shopping season. Warnings are posted about the phony money. Now, if I have some twenties, fifties and hundreds in my wallet, would it make sense to burn them all on the chance one or more might be fake? No, neither is it fair to judge the good news of Jesus' salvation on the actions of fake Christians!"

Hadassah was very quiet for what seemed to be an eternity. She studied Sam closely. "I know that this means a great deal to you, my darling. I know that you have made a serious commitment to this...this Jesus. I'm not prepared to deal with this right now, but I promise you I will. Whether this will have some affect on our relationship I just can't say, but I am moved by your sincerity and I will read your **How to Recognize the Messiah** carefully. Meanwhile, I ask that you say nothing to my parents. It would upset them terribly and I loathe the day we have to tell them about your decision. I love you Sam, but this will take time to work through." Sam gathered her into his arms. She allowed him to kiss her, but she was tense with other emotions.

The telephone buzzed in the Weizmann home. It was Ari Avigdor. He apologized for interrupting Winston's weekend, but there was an emergency that needed immediate attention. Avigdor reported that the Israeli Army Commander for the Haifa District was in his office with a complaint about the legionnaires stationed near Akko. Colonel Nissim, by turns embarrassed and angry, informed Winston that since the legionnaires camped in northern Israel they were involved in almost daily breaches of the peace. Major Krueger received each complaint with the promise to look into the matter, but nothing ever came of it. Now, a legionnaire was being held by Israeli police for aggravated assault on a Palestinian shopkeeper. Krueger angrily insisted the man be turned over to him, but the police refused. Legionnaires were ready to riot. Nissim went on to say, that another legionnaire had been wounded by his comrades for some undisclosed offense. The legionnaire was treated by the Mogen David Adom, you know, like your Red Cross, for a bayonet wound through each hand. "We have that man in protective custody as well."

Winston mopped his forehead in frustration. He apologized on behalf of the European Union and agreed to meet with Nissim at the Foreign Legion headquarters the next morning at 0800. "I knew it was a mistake to send those men to Israel," he said with emphasis. "Legionnaires are the roughest, unruliest, men in anybody's army. To have them idle in a foreign country is a recipe for disaster. Darling, I have got to leave first thing in the morning." Hadassah smiled sympathetically, "it's a short drive from here, Sam. Leave after breakfast."

Nissim greeted Winston with a reserve conditioned by the gravity of the situation. He added the information that legionnaires had been reported for attempted rape, theft from Arab souks, drunkenness, failure to pay restaurant charges, disrespect to Israeli authorities and innumerable instances of antisemitic remarks. "If this was my Army, Colonel Winston, I would resign in a minute," Nissim said with feeling. "If possible I am more angry than you are, Colonel," Winston said with jaws clenched. "If you don't mind, sir, I would like to speak to Major Krueger alone. When I get his take on this mess, we will talk to him together. Is that acceptable to you?" "Quite," said Nissim.

Krueger lazily rose from his desk when Winston entered. He stood slackly; made no effort to salute. Krueger's Sergeant Major, Boris Massoit stood nearby. "What's going on here Major?" Winston demanded. "What has happened to military discipline in the Foreign Legion?" "Nothing has happened to Legion discipline, Colonel," Krueger said sharply. "This is the finest military unit in the world. To put my men here in this country with nothing to do, is to reduce them to rust in a hurry." "That's a pretty speech, Major, but it just won't wash. You are guests of a sovereign nation. You have the normal guest's requirements to obey the law, treat the natives with civility and in general behave yourself. As soldiers, you have an even greater responsibility to conduct yourselves like gentlemen. You have brought dishonor on your country, the European Union and you have made the Foreign Legion a stench in the nostrils of these people. As the commanding officer, you are totally responsible for everything these men do."

Winston turned sharply to confront Sergeant Massoit. The Sergeant Major was vintage Foreign Legion. He was barrel-chested, a shaven head perched on massive shoulders. He had beady, pig-eyes, set in a permanent sadistic twinkle. Massoit was the reigning wrestling champion of the Foreign Legion. Winston wondered how many men Massoit had killed with those immense, ham-like fists. His gold chevrons testified to long years of service in many parts of the world.

"Tell me, Sergeant Major," Winston demanded, "how your man received those wounds in his hands?" "Mon Colonel," Massoit began, "it is a long tradition in La Legion, for men to discipline a comrade who steals from his barrack mates. Pinning the couchon, the pig, to a table with bayonets has been our way to handle small problems for more than two hundred years." "Did you conduct an investigation?" Winston asked. "What did the man steal? Who initiated this disciplinary action?" "Mais oui, Colonel, I investigated carefully" Massoit replied, clearly indifferent to the matter. "To a man, his squad said they did not lose anything to the culprit and no one could identify those who carried out the punishment. I placed eight men on bread and water for a week."

Krueger tried a more conciliatory tone. "Colonel Winston, you are a soldier. You understand that these are just the normal, how-do-you-say-it, high-jinks of spirited young men, far from home." Unmoved by the tactic, Winston replied, "Major, I am going to bring Colonel Nissim of the IDF in and I want you to apologize to him verbally and then give him a letter of apology. More than that, you will make preparations to send the enlisted man in their custody home to France for court-martial if the Israelis are willing to give him up. No," Winston countered, "I will do that. I will send the prisoner home and the wounded man as well. I will make a full report to the commander of the 6th Legion Brigade of your less-than satisfactory handling of your men. You will take steps at once to prevent any further offenses. There will be zero tolerance from this moment forward for any kind of misconduct. Start with no leave, no passes off the cantonment area for thirty days, for the entire company. That's an order."

Krueger burned. He spit out an apology to Nissim through clenched teeth. Nissim agreed to see about a release for the legionnaire in custody and Winston made arrangements to fly him and the wounded man back to France. Winston found plenty to reproach himself about for the conduct of the soldiers he technically had under his command. What a mess! Driving south to Jerusalem, he had the sticky feeling his troubles were not over with the Foreign Legion. "Those sharks are bottom-feeders," he said to himself.

# Chapter Eleven
*Sam and Hadassah united*

"Mazal Tov, Sam," said General Roy, in an internet transmission to Winston's Jerusalem office. "I just learned of your impending marriage. You should have told me at once, old friend. I share your joy at this important new chapter in your life. Please assure Mademoiselle Weizmann of my sincere best wishes " "I will, General, thank you," Winston said weakly. Roy went on to say, "Sam take your bride to the States for an extended honeymoon as my guests. But please stop here in Brussels on the way. I have an important task for you in New York and Washington. You will have plenty of time for a honeymoon. You have done a splendid job facilitating construction of the new Temple. I am sorry you will miss the dedication, but your honeymoon and the short assignment I have for you in the States is too important to postpone. Mazal Tov, Sam, you lucky dog!"

Sam felt one of his panic attacks coming on. "Has anyone ever been in a pickle like this?" he asked himself. I'm a believer in Jesus Christ, about to marry a girl who is not a believer and our honeymoon is to be paid for by the Antichrist! Sam remembered the old TV ad for a pain reliever. "This is Excedrin Headache number 38." In spite of the intersection of these life and death issues, Sam Winston was growing in the conviction that Jesus was in control and that somehow everything would work out. Perhaps not for Sam and Hadassah in this life, but in that great life to come. Sam's main concern was longing to see Hadassah turn to the Lord.

Hadassah was busy. Her days swung like the rotor on her chopper. One day she was ferrying supplies to IDF units battling Hezbollah guerrillas on the Lebanese border. The next day she was prowling the best stores in Tel Aviv building a trousseau. Winston's news that they were to honeymoon in the United States meant new headaches. Could she dress to American standards? Would they take her for a - oh, what do Americans call a country girl? A hayseed?

A liveried chauffeur from an up-scale Tel Aviv jeweler, delivered the very first wedding gift to the Weizmann home in Kfar Halutz. It was from General Roy. A genuine leather jewel case was opened to reveal a replica of the European Union Army cap badge. Each of the twelve stars in the circle clutched a diamond of at least one karat weight. The gems were of unusual clarity and brilliance. The swords piercing the circle were platinum. The note enclosed read, "The Holy Father blessed this badge of honor." It was signed "Roy" followed by the Greek letters for "666." It was a breath-taking gift. Winston fingered it carefully, wondering how best to dispose of it.

The tune-up for the wedding came in the discharge of Lieutenant Hadassah Weizmann from active duty in the Israel Defense Forces. She was now a Captain in the Reserves, liable for recall at any time. With Sam at her side, Hadassah received an impressive looking certificate from the President testifying of her long and faithful service to her country. He shook her hand and bussed her on the cheek. Winston beamed with pride. Her chopper crew threw her into a blanket and tossed her in the air until she squealed for relief.

Hadassah was strangely silent on the drive home to Galilee. Sam thought he would feel the same way on the day he separated from the Army, but there seemed to be something else on Hadassah's mind. Hadassah's eyes were glued on the road. Finally, Sam suggested they pull over and talk. She sunk down in her seat and closed her eyes. "Well, let me have it," Sam exclaimed, like a prisoner awaiting sentence. Hadassah said nothing for a few minutes and then turned to face her lover. "I've read **How to Recognize the Messiah,**" several times. I really have and I just don't know what to think about it. But here is my pledge, like Ruth of the Bible, your God shall be my God. Is that good enough for now? she implored. Tears welled up in Sam's eyes. He collapsed on her shoulder. "What a wonderful girl you are, my darling. I will take you on any terms. I believe God will lead us together." Relieved, Sam drove on to Kfar Halutz, the lovers chattering like magpies. Later Sam remembered the warning he found in that morning's devotions, "be not unequally yoked together with unbelievers" (2 Corinthians 6:14).

Kfar Halutz was a good place to think. They had the endless round of social amenities with the Weizmanns and kibbutz well-wishers. There weren't enough hours to be with Hadassah, but it was a good place to think. Marrying must write "finis" to my relations with the Antichrist, he resolved. I should march right into Roy's office, give my testimony of faith in Jesus Christ and let the chips fall where they may. No, I would simply be dead and Hadassah would be a widow. No, I've got to play this out, until Hadassah is saved and we are in the USA.

Thinking about the honeymoon and the USA, prompted Winston to call Major La Farge in Brussels. "Major, I need money for travel to Brussels and the United States. Will you please arrange travel vouchers for my wife and me? "All done, Colonel," La Farge replied. "One other thing, Major," Winston continued, "could you do something to get me some extra cash from my U.S. Army account?" "I'm afraid I have no communication with your Army finance, Colonel," replied La Farge, "as you know, they have not sent a single draft for your pay since you went on duty with the EU." "What?" cried Winston. "I've been getting euros at the Barclay Bank here on a regular basis." "That's right, sir, General Roy directed that you be paid from EU budgeting sources." "What is going on here," Winston said with alarm. "Major, can you put me in touch with the US Army NATO Section?" "That section is no longer in official existence, sir. You might try Major Rita Brown, the very last US liaison officer here in Brussels."

Rita Brown, a newly-minted field grade officer, was delighted to hear from Sam. "Congratulations, Major," Winston said hurriedly. "Do you have any idea what happened to my U.S. Army pay and allowances?" Winston thought he had been cut off, for there was nothing but silence on the line for a couple of minutes. "You really don't know, do you?" Rita said at last. "Know what?" Sam all but screamed. "Sam, I almost got turfed out for talking off the record to you. That shouldn't happen to a nice West Point grad, like me. I'm sorry, I can't help you. I suggest you call ARPERCEN, the Army Personnel Center in Saint Louis, your home town." Without waiting for a reply, Major Brown hung up, wishing she had put a move on Sam Winston when conditions were right.

Civilian employee, GSA 12, Personnel Tech, Jason Handley, ARPERCEN, Saint Louis, was courteous to the caller from Israel, but the man's story was confusing. "Please slow down sir," Handley appealed. "I've got it now, sir. You are LTC Winston, Samuel R. and your SSAN, sir? Right, that's what I show. Let's see what the computer brings up. Yes, here you are. You were an O-5, regular commission. You went to the Army of the European Union. Is that correct sir?" "Yes," Winston replied. "What I need to know is why my pay and allowances have been held up for the period I have been on loan to the European Union?" "Pay and allowances, sir? There is no indication that you are due anything, sir," Handley answered. "Supposing I pull up your complete file," suggested Handley. "O.K, here we are," he continued, "you resigned your commission to accept a commission in the EU Army." "Resigned?" protested Winston, "I did nothing of the kind. Special Order 27, Paragraph 39, is right here in my hand and it says I was transferred to the EU on loan and that U.S. Army pay and allowances were to be paid in Eurodollars." Wordlessly, Handley brought up a short note of resignation over Winston's signature. On the screen, Special Order 27, Paragraph 39, was worded differently from the copy Winston was holding. Handley next showed DD Form 214, Report of Separation. It showed eighteen years, seven months and twelve days of service. Handley added, "I even have your last final-type physical examination, Mr. Winston, done at Stuttgart three days before your ets." "Mr. Handley," Winston said slowly, "I have not been in Stuttgart for months and I was not due for a physical, before I went to the EU. Every document you pulled up is a forgery." Handley looked at his cubicle partner, raised a hand to his temple and twirled a finger in a circle. "I don't know about that Mr. Winston, but I can tell you, you are not in our Army."

Winston stared at the phone for what seemed to be an hour. What is going on here? he asked over and over. The United States Army just doesn't do things like this. But this must be what Rita Brown was referring to when she said, "you just don't know do you?" Winston was angry. He slammed a file drawer and kicked the desk. A verse he was memorizing came to mind: "Yea doubtless, and I count all things but loss for the excellency of the knowledge of Christ Jesus my Lord: for whom I have suffered the loss of all things, and do count them but dung, that I may win Christ" (Philippians 3:8). Winston, surprised at his change of attitude, chuckled aloud, recalling that he was wearing a uniform that he was not entitled to wear. That puts me in the company of every trash hauler in the world who wears his old Army uniform to work.

Winston was reasonably thrifty for a bachelor. Through Barclay's Bank, Jerusalem, he was able to transfer a sizeable sum of money from savings in Saint Louis. There was a 20% bite out of the funds for something called the Universal Peace Tax. Barclay's expressed their regrets about the tax, but explained that everyone gets hit with the tax on international fund transfers.

It would have been nice to spend the weeks before the wedding squiring Hadassah around to the expensive stores, but the Temple Mount had first claim on his time. The building was nearly complete. Interior decoration was superbly done. Rabbinical authorities had combed the world for the finest orientalists money could buy. Many were Jews, only too grateful to have some of their handiwork in the Third Temple. The authentic sometimes gave place to the aesthetic, but everyone seemed pleased with the result. The dedication committee got in everyone's hair, with interminable questions Winston and the engineers could not answer. General Roy was to deliver the dedicatory address, after a long, boring ritual and the rabbis' sermons.

There was time to play. Hadassah worked hard on the details for the Kidushin, the wedding ceremony. She tried to make the work as much fun as possible for Sam. She joshed him about the *Tenaim*, the terms of the dowry in the marriage agreement. "We have to ask my father how much he will require for my hand." Sam offered one dry milch cow and two goats. "Offer rejected," Hadassah replied, with the laughter of a happy child.

The big day arrived at last. The invitation list dictated Degania as the site. Degania was beautiful, wearing nature's best colors in her hair. The *hupah*, the canopied prayer shawl for the service, was supported by four posts, made from a tree planted the year Hadassah was born and a tree that older kibbutzniks thought was from about the time of Sam's natal year. Hadassah was radiant. Her gossamer dress of white, shimmered like the clouds over Galilee. Her olive skin, flawless complexion and shiny black hair, showed to perfection. A wreath of cornflowers in her hair and her veil completed the picture. Sam had reluctantly laid aside his Army dress blues and wore an ill-fitting cream-colored suit culled from a rack in a back street Tel Aviv men's store. Somehow, his natty Brooks Brother suit would be out of place in Degania. A purple fuchsia four-in-hand, a borrowed tallis and a yarmulke made him a passable groom. Sam knew he was poorly dressed, but rested in the thought that all eyes would be on Hadassah anyway. Of course, his boutonniere was a cornflower.

Ari Avigdor led Sam under the hupah. Hadassah was escorted by her father and mother. The Mesader Kidushin, an army chaplain , welcomed the couple with the words, "Blessed be he who comes in the name of the Lord. We bless you from the house of the Lord." Winston placed a ring on Hadassah's right forefinger. It was the same cheap Eilat stone he had given her at dinner in Tel Aviv. She had adamantly refused any other ring. "You are hereby betrothed to me by token of this ring in accordance with the law of Moses and Israel," Sam intoned, his voice breaking with emotion. The *Ketubah*, the marriage contract and the seven blessings were offered by a *Hazan*, a retired helicopter crew chief from Hadassah's unit.

The traditional wine glass was crushed under Sam's heel, to cries of Mazal Tov! A kibbutznik, much in demand as a *Badchan*, a minstrel, sang humorous songs and cracked jokes at the expense of the newlyweds. Degania celebrated well into the night. The Winstons stole off into the sunset and drove to a luxury hotel near the Dead Sea.

You really don't know a person until you live with them. Hadassah had no real preparation for Sam Winston. In truth, Sam Winston was only beginning to know himself, the result of coming to faith in Christ. Hadassah knew Sam would be gentle, loving and sensitive to her needs. She was all but blown away by a man who insisted on praying with her and reading the Bible before retiring. She was startled to find him up before dawn to pray again. He insisted on holding her hand to pray before meals. He described in detail everything he had learned from the Bible that day. At first, she joshed him for being extreme in his devotional life. "Ease up on the Bible stuff, Sam," she pleaded. "You are not going to a Yeshiva or a Seminary are you? Even rabbis take a day off." Sam apologized, but felt there was so much he did not know. It gave him a chance to tell her once again how much Jesus meant to him. The Bible, prayer and talk about Jesus as a personal friend, were difficult for Hadassah to grasp, but she never again criticized her husband's walk with the Lord.

Seven days in En Gedi flew by like a weaver's shuttle. Their last morning there, Hadassah shyly approached Sam and said, "darling, would you help me to be a follower of Jesus?" Sam sank to his knees, clutching her hands. Softly he asked, "do you mean you want to be saved, sweetheart?" "I think I'm ready, Sam." Sam took his Bible and guided Hadassah to the sofa. With his best instructor's voice, Sam began with the statement: "every human being is a sinner by nature and by choice. Do you understand the concept of sin, Hadassah?" "That's bad stuff." "Yes," he agreed with a smile, "but it goes deeper than that. Sin is any failure to live up to God's standards, to God's glory. A person may strive to be good all of the time, but his nature is fallen and he has no approach to God on his own merits." Sam read from Ephesians 2:1-3:

"And you hath he quickened [made alive], who were dead in trespasses and sins; wherein in time past ye walked according to the course of this world, according to the prince of the power of the air [that's Satan!] the spirit that         now worketh in the children of disobedience: among whom also we had our         conversation [citizenship] in times past in the lusts of our flesh, fulfilling the desires of the flesh and of the mind; and were by nature the children of wrath, even as others."

(Ephesians 2:1-3)

95

"The key there is 'by nature,' darling. We sin by choice, because of our sin nature. We are hell-bound and hell-deserving. But notice, God took the initiative to remedy our condition in a way that was impossible for us to do ourselves.

"Not by works of righteousness which we have done, but according to his mercy he saved us..."

(Titus 3:5)

Notice the words of *Yeshaiah Ha-Novi*, Isaiah the prophet:

"But we are all as an unclean thing, and all our righteousnesses are as filthy rags; and we all do fade as a leaf; and our iniquities, like the wind, have taken us away. And there is none that calleth upon thy name, that stirreth up himself to take hold of thee: for thou hast hid thy face from us, and hast consumed us, because of our iniquities."

(Isaiah 64:6-7)

Hadassah, you could be the Chief Rabbi of Israel, the Pope of Rome or a Protestant minister and those distinctions could not save you. But Adonai, God, saw your need and mine, and He sent Jesus the Messiah, the sinless Son of God, to pay the full penalty for your sins.    Reading a little further in Ephesians Chapter two, we find:

"But God, who is rich in mercy, for his great love wherewith he loved us Even when we were dead in sins, hath quickened [made us alive] together with Christ [the Messiah], (by grace ye are saved)."

(Ephesians 2:4-5)

So you see you must respond in faith to God's gracious offer of salvation.

"That if thou shalt confess with thy mouth the Lord Jesus, and shalt believe in thine heart that God hath raised him from the dead, thou shalt be saved. For with the heart man believeth unto righteousness; and with the mouth confession is made unto salvation. For the scripture saith, whosoever believeth on him shall not be ashamed."

(Romans 10:9-11)

"Are you ready to be saved, darling?" Sam asked, trying hard to conceal a tremble. "Sam," Hadassah said bravely, "I know that something great has happened in your life. I believe you have the Messiah living within you and, yes, I want that too. I don't understand it all, but I believe everything the Bible has to say about God, about Jesus and about me, must be true. I want Jesus to save me." Sam, smiling through tears, invited Hadassah to kneel with him. He led her line-by-line through a prayer of commitment. She cast herself upon the Lord for salvation. Afterward, Sam shared a scripture of assurance that she now belonged to the Lord:

"I am the door: by me if any man enter in, he shall be saved, and shall go       in and out, and find pasture. My sheep here my voice, and I know them, and they follow me: And I give unto them eternal life; and they shall never perish, neither shall any man pluck them out of my hand. My Father, which gave them me, is greater than all; and no man is able to pluck them out of my hand."

(John 10:9, 27-29)

Sam, grinning from ear to ear said, "you are now a new creation in Jesus Christ, my darling. We are one in Him!" Easily one of the best days of his life, Sam realized he would have to begin schooling his wife in the long story of the Great Tribulation. Hadassah had a more pressing concern. "Am I still a Jew, Sam?" "Of course you are, and perhaps for the first time in your life you will understand the faith of our fathers. You now share their faith, the faith of Abraham, Isaac, and Jacob. David the sweet singer of Israel will sing for you. The prophets of Israel will have a message you can understand. Sarah, Rachel, Ruth, Elkanah and a host of other mothers in Israel will touch your life forever. You will find rest with other Jews for Jesus, like my niece Simone. Honey, I was really never a Jew, oh, perhaps I was a Jew culturally, but the synagogue was only the place where I expressed my own particular brand of Jewishness to other Jews. Now we have come home to the faithful remnant in every age." "But Sam," Hadassah protested, "haven't our people always reserved the right to say who is a Jew and who is not? Doesn't that mean Jews who follow Jesus are no longer Jews?" "Sadly, my dear, Jewish followers of Jesus have been mistreated and shut out of Jewish life for centuries. It is part of our people's rejection of the Messiah. You may be discriminated against, but every born again Jew knows beyond any doubt, that he or she really is a completed Jew for the very first time." "If you can handle the rejection, I can too, Colonel," Hadassah said with a jaunty salute.

# Chapter Twelve
*Honeymoon to terror*

"Sam, have you seen my purse?" Hadassah, obviously agitated, called from the living room. Rushing around to check out of their honeymoon suite, Winston was too busy to answer. In some kind of freak accident, his razor fell from the faucet to the floor, nicking his foot. Sam dabbed at the wound. "No, dear, I do not know where your purse is."

Then there was the matter of the missing theater tickets. The tickets for the single night performance of Inbal, the celebrated Israeli National Ballet, were obtained through Sam's government connections. They sat on the coffee table for two days. An hour before show time the tickets were nowhere to be found. Sam and Hadassah thought carefully about the maids, waiters and bellmen who came to the suite, but none had an opportunity to steal the precious tickets.

Someone might have taken the purse, but no one was around to knock the razor to the floor. It was not the end of annoying events. Hadassah's car turned up with every tire flat, but with no punctures or evident tread damage. A kind of dust devil blew through the suite one afternoon, the maelstrom spreading Rosie Carver's notes all over the room. After a long season on his knees in prayer, Sam felt sure they were under demonic assault. "Talk to me about demons," Hadassah demanded. "Well, I don't know much about them, but I understand they are fallen angels who joined Satan in his rebellion against God. There are many of them and they have great power, power greater than any human. But they are limited. They would kill us if they could, but they can't. Mostly, they are just irritating to believers, but they are cruel task-masters of the unsaved. Rosie Carver said there are four ranks of demons in view in Ephesians 6:10-13. There are demons in charge of whole countries according to Daniel Chapter 10. There are also demons involved in violence, some in black magic and many involved in tricking born again believers and attempting to destroy their witness for Christ."

Hadassah related that Yiddishkeit, the language, culture and lore of Jews that came out of Eastern and Central Europe, contains references to Dybbuks, malevolent beings that Hadassah believed to be exactly what Sam described. She went on to say that the rabbis say when a Dybbuk leaves a human he leaves a pinhole size blood spot on the pinky finger of the right hand or a crack in a window. "Well, the Dybbuk drew blood, all right, but on the foot not the finger." "What do we do about demonic activity, Sam?" Hadassah asked with some concern. We trust in the Lord and the power of His might. The Bible says,

"Ye are of God, little children, and have overcome them: because greater is he that is in you, than he that is in the world."

(1 John 4:4)

Sam confided in Hadassah that he had the feeling the strange events were some-how related to the wedding gift from General Roy. The pope had blessed it. Could that mean that it was charmed? "Darling, I have been uneasy about that diamond-encrusted badge since we received it." They agreed it made sense to get rid of it, but how? Sam hit on the idea of mailing it to himself, in care of Major La Farge in Brussels with a "hold for arrival" note on the address label. Sam mailed it the next day at the slowest delivery promised and the lowest class of service. What if it is lost? Well, blame it on the mails.

After the package was on its way, there were no further strange events. Sam's wound healed. The doorman found Hadassah's purse, with nothing missing. The ballet tickets never turned up. It was Hadassah's introduction to the Great Tribulation. It was time to give her the big picture. Sam took a piece of paper and drew a flat representation of the ages described in the Bible. A long horizontal line represented the 2,000 plus years of the Church Age, or the Christian era, including all the saved people from Shavuos, Pentecost, in about 33 B.C.E. through the recent Rapture. Sam read from Acts Chapter Two and First Thessalonians 4:13-18 about the beginning and the end of that period. "Did you tell me that Jesus came in the air at the Rapture, when those millions of people vanished?" Hadassah asked. "Yes, he came in the air," Sam replied. "Did anyone see him?" Hadassah pressed. "I think only the saved saw him, honey. When he rose from the dead after the crucifixion, apparently only believers saw him alive during the forty days before He went back to heaven. I believe no one saw him in the Rapture, but his own people."

Hadassah strained to remember how the story of the vanished was received in her military unit. "Oh, yes," she brightened, "there was a young, American Jewish boy in a maintenance unit. He was posted as a deserter for a couple of weeks. Some of his barracks mates said he was a Messianist. Then we never heard anymore about the matter." Hadassah knew a little about Rosie Carver and Sam's niece Simone. He reminded her they were caught away to heaven with Jesus.

Returning to his diagram of the ages, Sam drew a short horizontal line and labeled it **"The Great Tribulation"** above the line and **"Seven Years"** under the line. He drew two stick figures on the line. "That's you and me. Now let me show you the Bible outline of this period:"

### Matthew Chapter 24

I. Verses 4-8 - Describes the first 3 1/2 years of the Great Tribulation. It is a peri-od marked by false Messiahs, wars, civil disturbances, famine, disease and earth-quakes in unparalleled numbers. Sam paused and said, this is where we are right now. But add to the mix that the Third Temple is under construction in Jerusalem. The Temple construction is not God's project. It is the Devil's. Hadassah squirmed to say something, but kept quiet.

II. Verses 9-14 - Describe events at the mid-point of the Great Tribulation or 3 1/2 years after the dedication of the Temple. Hadassah interrupted, "Sam, you are in great danger working on the Temple," Hadassah said with alarm. "I don't think so, dear. The Lord's hand is upon us. Besides, my work there is over. But listen carefully, darling, General Roy secured the Temple Mount from the Muslims. He has given the right of Old Testament sacrifice back to our people. Scripture clearly states this is one means of identification of the **"Antichrist."** With a frown, Hadassah asked, "explain the title "Antichrist." "Well, Sam began, "as you know, the prefix *anti* means to be against something or someone. General Roy under the control of Satan is against Jesus Christ. *Anti* may also mean someone who takes the place of another. The Antichrist is one who endeavors to take the place of Christ as the object of worship. Both uses of anti apply in description of the Antichrist. Hadassah wanted to hear more about the Antichrist, but again deferred her questions.

Returning to his outline, Sam said, "that takes us to point number three:"

III. Verses 15-21 - The second half of the Great Tribulation, verse 21, (3 1/2 years duration), includes a number of events:

a. Verse 15 - The Antichrist puts an end to Jewish worship and makes himself the object of worship in the Holy of Holies of the Temple.

b. Verses 16 - 20 - Jews are persecuted. The readers of the passage at the time of the breaking of the covenant are warned to flee to the mountains, traditionally to Petra in the southeastern wilderness of the Kingdom of Jordan. Flight in the winter or on Shabbat is said to be especially hazardous.

c. Verses 23-26 - Many false Messiahs in the world. False rumors will abound that the Messiah has returned to earth,

d. Verses 27 - 31 - The Close of the Great Tribulation is marked by:

1. Verses 27-29 - Frightful natural phenomena and catastrophes worldwide.

2. Verses 30-31 - The Messiah returns to earth, vanquishing the Gentile armies.

Sam closed his notebook and Bible. "Darling, you and I are saints of God in the Tribulation. A great number of people, Jews and Gentiles, will be saved in this Great Tribulation. God has 144,000 saved Jews witnessing for him and winning people to faith in Christ. I met one in Jerusalem. I know him only as Ben-Zion. I met him for the first time in that little Turkish coffee shop you took me to. He gave me the leaflet, **How to Recognize the Messiah.** Later, I met him at midnight in a kind of safehouse. He baptized me and for the first time, I had communion.

"Communion? what's that?" Hadassah asked. "Well, I won't go into that just now. That's a treat I will share with you real soon. We talked only about Jesus and what it means to be saved. I have an idea I was followed to the meeting with Ben-Zion and I think I know who tipped off the authorities."

"You need to know, my love, that Rosie Carver and my niece Simone were saved in what was called the Church Age. It didn't cost much to trust Jesus Christ in the United States in those days. Many other believers in the Church Age suffered for their faith. The Bible seems to indicate that believers in the Great Tribulation, perhaps you and me, will be called upon to seal our testimony for Jesus with our blood." "Captain Winston is ready, Colonel," Hadassah exclaimed with a salute, "Jesus died for me. I can die for him." Sam brightened. "Don't forget, He rose from the dead and we will rise with him. But now, we have got to meet Roy the Antichrist. This man is energized by Satan, according to Second Thessalonians 2:9-10. I'm sure that means he is demon-possessed. Meeting him will be a real test because we have the Spirit of God living within us and as we may have already discovered, it gives the demons fits." "Next time, I'll hold on to my Inbal tickets," Hadassah said with a frown.

It took Winston several days to tidy up details of the Temple construction. Supplies and equipment flowed with fair efficiency to the job site. The air was charged with excitement as the dedication approached. Hadassah moved to Sam's Jerusalem hotel, packing and repacking for the United States. She made endless lists of everything from cards to be sent home to day-by-day matches of clothing and shoes. Sam was reminded that she was a scientist.

The English language edition of the Jerusalem Post featured a government wanted poster bearing the headline, "Have you seen this man?" It featured an artist's drawing, a passable likeness of Ben-Zion. The accompanying articles said the unidentified man was suspected of Temple Mount sabotage. A reward was offered for information leading to his apprehension and arrest. "They'll never get him," Winston said confidently. "Tell me about Ben-Zion," asked Hadassah. "I don't know much, honey," Sam replied. "I cannot even say for sure, that Ben-Zion is one of the 144,000 Jewish witnesses described in Revelation Chapters 7 and 14, but I have a hunch he is one of them. I don't know where he hides out or how he moves around, but if he is one of the Lord's Tribulation missionaries he must be immune to death for they are pictured beginning their work in Revelation 7:4-8 and the same group is alive with the Messiah when He returns at the end of the Great Tribulation, as seen in Revelation 14:1-6." Hadassah read those passages and noted, "according to Revelation 7:4-8 the witnesses are drawn from the twelve tribes of Israel. By name! Isn't that impossible? What Jew knows what tribe he belongs to?" "I know what you are saying, honey, all I can suggest is that God knows what tribes we belong to.

Wait a minute," Sam exclaimed, "Ben-Zion knew that my maternal grandmother was named Katz. He told me that Katz was a contraction of "Kahn," priest and

"Zedakah," holy. He said that made me a member of the family of Aaron, the high priest of Israel. Ben-Zion added that I would be a priest in the Kingdom reign of the Messiah." Hadassah brightened, "do you know that I am a Cohen too." "Wow," said Sam, "that makes us a priestly family." Hadassah frowned again. "I still find it hard to believe that every Jew can be identified with his family's tribe." "In Jeremiah 32, sweetheart," the prophet asks, "is there anything too hard for God?" God answers, "is there anything too hard for me?" God knows all things. Keeping His chosen people in their tribes should be easy for God. But in a practical way, Hadassah, you know Jews named Rubin. Would it make sense to think they belong to the tribe of Reuben? How many variations of Levi are in the world? I know Levys, Levines, Levins, Levitskys, Levinsons and so on." "That's true, Sam. I had an Asher and a Simeon in my crew."

Major La Farge on the internet directed that Sam be in Brussels in eight days. "Call me when you and Mrs. Winston arrive, to arrange an appointment with General Roy. You have reservations at the Hotel du Lac, compliments of the general." The conversation over, Sam said, "I would rather have a root canal than see the general."

Ari Avigdor arranged for a car and driver to take the Winstons to Ben Gurion airport. Security was tight as usual. It took two full hours to clear inspection. They were off to London on an El Al Israel flight. Nestled in their seats, Hadassah said she had two questions for Sam that really troubled her. "Tell me about the war that we are into. Secondly, how come the Jews are the principal victims in every war?" Sam rubbed his eyes. The questions were good ones. It was another occasion to regret that he had not spent more time in study with Rosie Carver. "Well, here goes, my lady. It seems that Satan, once a very high-ranking angel, rebelled against God. He recruited an army of other angels and began the war to take over God's throne. Of course, he cannot win, but he passionately believes that he can and so he fights on." Sam read from Isaiah 14:12-17. For emphasis he twice read Satan's words in verse fourteen:

"I will be like the most High [God!]"

(Isaiah 14:14)

Ezekiel 28:11-19, indicates that Satan will lose the war, but in the effort he has brought misery upon millions of people. Right now, it looks like he is in control, but not according to Revelation 6:16-17:

"And the kings of the earth, and the great men, and the rich men, and the chief captains, and the mighty men, and every bondman, and every free man...said to the mountains and rocks, Fall on us, and hide us from the face of him that sitteth on the throne, and from the wrath of the Lamb: For the great day of his [Jesus'] wrath is come; and who shall be able to stand?"

(Revelation 6:15-17)

I John 5:19 indicates there are two sides in this war. The verse begins,

"And we know that we are of God..."

(1 John 5:19a)

"That's us, darling, the born again believers. The rest of the verse says:

"...and the whole world lieth in wickedness, [or in the wicked one]"

(1 John 5:19b)

Adam and Eve fell into sin and the world they were charged with keeping, fell under Satan's control. He ordered the world and arranged it to enslave humankind. He introduced alcohol, drugs, immorality, violence and warfare, the sources of human misery throughout history. He ordered and arranged the world to entice us into lifestyles that could keep us from God. The Antichrist in the Great Tribulation is his final gamble in the bid for God's throne. He believes that a one-world religion, a one-world government and a one-world economic order will finally turn humankind against God forever. God will answer with unimaginable natural and supernatural catastrophes."

Satisfied with the answer, Hadassah asked again, "why do the Jews take a hit in the world's crises?" Sam replied, "let me ask you to supply the answer. Point number one: who gave the Bible to the world?" "The Jews," Hadassah answered without hesitation. "O.K., what nation was given the Messiah?" "Israel," Hadassah answered. "Good work." "Now to what nation will Jesus return to rule and reign?" "I believe that is Israel, too," Hadassah replied. "Do you get the picture now?" Sam queried. "Satan hates the Jews because they gave us the Bible, the Savior/Messiah and a future kingdom. Every person who is saved was a slave of sin and Satan, set free by the finished work of Christ on the cross. Satan can't touch Jesus any longer, but he can wreak vengeance on the Jews for their part in salvation and he will do what he can to destroy the testimony of born again believers." "Whew," Hadassah said, weighed down by the information, "that's a lot to think about."

On the taxi ride in from the airport, Sam had an eerie feeling they were being tailed. The bridal suite at the du Lac was fit for a king and a queen. Hadassah pirouetted around the room like a little girl in a new playhouse. Sam studied the elegant rooms thoughtfully and turned to Hadassah with an index finger over his lips. Sam inspected the light fixtures, the original French Impressionist paintings and the soffit above the draperies. The rooms were bugged. He found three and felt sure there were more. It was a letdown. Hadassah frowned. It wouldn't be any fun in these luxurious surroundings if you had to watch what you say. Sam thought about the larger implications. It could be the Antichrist's paranoia. Perhaps everyone in his service was under surveillance. On the other hand, Sam remembered, it seems Dupin is never very far away.

Brussels was alive with a new vibrancy, Winston had not seen before. The European Union was growing in power. Gutting the NATO alliance at last gave the coalition an army of its own. General Roy was much more powerful than a mere general in the French Army. At a dizzying velocity, he had consolidated his influence and power in every aspect of the multi-nation complex. He now had the power to crush any abortive rebellion in the ranks of member nations.

There were other changes in Brussels that Winston guessed were now the experience in every major city of the western world. There was a swagger in the step of West Europeans. So long under American cultural and financial domination, the United States was fast becoming a second rate power and the Europeans were on an emotional high. At the street level, things were not so good. Muslims, nearly 100,000 in Belgium alone, provided relatively cheap labor for the automobile industry. They were hated, tolerated and watched closely.

The Jews, loyal to the society they served well in the professions, business and industry and at every level of government, were under pressure to return to Israel and participate in the Temple Mount peace program. Some Jews saw the suggestion as the beginnings of an effort to make the EU, *Judenrein*, free of Jews. The spurious "Protocols of Zion," the fabrication of antisemites of two centuries before, was in wide distribution. The false screed charged Jewish international bankers were working to overthrow Christian institutions and make the Jews the rulers of the world. It was the same satanically inspired antisemitism of pharaonic Egypt, Babylon and Nazi Germany. Ironically, many Jews are the very last to believe the awful truth about their host nations. Winston shook his head in disbelief, for many Jews seemed blinded to their imminent danger.

Posters in several languages were everywhere featuring a smiling Roy and a seraphic pope. The duo urged allegiance to the One, True Universal church. It was a religion for all, the poster explained, including Jews not migrating to Israel. The irenic tone of the propaganda was a contradiction to life on the streets. Synagogues and the few Protestant houses of worship were closely watched, subject to search and seizure. Evangelical churches, abandoned in the Rapture, were now under the interim custody of the universal church. The fine print suggested freedom of religion was tolerated, but freedom of assembly was discouraged for nonconformist cults and movements. These cults and movements were to be officially registered by a given date. Rumor had it that Jews and those suspected of loyalty to Christ and the Bible, were randomly arrested and held on flimsy charges. It could be 1938 in Germany all over again, a few Jews concluded. Those who paid careful attention to the signs saw that they were on the brink of the days leading up to the Holocaust.

The Guardian reported stress cracks in the world economy due to adverse weather conditions from the Ukraine to Patagonia. The middle class in Europe and North America was slowly eroding away, global economists reported. It was increasingly a "haves and have-nots" society. Winston found a passage in Revelation 6:6 that foretold a Great Tribulation economy in which it would take a whole day's pay for a laborer in the formerly affluent west, to feed his family on a basic subsistence diet. The "haves" would find luxury items plentiful and affordable.

Winston discovered from notes in his Bible that wide-spread drug use was also a characteristic of the Great Tribulation. The notes related that sorceries, in Revelation 9:21 the Greek word "pharmakeia," gives us the transliterated word pharmacy in English. This reference seems to speak of the drug users. Revelation 18:23 describes the narcotic use in sorceries as the means by which the end-time drug dealers working on behalf of mercantile conglomerates will be able to control the world. The promise of Revelation 21:8 is that the drug users and dealers will ultimately meet God's final judgment.

The media made no mention of widespread famine and disease in the Third World, now under quarantine. Nations were added to the "no-travel, no-contact" list every few months. Medical authorities formerly among the first to provide humanitarian relief to underprivileged nations now were tasked with preventing the influx of disease-prone Third World people. Strong measures were employed to prevent the importation of products from blacklisted countries. Fines and imprisonment were leveled against the most ardent humanitarians. The southern half of the globe was sentenced to death.

The Winstons dined in their room in the Hotel du Lac a nicer place than the hotel where their romance had budded. It was soft living compared to the spartan back street hotel in Jerusalem. On the dinner tray Hadassah found the package postmarked Jerusalem. It was Roy's wedding gift. Careful to guard their words in the bridal suite, Hadassah, with a twinkle, said "don't forget to thank the general for his kindness, Sam."

Hadassah grew spiritually. Each day she took time to read her Bible. She preferred the Brit HaChodoshoh, the New Testament in Hebrew. Sam had suggested she start in the Gospel according to John. She devoured it quickly and then went back and read it carefully. She took time to pray, mostly for wisdom and safety for themselves, but she remembered that her parents, Kfar Harlutz and Degania were in jeopardy. She took them to the throne of grace in prayer every day. Hadassah made sure there was time for prayer and Bible study with Sam. Joint devotions, where every word was recorded in another part of the hotel was a real question for Sam. They decided this was a spiritual test. They would raise their voices in the right places and whisper and write out specific prayer requests on sensitive issues.

La Farge called to give directions for a 2000 hours meeting with General Roy. Roy was now ensconced in a chateau thirty kilometers from Brussels on the old Antwerp Road. "Of course," La Farge said unctuously, "the General is looking forward to renewing acquaintance with Mrs. Winston." Winston surveyed the garments in his closet. There was the painful reminder he was no longer eligible to wear an American uniform. He chose the suit he had worn the night he and Hadassah walked the streets of the city.

Ten Sing walked slowly through the great hall of the chateau. Everything was in readiness. Roy is gone, I am in charge, he mused. "Don't rough them up too much, Lord Ten Sing," Roy had ordered, "If Winston is a Christian, you will know it. If he is, I will dispose of him in his own country. It would make me look bad to have the man in charge of the Temple construction exposed here as disloyal. If Dupin is wrong, Winston can be of use to me at the United Nations and on Capitol Hill." "Oh yes, I am ready for the Colonel and his lady," Ten Sing said aloud, rubbing his hands in satisfaction.

At 7:15, the Winstons were ready for the drive to Roy's chateau. In the hotel lobby, an inebriated Major Rita Brown, swayed over to greet them. "I see you aren't wearing your greens, Colonel. In the States you can wear it down at the VFW or to the American Legion hall on the Fourth of July. 'Stoo bad," she slurred, "'stoo bad that you resigned your commission at the height of your career, but we all make mistakes, don't we, Sam." Lurching to Hadassah, Brown slobbered, "honey, take care of this guy. The Army is so sore over NATO's closing, Sam is a scapegoat. Watch out for the wolves, Mrs. Winston." Rita Brown swayed off into the bar room. Sam could see Monsignor Cormac O'Brien beckoning to her.

La Farge's vehicle and driver sped the Winstons to an imposing chateau in a forested park. A long winding road from the guarded front gate, past a weathered fountain, took them to a formidable three-story, gray stone show-place with long windows and a gabled roof. It was straight out of a Hitchcock movie. It seemed appropriate for the official residence of the Antichrist. The driver dropped the Winstons at the front door and drove off to a well-concealed motor pool.

The monstrous doors of the chateau opened on the great hall. Dimly lit, the massive room was dominated by open beams and tapestried walls. Mounted heads of stags, vied for space with medieval armor and weapons. There was the inevitable Catholic statuary, Marian icons and a number of wretched dying figures on crosses. A table, longer than any Hadassah had ever seen, filled the room. A liveried retainer left the Winstons to gape at their surroundings. There was something definitely eerie about the house. It was chilly, colder than outdoors. Lights flickered occasionally. Sam drew Hadassah, wide-eyed, close to his side. Sam felt the atmosphere was just what he expected in the lair of the Antichrist. He remembered reading Revelation 18:2, that Roy's modern Babylon would be "the habitation of demons, and the hold of every foul spirit, and a cage of every unclean bird." Everything about the chateau suggested the future Babylon of Revelation 18 exactly.

A blood-curdling scream shook them both. A voice from the stairwell above cried "no, no, no more." The plea was punctuated by another scream. Hadassah had coolly faced RPG fire from Hezbollah gunners, but she recoiled at the unearthly screams. Sam was little better. He had looked death in the face a number of times, but this was a new experience. A new figure, an oriental motioned to Winston to follow him. Down a long hallway with innumerable turns they were shown into a large room. Dimly-lit, it was furnished with a silk brocade sofa, two chairs and a small round table topped by a Madonna and child. They seated themselves and silently waited. Hadassah was the first to notice a vapor seeping under the door that slowly covered the floor and began to rise around them. Weird music seemed to surround them. Shadowy figures and lights danced on the ceiling. A low moan carried on an air flow, punctuated the scene. Sam's chair began to spin as if by some unseen hand. Lifted up four or five feet and still spinning, Sam held on tightly. Hadassah was pulled from her chair. A phantom hand cupped her breast. A second, claw-like, lacerated her thigh. In anger and terror, she flailed and screamed at nothing. Sam, unable to focus, shouted, "in the name of Jesus Christ, be gone!" Immediately, he dropped to the floor, blood dripping from two fang-like wounds in his left hand. Hadassah held her face in her hands and sobbed uncontrollably. Groggy, Sam reached for her. Her head buried in his shoulder she stammered, "I was groped!" How? and by whom? "Honey," Sam purred, "we're safe. We just met Satan and his henchmen, but the Lord rescued us." His arm sheltering his wife, they looked the room over carefully. The chairs were overturned. The sofa was ripped. The table was unmoved, but the plaster Madonna was broken into several pieces.

The door was locked. Sam pounded, livid with rage. There was a click, the door swung open. Ten Sing stood there, four Orientals behind him. "Well, if it isn't the prime minister of hell, himself," Winston exclaimed. He was angry enough to go for his throat, but restrained himself. Ten Sing smiled sardonically, "well, Mr. Winston, seeing your wife's wounds and your hand, it look's like you had an interesting visit to General Roy's home." Hadassah reached out instinctively to restrain Sam. Composed, Sam replied, "Satan and you threw something at us in here. It was devilish, ghoulish and straight out of the pit of hell, but you know we beat you in the name of Jesus Christ. There is a lesson for you in this. The Bible says in Philippians 2:9-11, "wherefore God hath highly exalted him and given him a name that is above every name, that at the name of Jesus every knee should bow, of things in heaven, and things in earth, and every tongue should confess that Jesus Christ is Lord, to the glory of God." Ten Sing reeled under the power of the name of Jesus. "Get out Winston, get out," he screamed.

The driver was waiting. From a top-story a window was thrown open. A shadowy figure with arms upraised cried out, "Jews and Christians. You will die." The cry was followed by a piercing scream like the one that initially greeted them. The driver, visibly shaken, quickly returned the Winstons to the du Lac. It took time before they could talk about the chateau. They treated the lacerations on Hadassah's thigh. The horror of it all made it hard to look at the five long red rivers of pain that encircled her leg. Sam dabbed peroxide on the wounds. "When I was in college," Sam commented, "I read Thomas Aquinas on the Incubus, a demon described in the middle ages as one who sought to have sexual intercourse with women. There was also said to be a Succubae, a female demon, if there are such things, who sought sex with sleeping men. Hadassah shuddered at the thought. She pressed Sam for a promise they would never again get into a scrape with demons. "I can't promise that, honey, but you can rest assured I will duck them if I can." He poured iodine on his own wounds. Sam was disgusted with himself. He had failed to pray before they entered the chateau. He vowed never to fail to pray in any future encounters with the unseen world. He drew Hadassah close and prayed aloud, "Lord, thank you for keeping us from the wicked one. The guys in the next room need to hear us glorify the Lord," Sam said with feeling.

Early the next morning, La Farge called to say that he was sorry Roy was not at home the evening before. "He was called to the Bilderberg and I did not get the message. I apologize, Colonel, for any inconvenience it may have caused you. Your orders will be delivered to you, sir. You will hear from the general in due time." Sam cradled the phone and smiled. "Well, my dear, the official story is that Roy was not even there last night." "You should have asked him who screamed and who molested us?" Hadassah said, loud enough for the tappers.

Sam's thoughts were elsewhere. "Bilderberg, Bilderberg, what do I know about Bilderberg? I've heard the name before, but where?" Sam brightened, "Oh yes, I recall. I did a paper in College on the Illuminati. The modern day Illuminati is the Council on Foreign Relations and its spin-off the Tri-Lateral Commission. The organization was launched in 1958 by Queen Beatrix of the Netherlands and her Consort, Prince Bernhard Leopold. The Tri-Lateral Commission meets annually at the Bilderberg, a hotel in the Netherlands, not far from here. The one hundred twenty members of the Commission are called "the Bilderbergs." "What does the commission do? Is that another gathering of demons?" Hadassah asked. "The demons are probably in attendance," Sam explained, "for that group has always been involved in the drive for a one-world government and a one-world economy. As I recall, it was a Jakob Weishaupt, a Jew who became a Catholic and later a Catholic priest who hatched the scheme in the mid-1770's. He borrowed the idea of a one-world organization from the Knights Templar of the Crusades. Weishaupt defected from the Catholic church, joined the international bankers, the Rothschilds, and systematically worked his disciples into every field of endeavor known to man. Weishaupt had the single purpose of controlling the world. This was the "Illuminati," the enlightened ones. The Freemasons figure in the history, too. So many good men in the States are in the Masonic order, once-upon-a-time even me. I was a thirty-second degree mason. I wore an apron, carried a spear and never knew I was in anything, but the most refined organization in the world. The Masons said, "we make good men, better men." We were the enlightened ones, a staple in Masonic teaching, but we had no idea that there was a dark underside to the movement. I was shocked to learn a few years ago that there is a Masonic organization in Italy that includes many Catholic prelates. Let me think, yes, it was known by the strange name "P-2."

The name Illuminati was too old world for American tastes, so it became the Council on Foreign Relations after World War II. In England, I believe it is called "the British Institute of International Affairs." The amazing thing, Hadassah, is that many outstanding American conservatives have been counted in the membership. While I was stationed in Germany, I read of four hundred and fifty who met right here in the Hotel du Lac one year. Most of them were anything but "one-worlders." I don't know how they got into a group that plays the devil's game." In a whisper Sam added, "Roy, I will guess, is either the presiding officer now or soon will be." "What makes you say that?" Hadassah inquired. "Easy. The Antichrist is Satan's man. Satan will manipulate his slaves to give the leadership to his man." "But why were we the object of demonic attack?" asked Hadassah. "You were Roy's fair-haired boy." Sam's eyes narrowed in thought. "I'm going to guess Dupin knows that we are Christians." Our visit to the chateau was a warning. Sam did not share that conclusion with Hadassah. Roy could kill us here, but it will be easier to get us when we are in the States.

Maurice Dupin parked his Citroen a block from the du Lac. He was joined by two agents near the entrance and strode into the hotel. On the lift to the ninth floor, Dupin thought over his early morning conversation by phone with Roy. "Dupin," the general said, "the Winstons are traitors. Ten Sing is sure their allegiance is to *That Man*. The remarks they made on your wire-taps offer conclusive proof. They must be dealt with, but not in Europe. Pick up Winston's orders from LaFarge. Act as though everything is in order for him to meet with our people at the United Nations three days from now. Escort them to the plane. They must not be allowed to escape. I hold you and your action group responsible to see that they get to New York where I will consider just how to dispose of them."

Dupin rapped on nine seventeen. Hadassah admitted him. He removed his hat and quickly took in everything in the room. A book, perhaps a Bible, was partially visible under a love seat. He declined coffee and produced a packet of information from a briefcase carried by one of his men. "Your orders are purposely vague, Colonel. You are to meet EU representatives at the United Nations in New York and Department of State people in Washington D.C., to outline the Temple Mount project. As the director of the Temple Mount project you know it is the linchpin in the general's worldwide promotion of the "Universal Peace and Safety Campaign." The Temple Mount project, a coup in achieving peace in the Middle East, should lure the reluctant Americans back into an EU military expansion, on hold since the Americans withdrew needed weapons, personnel and money from the now defunct NATO alliance. If the Temple Mount brought Muslims and Jews together, who may doubt that a strong leader would bring the most reluctant to the table. Peace and Safety is just around the corner. Your contact person in New York is my agent, R. Poncet. Agent Poncet will meet you at JFK customs. Any questions?" Sam looked at Hadassah and back to Dupin. "No questions." "Good," Dupin replied, my men will pick you up tomorrow at 0800 and drive you to the plane." "We'll be ready," Sam said slowly.

After Dupin's exit, Sam secured his Bible from the floor and turned to the first epistle to the Thessalonians. Wordlessly, he ran his finger along the line so Hadassah could read:

"For when they shall say, Peace and safety; then sudden destruction cometh upon them, as travail upon a woman with child; and they shall not escape."

(1 Thessalonians 5:3)

# Chapter Thirteen
## *New York*

The Citroen, the Winstons' luggage carefully stowed in the trunk, made it out to the airport with time to spare. Dupin's agents, looking every inch like intelligence types, said nothing. At the airport, one handed a plastic pouch to Hadassah, passed a handcuff over her left wrist and secured it to the handle of the pouch. A chain was passed around her waist and locked in place. Hadassah was too stunned to protest. Sam numbly said nothing.

"What does an unemployed ex-soldier do now"? Sam wondered. He had plenty of time to pray and think about it, for his usual air travel panic attack kicked in and sleep was gone. Hadassah curled up on his shoulder, sleeping like a baby. Sam was convinced God would take care of them. He reveled in the thought that a believer is really living by faith when he has no idea how God will supply his needs. The need escalated the very next morning. The flight attendant had just cleared away the breakfast dishes when Hadassah in a coquettish mood Sam had never seen before, purred, "I've got a secret." "That's nice honey," Sam said, without looking up from his newspaper. "You've got to guess my secret." Hadassah slapped at his paper. Sam, obviously annoyed crowed, "how am I supposed to guess your secret? I have no clue." "Think nine months," she said in disgust. The light turned on. "You're pregnant!" he exclaimed, loud enough to be heard all over their section of the plane. "Yes, Samuel R. Winston, you are going to be a daddy." Some passengers clapped. Sam embraced her so hard she gasped for air. "Thank you Lord" is all the prospective father could say. Hadassah wore that mysterious Mona Lisa glow.

Sam wasn't prepared for the changes he found in the United States. At the passport control office at JFK, a grim-looking immigration officer scrutinized Hadassah's passport and Sam's EU identification. "Are you Jewish, Mrs. Winston? And you Mr. Winston?" "Why do you ask?" Sam demanded angrily. "The Protection of Minorities Act requires us to ask, Mister," was the hard-bitten reply. "Never heard of it," Sam shot back. "You've been out of the country a long time, Mr. Winston. It is now a law that all official papers carry a designation of race, religion or ethnic origin. I assume you are Jews." Winston's objection was construed as an admission. The officer placed Hadassah's passport under a printer. A black "J" scored the edge of her photograph and a portion of the physical description. "That's got to be against the law," Sam protested. "Not any more, Mr. Winston, you Jews are under government protection now. We'll see to it nothing happens to you," he said with a sneer. "Oh, I must mark your Social Security card as well." "I refuse," Sam exclaimed. "Suit yourself, Mr. Winston. I can call the security officer and we'll mark your card while you languish in jail."

Two official looking people, one a woman in a black leather coat and a leather hat turned down fore and aft, closely watched the Winstons. Her companion was dressed in a London Fog trench coat, probably an FBI agent Sam decided. The man flashed his FBI I.D. and introduced himself as Sam Flagler. He introduced Renee Poncet of the French SDECE. A grim-faced woman of about forty, Poncet produced a key to unlock Hadassah's handcuff, chain, and security pouch. Sam and Hadassah had made it up before hand that this would be their break with Roy. Agent Poncet held out the security pouch to Sam, but he refused to take it. "Miss Poncet, please tell your boss that Sam Winston has formally quit the service of General Roy. He laid his EU identity card on the pouch. From his attaché case, Sam produced his white beret and the general's wedding gift, the cap badge carefully wrapped. He handed over a certified check for $50,000 to the stunned Poncet. "That is reimbursement for my pay and allowances and our air fare on this flight." "You can't do that man," Flagler insisted. "No? I just did it. I am home in my country and I can do what free men do, I can quit working for General Jean-Luc Armand Roy."

At carousel D, Sam, feeling free at last, reclaimed their luggage. It showed all the marks of having been carefully rifled. Hadassah broke her silence, "do you know what the "J" on our papers really means, Sam?" "Yeah, " he answered coarsely, "the cherished American right of privacy has been violated." "It's more than that," she continued. "In the early years of Nazi persecution, many Jews fled to neutral Switzerland. The Germans objected to the Swiss harboring refugees and the Swiss, not the Germans, hit on the idea of having the Germans identify Jews with a bold "J" on their identity papers. This made it easy for Swiss border control agents to refuse Jewish immigration. The letter "J" was more effective than barbed wire in keeping our people from freedom. Later, it made it easy to round them up."

Sam was euphoric over his resignation from Roy's service. New York was both exciting and frightening for the young Jewish girl from Galilee. The tall buildings, the stores, the sights and sounds of the streets were an unforgettable experience. They visited Times Square, Wall Street, Ellis Island, the Statue of Liberty. Hadassah knew all about Emma Lazarus, the Jewess who penned the lines pledging the country to open arms for the poor, persecuted immigrants to the New World. They paused and observed a moment of silence at the World Trade Center Shrine. They toured the United Nations just to say they did it all. The UN had the Chagall art works and a few other things worth seeing. Sam explained that the UN was a never-ending source of difficulty for the FBI and the intelligence agencies because UN membership gave rogue states an open access to spy on the United States. Sam recalled his friend Carver remarked that the UN was thought to be the confederation out of which the Antichrist would rise, but the best scholars thought of the forum as simply one that would soften the world up for the idea that constitutional republics, patriotism, and conservatism would have to give way to a global mindset. Left-wing elements promoted that scheme throughout the lifetime of the organization.

New York is a city that comes alive after nightfall. Sam thought it would help to put Roy out of their minds if they saw the sights of the city. Wandering from their quarters in the Ambassador Hotel, the Winstons were jostled by the crowds, dodged taxis and laughed all along the Gay White Way. Window-shopping, they were accosted by a dissipated young man in his late twenties, under the influence of something. He laid clammy hands on Hadassah. He slobbered, "get rid of the old geezer, babe, and I'll show you some real fun." Hadassah pushed him away. Sam, lightning fast, grabbed the young man, bent his arm behind his back and slammed him into a brick wall. His nose broken, blood streamed from both nostrils. "You violated my civil rights," the assailant cried. "Boy," Sam said sharply, "you are fortunate I belong to Jesus Christ. A few years ago, you would not have lived to see day light." One of New York's finest happened on the scene and demanded to know what happened. Sam related the incident and pointed to Hadassah's torn blouse. The young man blubbered his civil rights charge again. The officer spoke roughly to Winston, "why did you beat this kid up? He was just out having a little fun." The officer looked Hadassah up and down lewdly. He smiled, tapped her with his nightstick and smirked, "I could go for you myself, sweetie." Sam clenched his fists until they turned white. He was sorely tempted to give the policeman the same treatment he gave the boy, but decided against it. "You and this doll better get on down the street, Mister," the officer warned, "and let boys be boys."

New York had changed radically since Winston went to the European Union. Full-front nudity was advertised on the Gay White Way. "X-rated" movies did a land office business. Liquor and drug traffic were unimpeded by the law. Violence was everywhere; the air filled with four letter words and racial slurs. It was a New York Sam Winston had never seen before. He remembered the ominous prophecy of Second Thessalonians 2:6 that in the Great Tribulation the restraining ministry of the Holy Spirit would be withdrawn. It was clear public disapproval of immorality was a thing of the past. Laws to protect the innocent were ignored. The Rapture had signaled the gradual withdrawal of the Spirit's restraining influence. Things would get worse.

Things got worse for the Winstons the next day. A walking tour of Greenwich Village was a mistake. This time it was Sam who was the target of a sexual assault. Two young men dressed in leather and chains were all over the sidewalk, locked in an embrace. They parted to look Winston over carefully. One made a move. Sam kicked him in the groin, doubling the assailant, groaning in pain. That made it easy to give him a knee lift to the jaw followed by a two-handed karate chop. The man folded like a house of cards. The other gay looked for a weapon to help his friend, thought better of it and ran down the street. A crowd started to gather. A siren wailed. Sam grabbed Hadassah. They managed to lose themselves in the press of the sidewalk traffic.

Back at the hotel, Sam sensed there was something wrong. Hadassah played with her coffee, said nothing and studiously avoided looking at him. Anxious to clear the air, Sam blurted out, "O. K., give it to me." Mrs. Winston, arms akimbo, looked at him steadily for what seemed an eternity. "I don't like the man I've seen lately. The beating you gave those men scared me. I've faced down the Hezbollah and angry Palestinians, but I never felt the hatred for them that you showed those guys." "Honey," Sam protested, "I was defending you and defending myself against those drunks and perverts." "No, Sam," Hadassah replied coldly, "first of all you didn't defend me. You beat a man who dared to touch your property. And today, you didn't defend yourself. You have hated gays all your life. Here was your chance to smash one of them. I've only been a believer about fifteen minutes, but I don't read of Jesus beating up the people who treated him badly." "Hadassah, I've got to be a man. I will continue to fight with all my strength against those scum bags." "Well," Hadassah replied softly, "if you fight again, don't fight like that for me, for I do not want that kind of defense. And since you told the kid under drugs that he was fortunate you are a Christian now, you ought to check with heaven, because I doubt Jesus wants you defending Him."

Thoroughly chastened, Sam sank to his knees and prayed, "Lord, forgive me for Jesus' sake. I have sinned against you, for I have sinned and beaten men who need your salvation. They got nothing from me but my hatred. I have sinned against my wife, Lord, and shamed her before the world. Oh, Lord, forgive me please and restore unto me the joy of thy salvation, in Jesus name." Tears welled up in his eyes as Hadassah knelt beside him and kissed him tenderly.

If Hadassah was nervous about walking New York streets after the encounters with the street people, she did not show it. She loved the shops, spent too much money and loved the restaurants. They dined in a cavernous place, a pitch-black restaurant, filled with a typical Manhattan lunch-hour crowd. Big menus were thrust into their hands. They were pinioned against a wall behind a sandwich-size table. "Your eyes get used to the dark, honey," Sam reassured her. He immediately thought to himself that his words were a parable of the believer growing used to a sin-cursed world and its temptations.

The New York Times was filled with reports of the alarming changes in American life and culture. There was frequent mention of the Protection of Minorities Act, known by its acronym POMA. One story related that 5,000 New York Haitian immigrants were taken to a camp in West Virginia for training in American lifestyles. The Coast Guard had shot up a boatload of Cubans seeking asylum in Florida. A detention zone, said to be purely voluntary, was opening near the Mexican border for settlement of indigent Hispanics. "That sounds like a concentration camp to me," Sam said with disgust.

Sam read carefully the details of a pending congressional bill called "The Quality of Life Act." It provided for unrestricted abortion through the expected time of delivery. In the opinion of a physician a fetus, officially not a baby, should be terminated by any means at any time during gestation. Another provision held that euthanasia was to be open to any age, without notification of family. Any American who was deemed to have a diminished quality of life through accident, illness or seniority, could be solicited for undergoing a painless death and the harvesting of vital organs. The implication of the entire act was that Americans were the property of the State and the collective good exceeded the wishes of the individual. The bill spelled out the truth that this world is the ultimate reality. "God seems to have allowed the humanists and evolutionists to have their way for a little time," Sam concluded.

Hadassah was surprised to learn there was an Hasidic community in Williamsburg, the borough of Brooklyn. Hadassah was familiar with the Mea Shearim community in Jerusalem. The Hasidim in Williamsburg migrated to the United States after World War II. The men wear payess, the side locks, and wide hats. Some effect black coats and distinctive trousers or knickers. "We saw growing evidence in Brussels that the Jews of the world may be in jeopardy," Hadassah said with alarm. "I think we ought to go to Williamsburg tomorrow and see how our people are doing." Sam nodded, "I guess that some synagogues and yeshivas, religious schools have moved to Israel since the Temple is about to open." As he thought about it, Sam was surprised that he felt a kinship to every Jew in the world, a sensation he had never known before.

Williamsburg was a kind of cultural ghetto of the Hasidim's own making. The ultra-Orthodox sacralized everything they own and everything they do. Their homes, clothes, automobiles, and especially the food they eat, were incorporated into a life-style designed to insulate the faithful against the world outside. The insulation was especially useful in locking out the influence of non-observant Jews like Sam Winston and secular Jews like Hadassah.

Walking up from the underground, the Winstons were alarmed to find Williamsburg was already under police guard. Yellow crime scene tape and barricades channeled vehicular and foot traffic past a check-point. Entry was denied to any who were not Williamsburg residents or who had no good reason for being there. The NYPD officers were hard to convince that a couple of non-Hasidic Jews should be admitted. Hard talking and the fact they were Jews got them through the check-point. An alarmed Hadassah remarked softly, "Sam, this community could be walled in overnight! This is a heart beat away from becoming a Warsaw ghetto. Our people are in danger here. What can we do?" "I don't know honey. Oh, how I wish Ben-Zion was here. But then," Sam recalled, "the Lord's 144,000 Jewish evangelists are everywhere. Rest assured, there is a witness for the Messiah somewhere in this community."

Fairly fluent in Yiddish and used to rubbing shoulders with the ultra-Orthodox, Williamsburg's sights, sounds and smells meant more to Hadassah than to Sam. Hadassah pointed to the Hebrew letters on a store window. "Those are Hebrew letters, Sam, but Yiddish words. Yiddish is a corruption of middle high German.

Interestingly, your German forefathers wouldn't speak Yiddish. That was the language of the ghettoes and shtetls of my people in Eastern Europe," Hadassah explained. "That's a *Glat Kosher* meat market Sam. Glat means "smooth." It tells the faithful that it is far more scrupulous in the blessing, slaughtering and handling of meat than say a kosher market outside of Williamsburg. They have less exacting standards of kosher preparation in Degania, for instance. That would be *hashash* to these Jews." Hadassah pointed to a line of Yiddish and translated it as "zealous of kosher requirements more than the most zealous."

Sam tried hard to get passers-by, to talk, but without success. Feeling it might be that he was walking with a woman, Hadassah strolled off by herself, but that didn't work. The Hasids, had nothing to say to an outsider. "If I only had a ton of **How to Recognize the Messiah**, in Yiddish," he said with regret. They left colorful Williamsburg with heavy hearts. If the Jews are in for a time of persecution it seemed certain the dress and customs of the Hasidim would attract immediate attention. Hadassah remembered a Japanese axiom from her college days that holds, "the nail that sticks up gets hammered down."

A visit to the famous Saint Patrick's Cathedral on Fifth Avenue, opened the Winstons' eyes to the new Universal Church. On the outside it was a typical Catholic Church. Inside, the sanctuary featured a female priest, in fact, several female priests. An aggressive women's organization in the progressive Catholic movement was combing the nation for Catholic feminists willing to take the priest's stole. Ordination for women was as rapid as a weary diocesan bishop could lay hands on them. Married priests were in vogue after long struggles over compulsory celibacy. Catholic sources privately agreed the numbers of gay priests remained about the same as it had since the 1970's.

A nun took them on a tour, pointing out the features of the ornate sanctuary. Sam was hardly prepared for the changes in the Roman church. The Mormon Temple in Salt Lake City had just provided a new statue of Joseph Smith, the founder of the Latter Day Saints, for the narthex. The nun explained rapturously that Smith had made a lasting contribution to family values. A shrine dedicated to Mary Baker Eddy, the leading figure in the Christian Science movement, extolled her teachings on healing by faith. Russell and Rutherford of the Jehovah's Witnesses received honor as inspired teachers. A host of other men and women including Mohammed and Confucius were honored with portraits and statuary. The most interesting acquisition was a reclining Gautama Buddha in gold leaf, a satisfied smile upon his face. There were quotations on the walls in gold from free thinkers and other philosophers like Kingsley, Darwin, Bertrand Russell and even the atheist Robert Ingersoll. One wall was devoted to the words of the late Saint John Paul II, the former pope, who wrote on December 12, 2000, "All the just of the earth, including those who do not know Christ and His Church, who, under the influence of grace, seek God with a sincere heart, are thus called to build the kingdom of God by working with the Lord, who is its first and decisive builder."

Sam couldn't resist witnessing to the nun of his faith in Jesus Christ. He did it gently with a question. "Sister, I am an honest seeker after truth. Would you please tell me what I need to know and what I must do in order to make it to heaven?" The nun frowned and then brightened. "I would say sir, that you need to be honest and sincere in your dealings with your fellow man. The Holy Father has taught us to love one another. You mention heaven. Is there such a place? I once believed there was, but now I believe that we make our own heaven or hell right here on earth. Take any one of the ways to heaven on earth, such as the Catholic way, the Buddhist way, the Muslim way and you will realize your goal. The fact that we are all together in one great, Universal Church, makes it easy for everyone to choose their path and follow it." "Thank you, Sister," Winston said with feigned apprecia-tion, "but what role does the Bible play in the quest for heaven?" "Well, it has little relevance in modern faith, but it would not hurt to read it I suppose, provided one did not become fanatical about it. Fortunately, we have rooted out most of the Bible-thumpers and our leaders continue to educate the people above the letter of the law," the nun explained. "Tell me, then dear lady," Winston pressed, "are you sure of heaven right now?" "No, I'm not sure of heaven. As I said, I'm not really sure there is such a place." "Thank you for your kind indulgence, Sister. Let me say, I was a Jew who cared nothing for religion of any brand. Recently, I was introduced to the truth that Jesus fulfilled every Messianic prophecy of the Old Testament. Our people longed for His coming. The Bible says,

"He came unto his own, and his own received him not. But as many as received him, to them gave he power to become the sons [children] of God, even to them that believe on his name."

(John 1:11-12)

"This was news to me, Sister, good news, but the best news of all was that this Messiah Jesus had come to seek and to save that which was lost. He died my death. The man you call your first pope wrote,

"Who his own self bare our sins in his own body on the tree, that we, being dead to sins, should live unto righteousness: by whose stripes ye were healed."

(1 Peter 2:24)

"Dear Sister, for the first time, I saw myself as a sinner, bound for hell and deserv-ing hell. I cast myself upon the Lord and asked Him to save me and He did! Would you like to receive Him as your Savior and Lord right now?" Numbed to silence, the nun stammered something unintelligible and turned to run off. "Please wait, Sister, you just received a clumsy, but true presentation of the saving message of Jesus Christ. You need to hear a couple of more verses.

"For if we sin willfully after that we have received the knowledge of the truth, there remaineth no more sacrifice for sins, but a certain fearful looking for of judgment and fiery indignation, which shall devour the adversaries."

(Hebrew 10:26-29)

"You are now responsible for that message. You need to be saved. You can be saved. It is perilous to your eternal soul to ignore it or reject it. Turn to Jesus Christ, I implore you." The nun turned and fled. Too bad," Sam said, "I guess I muffed that one." "No, you didn't honey, it would have been easy to ignore her ridiculous assertions about religion and heaven on earth. You persisted and gave her a lot to think and worry about."

Mary, hailed as co-mediatrix and co-redemptoress was easily the winner in terms of numbers of statues, pictures and votive lights in Saint Patrick's. In some she was encircled by angels, clad in shimmering white, a solid gold crown on her head. Others featured her as the peasant girl of Guadeloupe. In a few she was the black virgin of Poland. The places of her apparitions, Lourdes, LaSallette, Medjugorje and scores of others were depicted on a globe in motion, under the legend Regina Mundi, Queen of the World. Sam and Hadassah turned away in disgust. "Hadassah," Sam asked, "what would Isaiah, Daniel and Ezekiel do if they were to wander into this building?" "They would run out the door, Sam. Our people were so thoroughly cured of idolatry many Jew won't put up pictures of their own families."

Sam and Hadassah watched as a class of about one hundred converts to the Universal Church received their first communion. The moderator explained that they were in training for full membership in the church. The program, she explained is known as "the Rite of Spiritual Initiation of Adults." Formerly it was the Rite of Christian Initiation, but the term "Christian" was inappropriate in the new enlightenment so the more imposing term "spiritual" was now used. Hadassah was sure that a number of the communicants were Jews. She asked a nun about it and learned, "oh yes, there are Jews in great numbers now. Since the Holy Father and General Roy have opened up worship for Jews in Jerusalem, those who choose to live outside of Israel should place themselves under the Universal Church. Synagogues must be closed and Jewish religious practices curtailed or brought under the umbrella of the one, true church." "Are the Jews or any others in training here against their will?" Hadassah asked. "Of course not," the nun snapped, "if some should feel that way, they better understand that they are giving up an apostate faith for the grace of a new beginning." "Sam, our people are in trouble," Hadassah said with conviction.

Hadassah grappled with the nun's statement about the Jews. "I just don't get it," Hadassah said. "Why does this Universal Church speak so warmly of their new church as one big happy family, inclusive of everyone and everything, but they want to shut down synagogues and force the Jews to join them? Why?" "Hadassah, you know more about the history of our people than I do. Remember that most of the persecution of our people has been at the hands of false Christians. The Roman Catholic Church systematically persecuted our people in Western Europe. Their inquisition was even exported to the New World. Anglicans killed Jews. Lutherans killed Jews. All kinds of dreadful things were done to our people in the name of Jesus. The problem for the Catholics, indeed for all false Christians, was that the Jews, the Chosen People, refused to recognize their claims to be God's church. That posed a dilemma for Rome, the dominant of the false faiths, that they have never been able to solve. Since the Jews failed to recognize Rome's spiritual authority, it suggested the Catholic claims were bogus. If then the church annihilated the Jews it would say, since you couldn't convince them of your divine mandate you felt compelled to kill them to silence their indifference. Therefore, periodically they followed a policy of reluctant toleration. That hasn't changed. Their hatred for the Jews is as keen today as it ever was. It reminds me of the hatred Haman felt for Mordecai, because Mordecai would not bow down to him. Our people are Mordecai's children."

The last day in New York, the Winstons spent in their hotel room. Every television channel carried live reports of the dedication of the Third Temple in Jerusalem. It was an impressive ceremony. It began with the ceremonial entry of the Ark of the Covenant. It was followed by a procession of priests carrying the menorah and the holy vessels. They were accompanied by scores of trumpeters and white robed Levites playing cymbals, psalteries and harps. Unlike the dedication of Solomon's Temple there was no cloud, signaling the entrance of the glory of God. Brief glimpses of a sacrifice and the spilling of blood at the base of the altar of burnt offering, completed the ritual phase of the ceremony.

General Roy, basking in the adulation of a mostly Jewish crowd and a sizeable number of foreign dignitaries, spoke for nearly an hour on his "Peace and Safety Program." The program, he explained, embodied the Temple worship and the unification of churches in the West. With a bow to the Holy Father, he mentioned the Sistine Chapel as an example of a new, higher plateau in religious expression. He predicted lasting world peace through his three-fold initiative in a one-world religion, one-world government and one-world economic order. The applause was deafening. The networks cut to simulcasts in Europe, Africa, Asia and North America where an estimated two billion people cheered and screamed. Roy said that poverty would be shortly erased. He called upon world citizenry to take another notch in their belts until world hunger and disease, the final elements in his economic program were complete. He then introduced the director of the International Peace and Safety Program, Lord Ten Sing. Sam and Hadassah were aghast. It was easy to see that most of the visiting dignitaries were more than a little surprised to learn an oriental would head up the worldwide appeal. "Mother Castaldi was right, "Sam remarked, "she told me he was destined for big things."

"Babylon is in full flower, "Sam exclaimed. "Tell me about it," replied Hadassah. "The new Babylon is the old Babylon, honey. In Genesis Chapters ten and eleven we read of an aspiring world leader named Nimrod, who built cities and planted a dictatorship in the known world of the Middle East. His wife headed up the only religious worship permitted. Secular historians of the day suggest it was a slave economy. The cities were built on the backs of captive labor. Satan was behind the scheme. God dealt with this rebellion, but the idea never died. The three-fold dream was alive when Christ was on earth and it is alive today. General Roy, directed by his majesty Satan, has engineered a deal to make a rebuilt Babylon. The plan is working, but God is in control. My great sorrow is that I did what I could to make the religious hoax a reality, in the building of the Third Temple." It was a timely reflection, for Roy concluded his speech by unfurling a banner in red and black bearing the legend Key Ky Sigma and it's interpretation **666.**

# Chapter Fourteen
*Washington, D.C.*

The rental agency sedan was adequate for the drive to Washington. They found a down-at-the-heels motel and dropped their luggage in room 218. Sam closed the door behind him and paused. "C'mere honey." Sam reached for her shiny black hair. "What are you doing?" she demanded. "I need one hair." He pulled hard. Hadassah uttered a protesting "ouch." Sam knelt and placed the hair along the frame and threshold. He removed chewing gum from his mouth and secured both ends of the hair. "Do we need that Sam?" "I dunno," Sam replied, "but it can't hurt."

After a quick motor tour around the Beltway, Sam thought his wife needed to see the Israeli embassy. Hadassah flushed with pride as she walked under the white and blue striped flag with the blue Star of David. A Technion classmate, squealed with delight and smothered Hadassah with a bear hug. They chattered in Hebrew for longer than Sam wanted to stay. The third secretary, Yael Kaplan, recognized Sam and invited him into his office. Kaplan congratulated Winston on his work on the Temple. He feigned surprise that Winston had resigned from Roy's staff. Sam realized Kaplan knew more about it than he let on.

Sam remembered his mission. *Somehow I've got to witness to this man.* After the pleasantries, Kaplan seized the initiative and talked about the growing uncertainty for the Jews worldwide. "The Temple is a great thing for our people, but there are disturbing reports from *bahutz l'aretz*," a term in Hebrew Sam remembered means "outside the land." To the Jews, everything beyond the borders of Israel is outside the land. "We hear," Kaplan continued, "of synagogues in Europe closed down on one pretext or another. We are told of some Jewish rabbis and Jewish community leaders held incommunicado and some who are simply unaccounted for. What have you seen, Mr. Winston?" "Just as you say, Mr. Kaplan, we found those absurd Protocols of the Elders of Zion distributed in great numbers all over Brussels. My wife and I were alarmed to see that the Jews of the Williamsburg district of Brooklyn have check-points and round-the-clock police surveillance. Hadassah had the frightening thought that it could be walled up like Warsaw overnight." "We know about Williamsburg," Kaplan said with evident concern, "but there are no Israelis there. We cannot officially even inquire about the restrictions on entry and exit from the community."

"Are you under pressure to get American Jews to migrate to Israel," Sam asked. "We have had a flurry of applications since you began work on the Temple. However over many years, American Jews have little stomach for the often spartan and sometimes dangerous life in Israel. It is no Miami Beach and so an aliyah is not very appealing. We sent a few thousand Orthodox Jews home to Israel in recent months. Only about 10 -15% of the more dedicated Jews will stick it out." "Well,

Mr. Kaplan, I've not announced my plans to my wife as yet, but I'm going home to Israel as soon as my mission is complete in this country." "And what is that mission, Mr. Winston?" "Mr. Kaplan, I am a believer in the Messiah Jesus. I have come to warn my people of the wrath to come." "The wrath?" said Kaplan with some evident alarm. "Hmm, the wrath to come, you say?" "What do you see our people facing, Mr. Winston?" Sam leaned across the desk and said in a low voice, "this is the time of Jacob's trouble, Mr. Kaplan. The prophet Jeremiah says in Jeremiah 30:4-6:

"For thus saith the Lord; we have heard a voice of trembling, of fear, and not of peace. Ask ye now, and see whether a man doth travail with child? wherefore do I see every man with his hands on his loins, as a woman in travail, and all faces are turned into paleness? Alas! for that day is great, so that none is like it: it is even the time of Jacob's trouble; but he shall be saved out of it."

(Jeremiah 30:5-7)


"The days grow dark for our people Mr. Kaplan. Notice the imagery. It is a man who has birth pangs. That's out of the order of nature, isn't it? These will not be ordinary times. And the analogy of birth is that we always know it is coming in nine months, but it always seems to take us by surprise. The teaching is this. Our people, in Israel and in the diaspora are going to become the victims of the most ungodly pogrom we have ever faced. Pharaoh, Haman, Petlura, Bogdan Chmielnicki and Adolph Hitler are nothing to the monster that is already on the scene!" "And who is this monster?" Kaplan asked with annoyance. Winston straightened his back with the force of his answer. "General Jean-Luc Armand Roy! In Christian literature he is called the Antichrist!" Kaplan jumped to his feet. "Out of here, Mr. Winston, take your wife and never come back. General Roy cannot be responsible for the attitude of traditional antisemites. For decades you Messianic Jews have been the real menace to our people. Messianists have no place in Israeli territory and this is Israeli territory!"

Hadassah was not happy at being hustled out of her nation's embassy, but by now she was as committed as Sam to their mission. They had done the Capitol, the Washington monument and the Lincoln memorial, the Vietnam Memorial Wall and the Smithsonian and of course the only open residence in the world of a nation's chief executive, the White House. Sam was tired. Hadassah was fresh, animated, and ready for the stores. She was off on a shopping tour looking for gifts to send home to family and friends. Winston relaxed on a park bench in Lafayette Square. How did the interview with Kaplan go so badly? Sam knew the answer. He regretted he had not stuck to his gospel witness. Kaplan couldn't handle the truth about Roy when he had no opportunity to know the truth of biblical salvation.

Official Washington was an interesting study. After a century of world leadership, the United States was slipping into the unaccustomed role of a second-rate power.

The decline had come in four short years. Winston relived a brief tour in the White House as an aide to then President Lucinda Chavez. "Lucy" Chavez was the first Hispanic president of the United States and only the second woman chief executive. Chavez had done a great job through two terms. A graduate of Annapolis, Lieutenant Commander Chavez was a Navy SEAL. She brought muscle to the Oval Office and quickly rejuvenated the Armed Forces. The old saying that the U S trained for the next war by re-fighting the last one was true. President Chavez changed that and the nation cheered. But it was short-lived. Her successor, William T. Cameron was a weak man, bedeviled by a House and Senate in the hands of the other party. A flawed foreign policy saw Roy and the European Union do an end-run on just about every US initiative in the world. American trade balances were in a shambles. Unemployment was near double digits and soaring interest rates reminded Wall Street of the Carter administration. Crime, always a problem, was now out of control. The Protection of Minorities Acts,(POMA) reinforced the walls between whites and minorities, the rich and the poor, and in the opinion of many, legitimized bigotry and hatred. Like puppets, the Americans cowered before Roy's demand for an American Expeditionary Force to augment his EU army. Threat of a worldwide boycott of American goods and services brought the national leadership to their knees. Washington was putting together an Army Corps of men culled from already under strength units. The U S Air Force had nothing to contribute and a Navy long on capital ships with only skeleton crews asked to be excused from operations in foreign waters.

Nothing signaled the end of American dominance in world affairs like the  boot-licking underway in  Roy's Peace and Safety initiative. The EU mission Sam was to join was received like the Second Coming. The program promised peace for a piece of the action. The program was nothing less than a demand that national interests be subordinated to a one-world government and a one-world economic order. Roy promised a cashless society at the cost of American economic sovereignty. Money that once flowed to Washington and stopped, now had to be transferred to Brussels. According to Father Cormac O'Brien's early revelations, ultimately to a new Babylon.

Sam was surprised to see Monsignor Cormac O'Brien sidle up and take a seat next to him. The priest's cherubic good looks, florid face, wreathed by unmanageable white hair, was an advertisement for shamrocks. He effected a gray jacket rather than his customary black, but the trousers, long without a crease, were the customary black to match his vest. The Roman collar, good for evading traffic tickets, supported heavy jowls. "The ubiquitous Father O'Brien," Winston exclaimed. "How surprised I am to see you, Father." "Oh, well, I am not surprised to see you, Colonel, inasmuch as you have been shadowed since you left Brussels." "I have?" Sam replied in mock alarm. "How does a discredited U.S. Army officer rate that kind of attention?" "These are difficult times, Colonel," O'Brien said gravely, "today's friends are tomorrow's enemies. You think you have managed to escape a web of intrigue. I, on the other hand, thought I was in on the ground floor of something good for holy, mother church. Now, well, I just don't know."

"What brought you to the U.S. and Washington?" inquired Winston. O'Brien looked over his shoulder as though looking for someone and began, "you were tapped to give a testimonial for the Universal Peace and Safety program here and at the UN, but when you ran out, General Roy secured the permission of the Holy Father to send me in your place. For the moment they are quite happy with me. I wear well at cocktail parties and on the tomato aspic luncheon circuit. All I do is pray over the salad, make the sign of the cross and then tell stories about the blessings world-wide of General Roy's program." "That gives you time, then, to raise money for the Irish Republican Army," Winston said with a smile. "No, no, my boy, the IRA bagman, as you once called me, is no more. The IRA is nothing today. The big thing is the change in holy, mother church." "I saw those changes up close at Saint Patrick's in New York," Winston replied. O'Brien mopped his brow of imaginary perspiration. "You may recall, Sam, that I am a member of OPUS DEI, the most conservative movement within the Catholic Church. We opposed the progressives plan to open the church to all kinds of false gods and - saints preserve us - female and faggot priests. We are beset by hosts of laity unconfessed and unworthy of the holy eucharist. Purgatory is no more. Penance is a joke and indulgences have gone by the board. As an OPUS DEI member, my confessor must be a member. The confessional is my only opportunity to pour out my heart to a brother priest who is as shocked as I am at what is taking place."

Sam felt genuine compassion for the distressed priest. "Father, I am a Jew. I was never much of a Jew religiously. When I grew up and left home I left Judaism far behind. I didn't need it. Then I met a wonderful young Gentile believer who showed me from God's Word that every mortal is a sinner, hell-bound and hell-deserving. He insisted I couldn't do anything about my sinful nature and he proved it to me from the Bible. He then showed me that God saw my lost condition, took the initiative and sent Jesus Christ to die for me. One day, I went to my knees and I asked the Lord to save me for Jesus' sake and He did, Father, He really did. That is the reason I left Roy and his program. Father, did you ever hear of the Great Tribulation?" "Sam", O'Brien replied, "in the twelfth century, Saint Malachy, the Bishop of Armagh, in my native Ireland, was a gifted prophet. He had visions of the popes far into the future. Let me see if I can recall his vision of the last pope. Ah, yes," he continued, "Petrus Romanus, Peter the Roman, will reign in the final persecution of the Holy Roman Church. He will feed his flock among many tribulations; after which the seven-hilled city will be destroyed and the dreadful Judge will judge the people." The present pope is very ill. A Benedictine, he will be succeeded by Peter the Roman. If Malachy was right, he should be ascending to the throne very soon."

"Father, this is the Great Tribulation Bishop Malachy may have foreseen. Jesus spoke of it in Matthew Chapter 24. Would you read it soon, please. Also read Revelation Chapters 13, 17, and 18. Your church has only about two more years and then Roy will loot it and destroy it for it does not fit into his plans or those of his master, Satan." "Roy? Satan? What are you talking about Sam?" the incredulous priest asked. "Father," Sam replied gravely, "Roy is the Antichrist. He is Satan's man to forge a one-world church. Look at the evidence. A one-world government, is underway. And a one-world economic order that you first told me about, centering in Babylon." "Sam, Sam," O'Brien clucked, "you've had too much sun. I don't know if it's Malachy's Tribulation, but we're talking about Roy, a decent man; a man working for the good of all mankind." "You just described the magnitude of the deception, Father. Who really can do good to all mankind? Only the Prince of Peace, Jesus Christ. The counterfeit program we see today, is the work of the Antichrist."

Sam searched the face of Cormac O'Brien. "Father, if you died today where would you spend eternity?" "Oh, I don't know, my boy, I've lived by the love of God and the laws of my church for lo, sixty years now. I suppose my soul will be weighed in the balance and if I am found worthy I will pass into purgatory for my final cleansing as a friend of God and then one day, paradise!" O'Brien's statement dripped with sorrow, uncertainty and fatalism. "Father, you can know you are saved and sealed for heaven simply by laying your sinful soul at the foot of the cross, casting yourself upon Jesus Christ to save you and receiving him to make your justification sure. Give up any pretense of trying to make it to heaven by what you can do for Him. The dear friend who introduced me to Jesus Christ used to say, "Sam the only thing you can provide God is a sinner, because he has already provided the Savior." O'Brien smiled, "you are a good man, Samuel Winston. I am grateful for your concern for my soul. In God's good time, we shall speak of this again. But for now, I must tell you that General Roy is very, very angry with you. You will have to face him at some point. I happen to know French SDECE agents followed you to the Israeli embassy. Roy has delayed apprehending you until the right opportunity. Be on your guard. Your faith in the Blessed Jesus will see you through." With that, O'Brien hurried off across the square.

All smiles, Hadassah walked to Sam's park bench waving her shopping bags, trophies of war in the shop 'til you drop competition. Hand in hand, they walked the few blocks to their rented automobile. On the way Hadassah's countenance darkened. "A terrible thing happened at Nieman Marcus." "That's nice honey, Sam said vacantly. "I was in a big line at the…" Hadassah fished for the English word. "You know, we call it the cash, but what do you call it? Oh yes, the cashier. Any way, I was talking to a nice lady carrying an umbrella when a big lady pushed in ahead of me. She yelled, "I've go to go to work" and she began pushing the line toward the cashier. Suddenly, she cried out and slumped to the floor. I turned to ask the lady with the umbrella what had happened, but she was gone. Store security said the big lady was dead." Sam turned in alarm. "Honey, the umbrella was not for rain, it was a lethal weapon. The tip of that instrument holds a retractable needle filled with poison. The poison was intended for you. They waited until you were in a crowd. The impatient lady got it and the assailant escaped." Hadassah hung her head. "That lady died in my place."

"There's our car at the end of the block," Hadassah pointed. Trying to think of what to do, Sam was not ready for a cheery greeting from a burgher, taking the afternoon sun on his front porch. "They fixed your car, ma'm. A tow truck mechanic drove up, crawled underneath and worked for about fifteen minutes." If the umbrella episode got Sam's attention this innocent remark galvanized him to action. He grabbed Hadassah's arm and ran back toward the mall. "That car is a bomb. The minute we would have turned the key we would have been with the Lord."

Sam found a convenience store and called 9-1-1 to report the car was a bomb. He realized the call would be traced. They hurried out of the area. A weary 9-1-1 clerk filed it as a crank call.

"We've got to get our luggage out of the motel. Roy's men are determined to get us." Sam looked around carefully for a tail on the taxi ride to the motel. He left Hadassah in the lobby and walked softly to the second floor. Would it be another bomb or would it be some other device? Tip toeing to their room Sam found Hadassah's hair in place, but it was not quite the way he had secured it. Sloppy work, Dupin, he thought. Looking around for some heavy object, he opened the glass fire extinguisher case and removed the heavy container. He hurled it at the door. It crunched under the weight of the extinguisher as both barrels of a .410 shotgun spewed double-ought shot into a cheap watercolor on the corridor wall.

Carefully moving through the room, Winston looked for secondary devices. He was surprised to find their luggage untouched. Hadassah ran up the stairs. She clutched Sam, fighting to suppress her sobs. "Honey," Sam explained, "we will have to leave our hang-up clothes. We can't carry any more than our bags." The room clerk came into the room, saw the shotgun wired to the ceiling and ran out shrieking. Sam and Hadassah quietly slipped out the back way and headed for a taxi stand.

It was a long taxi ride to Fort Myers and the quarters of Dan and Tova Shapiro. Sam met Dan at Indiana U. Dan was a promising ROTC cadet. He had hung on Captain Winston's every word. Now, Dan was a battalion adjutant in the famous Third Infantry Regiment, the Old Guard, the unit on duty at Arlington National Cemetery and the tomb of the unknown soldier.

Dan Shapiro met the Winstons at the door. "I can't let you come in Colonel. I'm sorry, but I've got my career to think of." Desperate, Sam rushed his words. "Dan I need a car. It's a matter of life or death. There have been attempts on our lives this afternoon. Apparently unmoved, Dan shook his head slowly.

Ready to turn and walk away, Sam remembered his mission. "Dan, we are believers in the Messiah Jesus. Because of our faith, General Roy wants to kill us. If that is what the Lord has for us we are ready, but I want your people and mine and anyone that will listen, to turn to Jesus the Messiah while there is still time." "Come

126

in," Dan said suddenly. Once inside, he brightened and said, "Tova and I and our three kids are believers." A dam broke in Sam's heart and he wept unashamed. The old friends hugged and Sam remembered to introduce Hadassah. Tova hugged and kissed Hadassah on the cheek.

"I had to be sure, Sam. The conversation in the latrines at the Pentagon, places you as the archenemy of the U S Army, by selling out to the EU. "Dan, believe me my appointment to Roy's staff was approved right in the White House. I got out when I got saved and I woke up to the monstrous conspiracy that is swallowing more than half the world. But tell me, how did you meet the Messiah?"

"Tova picked up a used paperback for fifty cents at the Officers Club book sale," Dan explained. "It was "The Late Great Planet Earth." Tova read it, I read it and then we read it together. Hal Lindsey opened our eyes to things it is hard for Jews to believe. We looked at one another and then we did the only thing we could do. We asked the Lord to save us."

"Baruch Ha Shem," exclaimed Hadassah. "Blessed be the name of the Lord." "That is great," Sam added. "But tell me have you seen the noose tightening around our people?" Dan's lips turned down. "Noose is right Sam, after ten years of superior OER's my annual ratings dropped to satisfactory for the last two years. I'm out as adjutant of the second battalion." Tova dabbed at her eyes as Dan added, "just yesterday I was placed on orders for the Middle East." Sam shook his head in concern. "In addition to those unexplained things, out of the clouds I start hearing whispers of "kike," and "Christ-killer" stuff. "I'm sending Tova back to her folks in Rapid City. You better think about going underground yourself, Sam."

"Dan, Hadassah and I have a job to do. We must reach as many Jews and Goyim as we can in the time that remains. From your own study you know that things will get worse and worse for everyone on earth. I have lost loved ones. Hadassah is a sabra and she has a family that has never really heard the Gospel. I need wheels to get to Saint Louis. "I have a car I will give you," volunteered Dan. "It's not much. It's an old Dodge Stratus, but I've tinkered with it and it's basic, very basic transportation." "What do you want for it," Sam asked. "Not a penny," he replied, "this is my part in the Winston reach-the-world movement. Take it with our love and prayers."

# Chapter Fifteen
*Saint Louis*

Sam took the 123 Dolly Madison west out of McLean. He made swift lane changes, took exit lanes without notice and doubled back repeatedly. It attracted a State patrolman's attention, but it was near the end of his shift and he decided to let the crazy guy go. When Sam felt that they were not being followed, he headed south to Interstate 64 and pointed the car west. Perhaps there was no need for evasive action, but he remembered, vigilance is the price of freedom.

It was good to be on the open road. The miles slipped by. Driving the speed limit, with Hadassah at the wheel, they rolled through the beautiful Appalachian Mountains, then north on the West Virginia turnpike. Hadassah was enchanted with the white fences framing the horse country of Lexington, Kentucky. She marveled at the natural verdancy of Indiana and Illinois. She reminded Sam of how hard the first Jewish kibbutzniks had to work to eke a living from the soil of Israel. She recounted how her grandfather led the company that drained the Lake Huleh district north of Galilee. A pestilential swamp, back-breaking labor made it into a rich, productive area fed by cool waters.

They broke up the trip with what was for Hadassah a loathsome round of fast food and truck stop restaurants. Sam thoughtlessly ordered egg dishes every morning, an aroma guaranteed to send Hadassah to the rest room to lose whatever she had on her stomach. "One more egg sandwich, Samuel Winston, and I'm going back to Israel, alone!" she announced with finality.

The mention of Israel reawakened Sam's worries about the senior Weizmanns. It was time to school Hadassah on some of the details of the Great Tribulation. She needed to know what lay ahead for her homeland. "Honey, just before the Antichrist stops the worship of our people in the Third Temple, he will begin military operations in the Middle East. Revelation 16:14 speaks of the use of demons to summon the nations to a series of great battles in an end-time campaign.

"For they are the spirits of demons, working miracles, which go forth unto the kings of the earth and of the whole world, to gather them to the battle of that great day of God Almighty."

(Revelation 16:14)

"To understand the closing episodes of this world-wide drama, we must understand the beginnings of that great day. Satan has a consuming desire to take over the throne of God. His plan got under way in Babylon before Abraham's journeys in the Promised Land. In Genesis Chapters 10 and 11, we have the record of Satan's agent, a ruler named Nimrod, who was a city builder and a great hunter. Ancient historians tell us this man trained an army ostensibly to control vicious animals that stalked the land. He was the first known animal control officer." "You're joking," Hadassah smirked. "No, really, he was an animal control officer in what is now the desert of Iraq. At any rate, the training paid off and his Army swept to the Mediterranean, right through what is now Kfar Halutz and Degania, I suppose. Well, his wife Semiramis, not mentioned in scripture by name, was the object of worship in Babel, Genesis 11. There was only one universal language then and God confounded the language in order to halt the building of what was a center of idolatry and unbridled lust. For a little time, Satan had his one world government under Nimrod and one-world worship under Semiramis. The building of cities and the operation of the empire was a slave-based, one-world economy. Babylon is a second home to Satan and the cradle of his ambitions.

Our people went into captivity to Babylon in the Sixth Century before Messiah. They were cured of idolatry in that land. When the remnant returned, they had kicked the idolatry habit and are still free of that sin to this day. I think I showed you the mizrach from my Uncle Leopold's apartment. The direction for prayer to Jerusalem was the only wall decoration of any kind." Hadassah nodded, "we have no pictures on our walls at home, if you noticed."

Returning to the Bible study, Sam remarked, "a note in my Bible at Zechariah Chapter 5, points out that the Jews did bring home to Israel some elements of Babylonian culture that were not helpful to us, namely the desire for riches. In the prophecies of Zechariah 5:5-11, the symbolic story is of an ephah, a large basket for dry measure in use among the Jews of that day. The ephah contains a woman, identified as "the wickedness" in verse 8. She attempts to get out of the ephah and an angel pushes her into the basket and places a talent, a circle of lead, as a lid on the container. The ephah was capacity; the talent was quantity. Now the ephah represents commerce. Financiers might have placed an ephah above the main entrance of the New York Stock Exchange for in the Middle East of that day, it was the logo of commercial enterprise. Well, two women, with the wings of storks carry the woman in the ephah away into Shinar, the ancient name for the land of Babylon. The note in my Bible suggests this is a cleansing in the last days of the sin of avarice and greed, brought back from Babylon after the Captivity." "Sam," Hadassah protested, "you're buying into the same old goyish charge that the Jews are the money-grubbers, the sinister international bankers out to control the world." "No, I'm not honey. Every Jew knows that our people got into banking, jewelry, furs, pawn-brokerage, because we were shut out of all the pastoral and agricultural pursuits that were natural for us. The woman in the ephah, "wickedness," is universal. It is a sin that has engulfed all mankind. God is cleansing His people from this contamination. When we look at the commercial Babylon in Revelation Chapter 18, the Jews are not said to be the proprietors of the empire, it is the Antichrist and the goyim. You wrongly charge me with joining in the smear on our people. Again and again that chapter speaks of the "nations" and the "kings of the earth," who are into business of every description including "the souls of men." But God has a special word for the Jews in the snare of this financial colossus,

"And I heard another voice from heaven, saying, Come out of her, my people, that ye be not partakers of her sins, and that ye receive not of her plagues."
(Revelation 18:4)

Now to bring this down to where we live, many Bible scholars believe the prophecy of Zechariah 5, involves the rebuilding of Babylon as a reconstituted commercial center. Brussels could not fill the bill for anything except Europe. In a commercial Babylon in the Middle East, it would tie together Middle East oil and oil-dependent nations of the Pacific rim. It renders the city the queen of the seas for its transportation possibilities are unlimited. It is the center of the earth. It would be a jewel for Satan's crown. Monsignor O'Brien was the first to tell me about the dream of rebuilding Babylon and in Washington the other day, he told me it is well underway. The Catholic Church put up nearly one trillion dollars according to O'Brien. For the time being, the Antichrist is able to buy off the Saudis and Husseinis, but the Islamic fundamentalists don't want an infidel presence in the heart of Arab territory so they are ready to fight. Antichrist and his army will have to fight to protect this long-cherished dream.

Now we know a great deal about the fighting that will take place in the last days. We normally think of a battle as one single engagement. A war consists of many battles and so it is here. The word for battle in Greek is *polemos* and means a campaign. The teaching is that there will be a succession of battles part of God's plan for the wind-up of the career of the Antichrist." Uneasy about telling her the location of two of the battles, Sam pressed on with an outline of the campaign. "First, Daniel 11:40 tells us,

"And at the time of the end shall the king of the south push at him;"

In Daniel 11:42-43, we learn the king of the south prefigures a North African confederation.

"He [the Antichrist] shall stretch forth his hand also upon the countries: and the land of Egypt shall not escape. But he shall have power over the treasures of gold and of silver, and over all the precious things of Egypt: and the Libyans and the Ethiopians shall be at his steps."

It appears North Africa is looted for the resources to finance the war. Libyan oil provides the fuel for Roy's war machine. In his first major command, Roy will be worried. Does he have the men and materiel to carry out the reduction of the vast armies and staggering array of armaments in the hands of the Arabs? His master Satan drives him on. The North Africans will "be at his steps," signifying that they sue for peace. The next step for Roy is fraught with danger. The scriptures tell us,

"But tidings out of the east and out of the north shall trouble him: therefore he shall go forth with great fury to destroy, and utterly to make away many."
(Daniel 11:44)

130

The Antichrist is spoiling for a fight, but does he have the manpower to take on the Muslim world? He figures history is on his side. The Islamic world has a preternatural religious unity, but it is only as deep as their prayer rugs. Families, clans, tribes and nations in the world of the Prophet have agreed on very little except their hatred of Israel. In successive wars, you Israelis have outsmarted, outmaneuvered and outfought armies many times your size and won. The IDF is forced to win its wars within two weeks or be worn down to annihilation, right? Israel counts on rivalry, bickering and suspicion in the Muslim alliance to work in Israel's favor. For more than half a century, Arab bombast and threats of the extermination of the tiny State of Israel have been the staple of mullahs on Fridays in the Islamic world. "It is time to pull out this cancerous tumor [Israel] from the body of the Muslim world," railed Hashemi Rafsanjani, President of Iran, in October, 1990. Arab rhetoric focuses on the smarting defeats at the hands of the Israelis. The age-old "follow the money" principle works here. Israel has an estimated three trillion dollars of untapped mineral resources in the basin of the Dead Sea. These resources include "rare earths," the exotic minerals valuable in space craft development. Ezekiel discloses the mind of the Arab in Ezekiel 38:11-12,

"And thou shalt say, I will go up to the land of unwalled villages; I will go to them that are at rest, that dwell safely, all of them dwelling without walls, and having neither bars nor gates. To take a spoil, and to take a prey; to turn thine hand upon the desolate places that are now inhabited, and upon the people that are gathered out of the nations, which have gotten cattle and goods, that dwell in the midst of the land."

"Sam," Hadassah cried, her hand to her mouth in horror, "that's Kfar Halutz! We have no walls, no gates to amount to anything. Our people, gathered out of the nations, carved a land out of the desolate places. That's us, Sam, that's us! Oh, Sam, what can we do?" Her eyes welled up with tears. "Hold on honey, hear the rest of the prophecy of Ezekiel. Let me see, where was I? Oh, yes, the northern confederation is a formidable military coalition, probably including Turkey, Syria, Lebanon, the former Soviet republics with Muslim majorities, Iraq, Iran, Afghanistan and Pakistan. My Bible notes say that for years, Bible commentators identified this northern confederation as Russia and the former Soviet satellites. Later commentators seem to feel that such an alignment did not have good textual support. Now the feeling is that it is a Muslim confederation in two parts. A confederation comprised of nations directly menacing Israel on the north. A second Army, those Muslim nations that would sweep down from the north and east seem to represent a troubling eastern confederacy. Ezekiel describes the invasion of Israel in this way, in Ezekiel 38:9:

"Thou shalt ascend and come like a storm, thou shalt be like a cloud to cover the land, thou, and all thy bands, and many people with thee."

Now here is the best part, honey, listen to what God does to this northern invader according to Ezekiel 39:4-5:

"Thou shalt fall upon the mountains of Israel, thou, and all thy bands, and the people that is with thee: I will give thee unto the ravenous birds of every sort, and to the beasts of the field to be devoured. Thou shalt fall upon the open field: for I have spoken it, saith the Lord God."

Hadassah, God is going to destroy the northern invaders with natural disasters, fire and brimstone. General Roy won't have to fire a shot in that battle. Isn't God good?" Sam exclaimed with excitement. "Yes," Hadassah replied hesitatingly, "but will my home go before God strikes?" Sam had dreaded the question for a long time and did not answer immediately. He continued, "the timing is important here. Before God judges the northern confederacy, Roy will move his expeditionary forces into Israel. Daniel tells us in Chapter 11 and verse 41:

"He shall enter also into the glorious land, and many countries shall be overthrown: but these shall escape out of his hand, even Edom, and Moab, and the chief of the children of Ammon."

(Daniel 11:41)

We have no record of Israeli opposition. It may mean the Israelis are so grateful for an ally to confront the Muslim hordes that Roy is welcomed into eretz Yisroel. The order of battle is set. The Arabs stretch in a single, long column from Bozrah in Edom up through the valley of Jehoshaphat and over the plains of Jezreel to Armageddon. Megiddo to you, honey. There to meet them is Roy, the Antichrist and his armies, directed by Satan and his hordes. It shapes up as the most desperate battle of all time. But that is really deceiving." "Sam, the route you describe for the eastern army runs right through Halutz and Degania, doesn't it?" Sam dodged the question again. He continued, "my notes say, that the Antichrist and the eastern army will never fight one another, for the Book of Revelation tells us in Chapter 19 and verse eleven:

"And I saw heaven opened, and behold a white horse; and he that sat upon him was called Faithful and True, and in righteousness he doth judge and make war."

(Revelation 19:11)

Verse 15 tells of the results of this war:

"And out of his mouth goeth a sharp sword, that with it he should smite the nations; and he shall rule them with a rod of iron: and he treadeth the winepress of the fierceness and wrath of Almighty God."

(Revelation 19:15)

132

Hadassah that ends the war! The Great Tribulation ends in the destruction of the Antichrist and his armies and the Muslim hordes from the east. Jesus Christ is the winner!" Sam pronounced with the enthusiasm of a football fan at his alma mater's come-from-behind victory. Hadassah, her brow furrowed with concern, her voice a whisper, "you never answered my questions about Halutz and Degania. My home, probably my family and everyone I know is doomed. Right?" "I just don't know honey. It is true the farm is on the invasion route. We are going to pray that the Lord spares your family. Somehow, we will reach them for the Messiah." Sam turned back to his Bible. "Honey, there is another very sad episode I omitted in the account of Roy's invasion of Israel. Zechariah tells us in his prophecy, Zechariah 14:2-3:

"For I will gather all nations against Jerusalem to battle; and the city shall be taken, and the houses rifled, and the women ravished; and half of the city shall go forth into captivity, and the residue of the people shall not be cut off from the city. Then shall the Lord go forth, and fight against those nations, as when he fought in the day of battle."

Sam made no effort to provide any further interpretation of the passage. Hadassah wept unashamedly. "*Yerushalayim shel zahav*, Jerusalem of gold," Hadassah said softly. "My people, gone in a moment of time. Could not the Messiah prevent such dreadful things?" Tears rolled down Sam's cheeks. "Man's sin and Satan's venom is the direct cause of all of our troubles. Our responsibility is to live for Him in a dreadful time and bear witness of His grace."

Hadassah's first view of the "Father of Waters," the Mississippi, was disappointing. "Too muddy," she exclaimed. Sam was shocked to see how much Saint Louis had suffered from the recent earthquake. Sam related "in the early Nineteenth Century, the town of New Madrid, one hundred and fifty miles to the south literally disappeared in a monster earthquake. It was so devastating, the Mississippi actually flowed north for a time. Ever since, the New Madrid fault line has been a source of concern." The latest earthquake had taken a toll. Two of the bridges spanning the river were closed for repairs. The waterfront Arch was cracked. Tape and barricades warned the tourists. The Old Courthouse, site of the Dred Scott decision, was also heavily damaged. The Old Saint Louis Cathedral was untouched. Homes in the older sections of the Queen City of Missouri weathered the earthquake fairly well. The bedroom suburbs twenty minutes west were scenes of heavy damage.

Sam had to think hard about how to get into Sophie's house without driving up to the door. The first step was an out of the way parking spot on a supermarket parking lot six or eight blocks from the home. Late that night, they walked until Hadassah had to stop and sit for a minute. "This is James Bond stuff isn't it, Sam," she said cheerfully.

A block in rear of Sophie's, Sam strained to recall the way he got into the house when he was a kid. It was through the rear entrance. "Let's see, I crossed through Kirchner's backyard, went over the Levy's fence, walked down the culvert and through the hedge. That's it." Dogs barked and lights winked on, but no one challenged the trespassers. Hadassah took the fence and the other obstacles with the same vitality as in her IDF years. Sam was painfully conscious that he was out of shape.

Sophie's house had survived without a scratch. The home was ominously dark. Shades were drawn, no lights were visible anywhere. Sophie answered the knock with the challenge, "who is it?" Sam had made no effort to tell her of their coming. If the SDECE was on their trail it might place the family in jeopardy. It was clear what kind of treatment those involved would receive from an angry Roy. It was wise, to take every precaution.

Sophie's welcome was encouraging. The usually urbane Sophie was anything but composed this morning. The Jewish princess had her tiara in mothballs. Sam told her little about their situation, except that they were fugitives. That was easy, for Sophie had a feeling every Jew would shortly be a fugitive. All of the talk was of the growing rumors of repressive measures of the Universal Church. The first whispers of impending trouble were blown off as just talk. The Jews have an irrepressible conviction that good Gentiles will always reward the loyalty and the good behavior of the Jewish people. As the rumors persisted, the Jews looked to Washington and the White House for reassurances. They had voted for the president in impressive numbers because the Chief Executive was the liberal darling of the progressives in all walks of Jewish life. It cost them dearly in campaign contributions and other perks, but peace and prosperity was worth the price. Their champion did nothing. Now, rumors were rife and the Jews were concerned. Some were scared, Sophie among them.

Sophie was glad to see Sam. She had blamed him for Simone's vanishing, but that was a dead issue now. It was good to have big brother around. He would know what to do. In spite of his own problems she reasoned, he is a high-ranking Army officer and must have important friends. His wife? Sophie looked her over carefully a number of times and decided she was not up to the Reform Temple women's group. She didn't meet Ladue standards, by any means. She was a helicopter pilot in the Israeli Army! She was an agronomist! How gauche! And now she's p.g. I cannot imagine Samuel as a father, she said to herself.

Over breakfast, Sophie related that their temple was closed on the bogus claim that it was structurally unsafe. One tiny crack was evident high up in a sanctuary wall. Engineers in the congregation looked over the damage and pronounced it a non-factor. The city closed it anyway. The congregation took it as a step in the repression of Jews. Sophie called Rabbi Kravitz and told her of Sam's arrival. Kravitz was anxious to talk to Sam and would be there for lunch. Dog-tired, Sam and Hadassah retired to Sophie's guest room. Tugging off his loafers, Sam told himself again that missing salvation before the Rapture was the worst mistake he ever made. Hadassah was already asleep.

"Shalom, Rav," Winston greeted the harried Rona Kravitz. "Mazal tov to you and Mrs. Winston, Sam" she replied, as she offered her cheek to Winston for a buss. She chattered away in Hebrew with Hadassah, breaking into English to say, "I know Galilee is beautiful at this time of year."

Rona Kravitz picked at her bagel. Coyly, she asked Winston why he quit the Temple project. He was guarded, thinking it was not the right time to be too bold about his reasons for deserting Roy's employ. The rabbi was concerned about current affairs in Israel and Europe. Sam was sure she really wanted to learn of his reaction to the coercive acts against the Jews. "I guess Sophie told you the authorities closed down our temple," Kravitz remarked. "Yes," Sam replied, "I'm sorry about that rabbi. I'm sure that is a daily occurrence now. In Brussels there was an open letter to Jewish synagogues and what they call 'nonconformist groups' urging them to close down and join the Universal Church movement." "We got the same kind of letter here," Kravitz noted, "sweetly inviting us to move to Israel or to begin worshipping with the Universal Church. Where do you see this going, Sam?" she asked anxiously. "Rabbi, I am not a prophet, but our people have a great deal of history to consult on the slow strangulation of our civil rights. Once the process begins it always ends in a pogrom or something worse."

The rabbi began to pace. "This is the United States," she said with feeling, "we have been loyal Americans since 1654. This country won't turn her back on us now, will she?" It was more of a plea than a question. "Rabbi, your whole demeanor says that you really fear the worst. But let me make a very bold and perhaps a very rude suggestion to a spiritual leader. You need to look to God's Word for an understanding of the times." Kravitz nodded in agreement, "the Torah can be of great comfort in a time of uncertainty." "Indeed, Rabbi, but you need the New Testament with the Old, to get a really complete picture of the end-times," asserted Winston. "I don't read the testament of the Christians," Kravitz replied curtly. "Rabbi, three times in the Book of Jeremiah, we read the forecast of "fear on every side." The words were literally true in a Jerusalem under Babylonian siege, but they hold a prophetic message for our people, that our greatest menace is our failure to obey God and to heed His Word. Everything that can befall our people is spelled out so carefully in the two Testaments that it is folly to walk the floor wondering what will happen next." "You mean, Samuel Winston, that you can give an accurate forecast of what will happen to world Jewry in this present time of uncertainty?" "I mean exactly that, Rabbi. I mean exactly that. Will you allow me to present the prophetic program of the two Testaments?"

Kravitz weighed the suggestion without a word. "Sam, the congregation meets each Friday in the banquet room of Izzy Dolginoff's restaurant in Chesterfield.

Would you join us for our Shabbat service?" "Of course, rabbi, but there is something else I must tell you. Hadassah and I are Messianic Jews. We believe in the Messiah Jesus." Kravitz turned, thunderstruck, with her mouth open. She turned wordlessly to Sophie who wore a what else could happen to me look. Turning back she said, "your references to the New Testament should have been a tip-off to me that you were one of those Messianic people," Kravitz said with a sneer. "Forget what I said about meeting with the congregation, they would never approve of a Messianist in the Shabbat service." Sam received the news with a shrug of resignation. Kravitz offered her thanks to Sophie for the bagel and was off.

It was awkward. Sam figured he and Hadassah would have to leave Sophie's home. He prepared to go up and pack. Turning to Sophie, he asked, "do you have an obstetrician in your congregation?" "We have several, but Wolf Abramson is the best." "Hadassah, has not seen a doctor yet, and maybe it is too soon, but I would like to have one waiting in the wings. I don't know how long we will be in the States, but I would feel better about things, if I knew she and the baby were doing all right." "I'll call him for you, Sam. Of course, you are going to remain here for the duration of your stay." Sam faced his sister. "Sophie, it could be dangerous for you harboring fugitives and delicate for you to have Messianic Jews in your home. We will get some kind of quarters near here for a while. We don't want to make things difficult for you." "Sam," Sophie said with unaccustomed warmth, "this is your home. You and my sister-in-law are welcome here. I don't approve of your Jesus, but that is your business."

Sophie pulled strings to get Hadassah in to see Wolf Abramson. Hadassah wasn't mentally prepared for the consultation, but going relieved Sam's concerns for her and the baby. Sophie dropped Hadassah off at the doctor's office adjacent to the Jewish Hospital and took Sam to nearby Forest Park to jog.

It was great to be on the cinder path again. It had been too long. Winston began slowly, but with no wind resistance, it was tempting to step it up a notch. He did a 5-k run, cooled down and collapsed on a park bench. Wondering how Hadassah was doing, Sam remembered the ancient Jewish prayer, "thanks be to the Holy One that he did not make me a woman." I wouldn't want to be in a gown and stirrups, this morning, Sam thought, with relief.

Winston was barely conscious of the man who quietly seated himself on the other end of his park bench. The man carefully opened a paper bag and began to spread a handful of seed on the pathway. Without looking at Sam, the man said, "Mr. Winston, my name is Gershom. Ben-Zion sent me." Winston, wide-eyed, realized this was another of the 144,000 Jewish witnesses for the Messiah. The man was much younger than Ben-Zion, in his early thirties probably, with blue eyes, fair skin and a surprising shock of blonde hair. Gershom never looked up from the feeding of a growing flock of pigeons. "Mr. Winston," the visitor continued, "the *ruach Elohim*, the Holy Spirit, will give you favor in the eyes of the B'Nai El congregation. They will listen carefully to you. Warn them not to accept any invitation to move to Israel. If they remain here, some will survive. Give them a clear invitation to turn to the Messiah Y'Shuah. One more thing, Mr. Winston, there is a home prepared for you and your wife in the town of Crescent." "I know it well," Winston said eagerly. "Ask for the home of Doctor Boyd." Gershom closed his bag of seed and sauntered off down the path. "Wait," Winston cried, "how will I contact you?" The cry went unheeded.

The medical exam proved what Hadassah already knew. She was pregnant. Mother and child were doing well. "He wants to see you on my next visit." "Why?" Sam asked with annoyance. "Oh, I think he wants to see how a man your age was able to father a child." Hadassah dissolved in gales of laughter. Sam reddened, clearly troubled by the difference in their ages.

Sophie warmed to Sam and found she genuinely liked Hadassah. She kept shades drawn, lights dimmed. Periodically Sophie looked the cul-de-sac over for unusual vehicles or foot traffic. Sophie gave them little opportunity to witness to her. Sam's nephew Derek was interested in everything. He plied Hadassah with endless questions about life on the kibbutz and about her adventures in combat. He had a marginal interest in the United States Army, but only for the travel advantages it might represent. The dangers and physical exertions of military service were a turn-off for him. Hadassah primed the pump spiritually with Derek by relating how excited she was to be studying the Bible.

Sam was eager to get to Crescent and the home of Doctor Boyd. Sam knew Crescent. As a kid, he had swung from a cable suspended beneath the Missouri-Pacific Railroad bridge spanning the Meramec River. Twenty minutes west of Saint Louis, Crescent is an unincorporated cluster of homes on a wooded knoll. In a parody of an old song, Sam recalled, "It ain't no town and it ain't no city; it's awful small, but it's awful pretty."

They left the Shapiro's Stratus with Sophie. In Derek's ten-year old car, a varicolored collection of dings and an engine that knocked, Sam and Hadassah drove to the home promised by Gershom. They took the road up from the interstate. The community had managed to escape the crush of the bedroom suburbs. A great place to raise a boy, Sam thought to himself. Maybe even a girl. Thinking about his latest encounter with Gershom, Winston recalled Gershom means "a stranger here." We are strangers. Israel is our home now. Our future is there with the Messiah. A man on the road directed Sam. "Stay on this road, go past the old general store and cross the railroad tracks. Go about three quarters of a mile and turn right into Quail Run Lane. His is the only house on the lane. You can't miss it. But he ain't there," he added.

The Boyd residence had home written all over it. A single-story, log house with a veranda encircling it on all sides, it was unpretentious, but inviting. Big trees had been preserved for shade. Chintz-curtained windows admitted sunlight from every direction. The door was unlocked. Hadassah restrained Sam from entering. "This is my first home. Isn't it an American custom to carry the bride over the threshold? You better do it now, Colonel, before I get too big to pick up." Laughing, Sam feigned struggling to gather his bride into his arms. "Hadassah," he exclaimed, "you have really picked up weight!" She slapped at him, and said "get on with it."

It was puzzling. The dinner table was set as though the Boyds had planned on dinner at home. Vegetables and meat on the stove had long spoiled and the bread was as hard as shingles. Milk in the refrigerator was sour. Sam was interested in the desk neatly piled with Bibles and commentaries. They told a story. Dr. James Boyd was a minister of the Gospel. He was working on a sermon, with little more than the title, "The Judgment Seat of Christ." "What happened to these people, Sam? "Hadassah asked. "I will guess that they were Raptured, honey. Yes, I'm sure of it. These dear people are with the Lord."

There were two bedrooms. There was no evidence of Boyd children. The clothes closets showed Linda Boyd had a few nice things, but her wardrobe consisted mainly of Sunday-go-to-meetin' clothes, plus some old things that said she was a gardener. Doctor Boyd had a few nice suits, ties that needed to be retired and shirts that were on their last legs. Shoes were carefully lined up under the bed, polished and ready for wear.

Doctor Boyd was a graduate of the distinguished Calvary Bible College and a highly respected seminary. His writings and sermons filled several volumes in a bookcase that had the classics of Christian devotional and doctrinal literature. Sam spent every waking hour in the rich resources of Boyd's library. Every day, Bible passages that had nagged at him for an interpretation opened up with meaning. For the first time, Sam had an opportunity to grow in knowledge to match his growth in spirituality. Hadassah had her first introduction to Christian music. Mrs. Boyd had a good supply of traditional and more modern gospel music, most by highly qualified musicians.

Sophie used her influence and her credit cards to get telephone, heating and electrical service restored to the Crescent address in her name. It was good for security. There was nothing with the Winston name on it. Sam had to satisfy some of the Boyd's unpaid bills. He wondered when someone in authority would walk in and charge them with illegal entry. Officially, all of the properties of the vanished, were under the interim care of the State or the Universal Church. No one had noticed the Boyd home was unoccupied. Miraculously it escaped the vandalism and looting that had taken place all around the world after word got out that millions had left everything they owned.

Sophie drove out to see the Crescent Winstons. She found Hadassah the agronomist working in the garden, coaxing some reluctant spring flowers to grow. Sophie brought what she considered the startling news that the B'Nai El congregation wanted Sam to speak at the Friday evening service at Dolginoff's restaurant. "Are there restrictions I should know about, Sophie? " he asked solemnly. "None were mentioned, Sammy. But you know I have to go on living here, so please be careful what you say." "I promise you this, Sophie, I will only say what the Lord directs me to say." Sophie stayed for dinner. She had to endure Sam's from-the-heart prayer of thanksgiving over the meal. After dinner she had to sit through Hadassah's Bible reading and then another time of prayer. There was prayer for the peace of Jerusalem. There was prayer for Hadasssah's folks in Galilee. There was prayer for Sophie and thanks was offered to God for her help in putting the home together. There was prayer for Rabbi Rona Kravitz and B'Nai El. There was prayer for believers everywhere. The most moving prayer was for the Jews and the peace of Jerusalem.

Sam finished by quoting a scripture designed especially for Sophie.

"And this is life eternal, that they might know the only true God, and Jesus Christ whom thou hast sent."

(John 17:3)

Were they getting anywhere with Sophie? "Only the Lord knows," Sam concluded. To be sure, she was sweet and gracious when she had to be. Sam made up his mind that he would sit down with her soon and explain the Gospel message point by point.

Hadassah was a good cook. She felt it was worth the long drive to the nearest supermarket for variety. She quickly learned to decipher the unfamiliar packaging and labeling of American food products. For security reasons, she did her shopping as much before dawn as possible. A problem immediately arose. Hadassah and Sam grew up with table wines. Sam, a modest drinker before his salvation suggested they had a freedom to say "no" to alcoholic beverages of every kind including wine. Hadassah agreed.

The prospect of speaking to the B'Nai El congregation daunted Sam Winston. "I'm not up to that, honey," he pleaded. Hadassah's eyes narrowed to slits as she jabbed him with her forefinger. "Didn't Gershom promise you the Holy Spirit would give you favor in their eyes?" "Yes, he did," Sam replied slowly. "How do you think you got the invitation then?" she probed. "Of course, you are right. Unless the Holy Spirit had moved them to have me speak, it would never have happened." Sam brightened. His fear of facing them was gone in an instant. Now, he could concentrate on the Spirit's message to those who needed God's Word so desperately. The congregation would be looking for something encouraging in the face of grim forecasts of pressure on Jews worldwide. Could Sam meet that desire for information and still give them the Gospel?

The message went through three drafts before Sam was satisfied with the final product. He tried it out on Hadassah. She waggishly feigned a yawn and shook herself out of an imaginary nap. "Whaddya think?" Sam asked, longing for applause. "Oh, it was great," said play-acting Hadassah. She added, "what did you say after Ladies and Gentlemen?" Sam tossed a pillow she easily dodged.

The drive in to Dolginoff's seemed to take forever. Sam went over his message again and again, lacing it with prayer in the most sensitive elements. He chuckled to himself as he thought of something he read in one of Dr. Boyd's books. An English preacher named Charles Spurgeon, evidently a very able Bible expositor, had a note in one of his sermons, "pound pulpit - weak point." Hadassah was mulling over her own concerns about B'Nai El. How would she fit in? She realized she was not dressed to Sophie's standards. Leaving her best clothes in Washington left her with little for a dress-up occasion. Would the B'Nai El ladies look down their noses at a lowly kibbutznik? She prayed for the same favor in their eyes that she was confident the Holy Spirit would give to Sam.

# Chapter Sixteen
*Teaching at B'Nai El*

Doginoff's was a Chesterfield landmark. A bedroom suburb of Saint Louis, it attracted the mobile upward crowd of fast cars and big mortgages. In World War II Chesterfield was home to a Prisoner of War compound for Italians taken in North Africa. Young executives now mowed lawns once sown in sugar beets by experts from the Rapido valley. Dolginoff's bore the marks of a rising tide of antisemitism. One window was boarded up, a victim of rock-throwing youth spurred on by the news it was now a part-time synagogue. But the food was good and Gentiles with no natural taste for Kreplach and other culinary creations braved waiting lists to get into the dining room.

Sam scooped a yarmulke from a pasteboard box near the door. Rabbi Kravitz introduced him again to the Parnas, Herbert Waxman. Waxman was cold to Sam, saving his only smile for Hadassah. He didn't vote for me to come, Winston concluded. The service began with Rabbi Kravitz begging the congregation to take their seats. In a calculated affront to Winston, the Messianist, Sam was not seated on the platform as custom dictated. He was grateful to be in the first row pressing Hadassah's hand as the tension mounted for him. *The Shema* was intoned and sung beautifully by an immaculately dressed young woman. Torah and Talmud portions were read from a printed leaflet. A long list of deceased members consumed the greatest amount of time. Sam was introduced by Rona Kravitz as a former member of the congregation, the son of Irvin and Sylvia Winston, of blessed memory. "He is the brother of Mrs. Sophie Bernstein and the relative of a number of local families." Sam was on. He withdrew his prepared message from an inner pocket of the ill-fitting suit coat, Sophie provided from the clothing of her late husband. Sam calmly looked over the congregation and began.

"Shalom, ladies and gentlemen. I am grateful for your invitation to speak tonight. I am conscious that I am not the choice of some of you. Probably I am not the choice of most of you, but I am here as a Jew, one bound with you in our commitment to Israel and to the rescue of our people from the peril that has encircled us since slavery in Egypt." Winston was interrupted by an outburst from a bearded man near the back of the room. "How can a believer in the mamzer, the illegitimate one, be committed to the traditions of our people?" "Dry up, Leon," someone pleaded, "let the man talk." "Thank you," Sam responded and resumed his speech. "I lately came from Eretz Yisroel with my new wife, Hadassah Weizmann of Kfar Halutz." There was a mild ripple of applause for Hadassah. "I worked on the construction of the Third Temple, under the authority of General Jean-Luc Roy of the European Union. I quit working for General Roy because I realized that our people are placing their trust in a man who will bring about the time of Jacob's trouble, envisioned by the prophet Jeremiah."

Warming to his subject, Winston continued. "I understand your excitement at the rebuilding of a Temple after centuries lying in ruin. Like you, I crushed the wine glass under my heel at the time of my vows as a married Jew, but the Temple that has just been constructed in Jerusalem is not the Temple the Fathers of Israel looked for. Many of our contemporary Orthodox brothers agree that this Third Temple was built without divine authorization. The Temple we look for is one that will be raised up in the days of the Messiah." That statement raised another round of grumbling and shuffling of feet. "But I did not come here to argue the legitimacy of a Temple, dear people of B'Nai El. I have come to challenge the legitimacy of the one who contrived the building of the Temple. I have come to warn you that this man will be the eye of the storm that is about to fall upon our people."

Those in the congregation enraptured with the Third Temple, rose up in a body at this point and jeered at Winston. "This is classic chutzpadik and narishkeit. How dare you blacken the name of Roy, the righteous Gentile. You are not worthy to speak of the *Ha-Mikdash ha-gadohl*," one cried. "Take your Jews for Jesus' lies out of here." Rabbi Kravitz sunk down in her seat. Parnas Waxman looked at her in anger.

Winston continued, "I have known General Roy for a number of years. I was in the United States Army and he was an officer in the Canadian forces. We met from time to time in joint training exercises in various parts of the world. He was a good soldier. I liked him. Someone in the European Union in league with influential people in the Roman Catholic Church were searching for a leader for their new religious, political and financial movement. They hit upon the idea of bringing a distinguished French Canadian back to France. It was a symbolic return of a soldier from a French army that had been left to die in the wilderness of Acadia centuries before. Roy was that man. At some point in his new career as a general in the French Army, I believe he fell under the power of spirits not of this world, spirits that are antigod, antimessianic, antibible and antisemitic. I believe the man sold his soul for fame and fortune. He shot to the top, first as a political leader and now he is about to become the military leader of the Western World. Millions believe he secured the Temple Mount out of concern for the restoration of our cherished Temple worship. The Temple thrives as we speak. Why would a Gentile do this for our people? If it was done as an altruistic gift for the Jews, this is a gesture unmatched in human history. But from sources inside his own coterie, I learned that the Temple Mount was obtained to cement his reputation as a man of peace. Secondly, to secure Jewish financial support and ultimately it was part of a colossal scheme involving the rebuilding of ancient Babylon and the movement of the financial capital of the world to the Middle East. The Roman Catholic Church put up nearly one trillion U.S. dollars to seal this secret treaty with the Arab world. Believe me, the Catholic Church would not invest one cent in a project that does not promise a return for them."

Winston looked the congregation over closely. Silence reigned as Winston continued. "General Roy's treaty to obtain the Temple Mount had a number of secret accords. One of them gave to the so-called Universal Church, religious authority over all Jews and Gentiles living outside of Israel. Slowly but surely, our people in the diaspora are being pressured into either migrating to Israel or pressured into joining the Universal Church. The Protocols of Zion are widely distributed in Europe. That people can still be gulled by this ridiculous screed is beyond understanding, but it is true. The antisemites are grinding out their literature. Does General Roy object? No. He is no friend of the Jews. More and more synagogues are being closed, as yours has been, on one pretext or another. Jewish authorities say that Jewish spiritual life is interdicted in many parts of the world. Rumors mount daily of Jews who have vanished without a trace. And now, the General urges you to migrate. Free transportation is promised. My friends, don't listen to this appeal. I am convinced it is an invitation to death. This is another Umschlagplatz, the railroad station in the Warsaw Ghetto that was a one-way ticket to the gas chambers. Watch for the inducements. In the ghetto it was a loaf of bread and some ersatz marmalade. What will it take to induce you to migrate? Count on it, it is only a matter of time before you have an offer they will believe you cannot refuse. I tell you, all who take the bait will never see Israel. Never see home again.

Then, my people, if you do not follow the pied piper of death, you are betrayed into the hands of the Universal Church. It is the skeleton and sinew of the Roman Catholic Church with the addition of the Buddha, Confucius, and a host of other idols like the ones that were a snare to our people. Look for the day, not far distant, when you will be invited at the point of a sword to bow down before these images. But the end is not yet. The final chapter in this Third Temple scheme will have Roy, the Antichrist, put an end to the sacrifice and the oblation of the faithful and seat himself in the holy of holies as the object of worship. Daniel called this final calamity for the Jews, "the abomination of desolation."

Away with this meshumed," screamed a woman. Sam winced, recognizing her as a cousin. "He speaks lies. Roy is the greatest friend our people have ever had. The Catholic Church has changed and is now a friend to Israel and to our people."

Sam paused to look at his notes and said, "any day now, the United States under Roy's direction, will declare a cashless society. You will not be able to buy, sell or trade without a laser tattoo on your hand or forehead. Compliance will mean more than taking steps to feed your family or simply obedience to the laws of the land. Compliance means complicity in a denial of our God and submission to the devil. I pray that you will refuse the mark, although it may well cost you your life for your refusal. My fellow Jews, I am a believer in the Messiah Jesus. I was not as *frum* as many of you here this evening. A Gentile friend showed me from our own Bible that I am by nature and by choice a sinner, bound for God's judgment. I did not believe there was a place our people call Gan Eden, but the word of scripture quickly convinced me there is and that there is also a hell. I learned my sins would send me to that hell. It was then I learned that God sent Y'shuah HaMuschiach to be my kipporah, the sacrifice for my sins. Our father Abraham at the occasion of his offering of his son Isaac said, "God himself will provide a sacrifice." My friends He has done so. Y'shuah is the Lamb of God which takes away the sin of the world. It takes no *chutzpah*, guts, to believe in Him and the one who does, quickly learns it is not *narish*, foolishness, to do so."

"Away with this man," angry congregants demanded. Most of the congregation got up and filed out of the room. Some left with curses. Some voiced muffled threats. One man, fist cocked, came at Sam, thought better of it, and turned away. Rabbi Kravitz did not know what to say. She simply nodded to Winston and walked out.

Hadassah drove home. Sam said nothing. Hadassah decided it was best to leave him alone with his thoughts. Over tea at home, Sam asked, "well, honey, what did you think?" "It was your first sermon, Sam. I was impressed. I believe the Holy Spirit used you tonight. I'll make you a fearless prediction. You will hear from some of those people. Some will have bitter, angry things to say, but some will ask questions about your relationship with the Messiah. Mark my words." Sam swirled the tea in his cup and said slowly, "it is characteristic of our people that we are slow to react to danger. Did you know, Hadassah, that A.M. Rosenthal of the influential New York Times newspaper admitted in 1996 that the paper did little to publicize the fate of Europe's Jews at the height of the Holocaust? We Jews have a hard time believing our enemies would really want to destroy us and we have a harder time recognizing our friends."

# Chapter Seventeen
### Sam Winston, Evangelist

Rabbi Kravitz slumped over her coffee, concern etched on her face. It was a casual Monday for her, marked by her jeans and tennies and her sweatshirt with maroon letters and the great seal of the Ben Zakkai College and Institute of Religion. She had arrived at the Winstons early, refused breakfast and hemmed and hawed about Sam's warnings to the congregation Friday evening. Finally she made an allusion to Sam's relationship with the Messiah. It hardly seemed possible, Hadassah thought, but the rabbi was the first to confirm her prophecy that there would be some who would want to know more about faith in Jesus. Sam was ready for her.

"Did you watch the news before you left home, rabbi?" "No, Sam, I listened to the weather and the traffic reports. When you drive I-270 you need traffic reports." "Well, this morning's news told of some interesting activities on the Temple Mount in Jerusalem. Let's see if we can pick it up on the TV." Sam surfed through a few channels and then hit on one with a live report. A journalist standing near the eastern gate of the old walled city reported: "The morning sacrifice at the Temple was the scene of scuffling between members of the Temple Mount Faithful and Israeli soldiers detailed to protect the Temple and the Dome of the Rock and the Muslim holy places. The clash occurred as two men, here every day since the Temple was dedicated, showed up during the morning oblation and began preaching about Jesus. Identified as messianists, the men effect the sackcloth dress of the period of the prophets. They warned Jews to repent and turn from what they called the false worship in the Temple and to receive Jesus as Savior and Messiah. The Israeli officer in charge of Temple Mount security, Captain Ari Avigdor, said the Temple Mount Faithful were angry with the authorities for failing to prevent the men from disrupting holy services. Captain Avigdor claims the two preachers refuse to withdraw from the Temple Mount and he says he has no authority under the mutual worship agreements to forbid anyone to speak who is not directly hindering religious activities. He went on to say that he had received a number of reports of injuries to Jewish worshippers, who attempted to assault the two men, including some, unaccountably, with major burns. Avigdor said all attempts have failed to learn where the men stay while the Temple is closed. Reporting live from Jerusalem, I'm Slade Brock."

Sam snapped off the TV. He turned in his Bible to Revelation Chapter 11. "Just listen to this rabbi." He began in verse one:

"And there was given to me a reed like unto a rod: and the angel, stood, saying, Rise, and measure the temple of God, and the altar, and them that worship therein. But the court which is without the temple leave out, and measure it not; for it is given unto the Gentiles: and the holy city shall they tread under foot forty and two months."

(Revelation 11:1-2)

"There are two things we want to get hold of here, rabbi. First, I believe you will agree that the text seems to be talking about the Temple Mount for that is the only location for a Temple of God spoken of in any part of the Bible. Secondly, note that it speaks of the Gentiles in the city while the Temple stands. This did not take place in the past for in the siege under Nebuchadnezzar and the siege under Titus, both Temples were destroyed when the Gentiles captured Jerusalem. Incidentally, the Book of Revelation dates from about 96 A.D., a quarter century after the Romans destroyed the Temple so there was no Temple standing when this was written. Now let us read on:

"And I will give power unto my two witnesses, and they shall prophesy a thousand two hundred and threescore days, clothed in sackcloth. These are the two olive trees, and the two candlesticks standing before the God of the earth. And if any man will hurt them, fire proceedeth out of their mouth, and devoureth their enemies; and if any man will hurt them, he must in this manner be killed. These have power to shut heaven, that it rain not in the days of their prophecy: and have power over waters and to smite the earth with all plagues, as often as they will."
(Revelation 11:3-6)

Rabbi Kravitz was clearly shaken. "But, we cannot be sure that what we heard on the news is what is described here, although I must admit there are a number of points of similarity. What I want to know about is the content of their prophecy. The news says it is about Jesus being the Messiah. Good night, that's a very dangerous message to preach at the Temple," she exclaimed. "I agree," Sam replied, "but to your question about their message, note that they are said to be olive trees and candlesticks. Olive trees and candlesticks speak of God's message in the power of the Ruach Elohim, the Holy Spirit of God. The ministry of the two witnesses is like that of Joshua and Zerubabel, in Zechariah 4:1-7. They ministered at the Temple in the days of the return of the remnant from the Babylonian Captivity.

Rabbi, note that the newsman said the two men are dressed in sackcloth. Would anyone have been admitted to the Temple wearing sackcloth in Solomon's day?" Rabbi Kravitz thought for a moment and then said emphatically, "No." "According to notes here in Doctor Boyd's library," Sam continued, "sackcloth was a sign of mourning for sin, common to the Jews, especially the prophets. The men in the news report, by their dress and their message would seem to be Jews repenting of the sins of our people, in accepting a bogus ritual while rejecting the testimony of the Word of God about the Messiah Jesus."

"O.K., Sam, supposing they are Jews, you haven't given me much detail about their message. Do you have anything to offer in depth about what they might be saying?" "Indeed I do, Rabbi," he answered, "we have an outline of the message of ex-Rabbi Paul of Tarsus, formerly known as Saul, who was a believer after the death and resurrection of Jesus. He had access to synagogues all over the Roman world. He entered a synagogue in Thessalonica, Greece, and preached to the congregation. Let's analyze his approach."

"And Paul, as his manner was, went in unto them, and three Sabbath days reasoned with them out of the scriptures, opening and alleging, that Christ [Messiah] must needs have suffered, and risen again from the dead; and that this Jesus, whom I preach unto you, is Christ [or the Messiah]."

(Acts 17:2-3)

"His message was Bible-based. Considering the time here, about 53 A.D., it was the Old Testament that he used in his presentation. You are not surprised at that, rabbi, a Jewish version is all that he had. Secondly, we note that he "opened and alleged," certain truths. My notes say that to 'open and allege' means to set forth propositional truths. He had two. Initially, he presented a stream of evidence that the Old Testament speaks of a suffering, dying Messiah. Our report says:

"Opening and alleging, that Christ [the Messiah] must needs have suffered, and risen again from the dead..."

(Acts 17:3a)

I understand that some Jewish scholars perplexed by the facts of a suffering Messiah in the Old Testament, posited a two-fold Messianic presentation. One who was entitled to the throne of Israel, the Son of David, and a second Messiah, Son of Joseph, who died for sin. Whatever tack is taken, there seems to be a disconnect in Judaism when it comes to the Old Testament portrayal of the Messiah. Do you see it that way, rabbi?" Sam inquired. Rona Kravitz was silent for a few minutes. She had privately wrestled with this problem in seminary days. She accepted the dictum of her professors that the text was usually at fault in passages hard to interpret. It was easy to capitulate to the idea that if a passage seemed to speak of a literal, human Messiah, it had no authority and you simply ignored it. "Yes, I suppose we have closed our eyes to some passages that seem to point that way. Now, that does not say that the passages are literally true, but they are there." Sam continued, "Paul's second point is:

"...and that this Jesus, whom I preach unto you, is Christ [or the Messiah]."
(Acts 17:3b)

It seems to me, Rabbi, that no Jew is going to listen to me present the claims of Jesus as the Messiah, who has not first been prepared by examining the biographical sketch of the Messiah in the Bible of the Jews. Is that right?" "That makes sense," agreed Kravitz. "Well," Winston continued, "are you ready for this? The chances of Jesus accidentally or pointedly fulfilling more than 333 specific Messianic prophecies is astronomical. Rabbi, Jesus is the Messiah or Judaism must come up with a satisfactory answer to this imposing body of proof. Our people have been denying the undeniable since Jabneh in 70 A.D. when Rabbi Ben Zakkai asked Roman permission to reconstitute Judaism as a bloodless religion. Rabbi, we were never a bloodless religion. Modern Judaism's basis in Hosea 6:6, "For I desired mercy, and not sacrifice; and the knowledge of God more than burnt-offerings" misuses what is really an appeal to reality in ritual with heart-felt conviction." Rona Kravitz weighed Winston's words carefully. "Do you have a list of Old Testament Messianic prophecies and their fulfillment, she asked? It would save me a good deal of work." With a flourish, Winston presented a copy of Ben Zion's paper, **How to Recognize the Messiah.** Rabbi Kravitz thanked Winston, bussed Hadassah on the cheek and drove away.

"Whew," Sam said with a stretch. "That took a lot out of me, but it was a good opportunity with our friend Rona. What do you think, honey, do we have a chance of winning her to Christ?" "As I read it, Sam, we sow the seed. Perhaps someone else will water it, but it is God who must give the increase." "Oh, you have come so far, Hadassah. Your answer is right on."

Sam was genuinely delighted with Hadassah's spiritual progress. "You are really growing in the Lord, honey. You amaze me with your grasp of biblical truth." "Yeah, I'm growing all right," she replied, running her hand over an expanding mid-section. "Will you still love me lumpy and out-of-shape?" she asked plaintively. "I'll love you more," he said sincerely, "you are bearing our child. I am so proud." "But Sam, if I am growing spiritually why have you put off baptizing me?" Sam's hands went to his face in shame. Before dawn the next day, Sam drove Hadassah down to the Meramec. After a short explanation of the beautiful observance, Hadassah was immersed in the Name of the Father, and of the Son and of the Holy Spirit.

Sam was more than a little delighted with his own spiritual growth. Dr. Boyd's library helped immensely. There were hardly enough hours in a day to study all the Bible and doctrinal issues that consumed him. Disappointed with his presentation, he went back over the interview with Rona Kravitz. He determined to study harder.

Sam studied Purim, the commemoration of the deliverance of the Jews from Haman's death plot. It was a special feast day for Hadassah. Born on Purim, she was given Esther's Jewish name Hadassah, meaning "myrtle." The Winstons reminisced over the Purim of their childhood. "Ahoor, Haman," Hadassah cried in her best dramatic voice. It was a mirthful time recounting episodes of dreidels and hamantaschen, the cookies shaped like Haman's hat. Hadassah told of Purim parties while she was in the army. "Somehow it became the custom for our soldiers to drink alcohol until you couldn't tell Haman from Mordechai. One year I spent the sixteenth of Adar, collecting my crew from bars and house parties. All I ever got was a muffin with a candle in it and some hard spanks for my birthday." "I'm up for your muffin and your spanks, but no drinking," Sam said firmly. We will observe Purim as the scripture prescribes."

"And that these days should be remembered and kept throughout every generation, every family, every province, and every city; and that these days of

Purim should not fail from among the Jews, nor the memorial of them perish from their seed."

(Esther 9:28)

Observing the feasts of Israel offered good opportunities to remember the Lord's death at the communion table. Sam explained it would take on special significance in the Passover Seder.

The mysterious Gershom appeared at the Winston's. "Out of thin air," Hadassah concluded. Gershom seemed to know all about the synagogue meeting. He urged Winston to take heart in the encounter. "It will bear eternal results," he reassured them. He seemed to know about the interview with Rabbi Kravitz. "You will see her turn to the Messiah," Gershom prophesied. "But now, there is much to be done. I have groups in this general area that we must summon to the Gospel. They are mainly Gentiles." "Oh," exclaimed Winston, "they get a second chance. That's neat." "No," Gershom replied gravely, "no one gets a second chance. Those who denied Jesus before the Rapture, remain in their sins. They will not come to the Savior now. The ones you must minister to never rejected Jesus. They simply never had a good opportunity, for a variety of reasons, to act upon the truth. Your job is to present the truth: "Repent for the Kingdom of Heaven is at hand," and "Behold, the Lamb of God which takes away the sin of the world." Are you ready, Mr. Winston?" "Yessir, I'm ready, but I'm not trained for the job, " Sam replied. "Isn't that your ministry, Mar Gershom?" "Mr. Winston," he replied, "the Gospel is the ministry of everyone who is saved. You can count on me to make some contacts for you, but the Lord wants to use you in reaching others," Gershom explained. "Some will come to faith. You need to tell them that they will probably die for it. Some will say it is not for them. They will go out lost with the unbelieving world. Mr. Winston, wait for a call. You will receive careful instructions where and when to meet these groups."

Hadassah felt that some gesture of hospitality should be offered to Gershom. She proposed he stay for dinner. "No thank you Mrs. Winston. I have no need of such care. Thank you." With that he was gone, walking down the lane to the main road. Hadassah tried vainly to discover if there was a car waiting for him. Perhaps he took the train. Gershom vanished as quickly as he appeared. Hadassah had questions about Gershom and Ben-Zion. Sam pointed to the references to the 144,000 in Revelation 7 and Revelation 14. "It seems to me," Sam opined, "this host of Great Tribulation missionaries make it all the way through the seven years of trouble. None die. Apparently Satan and his hordes can't kill them. Perhaps angels protect them and transport them around. Gershom said he had no need of care. That suggests to me that God has His hand upon them."

Invitations for Sam to meet with certain groups were not long in coming. Take Hadassah with him? That was a thorny question. It was difficult to assess the hazards. For now, it was not unlawful to meet and discuss spiritual matters, but Winston knew it was only a matter of time before believers would be hunted down, imprisoned and, as Gershom said, probably killed. The crunch time would come when believers would have to refuse the Antichrist's tattoo on the forehead or the hand. Sam reviewed the scriptures on this important matter. The false prophet, the vicegerent of the Antichrist, will require the mark.

"And he causeth all, both small and great, rich and poor, free and bond, to receive a mark in their right hand, or in their foreheads: And that no man might buy or sell, save he that had the mark, or the name of the beast, or the number of his name."

(Revelation 13:16-17)

"What's the big deal on this mark, Sam?" Hadassah asked. "A purely business requirement should not impact believers should it?" "Honey, it seems to be a way of effecting some kind of loyalty to the Antichrist. I note that it is taken in the "right hand." That is the hand for taking an oath. The upraised hand or the laser tattoo on the forehead would be visible to anyone requiring allegiance to the Antichrist. That's bad. At least, God sees it that way. Look what scripture says about taking the mark

"And the third angel followed them, saying with a loud voice, If any man worship the beast [the Antichrist] and his image, and receive his mark in his forehead, or in his hand, The same shall drink of the wine of the wrath of God..."

(Revelation 14:9-10a)

"In Revelation Chapter 15 and verse two," Sam continued, "victorious believers of the Great Tribulation are those who do not take the mark. In the next chapter, verse two of Revelation 16 says,

"...and there fell a noisome and grievous sore upon the men which had the mark of the beast."

(Revelation 16:2)

"Should Hadassah travel with me on gospel assignments?" Sam asked the Lord in prayer. Concern for Hadassah won out. Sam drove alone the twenty-five minutes to his first meeting just over the Mississippi Bridge into Southwest City, Illinois. It was 8:30 in the evening and growing dark. Following his instructions, Winston waited at the Red Rooster, a restaurant that was the meeting place for everyone for miles around. A man of about fifty, dressed in blue work clothes, "Herb" stitched on his shirt, sat down opposite him. "We're at the garage two blocks down on the right, Mr. Winston. Supposing you follow me. It's Schultz's Handi-Lube in case you get lost."

Winston found seven men, most dressed like Herb in work clothes. One wore a seedy brown suit and one, a young fellow Sam judged to be about twenty-five, was dressed in a sweat suit. Herb introduced the men, providing only first names. He explained that they had been rare attendees at churches in the area until the Rapture. "Uhh," Herb caught himself, "except for Steve who is Jewish." Four had lost believing wives they were forced to think were now with the Lord. Two men spoke up, including the man in the brown suit, averring that they did not believe the Rapture story, but that they were willing to listen to what Sam had to say about Jesus. Steve, the young man in the sweat suit, his faced wreathed in smiles, said that he was sorry he had missed the Rapture, but he was grateful to be saved now. Sam later learned that Steve found Jesus the Messiah by reading the New Testament Herb's wife provided. He went through the book as soon as he realized Christ had returned.

The garage was not the best place to preach a sermon. The shop lights were extinguished except for a small light over the counter. The men stood around careful to remain in the shadows. It's amazing, Sam thought to himself, the fear that is gripping Americans who live in a land that so far has only marginal relations with the Antichrist. It must be the absence of the restraining Holy Spirit, he reasoned, plus the fact there were no churches loyal to the Word of God. Thank you Lord, Sam thought, for believers like Steve to witness to the grace of God.

Winston placed his Bible on the cash register. He turned to Matthew Chapter 3 and read:

"In those days came John the Baptist, preaching in the wilderness of Judea, And saying, Repent ye: for the kingdom of heaven is at hand."

(Matthew 3:1-2)

"Fellas, John the Baptist was God's man to bring his nation to faith in God and to prepare the world for His Son, Jesus Christ. John's message was simply that the days for business as usual, were numbered. He called them to repentance. Repentance is a change of mind and heart about sin. Every man is a sinner. God is sinless. The desire of God's heart is for every man, woman, and child to be cleansed from sin and made fit for heaven. Not one of us could do it for himself. The churches you fellas attended didn't save you. Churches could not save the wives you missed in the Rapture. No church can do that for you. God took the initiative and gave us the only means of salvation. He sent Jesus, His own sinless Son to pay the penalty for sin on the cross and to cleanse every sinner who comes to Him in faith. John the Baptist preached to the religious rulers of his day, to the hated tax-gatherers, soldiers and to common people. He pointed the way to Jesus.

"The next day John seeth Jesus coming unto him, and saith, Behold the Lamb of God which taketh away the sin of the world."

(John 1:29)

The lamb is an important symbol in the Bible. In the history of the Jews we read of their animal sacrifices. The sacrificial system was God's method of covering human sin until Jesus made full payment for sin. In the feasts of Israel, an innocent lamb was sacrificed for the guilty sinner. The Jews understood it that way. Then Jesus came and He was the innocent Lamb offered for the sins of all men, not simply to cover sin, but to wash it away. A simple, Jewish fisherman who had a lifetime of experience with animal sacrifices saw the importance of Jesus' sacrifice for us. He said:

"Neither is there salvation in any other: for there is none other name under heaven given among men, whereby we must be saved."

(Acts 4:12)

The same man spoke of the manner of Jesus death:

"Who his own self bare our sins in his own body on the tree [the cross], that we, being dead to sins, should live unto righteousness: by whose stripes ye were healed."

(1 Peter 2:24)

Fellas, this sacrifice for our sins is the message of the Word of God. I cannot emphasize enough the role of the Bible in the salvation of men. The same man, Peter wrote:

"Being born again, not of corruptible seed, but of incorruptible, by the word of God, which liveth and abideth forever."

(1 Peter 1:23)

"Explain this born again stuff, Mr. Winston? My wife use to hit me with that term 'born again.' I can hear it as if it was yesterday. She said "ye must be born again." She also spoke freely of being saved." These questions were raised at just the right time. They were raised by one of the men who related that he had turned from speaking to his wife to surf the television that momentous day, and when he turned back, his wife was gone. "Thanks for that question, my friend. Jesus had an interview with a religious leader one evening. The man had come to see Jesus under cover of darkness, much like we are meeting here. The man had some flowery things to say about Jesus. All of his remarks were true, but Jesus saw the man's real need was a spiritual rebirth. His old sin nature, despite years of religious training and good deeds, could not change the man.

"Jesus answered and said unto him, Verily, verily, I say unto thee, Except a man be born again, he cannot see the kingdom of God. Marvel not that I said unto thee,

Ye must be born again."

(John 3:3,7)
The words born again can also be translated "born from above." You are born again when you see yourself as a sinner, lost, bound in sin and deserving of hell. And then you realize you cannot do anything about your lost condition. The good news comes to you that Jesus Christ died for sinners and He died for you. The proper response is to cast yourself upon the Lord and invite Him to save you. You can be "born from above." Like you guys, I didn't go in the Rapture. I was not saved. Not many months ago I received the salvation I did not deserve. I did not for a moment expect He would save me. But He did and I praise His Name."

There is one more feature to the Good News of salvation. The death Christ died on the cross was a very real death, but death could not hold the Son of God. He rose from the dead, my friends. He rose from the dead. It is the best attested fact in ancient history.

"For I delivered unto you first of all that which I also received, how that Christ died for our sins according to the scriptures; And that he was buried, and that he rose again the third day according to the scriptures: And that he was seen of Peter, then of the twelve [disciples]: After that he was seen of above five hundred brethren at once; of whom the greater part remain unto this present, but some are fallen asleep."

(1 Corinthians 15:3-6)

An enthusiastic Winston proclaimed, "He's alive! He's alive!" And He is coming again." Steve was ready to break into cheers. "There is one further point I must make," Sam said gravely, we are on the very brink of the end of life as we know it. Jesus prophesied of this time saying to His generation,

"the kingdom of heaven is at hand."

(Matthew 10:7)

"Jesus will return again very soon. Sin was dealt with at the cross. Sinners will be dealt with at this coming. If you have never been saved. This is the hour for you to make that eternal decision to trust Him as Savior and Lord."

The two men who earlier claimed that they did not believe the Rapture story were deeply moved by the message. Jim, one of the two, said the story just wasn't for him. He nodded to Herb and slipped out the back door. The other man, Leo, shifted from foot to foot, holding his face in his hands. Sam felt it was time to put them all on the spot. "Who wants to be saved? It is time to fish or cut bait, guys. What will it be? Jesus died for your sins. He is here tonight pleading with you to accept His no-cost-to-you offer to save you from your sins. Who will be the first?" "I guess that's me, Mr. Winston," Leon said softly, "I'll never see Jo Ellen again, unless I come to Christ now. I'm sorry Jim left." he added, "but I have been taking my signals from him for years. It is time for me to act." He picked out a dry spot on the oily floor and went to his knees. That seemed to be a signal for the others to kneel. Steve was already bowed in prayer, thanking the Lord.

Winston took them through the steps of salvation and invited them, one by one to, cast themselves upon the Lord for His salvation. Every man cried out for mercy. After a prayer of thanksgiving, Sam distributed some of Doctor Boyd's Gospel literature. He urged the men to distribute the tracts to family, friends, neighbors and anyone they could get to listen to the plan of salvation. Winston promised to pray for them and urged them to return at the same time next week. "Bring lost friends with you," he urged.

Sam thanked Herb for hosting the meeting. Herb told him, "this fella Grisham or somethin' like that, dropped in to the shop last week." "You mean Gershom," Sam interjected. "Yeah, he had some stuff for me to read. He came back every day. A real persistent guy. Finally, he said he had this friend who would come by and talk with anyone I could get to meet with us. Some of us used to go to church around here and some of us lost wives in that Rapture stuff. I was kinda scared for some reason, but I'm glad we got together. You're welcome here, anytime. Thanks, Mr. Winston. Sam drove back home, weary but rejoicing.

# Chapter Eighteen
*Opposition*

Debating whether to stop or go on, Sam circled the Army Personnel Center for the third time. The only blight on his joy of finding Christ was the way he was fraudulently separated from the service. Winston ached to see the records of his Army discharge. He decided it was time to get to the bottom of it all. It took a few minutes in the waiting room before Captain Miles Jensen summoned him. Jensen called up Winston's records on the computer and then printed out the DD Form 214 Report of Separation. Sam asked permission to view his military pay record and his final physical examination. Jensen turned the computer screen around. Winston scrutinized the records carefully. The Report of Separation in his hand and the records on the screen looked authentic. It was his signature all right, lifted from any one of perhaps thousands of documents he had signed over eighteen years. Winston began to laugh. Startled, Jensen asked, "uhhh, what's funny, Mr. Winston?" "You take a look, Captain. Do you see anything peculiar in these papers?" Jensen scanned the documents and said, "no, sir. I don't see anything." "Well, somehow, I got around pretty well on the day I was discharged. Note the date on every document. I had a physical exam in Stuttgart, Germany. I got my final pay in Eurodollars and signed my Report of Separation, in Brussels, Belgium. All on the same day!" "Well, I guess you flew from one venue to another that day, Colonel," Jensen replied, plainly embarrassed over the issue.

"It doesn't matter, now, Captain. I am in a different, more powerful army. While on duty in Israel I met Jesus Christ. He took a miserable sinner with silver leaves and a black heart, washed him from his sins in Jesus' blood and gave him a new life. I am saved and bound for heaven, Captain. You may have Jesus as your Savior, too." Winston gave him a Gospel tract. Jensen flushed and asked for Winston's green I.D. card. "Leave your address at the clerk's station, Colonel, and your discharge certificate will be mailed to you in six to eight weeks."

Winston lost no time getting out of the city. It was over. The pain was gone. "At least they gave me an honorable discharge," he chuckled. "If you are going to do someone in with phony papers, you might think of giving him a bad conduct discharge. Hmmm, I bet they had to wrestle with that question."

Captain Jensen watched Winston exit his office and slowly walked back to the department break room for a cup of coffee. When he returned to his desk there was a red-edged message on the screen: "Stop and Detain," the message ordered, "former USA officer Samuel R Winston wanted for high crimes and misdemeanors. Advise HQ NSA or nearest FBI field office." Jensen checked with the clerk, but Winston had not left a forwarding address.

General Roy, the Antichrist, was all over the news of the day. He was honored at mass in the Vatican's Sistine Chapel. The pope urged the world to enlist in Roy's crusade for Peace and Safety. The U.S. got the message at the same time the House and Senate passed unanimous resolutions making the Peace and Safety program the law of the land. There were a number of reports of arrests for violation of the Protection of Minorities Act. Several thousand undocumented aliens were ordered deported to unnamed countries of origin. An excursion boat was due to leave Miami later in the week with several thousand Jews migrating to the Holy Land.

On the international scene, the rebuilding of Babylon was reported to be well ahead of the target dates for the completion of the commercial phase of the project. Events were stormy in Europe. Two Scandinavian countries had dropped out of the European Union. Three weak nations were in Roy's doghouse. He forcibly merged those nations with stronger neighbors. There were now ten nations in the confederacy. Winston remembered,

"These have one mind, and shall give their power and strength unto the beast."

(Revelation 17:13)

The Winstons felt it was important to observe the seven major feasts through the Jewish religious year. Passover and Shavuos, Pentecost, seemed to merit special emphasis. They added a special home observance of Resurrection Sunday and Ascension Sunday.

Hadassah in the blush of emerging motherhood, was growing more beautiful. Swelling with child, she jogged and ran every day and felt fine. She could even handle a fast food egg sandwich, indulging them for Sam's sake. He seemed to care nothing about the hazards to his health. Hadassah loved Crescent, at least Quail Run Lane. She delighted in an occasional dip in the Meramec. It was silt brown most of the time and had an annoying abundance of blood-sucking leeches, but it was wet and cooling. With a built-in heater, Hadassah suffered through mid-America's summer.

Rabbi Kravitz worked to keep the synagogue together. She faithfully led in the Torah portion, the prayer book and *yahrzeit* observance each Friday. Sam and Hadassah decided they would be there each Friday regardless of the congregation's reaction. The Lord had given Sam Winston an inexplicable favor in the eyes of the temple faithful. While they *kvetched* and bickered many wanted to hear what the *meshumed* had to say. Dolginoff's was too public. They met in a palatial home in Ladue. Winston was surprised to see some of the same faces that were ready to lynch him at the first meeting. Invited to speak, he decided it was time to talk frankly about the Bible prophecies concerning the last half of the Tribulation.

"My friends, I believe we must be mere days away from the ordinance requiring that all men have the laser tattoo in the hand or on the forehead. "It started in Brussels a week ago," a man in the congregation cried out. "There are notices in the paper and on television for the compulsory tattoo to be available next week in The Hague, Berlin and Paris." "Thank you," Winston continued. "Our time is coming. Perhaps you saw the television interview this morning with the new director of the International Peace and Safety program, an oriental named Ten Sing. He was seated before a full figure portrait of General Roy. You heard him speak glowingly of the tattoo identification mark. His polished Oxford diction and his formal, striped pants and swallow-tailed coat commanded attention. There was no hint of coercion or punishment for non-compliance with those who choose not to take the mark. It was a peaches and cream kind of message. My friends, that frightens me. There will be a death penalty for those who resist the tattoo."

Winston continued. "I met Ten Sing in Italy. He brought oriental spirit-guides, the dybbuks of Jewish legend, to the so-called miraculous healing of General Roy. The satanic drive for a one-world religion, one world government and a one world economic order is underway. I think that you need to look at this mark as something more than an annoying bureaucratic requirement. It is a means of reducing men to slavery. It facilitates the regulations already in place to grant life or deny it. There will be no place for the sick, the aged, the unproductive. Need I say there will be no place for Jews? Listen to what God has to say on the matter:

"...if any man worship the beast [the Antichrist] and his image, and receive his mark in his forehead, or in his hand, The same shall drink of the wine of the wrath of God, which is poured out without mixture into the cup of his indignation; and he shall be tormented with fire and brimstone in the presence of the holy angels, and in the presence of the Lamb."

(Revelation 14:9-10)

Worshipping the beast and his image was a real problem. No Jew would do that," cried one man. "May I defer answering that for a few moments, sir?" Winston responded. "I promise to deal with that in a sequential manner. But now, I want to emphasize that Adonai does not want anybody to receive the mark. It is treason against God. To take the mark means you are an enemy of God. You have sided with Satan and you will be separated from God forever." A well dressed lady rose and said, "it sounds to me like death if we do; death if we don't." "Well said, madam," Winston responded, "I am reminded of Moses' choice. The Bible says,

"By faith Moses, when he was come to years, refused to be called the son of Pharaoh's daughter; Choosing rather to suffer affliction with the people of God, than to enjoy the pleasures of sin for a season."

(Hebrews 11:24-25)

"Now to that question I deferred. Our people really got cured of idolatry in Babylon. It has never been a problem to this hour. At the same time, if you know Ezekiel Chapter 8, you know that the prophet Ezekiel could not believe God's people would fall into idolatry, but the Lord took him out of a Babylonian concentration camp and transported him back to the Temple at Jerusalem. There Ezekiel found Jews worshipping the sun, Jewish women weeping for Tammuz, the cult of immorality and portraying all kinds of painted figures on the walls of the Temple itself! In a time of uncertainty like this good men will fall into this dreadful sin in the name of feeding their families." The questioner seemed saddened, but satisfied with the answer.

"Let's move on to the next event in the prophetic revelations of the Word of God. According to Daniel 11:42-43, General Roy, the Antichrist, will launch a seaborne invasion of North Africa, Egypt, Libya and Ethiopia. The troublesome 'horn of Africa,' will be subdued. This will provide the oil resources and the financial support for his further military adventures in the Middle East. Then I believe, my friends, that we will be at the mid-point of this Great Tribulation that we are now beginning to see in bold relief.

In a swift sequence of events, I believe the Antichrist will stop the oblation and the sacrifice in the Temple at Jerusalem. Our people in Jerusalem will go one morning for the usual morning sacrifice and they will find that the Antichrist himself stands in the holy of holies and our people will be ordered to fall down before him in worship or die on the spot!" The congregation, in shock, rose as one. "I know how horrible that is to contemplate. Daniel calls it 'the abomination of desolation.' The worship of the image may mean that when the Antichrist cannot be there in person that the faithful will be obliged to worship a computerized, audio-animatronics image that moves and speaks. The despair and degradation of our people will be complete. Of course, the bravest of them will refuse this imposter and be slain. Some will capitulate.

I believe a simultaneous development in the rest of the world, will be the surprising end of the Universal Church. The Antichrist used the church to come to power. You saw General Roy as the pope's favorite. He visited the Vatican, was feted and dined at the pope's table. The Catholic Church heralded him as the long-desired Catholic leader and opened their coffers to him. The Church, suddenly included Mormons, Muslims, Buddhists and other religions and cults and yes, some Jews. In scripture this church is seen as a harlot, because of her spiritual adultery with the world. You may read about this union in Revelation Chapter 17. The Antichrist needs the financial resources and the church's amazing world organization in order to come to power. When he has the strength to go it alone, he will loot and destroy the harlot church. The Bible tells us:

"And the ten horns [a metaphor for the European Union] which thou sawest upon the beast, these shall hate the whore [the Universal Church], and shall make her desolate and naked, and shall eat her flesh, and burn her with fire."

(Revelation 17:16)

158

"I believe," Winston continued, "this must be the time at which a rebuilt Babylon, rather than Rome or any other European city, will be the new world headquarters of the Antichrist. If you have done any reading in recent weeks and months, you have seen reports of how this commercial colossus is coming together. Ironically, Catholic insiders told me a long while ago that it was Catholic money that bought the rights to a rebuilt Babylon in the heart of Islam, buying off the Muslims in the revival of Temple worship at Jerusalem."

"Friends, Israel will be in for a very bad time. After the successful invasion of North Africa, General Roy's expeditionary force will enter Erets Yisroel. If the idea of an image in the Temple was hard for the congregation to take, they fell into open despair over the idea of Gentile armies in the Holy Land. Winston continued, "Zechariah tells us,

"For I will gather all nations against Jerusalem to battle; and the city shall be taken, and the houses rifled, and the women ravished; and half of the city shall go forth into captivity, and the residue of the people shall not be cut off from the city."

(Zechariah 14:2)
One man protested, "that was fulfilled in 70 A.D., Mr. Winston, that cannot be a future event." Winston responded, "this is one of a host of passages in the Old Testament that have both an historic and a prophetic significance. I suggest this verse fits into the prophetic scheme because of the verse that follows:

"Then shall the Lord go forth, and fight against those nations, as when he fought in the day of battle."

(Zechariah 14:3)

That never happened in 70 A.D., but it will happen after General Roy sacks our holy city." "My daughter is on a kibbutz," a woman in tears cried out, "how bad will it be for out people in the Holy Land?" "I will have Zechariah answer you, ma'am.

"And it shall come to pass, that in all the land, saith the Lord, two parts therein shall be cut off and die; but the third shall be left therein."

(Zechariah 13:8)

Winston reverently bowed his head and said nothing for two or three minutes. "Friends," he announced solemnly, "two-thirds of the Jews of Israel would mean something on the order of a million and a quarter deaths. In a land 60 miles wide and 180 miles in length, Eretz Yisroel, will be one gigantic cemetery. That is why I say to you, don't migrate to the Holy Land. Life will be desperate enough in the diaspora. The scriptures tell us:

"And I looked, and behold a pale horse: and his name that sat on him was Death, and Hell [sheol in Hebrew] followed with him. And power was given unto them over the fourth part of the earth, to kill with sword, and with hunger, and with death, and with the beasts of the earth."

(Revelation 6:8)

God's Word tells us that one of every four of us in this room will die in the time that remains to us. I believe you are here by God's appointment to hear not only the grim details of events beyond our ken, but in order for you to make an intelligent decision about whom you will follow. To follow the Antichrist, by his mark or the worship of his image, means physical death now or physical death soon. Then you will face eternal death in the lake of fire. To follow Jesus the Messiah may well mean physical death, for Satan is determined to destroy anyone who belongs to Y'shuah HaMushiach. Following Jesus means eternal life at the end of this one. You must decide. To do nothing places you at Satan's mercy. It will likely mean death physically, with no one to say kaddish or observe your yahrzeit. Worst of all it means separation from God forever.

But let's go back to Zechariah," Winston said with a hopeful smile. "You will recall that he tells us of the remnant that will survive the Tribulation in Zechariah 13:8. Now, listen to the future for that remnant in verse nine.

"And I will bring the third part through the fire, and will refine them as silver is refined, and will try them as gold is tried: they shall call on my name, and I will hear them: I will say, It is my people: and they shall say, The Lord is my God."

(Zechariah 13:9)

"There is a great day coming for our people," Sam concluded. "I believe I have said enough for tonight. My friends, no one knows whether we shall be alive to meet again. Let me urge you to seriously pray,

"Adonai, is Y'shuah really your Son? Is He really the Messiah of Israel? Do you want me to become a completed Jew, one who believes in this Jesus as Savior and Messiah? Adonai, I will receive whatever you have for me by faith."

The meeting dissolved in a wholly different atmosphere than in Winston's first message to the congregation. They were silent, subdued, plainly reflecting on the momentous things they had heard. Rabbi Kravitz smiled wanly and said nothing. Four people grasped Winston's hand in a wordless expression of thanks. More than one wiped at tears.

Sam had a schedule of evangelistic meetings throughout the week. The men's group in Southwest City was now co-ed. Some women, co-workers, friends and a couple of wives, were coming on a regular basis. Souls were saved every week.

They never seemed to tire of the Gospel story, but Sam varied his presentation so it was worth coming again. Steve Rosen, who was in the first gathering at Schultz's Handi-Lube now hosted the meetings. A single young man, Rosen was the only Jew in Southwest City. He operated a successful branch of his father's Chicago-based insurance agency. He proudly showed Winston the work station of Geraldine Schultz, Herb's wife. Mrs. Schultz had been used of the Lord to get Steve into the New Testament. When Mrs. Schultz was Raptured, Steve knew immediately what he must do. He kept Mrs. Schultz's work-station exactly as she left it. Rosen confessed that he had not yet been able to tell his Jewish family about his decision. The entire town seemed to know that Rosen was now a Christian. The talk on the street was of the great number of people that attended the weekly Bible studies in the Rosen Insurance office. Winston was by turns elated and concerned. How long would the Universal Church tolerate an evangelical testimony?

Sam had a regular meeting a few miles from home. This was a group of mostly business people who had been too busy to listen to the Gospel message before the Rapture. They were paying off mortgages, sending the kids to college and replacing the family automobile. Gershom had them meet in a back room of the YMCA. About half were Roman Catholics, disillusioned with the movement that had brought all kinds of strange images into the churches they had sacrificed to build. Sam decided it was best to ignore their religious ties and simply concentrate on the Good News of the death, burial and resurrection of Jesus Christ. They were average, garden variety sinners, most with a dark room locked deep in the conscience. A number had suffered the death of marriage, some of the women were physically, emotionally and spiritually scarred by abortions in their youth. Some of the men had worked through infidelty, drug and alcohol habits and sexually transmitted diseases. All of them were far from God. Many were angry with God. Some felt God was angry with them and a few were convinced the ax of judgment could fall at any time. They were ready for the message that God was still in the saving business. Most of them made decisions for Christ in their first clear understanding of the Gospel. It became a growth group. There were first-time decisions every week. Winston was encouraged to learn that some were quietly witnessing in their own circles of acquaintance.

It was comic relief to visit the laundry room of the General Hospital, about twenty-five minutes from Crescent. Gershom had worked with the hospital housekeeping department for some weeks and a number had been saved. Winston was asked to be at the rear service entrance of the hospital about 10:15 in the evening to meet some eleven to seven shift workers. He slipped in and looked for a lanky African American named Jeff. Jeff, a ham-handed basketball player, right off the bricks of the ghetto, was smiles from ear to ear as he introduced Sam to the twelve people who kept the hospital in linens. It was easy to identify the believers. They were warm and effusive, all over Sam with bear hugs. "I ain't never listened to a honky preacher before," Rolinda Makepeace exclaimed, her body convulsed in laughter. "Me neither," said Jordan Humphreys.

There were no chairs in the laundry room. Some sat on washers, most leaned against appliances. Jeff told the group that Lisa on the desk upstairs had promised to buzz them if security was coming down. Winston explained that he was a new believer himself, and was trying to grow in the knowledge of the Lord Jesus. "I have selected the story of the Ethiopian for tonight, my friends. In the Acts of the Apostles, Chapter 8 we read of a eunuch, the treasurer of Ethiopia,if you please, who had been to Jerusalem to worship with the Jews. In his chariot on the way back home he was reading the Bible." "Eunuch? You mean this dude was neutered?" Rolinda asked. "Yes," Winston blushed, "that was common in the world of that time. At any rate," Sam continued, "the Ethiopian was reading Isaiah Chapter 53,which is a wonderful prophecy. The Lord sent an evangelist named Philip to help the man. Philip asked him, "do you understand what you are reading?" "How can I," he replied. "I need someone who knows the Bible to help me."

"The place of the scripture which he read was this, He was led as a sheep to the slaughter; and like a lamb dumb before his shearer, so opened he not his mouth: In his humiliation his judgment was taken away: and who shall declare his generation? for his life is taken from the earth."

(Isaiah 53:70-8 quoted in Acts 8:32-33)

"The Ethiopian asked Philip about the speaker. "Does the prophet speak of himself or of some other man?" The Bible says

"Then Philip opened his mouth, and began at the same scripture, and preached unto him Jesus."

(Acts 8:35)

My friends, the man who was led to slaughter, the lamb dumb before his shearers was no other than our Lord Jesus Christ, who made full payment for the sins of men. It was God's purpose in sending His Son, for the Son to die for miserable sinners. I am a sinner by nature and by choice friends, and the Lord saved me from my sins. And he longs to do that for you."

The phone buzzed twice. Jeff quickly cleared the linens off a gurney, opened a sheet and directed Winston to climb on. Jeff and Jordan covered him head to toe and pushed the gurney out into the corridor. The elevator opened at the end of the hall and a security officer eyed the two men as they passed him. "Morgue," Jeff said simply. Jordan clutched the sheet around Winston and pushed a little harder.

A Mrs. Gennaro, representing a group of Catholics dissidents from a parish in a bedroom suburb, called to invite Winston to speak to them. As an emissary of the group, she was personally reluctant to listen to a non-Catholic. Gershom had worked with them for some time, but no one in the group had been saved. A good deal more ultra-Catholic than any Winston would meet, these people were angry about Rome's sell-out to the Universal Church. Theoretically, the UC guaranteed all participants wide latitude in continuing the rituals they brought to the new faith. But it was a new scheme of things dependent on a Catholic infrastructure. Traditional Catholics, like Mrs. Gennaro's group detested the addition of pagan idols to their church. They were exercised about the errors of Protestants, Jehovah's Witnesses, the Mormons and Christian Science that came with the idols. Driving to the meeting in the Gennaro home, Winston was puzzled that these Catholics had resisted Gershom's witness and were now willing to listen to him. Studying materials in Doctor Boyd's library, Winston knew that the doctrines of purgatory, penance, indulgences and auricular confession to a priest were soft-pedaled. For many Catholics, this made the Universal Church more attractive. It had taken years, but the Anglicans, and the Eastern Orthodox communions were fully represented in the Universal Church.

Winston turned over in his mind what he knew about the attitude of the Catholic Church toward the Jews. He remembered reading Adolph Hitler's speech on the occasion of the Concordat with Germany in September, 1933. Hitler said, "I am only continuing the work of the Catholic Church: to isolate the Jews and fight their influence." Church silence largely sealed the fate of the Jews of the Third Reich and ultimately of most of Europe. It seemed clearer each day of the Tribulation, that Nazi-style antisemites were in control in Roy's regime. The world appeared eager to see the Jews suffer once again.

Eighteen were gathered in the Gennaro's family room. Almost every face registered the look: "you can't talk us out of our Catholic faith." It was a good opening for Sam Winston. "Friends, you were very happy with normative Catholic life and teachings." (Nods all over the room). "I am here simply to warn you of the wrath to come. We are on the brink of the wildest pattern of natural disasters, war on a global scale, viruses like Ebola and AIDS, famine, and the total collapse of life as we know it. And the people of your city will not escape. It is time, not to take on a more vigorous religious life, but rather to see yourself as God sees you. And then apply His answer to the question "where will you spend eternity?" Let me read the words of the man you consider to be the First Pope:

"Forasmuch as ye know that ye were not redeemed with corruptible things, as silver and gold, from your vain conversation received by tradition from your fathers; But with the precious blood of Christ, as of a lamb without blemish and without spot."

(1 Peter 1:18-19)

"Peter speaks of the essentials of salvation. You must be redeemed, bought out of the prison house of Satan and the price that was paid is the precious blood of Jesus Christ. Peter mentions tradition. Tradition is unreliable. Tradition usually supercedes and contradicts the Word of God. Peter hits that too."

"Being born again, not of corruptible seed, but of incorruptible, by the Word of God which liveth and abideth forever."

(1 Peter 1:23)

"Most of you became Catholics by baptism as infants. You were given first communion in your church. You consider yourself to have received Christ in the host. Is that right?" "Yes, that's what we believe," they choursed. "Then you were confirmed by the bishop. You probably went to confession and you would not miss mass. So that is a sketch of your faith journey. Somehow, I don't find the Word of God as the instrument of your faith. I don't see any reference to being redeemed. I have real questions about whether you really belong to God's forever family!" Winston paused to let the force of his words sink in. The words sunk in. Some were ready to stone him. Many were ready to throw him out of the house. He continued, "you can be part of God's forever family tonight. First of all you must see yourself as sinners. No, you were not cleansed of your original sin at baptism. Witnessing a good confession and acts of penance do not answer the sin question. You must see yourself as sinners, lost, undone, bound for hell forever. Then you must see yourself as totally unable to do anything about your sin. Your church cannot help you. Listen to Saint Paul:

"Not by works of righteousness which we have done, but according to His mercy He saved us..."

(Titus 3:5)

In another place, Saint Paul says:

"For by grace are ye saved through faith; and that not of yourselves: it is the gift of God: Not of works, lest any man should boast."

(Ephesians 2:8-9)

"I'm going to pray friends. I am going to pray that the Holy Spirit of God will open your hearts and minds to the truth of the Word. You cannot save yourselves. The best day you ever lived, filled with all kinds of deeds of kindness and worship, will not save you. Your church cannot save you. Only Jesus can save you and He waits for you to call upon Him right now. Who will be the first?" There was concern on a number of faces. There was agony on the face of a few. No one moved. No one raised a hand. The Gospel went unheeded. After prayer, Winston thanked them and promised they would be in his prayers. Sam Genera offered a handshake and said, "we believe Holy Mother Church will recover from her present troubles and we will be with her." Winston shook his hand, his heart as heavy as lead. On the way home, Winston cried out for forgiveness for doing what he felt was a poor job of presenting the Gospel.

Sam Gennaro thought about Winston and Gershom while munching on a thick prosciutto sandwich washed down by a glass of pilsner. He wiped his mouth and reached for the telephone. "FBI? I want to report a Jew from Israel named Winston. Sam Winston, came to my house tonight and talked against President Cameron, General Roy and the Universal Church. No, I don't know where he lives, but his car has Virginia tags. Yeah, LKX 356. Is there a reward?"

# Chapter Nineteen
*The noose tightens*

Rona Kravitz, wreathed in smiles, roused the Winston's early Monday morning. "I couldn't wait to tell you. Sam! Hadassah! I'm a believer, a completed Jew." The Winston's crushed her with kisses and hugs. "Tell us all about it," they pleaded. "Well, I went through the **How to Recognize the Messiah** paper forty or fifty times, I guess. Then I asked God, "is this true?" And suddenly, I knew it was! Now, here is the best part. I'm going to Israel. I'm going back with some of our people to witness to everyone who will listen." Winston, smitten with alarm, cried, "you can't do that. I don't believe any Jew makes it to Israel now. The shipload that left Miami days ago, is unreported. The Coast Guard says it vanished and it was not in the Bermuda Triangle." "That may be, Sam," Rona said with conviction, but I must go and win Jews on the boat, in Israel or wherever God sends me." Humbled by her words, Sam exclaimed, "Of course. You are right, rabbi, you must go where the Savior directs. Forgive me for being such a poor brother as to try and turn you from the Lord's will." Sam and Hadassah smothered Rona with kisses, wept and committed her into the hands of the Lord. Rona paused at the door and said, "Sam, I want you to have my car. Sophie will get it to you." Through tear-stained eyes, the Winstons watched the rabbi drive down the lane.

Winston hated to steal time from Bible study, but it seemed essential to keep abreast of the world news. The media was filled with reports of natural catastrophes all over the globe. Many reports went unconfirmed, or were officially denied for fear of widespread panic. Casualties mounted in areas visited by plague. The National Center for Disease Control was under a total news blackout ordered by the president. The big news was of victims of exposure to the sun. Correspondents told of burn victims in numbers never before recorded. Daytime temperatures in many places in the North Temperate Zone were said to approach 120 degrees Fahrenheit in morning readings!

The long-dreaded water problems in the Middle East were a reality. For years, water shortages were expected if Turkey went ahead with threats to build twenty-one dams on the Euphrates River. The dams were still on the drawing board as an unexplained drought began drying up the twin rivers of the Fertile Crescent. Hadassah was more than a little concerned about the water supply of Israel and particularly for Halutz, but from her agronomy background and her faith in Israeli agriculture, she reassured Sam the country would survive.

The big news was from Jerusalem. General Roy had somehow managed to kill the two Temple Mount preachers! For three and a half years, at the time of sacrifice each day the preachers were there. They had thwarted every effort to silence them. Officially, they were under the protection of the Israeli forces but, the two men needed no soldiers. They were said to be directly responsible for a drought in the immediate area. When waters flowed, eyewitnesses reported, they turned to blood. No one interfered with the two until General Roy somehow managed to slay them. The general strutted and gloated. He was at the zenith of his power. The Jews were elated and the Muslims mystified. The general ordered the bodies remain undisturbed over the weekend. Mullahs spoke of it on Fridays, Jews toasted one another on the Sabbath. Secret believers knew from Revelation 11:7-12 that God had called the witnesses to their ministry and that God permitted their death. The believers were confirmed in their faith when the two stood to their feet. Resurrected, a great voice ordered the two to come up to heaven. Chaos and panic reigned on the Temple Mount. Ten Sing, Roy's aide attempted to put the matter in perspective. He hotly denied that a resurrection had taken place, but the entire world had witnessed it. Hadassah remarked, "the Lord is certainly making His presence known in Israel and the world." Sam felt a chill as Ten Sing raised his arms toward heaven and commanded flames to fall. Out of a cerulean blue sky a long pillar of fire fell to earth. The curious screamed in terror and ran for cover. Roy and Ten Sing disappeared into the Temple. "Hmm," Winston said reflectively, "it is clear now that Ten Sing is the False Prophet, the principal agent of the Antichrist. Sam read to Hadassah,

"And he doeth great wonders, so that he maketh fire come down from heaven on the earth in the sight of men."

(Revelation 13:13)

Sam realized that the Antichrist would soon break his covenant and put an end to Temple sacrifice. It would mean the end of the Universal Church as well. Satan was nearly finished with worship of any kind except of himself and his Antichrist. A world-wide campaign to receive the mark would be in high-gear soon. Sam tried to visualize what that would mean for those who had recently come to faith in Christ. He was particularly concerned about the believers in Southwest City. They were much too open about their faith. Sam regretted his alarm for he had urged them to speak for Christ. Still, it was a time for caution.

Jade Cummins rubbed at an invisible spot on the long hardwood counter of the Red Rooster Grill and watched the comings and goings of her Southwest City customers. How many blue plate specials have I placed before the working stiffs of this town? She fingered again the folded stack of crisp new currency in her apron pocket. This dough could get me out of this two-by-four town, she thought. But she had to think again about the job that came with the money. The people of this town with their holier-than-thou attitude, looking down their noses at me; it just isn't right for today. Maybe in some way, I will be helping the town to lighten up and enjoy what we've got.

Jade's windfall had come early that morning. She had just served Cleve Martin his usual biscuits and gravy and refilled his coffee cup. "Sit down, willya Jade, I've got something to talk over with you," Martin said with a smile. "I can't right now, Cleve, I've got orders in. I'll go on break in about five minutes and I'll talk to you," Jade said, figuring Martin's bill.

It was more like ten minutes, but Cleve was patient. Jade sat opposite him and played with her fifth or sixth cup of coffee. "I need a favor, Jade," Martin said gravely, "and I think you owe me one." Jade's countenance clouded. Owe him? she thought, he gouged me for that divorce. I helped make Cleve Martin, attorney, a rich man. "Jade, some important people in this town have a problem with which you can help us. Do you know Steve Rosen?" "Yeah, I know him. He's Jewish, I think. He sells insurance. Now he sells Jesus," she replied rather curtly. "That's him. Well, he has been counseling a young woman, the daughter of a prominent local citizen, to keep the baby that is due sometime in the fall. The girl made a mistake, but Rosen tells her that it is wrong to take a life. You know what those people say. That's not all. This Rosen is trying to reform the world. He speaks out at city council meetings on every issue. He opposed granting a liquor license because it was too close to a public school. This guy has got to go," Martin said with emphasis. Now here's what we want you to do, Jade." They whispered conspiratorially for a few minutes. Martin placed a wad of bills under a menu and gently pushed it across the table to her.

"Hello, Mr. Rosen? This is Jade Cummins, you know, I wait tables down at the Red Rooster Grill?" She switched to the more familiar, "Steve, I've got a problem. I guess you would call it a spiritual problem. Could you drop by my place some evening soon. I'd like to talk to you. Oh, any night would be fine. Tonight? Sure, I'm at home right now. Just come on by." Jade hung up the phone, took a deep breath, applied lipstick, checked her hair-do in the mirror and smoothed out her blouse. That was easier than I thought it would be, she mused.

Steve Rosen was at Jade's home within an hour of her call. A spiritual problem? The Lord is certainly working miracles in this town, for Jade Cummins is the last person in the world I would ever expect to be interested in the Gospel, he thought. Jade received him at her door. The alarm bells immediately went off in Rosen's brain, for Jade was dressed in a shear, form-fitting, low-cut blouse. She wore thick makeup. He was assailed by her cheap perfume. "Won't you come in Steve?" she purred. "No, ma'am, it is unwise for a man to enter the home of a woman alone. Couldn't we talk right here on your porch?" "Well, I declare, I didn't realize I was such a man-trap, Steve. A poor ole working girl in a restaurant wouldn't do a man any harm, would she?" "I'm sure you wouldn't Ms. Cummins, but if you don't mind, I'll just talk to you out here." With resignation, Jade seated herself on the dilapidated porch swing. Steve stood on the top step of the veranda. "Now then, Ms. Cummins supposing you tell me what's on your mind." "Oh, Steve, I'm just troubled about getting old. I don't have anyone now, and you know a woman alone has needs and I just feel that maybe you could give me counsel on how to handle loneliness, fear of the future and an empty life." Steve really felt the alarm bells now. No one, he reasoned, would call you for counseling who had such a vague set of issues on their plate. If she even seemed on edge about her needs and fears it might make sense. There is something wrong with this interview! Suddenly, Jade Cummins jumped to her feet and attempted to kiss Rosen. He parried the effort, but wound up with a little lipstick on a cheek and a great deal of the red stuff on his collar. Jade ran into the house, dialed 9-1-1 and tore her blouse. Outside, Steve was vainly scrubbing at the lipstick with spit and a handkerchief. Later that night, he was apprehended and booked for sexual assault and suspicion of attempted rape.

Sam thanked the Lord for the books in Doctor's Boyd's library. He was preparing a message when he felt an overwhelming need to pray. He had no idea what to pray for so he spent time just praising God, assured that he would receive some kind of message soon. It was not long in coming. It was Herb Schultz in Southwest City. "Mr. Winston, Steve Rosen has been arrested on suspicion of rape and sexual assault." "What?" Winston exclaimed. "Yessir, he is in the Carroll County Jail." "What happened?" demanded Winston. "Well, the story isn't clear, but a waitress at the Red Rooster Grill says Steve came to her home to counsel her and he attacked her. I don't know if it will mean anything, but the County Sheriff is the waitress's cousin." "What kind of a woman is this waitress, Herb?" "Well, Mr. Winston, there has been a lot of whispering about her for a lotta years. Steve would show respect for any lady, regardless of her reputation. Steve is not the kind of guy to take advantage of a woman. He is so hyped on reaching people for Christ that is all he thinks about."

Somehow, Sam had to get across the river as soon as possible. He literally pulled Hadassah up out of the garden mulch. He gave her time to change and they were off. Winston had missed the news that the National Guard and the Reserves of the United States Armed Forces had been ordered to active duty, ostensibly in support of the European Union's military intervention in the Middle East. Southwest City was alive with uniforms. The arrest and confinement of Steve Rosen was on everyone's lips. Separating fact from rumor was not easy. Skirting the crowd, Sam and Hadassah slowly worked their way to Herb Schultz' shop. Herb added the information that there were small groups around town fomenting trouble. "There is a militia group here, anything but the patriots they claim to be. Guys who talk like the old Klan keep bringing up the fact that Rosen is a Jew. And Mr. Winston, I have heard there is talk of lynching Steve."

They found a quiet place to pray. "Lord, should I go to the authorities and face whatever comes, with Steve?" Sam asked. Hadassah allowed an urgent "no" to escape her lips. "Shh," he reassured her and continued to pray. Afterward, Herb said, "I don't think it would do a bit of good for you to visit the Sheriff, Mr. Winston. Sheriff Cummins is a decent man. I believe he knows the character of his cousin Jade, all too well. This is entrapment. I believe Steve will give a good account of himself." Silent for a time, Winston said he felt the Lord did not want him to go to the jail. But Sam felt he needed to remain in the area. He urged Herb to discreetly contact the other believers in the Bible study and urge them to quietly drift out of town until the matter blew over. It was dangerous for them to remain. When they drove into town more than one person had looked at Winston quizzically, as though trying to place him in Rosen's circle.

Sam and Hadassah took a motel room in Red Bud, a few miles from Southwest City. In the morning, television news related that during the night, Sheriff Cummins had smuggled the prisoner under guard out of the Carroll County jail intending to transfer him to the Sheriff of Logan County. The report went on to say that a large band of unidentified men, heavily armed, had intercepted the Sheriff's escort and forcibly taken Rosen. He was found by a farmer at daybreak just over the Logan County line. He was lynched. A paper pinned to the body read "Death to the international Jewish conspiracy." Sam broke down in tears. Hadassah weeping herself, consoled her husband. Sam opened his Bible and read,

"And when he had opened the fifth seal, I saw under the altar the souls of them that were slain for the Word of God, and for the testimony which they held: And they cried with a loud voice, saying, How long, O Lord, holy and true, dost thou not judge and avenge our blood on them that dwell on the earth? And white robes were given unto every one of them; and it was said unto them, that they should rest yet for a little season, until their fellow-servants also and their brethren, that should be killed as they were, should be fulfilled."

(Revelation 6:9-11)

Sam felt the noose was tightening. One by one, the members of Rosen's Bible study were brought back to Southwest City and placed under house arrest on trumped up charges. Jim Collins, the man who opted out of the first Bible study at Schultz' garage was the principal informant against the believers. Herb felt sure Collins lied to the authorities about Steve. He was also thought to be the one responsible for the fliers out for Sam's arrest. An unflattering artist's impression had him years older and about one hundred pounds heavier. Hadassah laughed, charging him with concealing his real age from her. "I want you to autograph that picture for me, honey," she exclaimed, "I'll send it to my folks." The jest helped her conceal her real fears for his safety. Sam was unmoved by his peril, but his concern was growing for Hadassah and their unborn child. There was little encouragement in scripture that believers in the Great Tribulation would survive physically. Sam and Hadassah covenanted together that if they were caught, they would go out like the martyr, Steve Rosen.

God's special witness, Gershom, came by the Boyd home to give Sam an assignment in Springfield, Missouri, two hundred and fifty miles southwest of Saint Louis. Sam would meet a pastor with a small flock disillusioned with the Universal Church. It would be a three-day operation. Sam was eager to go. Hadassah had a feeling of grim foreboding. She reluctantly agreed Sam should go alone. Sophie brought Rona's car. Three times on the drive south down Interstate 44, Sam was stopped by police and armed civilian vigilantes with blue **666** arm bands. They searched drivers and vehicles looking for "contraband." Contraband seemed to be anything they took a fancy to and seized on the spot. One of the mock police tore off Sam's wristwatch. They had the wanted flier with Winston's picture on it, but no one recognized him from the artist's drawing.

The pastor and his very frightened parishioners met Sam in the basement of what had been their Protestant Church. A few carried New Testaments in mint condition. Some had Gospel literature. Sam had to call for order as several asked for an explanation for a spate of natural disasters in the Ozark area. More wanted to know about the war in the Middle East and the two men on the Temple Mount. All were worried about vanishing American civil liberties. The pastor, Dr. Arch Patterson complained that he had no real standing in the Universal Church. "Roman bishops and priests call the shots. We're just around to squeeze our people for more money. He wept openly that he had informed on some of his own people as secret believers. "They were never seen again," Patterson cried.

"What about the Jews here in Springfield? Winston asked. "A couple of months ago," Patterson replied, "their synagogue was closed. I hear they were given the choice of joining the UC or facing deportation. Some joined, most resisted. The resisters were loaded on school buses and were never seen again." A man standing nearby, said, "there were fresh graves out west of the national cemetery. A neighbor of mine picked up what looked like remnant of that blue and white shawl the Jews wear."

It was hard to get going on the message. Winston went through the scriptures proving that every man is a sinner by nature and by choice. He showed that neither their Protestant Church, the Universal Church or any church could save a man. "The good news, friends, is that God saw your need and sent Jesus Christ to pay the full penalty for your sins." Sam brightened as he related, "He rose from the dead and is now at the right hand of God. He will return again in a matter of months!"

The return of Christ was a difficult teaching for church-goers who had never seriously considered the claims of Christ. "I use to teach that Jesus was an ordinary man," Patterson confessed, "so looking for Him to return was foolishness to me. I see now that He really will come in righteousness and great power." Winston spent two more days, answering questions with Bible answers and dealing with the congregation one-on-one. Fifteen made decisions for Christ. Six were unsure and put off their decisions. Winston warned believers of their peril, but urged them to think of the joy that would soon be theirs in the return of the Savior. Three decided the cost was too great and went back out into the world.

Driving home, Sam managed to skirt the road-blocks by detours on country roads. He got back to Crescent and Quail Run Road about dusk. The house was dark.

There was no sign of Hadassah. The front door was open. Then he saw it. A lighted cigarette glowed behind Doctor Boyd's desk. "Come in, Colonel Winston. You'll remember me, Maurice Dupin, French Intelligence." "What have you done with my wife?" Winston demanded. "We have her. She is safe. But we want you, Colonel," Dupin said with a sneer, "you're going back to Israel to face charges of treason, sedition, and a host of other capital crimes." "I'm an American citizen," Sam said defiantly, "you can't charge me without an extradition order." "Colonel," Dupin laughed, "who would defend you? The U.S. Army? They threw you out. Will the United States government come to your rescue? They have a warrant out for your arrest. No, you are a Christian, a subversive and a saboteur. They are executing people like you all over the world. Incidentally, Colonel, I knew you were a Christian that night I followed you to Border Street in Jerusalem. We could have saved a lot of time and money if we had arrested you that night. You slipped away then, but you won't get away this time."

Winston thought about assaulting Dupin, but strong arms reached out of the darkness to pinion his arms behind him. "Pat him down," Dupin ordered, "and put him in the car. The men walked Winston down to the main road where their car was carefully concealed. He was forced into the back seat and held down on the floor. At Lambert Airport, the car drove up to a waiting KLM Dutch Airline plane. Hustled on board, Sam found Hadassah held by two rough-looking women. Winston foolishly made a rush for her and was sapped for his trouble. When he regained consciousness, blood trickled from a cut on the head. Winston found there were only a dozen or so people on board. He was seated between Dupin's two musclemen. Hadassah was across the aisle between the two female guards. Two other passengers were apparently under guard. Winston picked up the information that one had embezzled millions in EU funds and the other man had collaborated in the conspiracy to assassinate Roy in the Jordan operation. "You'll all feel the headsman's ax," Dupin predicted.

The flight was uneventful. Signaling with their eyes and facial gestures, Sam learned Hadassah and the baby were well. Hadassah was cool as a cucumber. Sam tried, but could not match her apparent nonchalance. Winston marveled. She is probably thinking this is a way to get back to Israel without paying the air- fare. What a mess I've gotten her and the baby into, he said in frustration, but then the Lord is still on the throne. Roy, Dupin and the headsman's ax cannot frustrate God's plans. Sam went over and over again, the verses he had memorized,

"For I am persuaded that neither death, nor life, nor angels, nor principalities, nor powers, nor things present, nor things to come, nor height, nor depth, nor any other creature, shall be able to separate us from the love of God, which is in Christ Jesus our Lord."

(Romans 8:38-39)

With tailwinds much of the way, the KLM flight crew had them at Israel's Ben Gurion airport in record time. The prisoners were hustled into two waiting vans and trucked off to Akko, the ancient Crusader fort of Acre. During the Mandate period it was a British prison. The British held Stern gang and Irgun terrorists in the stone and iron keep. The Israelis used it as an asylum.

The prisoners were thrown into cells on the third floor. Hadassah was in a cell alone next to the cell Sam shared with the EU embezzler. Still groggy from the blow on the head, Winston realized for the first time that they were in the custody of the French Foreign Legion, the unit he had brought to Israel. The Legionnaires languidly strolled the block once every hour. The rest of the time they lounged, slept and cursed their prison duties. They said nothing, but reserved their most malevolent looks and gestures for Winston. Winston thanked the Lord that they had not taken his pocket Bible.

The prisoners received one slice of bread and a cup of water, bitter with iron rust. Sam whispered to Hadassah when he could. She remained calm and cheerful in the face of the unknown. Winston's cellmate, the embezzler Jonathan Grey, was English, about fifty with sallow, puffy cheeks. His suit was Saville Row. His shirt was torn and the four-in-hand was twisted, mute testimony to rough handling by Dupin's men. Grey was so frightened he could barely speak. He had cringed in a corner since the cell door slammed shut.

Grey was a London School of Economics don who had given years of devoted service to the Crown and then for the last couple of years, to the EU. Over time, he felt that Roy's Hitler-like tactics were ruinous to the goal of genuine world peace. Grey began to talk with other dissidents and the unanimous decision was that Roy had to go. Stealing substantial funds from EU accounts might do it. They were exposed. Some managed to escape. Grey made his way to the United States. With other dissidents in Boston, an FBI sting operation led to Grey's capture. He was turned over to Dupin at Kennedy Airport.

Sam told Grey the New Testament story of two men, believers in Jesus Christ, who were incarcerated on trumped-up charges. "These men," explained Winston, "were as calm in the face of danger as I would like to be. The men had no intention of trying to escape, but during an earthquake the prison doors flew open and the warden feared every prisoner would break for freedom. Under the penal code of that day, the warden's life was forfeit if his prisoners escaped. He decided suicide was his best choice." Winston read from his Bible,

"But Paul cried with a loud voice, saying, Do thyself no harm: for we are all here. Then he called for a light, and sprang in, and came trembling, and fell down before Paul and Silas, and brought them out, and said, Sirs, what must I do to be saved?" And they said, Believe on the Lord Jesus Christ, and thou shalt be saved, and thy house."

(Acts 16:28-31)

Warmed by Winston's relaxed attitude and the calmness in his voice, Grey asked, "did the man believe them? Winston read,

"And when he had brought them into his house, he set meat before them, and rejoiced, believing in God with all his house."

(Acts 16:34)

Grey brightened. Winston took his hand. "Mr. Grey, you can face whatever comes like those two believers and the warden by doing as Paul urged. "Believe on the Lord Jesus Christ and thou shalt be saved." "Believe what?" Grey asked, eagerly. "Believe God when He says Jonathan Grey is a sinner, unfit for heaven. Believe God when He says I sent Jesus Christ to pay the full penalty of Jonathan's sins. Then believe God when He invites you to receive Christ as your own, personal Savior." "I will, I will," Grey exulted,"If you are ready, pray after me Jonathan. "Oh, Lord, save me for Jesus' sake. I know I am a sinner, lost and undone, and I now give all of my sins to Jesus for His atoning death for me. Oh Lord, please save me for Jesus sake." Grey, his face bathed in tears, opened his eyes. A smile creased his face from ear to ear. "I'm saved," he exclaimed, pumping Winston's hand in gratitude. He seated himself on his bunk fully composed.

At 1800 hours, a legionnaire unlocked the cell to admit Major Rolf Krueger and his Sergeant Major, the bull-like Boris Massoit. "Well, well, the ex-Colonel Winston," Krueger gloated. "You are finally going to get what is coming to you for your insults to the Legion and for being the dirty Jew that you are." "Yes," Winston said defiantly, "I am a Jew. A completed Jew, a believer in the Messiah Jesus. Major, you need to turn to Jesus Christ before it is too late." Angered as much by Winston's coolness as his witness to him, Krueger replied, "A Jew who is a Christian? It is too bad you can't die twice. In the new world order, both of your loyalties - Christian and Jewish - are death sentences."

Massoit stripped off his heavy black garrison belt with the flaming grenade on the silver buckle. Krueger carefully wrapped the belt around his right hand, positioning the buckle over the knuckles. Krueger looked at Winston, hatred seething in his eyes. "My grandfather was in the SS. He died a hero's death for the Fatherland, but he took thousands of Jews with him. I dedicate your death, Jew Winston, to his memory." "Your Grandfather was a coward," Winston spat back, "He killed old people, sick and helpless infants. He was no man." "Hold him," Krueger shouted. The fist in the solar plexus exploded in Sam's brain and in his groin as white, hot pain. A second and a third and Winston quivered in agony. The final crushing buckle to the jaw and Winston collapsed. He smiled in triumph. He had not screamed.

"Put the Colonel to bed, Sergeant," Kruger ordered. His arms pinioning and encircling Winston's shoulders, Massoit in a classic wrestler's arm drag and a whip, hurled Winston against the wall of the cell. Bloodied and wracked with pain, Winston lapsed into unconsciousness.

Hadassah from her cell, screamed out her defiance. "You yellow-bellied cowards. I shot down Hezbollah terrorists that were better men than you," she cried. "Bring the Jewess to my quarters," Krueger sneered.

Winston came around to find Jonathan Grey had placed his jacket under his head. Grey dabbed at his facial wounds and moistened Sam's lips with his water ration. Sam lapsed back into unconsciousness. He came to, to find two legionnaires carrying Hadassah's limp body into his cell. "Here is what's left of her, Jew!" one said venomously. Half-conscious herself, Hadassah slowly covered the torn lower half of her dress, wet and crimson. She smiled wanly and reached out a hand to her husband. "Our baby Samuel is with the Lord, Sam. I named him Samuel after you. Like Hannah, we had already given him to the Lord." "Sam moaned loudly, the salt of his tears stinging the cuts on his face.

# Chapter Twenty
*Escape!*

Sam's injuries would heal in time. It would take God's grace to heal the wound in his heart for Hadassah's suffering and the loss of Samuel, the baby they would not hold in this life. Sam had no idea how badly Hadassah had been abused. She could not talk about it and Sam did not know how to ask. Losing the baby, Sam felt sure, was harder for a mother than any man could know.

He slammed his Bible shut and wiped tears from his eyes. I must share with Hadassah the material I learned from Doctor Boyd's studies about the death of infants. Sam strained to recall the substance of the teaching. Sam went back into the Bible and was delighted to find the passage. It involved the child born out of the sin of King David and Bathsheba. David prayed for the child through a lingering illness. The text he was looking for had this to say:

"Then said his servants unto him [David], What thing is that that thou has done? thou didst fast and weep for the child, while it was alive; but when the child was dead, thou didst rise and eat bread. And he said, while the child was yet alive, I fasted and wept; for I said, Who can tell whether God will be gracious to me, that the child may live? But now he is dead, wherefore should I fast? can I bring him back again? I shall go to him, but he shall not return to me."

(2 Samuel 12:21-23)

Sam felt good about the passage, but then it occurred to him that their child was not physically complete when he died. That must mean we may not share David's confidence that he would see his child one day. Hadassah did not share Sam's uncertainty about the baby. She whispered to Sam she had never had a shadow of a doubt that Samuel was with the Lord. Sam chose to believe her figuring God could easily take care of the details.

No one in Akko prison seemed to care if the Winstons lived or died. The guard came, placed bread and water on the floor and left as quietly as he came. Somehow they were content to allow Hadassah to remain in the cell with Sam and Jonathan. The cell was built for two. Jonathan Grey gave up his bunk to Hadassah and slept on the floor. He did everything he could for his injured cellmates. For the first twenty-four hours, Grey was sure Hadassah would hemorrhage to death. He could only wonder if Sam was bleeding internally. He forced them to take bread and water. Hadassah succeeded in keeping it down. At first, Sam wretched with every bite. Both slept fitfully, moaning occasionally. Jonathan Grey learned how to pray.

Two or three days after their ordeal, well before dawn, the night sounds of Akko prison were punctuated by the sound of gunfire and men running the galleries. Rolf Krueger in an alcoholic stupor rose unsteadily from his bunk and reached for his holstered revolver. He never made it. An Uzi burst caught him full in the chest. Blood and bullet holes in the wall above his bed his final epitaph. Massoit, the Sergeant Major, died as he had lived, grappling with an Israeli commando in a dance of death. The duo went off the third tier to their destruction.

A sharp firefight and it was all over. Captain Ari Avigdor went from cell to cell until he found the Winstons. He saw they would need help. A terse command into his handset and four men with stretchers quickly appeared. Sam, half awake, grasped Ari's hand and silently mouthed his thanks. "Sam, it's war now. The EU army invaded Israel last night. Jerusalem has fallen and the powerful peace party in the Knesset has decided to sue for peace. They are more concerned with the northern confederation than with Roy. Sam, listen carefully. My men are going to take you to a Druze village up north. Stay there until you and your wife are well. I am taking my column to Degania now. I will set up an ambush for the rest of Krueger's company. They will be looking for you. Kfar Halutz and Degania is the first place they will look. I will tell the Weizmanns that you are safe. Shalom."

On stretchers, Sam and Hadassah were placed in an ancient Volkswagen bus, decorated in all the garish colors typical of Palestinian taxis. They were covered with mounds of carpet and two soldiers in civilian clothes drove them out of Akko. They drove south to Kfar Ata, Shafaram, and then swung north by back roads to Safad and Rosh Pina at the north end of the Sea of Galilee. From there it was a short drive to the obscure Druze village of Deir Hakim. The Mukhtar of Deir Hakim, Ali Ibn Qureish, was a figure out of Lawrence of Arabia. Warm, friendly black eyes, leather cheeks, and full lips were framed by long black hair and a short beard frosted gray with age, white in places. He wore traditional Arab dress. The Mukhtar motioned and Druze hands picked up Sam and Hadassah gingerly and transported them into a small stone building with two beds and a small open cooking pit in the middle of the floor. The Israeli driver offered an Uzi machine gun and a revolver to Winston, but he declined. The soldiers promised that someone would be in touch with them as soon as possible. "Shalom."

Veiled women brought cold goat's milk and Feta cheese. Hadassah drank the milk as though it was nectar. Sam had a hard time getting it past his nose. It was good and Sam realized it was just what was needed to get them on their feet. "You are safe here," the Mukhtar explained, "we are subject to patrols without notice. We are under Israeli protection if that is meaningful now, but there are powerful Arab armies within a few miles east and north of here. We have no idea when they may move upon us. If you remain out of sight you should be safe. No one cares what the Druze do."

Hadassah knew the Druze people. She explained to Sam that they were a Muslim sect who lived in northern Israel, Lebanon and Syria. They were peaceful, bothered no one and lived quiet, industrious lives. They differ somewhat from the Islamic majority and incorporated some Christian teaching and some Judaistic principles into a religion that dominates their lives. The Druze village was named for the father of the Druze people, Hakim, a twelfth century prophet. When it was necessary, the Druze worshipped as Muslims. At times they worshipped as Christians. Jesus Christ was prominent in Druze belief as a divine incarnation. The important thing was that the Druze were neutral in all of the Arab-Israeli conflicts and everyone seemed to respect their choice.

Sam had never slept so much in his life. Hadassah wasn't use to it either. Every day they gained strength. Every day they soaked up sunshine, ate well on lamb, rich succulent vegetable dishes, couscous, Feta cheese and of course, goat's milk. Hadassah took on the bloom of youth once again. She stretched and walked around as much as the Mukhtar considered safe. She spoke Arabic fluently and joked with the Druze women. Sam did not know what was said, but the conversations always seemed to be about him followed by raucous laughter. They had been in the village six or seven weeks when Hadassah said to him, "Father Samuel, we need another child." Sam was floored. He had no idea how intimacy would ever be approached again. "Yes, we need another child," Hadassah said firmly. Sam replied uncertainly, "Honey, look what you have been through. This country has been invaded in the south. The northern confederacy only minutes from here is ready to march in. It just isn't a good time for us, for our people." "Sam Winston, or Weinstein, whatever your name is, the time has never been right for Jews to have children. They had them in Egypt, they had them in the Sinai desert and they have born them in slavery, fleeing for their lives and even in death camps. When is it ever the right time for Jews to have children? We need to have another child even if we know, well, even if our second baby goes to be with the Lord like the first." Sam had no argument to make.

Sam despaired of the loss of his large Bible. He had the pocket edition. He poured over it hours on end. He was getting stronger. His abdomen was no longer sore to the touch. He moved carefully, fearful of stretching. He was gaining weight. The goat milk was to blame. He needed to exercise and move around. The Mukhtar produced an ancient Philco radio. It crackled and popped, but you could get some news on it. It confirmed Israel had capitulated to General Roy. EU forces were concentrated mainly south of Galilee and west of the Jordan. The media was clearly in the hands of the EU army. The radio poured out praise for the general. Real information was rationed. The commentators seemed to convey the idea that the General was concerned about the mobilization of the Muslim armies in the north. These statements were punctuated with warnings to the Muslim nations to the east to cease their warlike movements or suffer the consequences. What had become of Jerusalem? The Temple Mount? Hadassah worried about Kfar Halutz. Sam expected any morning to wake up to find she had left to learn the condition of her folks.

It was the right time for a visit from Ben-Zion. Sam grasped him and hugged him like a long, lost friend. Sam longed to know how he knew where to find them, but by now Sam was used to the mysterious, unexplained ways of the 144,000 chosen missionaries. "Do you know why Ari Avigdor came to our rescue," Winston asked. "Captain Avigdor is a believer, Mr. Winston. He found your **How to Recognize the Messiah**, in your Jerusalem office. He read it carefully and asked the Lord to save Him. He is one of us. A radio message passed through his hands that related your capture and imprisonment. He had already led a number of his commandos to faith in the Messiah Jesus and since Israel was at war with General Roy they readily volunteered to aid him in the assault on the prison." Winston's eyes filled with tears of thanksgiving, first for the news of the salvation of Avigdor and his men and then for the commandos that fought to free them.

Ben-Zion had a Bible for Sam, (cause for another," how did he know?"). The Lord's messenger told him that Jerusalem was taken. EU forces had sacked and pillaged the city, mercilessly ravished the women and conscripted all of the able-bodied men as slaves to support the military occupation. Zechariah 14:2 was fulfilled to the letter. The Temple Mount? The Antichrist broke his covenant with the Jews and set himself up as the object of worship in the holy of holies. Sam nodded, an exact fulfillment of Matthew 24:15 and II Thessalonians 2:3-4. The big news from Europe was that the Antichrist broke with the Universal Church. He looted the Vatican and was holding the pope captive. The systematic looting and burning of convents, rectories, shrines and monasteries was underway. Priests and monks have been slaughtered and nuns ravished. Meanwhile, the world financial capital in rebuilt Babylon was a bonanza for the Antichrist, Ben Zion reported, but its days were numbered. Revelation 18 would be fulfilled in the coming invasion from the East.

Ben-Zion grimly reported that there was wide spread persecution of Christians. The death sentence is quickly passed on every believer who is taken. Christians are immediately beheaded. Jews are treated very badly. They have been murdered assembly-line fashion in every country. Ironically, the Jews age-long persecutors, the Catholic Church and other cults and world religions, have fared no better.

"The good news, Ben-Zion went on to say, "is that millions of people have been saved worldwide. Most seal their testimony with their blood, but you would be thrilled, Mr. Winston, at how many go to their deaths praising the Lord for the privilege of suffering for His name. I am pleased to tell you many have come to faith in Christ, Jews and Gentiles, through your bold witness." "What can you tell me of Herb Schultz and the Southwest City believers? Of Rona Kravitz? Of my sister?" "All with the Lord, my brother," Ben Zion said gravely. "That must mean, Sophie trusted the Messiah," Winston said almost gleefully. "She did, my brother, and her son as well." Winston jumped for joy and ran off to tell Hadassah.

Ben-Zion continued, "as you surmised, Ten Sing is the False Prophet of scripture, the official spokesman for the Antichrist. As Mother Castaldi told you, he is a Tibetan medium summoned to aid the healing of General Roy. He did more than use black arts to heal him, Satan used Ten Sing to seize upon Roy's ambition. Roy traded his soul for power and Satan consumed him. Ten Sing not only speaks for the Antichrist, he is Satan's guardian of this last ditch stand for the wicked one." "I thought the False Prophet would be a Roman prelate, but it became clear that Satan had plans to destroy organized religion," Winston said. "It made sense that he would go to the dark underside of evil for one of his slaves to partner with the Antichrist." "That is correct. Now Ten Sing will force worship of the Man of Sin and enforce the taking of the mark."

"When can I go back to work for the Lord?" Winston asked impatiently. "You must first fully recover, my brother," Ben Zion replied. "There will be opportunities for reaching people through the printed page. And there will be opportunities through radio. Meetings and soul-winning opportunities will not be as frequent as in America, but there will be some. Your ministry will require rapid movements from place to place for we are now in the last half of the Tribulation and it will be a difficult time for everyone. Conduct yourself with care." Ben-Zion rose to leave. "When will I see you again?" Winston asked. "When you need help, one of our number will be nearby," Ben-Zion replied cryptically.

A ministry in print? Gospel by radio? How could these things be? Winston wondered. "Sam," Hadassah admonished, "you have been rescued from the jaws of death, you've seen your ministry flourish in ways you never dreamed of. Now you are doubting the Lord's ability to use us?" Hadassah clucked, "look to the Lord, my husband." "Of course, you are right," Sam agreed, suddenly flushed with love and admiration for Hadassah who seemed years ahead of him in practical faith. "This is the time to sit back and watch as the Lord directs us in the last roundup." Hadassah said. Darkness passed over Sam's face for an instance as he thought of the peril for Hadassah and the child she was asking the Lord to give them. He brightened again with the thought that his wife and family were important parts of what he expected God to do.

Hadassah's weak spot in faith was concern for her family in Kfar Halutz. The Mukhtar made some cautious inquiries and learned that Avigdor's Israeli commando had destroyed the Foreign Legion column that drove on Degania. Avigdor and his men urged the settlers to leave. Only a few chose to do so, the Weizmanns not among them. Avigdor's unit moved south. With the surrender of the Israeli forces to Roy, Israeli settlements were virtually defenseless. Hadassah boldly suggested that she go south and bring her folks to Deir Hakim or urge them to flee. "I don't believe for a minute they will leave home, Sam, but I would like to try." "No, I'll go," Sam said. "Sam, you would never get past a patrol on these roads. They won't pay much attention to an Arab girl carrying baskets of grain." Reluctantly, Sam agreed and Hadassah set off down the Syrian side of Galilee with two other Druze women. Veiled, averting their eyes, they endured cat-calls from young soldiers on patrol. The long walk gave Hadassah time to think. The Weizmanns simply did not know what the Winstons were into. During their time in America, the need for secrecy kept Hadassah from revealing anything about their activities. Sanitized letters to Israel were sent to a postal drop Sophie had arranged. The letters spoke of the child they eagerly awaited, gardening, the weather, the house and the occasional swim in an unnamed river. Hadassah felt a spiritual burden for her folks. It was time they knew of her saving faith in Jesus the Messiah.

They made the eighteen miles around the Galilee bridges and Degania and into Kfar Halutz without incident. Hadassah could sense there was something wrong. There was an EU security unit permanently assigned to the central office. The EU forces were there to handle the flow of food to feed the thousands of foreign troops. The collective farms of Israel had been raided for all existing stocks. A convoy had appeared at the gates of the settlements three days before. It was the British again. The Israelis thought they had seen the last of the Brits when they hauled down the Union Jack in 1947. A very polite Lieutenant Colonel Desmond Endicott-Symes was there to loot their storehouses. Resistance was pointless. The well-stocked larder of Halutz and Degania Alef and Bet was carted off to feed an army in the south.

Hadassah thought it would be wise to stay with her Druze companions in the nearby Arab village of Samakh. It was easy to pass a message into the compound. Dov and Miriam strolled around to the village and greeted their daughter with hugs and kisses. It was hard to explain about the baby. Hadassah told her story leaving out most of the details. Miriam wept silently. Hadassah smiled and said, "his name is Samuel and he is with the Lord."

The senior Weizmanns listened carefully to Hadassah's plea for them to leave the kibbutz. Dov looked at Miriam and replied, "We know that the war is coming to Galilee once again, my daughter," the sage-like Dov Weizmann said, "but we have faced war before. We will defend our beloved farm as we have since the first spade of earth was turned here. But we cannot leave." "Father, you don't understand. You won't be able to defend the village. This time our village will be swept aside like leaves in the fall. There is a large Arab army massing on the Lebanese-Syrian frontier. There is an even larger army just east of the Tigris-Euphrates. These forces are not like that leprous Kaukji and his Iraqi rabble that attacked Israel in 1948. It is not the Syrian brigade that was stopped at our front door. These are massive armies and they have an appointment at Megiddo." "How do you know these things, my daughter?" Dov asked with unaccustomed petulance. Hadassah buried her head in her hands and prayed for grace to answer.

"Father, Mother," Hadassah said solemnly, "I am a believer in Y'shuah, the Messiah." The Weizmanns recoiled momentarily, but waited for Hadassah to continue. "I have studied the Torah and in fact, I daily study the Tenach, and I have come to the truth that Y'shuah fulfills all of the scriptures that tell us of the Anointed One whom Adonay would send. My dear parents, Y'shuah came and our people did not receive Him. He came and just like the lamb that once was on every table at Pesach, He died for our sins. He is my kipporah, Mother, Father, and I love

Him." "What does that have to do with an invasion from the north?" Dov asked impatiently. "Just this, Father, the Bible that tells us of Y'shuah, also tells us He is coming back again, but before he does there are earth-shaking events that will shortly come to pass. My Sam, who is also a believer, studies the Bible day and night. Like many other believers, he is convinced that the last battles of earth are about to be fought here." Angrily, Dov interrupted, "he must have influenced you in this way. When you met him he had no faith of his own." "You are right, Father, he had no faith of his own. Since he gave his heart to Y'shuah, he is a better Jew than any rabbi I have ever met. He now understands our people because he understands himself. From God's Word he learned he was a sinner, one who would never make it to Gan Eden. He confessed his sins to God and God saved him. God saved me too, Father, and He wants to save you."

"Get to the point about the invasion," Dov insisted, pulling away from Miriam's restraining arm. "Father, you may recall about four years ago, there were rumors that millions of people around the world had suddenly vanished." "Yes, yes, I remember," he replied. "Well, it really happened. Those people were believers in Y'shuah. Most were Gentiles, some were Jews. They went to Gan Eden. At any rate, Sam was not a believer then, but it caused him to think and to read carefully about what a goyish friend had told him of Y'shuah. It was not easy for Sam, but he studied and asked the Lord to make it clear to him and God heard his cry. Sam followed the Messiah just before we were married. He was working on the Temple Mount." "Aha, he did not share with you that he was *geschmat*, before he met you under the hupah," Dov said with a sneer. "No, he did not share with me until after we were married. But he loved me and trusted God would save me too. Well, Father, God did save me through the blood of Y'shuah, shed for me on the cross. I did not accept Y'shuah in order to please Sam Winston. I was saved because I was convicted of my own sin and I gratefully found God's salvation from my sins."

Dov seemed to relax, ready to hear about Hadassah's fears for his beloved home. "Father, General Roy of the European Union Army has taken the southern half of Israel. Our IDF is now a part of his army. Your food supply was stolen to feed foreign armies. Along with European and American armed forces, Israeli Jericho II missiles and ICBM's are poised to strike Amman, Damascus, Baghdad and Beirut. But the immediate problem is the Arab army just thirty-five miles away. These are not the Hezbollah terrorists I fought against, these are modern, well-equipped armies with their own missile capabilities. One air-to-ground missile and Halutz is history, Father. Now, the scriptures teach that this massive Muslim army to the north will be destroyed by God Himself. Not one shot will be fired by the IDF or General Roy's forces. God will destroy the northern army." Hadassah took her Hebrew Bible from her pack and read from the Hebrew text in Ezekiel 38:21-23. "God is speaking, Father,"

"And I will call for a sword against him throughout all my mountains, saith the Lord God: every man's sword shall be against his brother. And I will plead against him with pestilence and with blood; and I will rain upon him, and upon his bands, and upon the many people that are with him, an overflowing rain, and great hail-stones, fire, and brimstone. Thus will I magnify myself, and sanctify myself; and I will be known in the eyes of many nations, and they shall know that I am the Lord."

(Ezekiel 38:21-23)

"Then the Galilean settlements are safe," Dov ventured. "No, Father, our home will escape the Arabs to the north, but it will not escape a second battle. Roy is the sworn enemy of our people. He is butchering and killing Jews the world over. Did you hear what happened when he occupied Jerusalem?" "We heard, we heard," Dov said, wishing to duck an unpleasant subject. "Most of our men and some of our women will be conscripted to serve this monster on our soil. If our village survives to produce for Roy, it won't survive the Arab attack from the East. The Bible does not tell of a judgment from God on those forces. They have an appointment to meet Roy at Megiddo and the returning Jesus, just fifty kilometers from here."

"When will this come to pass?" Dov asked, much subdued. "I don't know the date, Father, but the time must be very close indeed. "We will speak more of this, Hadassah, but for now, sleep." Hadassah was exhausted. Warmed by the presence of her mother and father, Hadassah lay down on the ground to slumber peacefully.

It seemed like only minutes before an alarm sounded in Degania. Hadassah jumped up, galvanized for action as she had been all of her life. She ran into the compound, careful to avoid the British troops assembling their weapons. Endicott-Symes was grateful for the Degania self-defense force. He had secretly rearmed most of the younger men. It was dark beyond the razor-edged concertina wire, girdling the compound. Nothing could be seen on the ground. There were flashes of lightning and the growl of thunder she judged to be just over the Lebanese border. Has it started? she wondered, or is this just another terrorist move in a war of nerves? Eitan Hadas, a childhood friend of Hadassah's was the kibbutz security commander. He would be in charge tonight. "How futile this is!" Hadassah thought. We are dealing with an enemy to the north that is so strong, it will be destroyed by God Himself. To the east, an army numbering in the millions is poised to strike. Her parents were uppermost in her mind. What could Hadas do, Dov and Miriam or any of the kibbutzniks do in a situation like this?" The night passed uneventfully. A patrol returned having seen nothing. Hadassah crept back to Samakh. At dawn, Commander Hadas called for a stand-down. He offered the guess that it was anoth-er case of Arab jitters. Whenever they get excited they shoot wildly into the air, usually with casualties to their own side. Hadassah thanked the Lord for one more day with her parents.

The Weizmanns were even more resolved to stay in their home at any cost. Hadassah gave up pressing them to flee. It was better to try and make inroads on their lives spiritually. They were not hardened against the Gospel. They did not resist the testimony of Jesus Christ. It was simply a new idea never before presented to them. Dov and Miriam believed anything Hadassah was committed to must be good. Agreeably they said,"perhaps in time we will see this Jesus as you do." Hadassah extracted a promise from them that they would read her translation of **How to Recognize the Messiah.** Hadassah kissed and clung to her parents as though it might be the very last time. A real possibility, it moved her to tears. She walked out of Samakh and joined her Druze companions.

# Chapter Twenty-one
*Gospel allies*

As an occupied country, it was difficult to get any news from inside or outside of Israel. The Druze seemed to have accurate information about troop movements. The EU army was on a never-ending search for food and other supplies. A fugitive from Jerusalem told of the house arrest of the Grand Mufti of Jerusalem and the Chief Rabbis of the Sephardic and the Ashkenazic communities. The nation was shocked when General Roy had them hanged, the very worst punishment possible for a Jew and a great dishonor for a Muslim. In a show trial a number of Catholic prelates were sentenced to death, including Winston's informant, Monsignor Cormac O'Brien. O'Brien pleaded for mercy and was allowed to commit suicide. Suicide for a Catholic Winston said, is a dreaded end, but cyanide was better than the gallows and easier than the firing squad. The Pope was said to be a virtual prisoner in the Vatican. The most shocking rumor of all held that Roy had turned Mother Castaldi and her community out of their chateau on the Adriatic and expropriated it for himself as a memorial to his miracle recovery. The Antichrist's break with the One-World Church seemed to be complete.

Winston's study of the New Testament Book of Revelation pointed to a number of calamities that were about to hit the world. Things had been quiet for a time. Winston thought a lot about Ben-Zion's news that many people were turning to the Messiah Jesus, most paying for their faith with their lives. The unbelievers, he felt sure, were perhaps even more confirmed in their hardness of heart toward the Messiah. According to Revelation Chapter eight, natural catastrophes would follow swiftly. First, there would be frightening electrical storms. Lightning without rain. An earthquake felt round the world. The drought that began soon after the Rapture now gripped the most arable areas of earth.

The next round of natural catastrophes called for hail, balls of fire and blood (Revelation 8:7). Men's hearts would fail them. The sights would be spectacular, but the consequences would be grave. One-third of the trees and all green grass would be burned up. Winston thought about the scientists who for decades forecast global warming. "I'm sure they had no idea what kind of warming God had in mind."

Somewhere in the world, a mountain burning with fire would be cast into the sea. One-third of the sea would turn to blood. Perhaps blood red, Winston mused. It might be somewhat like the red tides, a poisonous wave of dead micro-organisms that for years hit the world's beaches from time to time. Highly toxic, Revelation 8:9 says that it will result in death for one-third of the world's sea creatures. Nations dependent on a marine economy will take an additional hit with one-third of the world's ships destroyed.

Winston was particularly interested in the prophecy of a star called Wormwood that would fall to earth and poison the drinking water. The Greek for Wormwood in Revelation 8:11 is *absinthos*. Winston recalled that in colonial New Orleans the most lethal drink was absinthe. It was a powerful alcoholic beverage aged in wormwood casks. The absinthe drinker ingested worms that lodged in the brain. Winston also recalled that the Russian word for Wormwood is *Chernobyl*, the place name of a tragic nuclear melt down late in the twentieth century.

According to the prophecy, one-third of the light of the sun, moon and stars would fail. This could cause a good deal of comment in scientific circles, but it will be frightening for everyone. Will man have a nagging sensation that he is dealing with an angry God?

Pain and discomfort will be at their zenith when demonic forces sting the world's inhabitants. Men will cry out for death, but death will be denied them. Suicide will be contemplated, sought after, but beyond reach. For five months, according to Revelation 9:5, the trials will have to be endured. Will men come to repentance in that time period? The silence of scripture on the matter forces the conclusion, no, no one will repent. Rather they will curse God for their trials.

Sam had come back to one passage of scripture again and again. Zechariah 13:8 states that two-thirds of Israelis would perish in the Great Tribulation. Meanwhile, Revelation 6:8 relates that one-fourth of the world's inhabitants would perish from all causes in that same dreadful period. How many had died already? Information was hard to come by, but it was clear that millions had already lost their lives.

The Mukhtar of Deir Hakim was impressed with Sam Winston. The Druze chieftain spent more and more time with his Jewish friend from another culture, another world. In the cool of the evening they walked together. One evening, it seemed the Druze chief had something it was difficult for him to share. The Mukhtar stopped and addressed Winston, "Effendi, you know that the Druze meet on Thursday evening, outside the village. We zealously guard the secrets of our faith. But we, I should say I, am very much interested in your teachings about ___how do you express it? The end-times? These images are real to you, are they not, Mr. Winston?" "Indeed, they are," Winston replied. The Mukhtar explained, "well, in Arabic we have a saying that images in dreams are a good thing, if you can bring something of value from them. Our word for it is *alam al-mithral*. On next Thursday after our services would you meet with our faithful ones? I want you to explain the curious events you say must come to pass." Winston's heart leaped. "I would be delighted to, Excellency. Indeed I would." "Let's say 2200 then, the Mukhtar proposed. Sam had to work to conceal his elation. He thought, "how good our Lord is to allow me to witness to a great people, but a people whom conventional wisdom would say are closed to the Gospel."

Sam poured out his joy to Hadasssah over the chance to speak to the Druze. Hadassah tried to enter into his excitement, but she was consumed with her parents' determination to remain in Kfar Halutz, come what may. Hadassah was teary-eyed as she related "they were no more excited about my testimony for the Messiah Jesus than they were about my going into the army." "Honey, "Sam said soothingly, "they expected you to go into the army. They did not expect their daughter to become a Christian. But consider they didn't cut you out of their will for being a believer. They did not forbid you to return home. Look at it that way. They received the news as graciously as anyone could. No one in my family greeted Simone's salvation with such grace. As far as remaining at home, you are not really surprised that a shell-burst over Lebanon could drive them out. We'll keep praying for their salvation and for their safety." Holding Hadassah close, Sam said, "you are maxed-out emotionally, honey. I read something by David just today that fits your case."

"Why art thou cast down, O my soul? and why art thou disquieted in me? hope thou in God: for I shall yet praise him for the help of his countenance."

(Psalm 42:5)

"You see, honey, the soul is comprised of your mind, emotions and will. David is challenging his mind that was in a whirl, emotions that were running on empty and a will that was probably paralyzed; unable to move him in a positive direction. He challenged all three and took an objective view. Look outside yourself to the limit-less provision of God. That's hope. Then like David you can praise God for His countenance, probably meaning God's actual presence with you." Hadassah brightened. "David was right, thou man of my life. A hot bath, a joint of lamb, some rice, honey and strong tea and I will be a model wife again."

Hadassah related how the EU army had confiscated the village food stores and weapons. "Sam the kibbutz is in real danger. If they dodge the northern invasion, how will they escape the army from the east?" Almost pleading, Hadassah asked, "how can we convince our people to flee?" "We can pray." Sam replied. "Jesus said, "men ought always to pray, and not to faint" Luke 18:1. Then we must get out the word concerning the great army that is about to descend upon our land. While you were at home, Ben-Zion of the 144,000 faithful witnesses visited me. He says that I will be used again in reaching lost people. This time it will be mainly through the printed page and wonder of wonders, through radio!" "Sam this is incredible" exclaimed Hadassah, her eyes dancing with delight. Here we are in a Druze village where no one reads or writes. As for radio, we have this ancient Philco that hisses and pops and may give up the ghost at any time. We are certainly on praying ground here, for God will have to work at least two miracles to give us a print and radio ministry."

Changing the subject, Hadassah asked, "how much time do we have, Sam?" "I hope you mean, how much time before the Messiah returns," Sam replied. "I believe Jesus will return to earth in just over two more years. The Lord has an appointment with the Antichrist and the eastern confederation at Megiddo. But first the northern confederation will be dealt with by God alone."

Winston was nervous as he followed the Mukhtar to the meeting with the Druze faithful. It was held just outside the village in a nondescript stone building Sam had thought was an enclosure for sheep. The traditional Thursday evening worship service was over. There was no Koran or even a prayer rug to be seen. Winston had a nodding acquaintance with most of the men. They sat impassively waiting to hear what the infidel had to say. The Mukhtar translated for him.

"Men of Deir Hakim," Winston began, "let me say how grateful I am for the safety you have provided my wife and me and for your gracious provision for our needs. We thank the Holy One for you and crave His richest blessings on you, your families, your homes and your flocks." There seemed to be a noticeable thaw in the reception of their infidel guest. Winston continued. "I serve Jesus, whom you recognize as one of the divine incarnations. We believe Jesus, a great prophet, has revealed what will shortly come to pass. A few kilometers to the north a massive army is waiting to pounce upon Palestine. Prophecy in the Bible of the Jews, dating back 2,000 years tells us a great army will be destroyed, not by guns in the hands of men, but by the Holy One Himself. The same Holy Writ tells us that another great army in the East will enter your land in less than two years from now. Your families will be in great danger from these fierce warriors. After they enter your land, Jesus will destroy them. He will then begin His reign as the King of Kings and Lord of Lords.

"My friends, I was a Jew who really had no religion. I was an infidel. Then I learned Jesus died for my sins. I know the Noble Koran in Chapter four says that another man died in His place, but I must tell you Jesus died for me and rose again from the dead. Very soon, I shall see Him, and so will all who believe."

Will I get out of here alive, Winston wondered. Well, these worthy men need to hear the Good News too. Winston had nothing to fear. The citation from the Noble Koran, thanks to Doctor Boyd's notes, had a salutary affect on the Druze. The Koran's statement of the substitute who died, Winston knew, was an ancient denial of the crucifixion, but the fact that Winston knew the Muslim teaching won him respect.

The Mukhtar broke the silence with "Friend Winston, we will hear you again of this matter" and it was over. Sam and Hadassah prayed that night and the next for the Lord to save the Druze. Three nights later, ear-splitting shell and rocket fire signaled the northern invasion of Israel had begun. The Arabs made a lot of noise, but hit nothing. "Allah Akbar," infantrymen cried, and leaped from their trenches on the Lebanese side of the border. Advance elements quickly drove off the Israeli and EU border detachments. And then it happened. A tremendous thundercloud, stygian black, with a red-hot core, rained molten steel down upon the tightly packed infantry-armored units. Whole formations disappeared in an instance, vaporized. Those were the fortunate ones. Others screamed in pain from the tidal wave of liquid fire miles in width and depth. Flesh melted from bones.

Abject terror at the front was matched by panic and confusion in the rear. Syrians blamed the Lebanese. Sunni's blamed Shiites. Tempers flared and delicate alliances were broken. Some lashed out in fear, some took their own lives, the easiest way out of a desperate situation. In Deir Hakim, close enough to feel the heat, everyone took cover as best they could. Animals bawled in terror. Mothers rocked screaming infants. Sam and Hadassah remained on the floor of their stone house all through the night. Flushed with a sense of the Lord's victory, Sam prayed that the Druze would be moved to trust Jesus the Great Prophet.

No one made any effort to visit the scene of the carnage for many days. Metal glowed red and white. It took no Geiger counters to understand the ground pulsed with radiation, mute testimony to the fierceness of God's judgment. No one questioned the fact that the army of the Antichrist played no part in the defeat of the northern confederation.

The Mukhtar invited Winston to the next Thursday meeting of the Druze congregation. Winston read from Ezekiel Chapter 38, verses nine to sixteen. He highlighted the statement in the text that it would take seven years to burn all the northern confederation weapons. Burying the invaders themselves would take seven months. A graveyard city would be necessary. The men of the village, passive the first time, were animated now. They were clearly moved by God's power as revealed in scripture. The destruction of the northern army left Winston impatient to produce literature pointing out what God had done to the northern army and warning of the imminent invasion from the East. It was time to implore men to turn to God in repentance and to cast themselves upon the Lord Jesus for salvation.

Winston was not surprised when Ben-Zion appeared at his door. "You must go to Haifa," Ben-Zion said, "it is time for you to resume your soul-winning operations. In Haifa, find one Baruch Yarmolinsky at Rehov Barak No.17. Tell him you are interested in buying a pair of boots. He will ask, "what size?" You will reply, "one size fits all." Yarmolinsky is a believer. He has printing facilities. He will produce the literature you may place in the hands of unbelievers. "That will take paper, ink, and some means of distribution, but most of all it will take money," Winston exclaimed; betraying his doubts about the feasibility of passing literature in an occupied country. Ben-Zion ignored the statement. "Yarmolinsky will introduce you to Dame Flora MacLeigh, a grand old lady and a believer. Yarmolinsky and MacLeigh will take care of everything."

"Brother Ben-Zion," Winston said gravely, "how can we get Hadassah's family out of Kfar Halutz?" "I cannot tell you that Samuel, but I can tell you it must be soon. As you know, the settlement is directly in the path of the eastern confederation moving to the last battle of the campaign of Armageddon." With that ominous warning, Ben-Zion was gone.

Getting to Haifa would not be easy. Israel was truly an occupied country. In the north, the hot zone of divine judgment stretched in an arc from Nahariyya on the Mediterranean coast, covered Qiryat Shemona on the Lebanese border and stretched to the long-contested Golan Heights' city of Quneitra. The only forces that dared approach the hot zone wore protective clothing, washed everything in decontaminant and hastily fled the scene. The Mediterranean coast road, the Via Maris, was firmly in the hands of an international unit of Marines from the United States, Britain, Italy and France, under the colors of the European Union. Winston would have to penetrate the Marine sector. He would also have to get beyond a defense line of EU armored units sprawled across the Israeli midsection from Hadera on the West to the Jordan River. Patrols kept a watchful eye on the roads to Haifa, Nazareth, Tiberias and Afula. Degania was visited almost daily for anything useful, until it was picked clean. Patrols then scavenged the countryside for anything else they might confiscate.

There was little news from the south. There was a great deal of propaganda. EU spin-doctors worked hard to deny that Jerusalem had been the scene of rape, robbery and murder in the occupation of the city. There were scattered rumors of Israeli guerrillas operating in Moab, Ammon and Edom. General Roy strictly prohibited any kind of ground patrolling east of the Jordan. Aerial units and global positioning satellites provided the only intelligence of the area.
The general loudly boasted that the northern confederacy had been destroyed by his preemptive strike. He gave phony facts and figures of the order of battle and the weapons that were used.

Roy's favorite propaganda bulletin was of the rebuilt Babylon. It was amazing how swiftly a European and Oriental conglomerate had put together a new global market place. Fed by vast commercial air and marine fleets, seaborne traffic was temporarily at a snail's pace due to the loss of one-third of the world's shipping in the recent oceanic catastrophes. The merchants of the new Babylon had more to watch than their bottom line. They were understandably nervous, caught between the state of siege in Israel and the sound of millions of marching men coming from the Hindu Kush mountains and beyond. General Roy bragged, "look what we did to the northern confederation. We will destroy the armies from the East in the same manner." He hinted at a new weapon, something called Red Mercury.

Hadassah was adamant. "I'm going to Haifa. You need me. I know the city. I went to the IIT, the Technion to you, for four years." She signaled the issue was settled by wrinkling her nose and folding her arms. Sam, cowed by her conviction, weakly protested. "Winston, my friend," the Mukhtar interjected, "I believe your wife is right. She would be valuable to you. In the high state of readiness of the occupiers of Palestine, you would be quickly exposed. You do not know the city and you don't speak Hebrew or Arabic."

Sam was slowly morphed into a Druze. It took several bags of tea gently applied to a very white, diaspora complexion to bring his face and hands to a proper olive hue. Winston had grown a beard during his recovery, alarmingly gray he discovered. The Druze supplied the robes. "One more detail, Effendi. You must have something to sell. A Druze without a commercial enterprise will attract the eye." The Mukhtar passed four coops of doves to Hadassah.

The Winstons walked south to Rosh Pina. Rosh Pina was the first Jewish settlement in Galilee. It had little importance in the state of siege engulfing Israel. Posters of Roy, saluting with his new marshal's baton were everywhere. A few military policemen lounged in jeeps, idling away another shift. Hadassah purchased tickets on the Arkia, the Israel Inland Airline. The Mukhtar had urged against flying, certain the airports would be closely watched. An Italian army sergeant examined their fake I.D.'s and passed them to an Israeli soldier. With a twinkle in his eye, he said in English, "they're all right they're Druze. But we must confiscate their birds." No one on the plane seemed to take much notice of the Druze couple. The Mukhtar had worked some very unpleasant odors into their robes. Passengers gave them a wide berth.

Lieutenant Danny Texeira of the IDF strolled down the airport concourse dreaming of wine and Bronya at the close of the day's tour. He noticed the Druze woman facing a mirror, combing her long black hair. Strangely, her hejab was draped around her shoulders. Do I know her? The lieutenant asked himself. Hadassah froze. Danny Texeira! We were in the same stick at airborne school. Instantly likeable, Texeira had run, studied and jumped with classmate Weizmann. "Stupid, stupid, stupid," Hadassah kept repeating. No Druze woman would ever comb her hair in public. Danny is in the EU coalition forces now. He could have recognized me.

*"Kah mah oleh cartees le Haifa?"* Hadassah asked the railway ticket agent. She paid for the tickets for the sixty-mile diesel run to the north. A helmeted U.S. Marine officer in camouflage gear slowly walked through the chair car, scrutinizing every face. He rudely yanked an Israeli from his seat and tore open the man's backpack. Out spilled two cans of army rations. "You're a thief. You are hiding contraband stolen from the armed forces." EU soldiers sold the stuff on the black market every day. The young man protested in Hebrew, but his pleas were ignored. "Take him away," the officer ordered. Two husky marines hustled the man out of the car and pushed him to the station platform. The man was dragged off to an open field next to the station. An NCO and six marines quickly formed a line and the Israeli was executed. Sam shook with rage. Hadassah pressed her hand over his and lowered her eyes. The train started off for Haifa.

Marine Lance Corporal Lee Dixon, looked closely at the wanted poster and began shading the face with a short beard. He showed the poster to the officer who had conducted the inspection. "Sir, I believe that the man on the train with the Arab robes, you know the one with the short beard, looks a whole lot like this ex-Colonel Winston they are looking for." "Nah," said the officer perusing Dixon's art work, "there is no resemblance."

Soldiers, many of them Americans, shuttled on and off at every stop to Haifa. Winston was shocked at the heavy guns and built up positions all along the route. Sam estimated Roy was just about ready for Megiddo. He would be outnumbered about fifty to one, but he had the superior armament. Hadassah wasn't interested in the military build-up. She went on and on to Sam about the towns they were passing, Apollonia, Caesarea, Atlit and the artists' village of Ein Hod. "One day, we'll come back here and tour these towns," Sam replied. Hadassah could only sigh.

From the Haifa station, the Winstons sauntered across Plumer's square to Independence Road. Hadassah found the side street, Rehov Barak and its collection of middle-eastern cafes, now deserted, that had once featured pita and shishkabobs vying for the shekels of passersby. Rehov Barak Number 17, was a down-at-the-heels storefront with a western boot over the door. Baruch Yarmolinsky was an American Jew, with twinkling eyes, olive skin and a scraggly black beard. Winston found him ensconced behind a scarred wooden counter, surrounded by Tony Lama, Acme and Nocona boots and a few dozen pairs of Levi and Wrangler jeans. Winston found it hard to place a western boot store in Israel in the hands of a man who could pass for an ultra-Orthodox Hasidic Jew. He greeted Winston warmly. "I'm looking for a pair of boots," Winston said, following Ben-Zion's security instructions. "What size?" Yarmolinsky countered. "One size fits all," said Winston. Both men collapsed in gales of laughter at Ben Zion's strange code words. Sam and Hadassah liked him at once.

Yarmolinsky was a Chicagoan. His father ran a shoe store on the legendary Maxwell Street in the windy city. The store was barely one shoe box plus four feet wide and twenty feet from the tiny display window to the backdoor.
    The Yankee entrepreneur borrowed money from his father and migrated to Israel during the Urban Cowboy western wear craze of the 1970's. Yarmolinsky tried to interest the Israelis in Tony Lama exotics with limited success. He sold a few pair to kibbutzniks who loved them. The tough sabra women went for the jeans, but sizes were difficult to come by.

If Yarmolinsky didn't look like a western boot salesman, he certainly didn't look like a computer wonk. Bruce, as he preferred to call himself, could have made his living in desk-top publishing. From his first look at a mother board, he was a captive of the technology. He scrimped and saved to buy the components for his first PC which he built from scratch.

Cheap Bible software opened up Yarmolinsky to the Word of God. For a long time, it was an intellectual pursuit, but news of the worldwide disappearance of millions of people, caused him to delve deeper into the scriptures and he was saved. His encounters with Ben-Zion led him to the next step, soul-winning. Yarmolinsky saw the Gospel in printed form as the means of piercing the rigid separatism of the Orthodox and the carelessness of the kibbutznik. He purchased piece by piece, two ancient printing presses. In a hostile world, tracts could leave a fingerprint, but were difficult to trace.

Ben-Zion had placed Yarmolinsky in touch with an unlikely ally, Dame Flora MacLeigh. A polished Scottish lady, Dame Flora was an unmarried, ageless, dowager. After World War II, as a small child, she accompanied her Grandfather to his new posting in Israel. Drummond MacLeigh was an officer in the Highland Light Infantry. Flora's mother had died in the London blitz. Her father fell in Burma fighting the Japanese. Drummond MacLeigh ignored the protests of his family and took his little granddaughter to the most troubled area in the world. MacLeigh died in the terrorist bombing of the King David Hotel in 1947. Menachem Begin, later the Prime Minister of Israel, was the prime suspect in the bombing. Flora was sent home to Scotland. Under the care of well-to-do, doting relatives Flora had the usual schooling for a young woman of the better class. She felt robbed and cheated of a daddy and a mother she could barely remember. Wandering Edinburgh's Royal Mile one Sunday afternoon she felt led to drop in on a service at the Carrubbers Close Mission. She heard the Gospel for the first time. One verse of scripture arrested her attention,

"Therefore if any man be in Christ, he is a new creature: old things are passed away; behold, all things are become new."

(2 Corinthians 5:17)

Perhaps grieving over parents lost to violence and longing for Israel, Flora made no decision that day. She wound up her affairs in Scotland and made a home for herself in the land she had sorely missed. Her palatial home caught every breeze off the blue Mediterranean. She served her adopted nation well. A volunteer in the Mogen David Adom, the Israeli Red Cross, Flora rolled bandages, served on disaster relief teams and made herself useful in the hospitals and nursing homes. Heavily taxed like all Israelis, she gave sacrificially to every cause, including Palestinian charities. Dame Flora was typically Scottish, with the trade mark sandy hair, still free of gray, and the inevitable brogue that seeped through a smile perpetually creased. She was lithe and energetic. The red sash and pin of a Dame of the British Empire was conferred upon her by the queen for her care of wounded British servicemen during the Gulf War. But it was not until the millions vanished in the Rapture that she knelt and did what should have been done years before in the Carrubbers Close Mission. At once, Dame Flora shared her Christian faith with anyone who would listen. Her favorite story was of the Duchess of Huntington, who said she was saved by an "m." The Apostle Paul wrote in First Corinthians 1:26, "for ye see your calling, brethren, how that not many wise men after the flesh, not many mighty, not many noble are called." "I am so glad," exclaimed Dame Flora" that Paul said "not many noble" rather than "not any." I was saved by an m."

The Holy Spirit put Yarmolinsky and MacLeigh, together by having them meet accidentally. On the fifth of Iyar, the Israeli Independence Day, they stood side by side at a patriotic rally. Yarmolinsky noted the obviously Gentile lady next to him carried a Bible. "Excuse me, ma'am" he asked politely in English, "what's that book you have there?" "This is the Bible, young man, God's Word to a troubled world. Do you know it?" she asked. "Hmm, I've read it some," Yarmolinsky replied coyly. "What do you find in it, ma'am? "I find that it tells the story of the coming Messiah of Israel. Here, let me give you this little leaflet, it will give you all you the essential truths about the Messiah." Yarmolinsky took the tract entitled, **"The Conversion of a Rabbi,"** by Myer Pearlman. He looked it over carefully and turned to the last page. "Well, ma'am I know everything that is in this paper." Dame Flora was satisfied this Orthodox Jew was simply making light of the message. "And how do you know?" "You see ma'am, I printed it." It was the beginning of a beautiful friendship. For a long time they never got beyond "ma'am" and "Mr.Yarmolinsky," but they had sweet fellowship in the things of the Lord. Dame Flora took time from her pressing round of charitable activities to do all the busy-work tasks in printing evangelistic literature. Distribution was the biggest problem. The Israelis were always vigilant in suppressing Christian literature. Yarmolinsky had endless contacts in every walk of life. Arab friends were the most reliable in circulating Christian tracts under the very noses of the Israeli police and now the EU army of occupation.

Bruce and Dame Flora had managed to avoid the mark of the beast. The occupation forces had registration centers in Jerusalem, Tel Aviv and Haifa. The regulations called for everyone in the western world and in Israel to be registered and tattooed. Compliance was uneven. Efforts to register Muslims, the Druze and wily people like Yarmolinsky and MacLeigh were largely unsuccessful. Unmarked Israelis were forced to buy on the black market for food and other necessities. The black market flourished despite the best efforts of Roy's organization to suppress the trade.

Yarmolinsky borrowed a sherut taxi from a friend. He dropped Hadassah off at the Technion to visit an old classmate, Tova Rudnick, now the food service director of the university. Sam was hesitant, as usual, to have them parted in a dangerous city, but he had given in to his wife a lot lately. Winston tried to be patient as Yarmolinsky negotiated the hairpin turns of the mountain road to Carmel. Gleaming white houses, cleaned and scrubbed, were the most beautiful site on the entire Mediterranean coast. High taxes kept the hoi polloi out. Dame Flora's home was second to none.

Winston was impressed with the Christian commitment of his new friends. Dame Flora would provide the funds for paper and ink and Bruce would print the tract **How to Recognize the Messiah.** Dame Flora felt it was time to move Bruce's best off-set press to the well-concealed bomb shelter in the spacious garden at the rear of her home. They would take the press apart, piece by piece, and traveling only at night, reassemble it in the deep, dry, shelter that had food, water and best of all, electric power. "The tract will reach some Jews," Winston said with satisfaction, "but what about the Muslims, the Druze and the thousands of soldiers of the occupation who are strangers to the Gospel?" Bruce excitedly told him of Dr. Jamal Aziz, a former Muslim, who came to Christ under Ben-Zion's witness. "Doctor Aziz is fluent in a score of languages. He can produce an exact translation for anything you can put on paper, Sam."

"And we have another weapon," Dame Flora said with unconcealed delight. "Excuse me and I will get something from the boot of my automobile." She shortly returned trailed by her servant, Jason, carrying two large suitcases. "I've carried these things around in my car for a couple of days. A dangerous thing to do, incidentally." Jason opened both suitcases to reveal carefully packed radio equipment. One was a line-of-sight FM set, with a range of up to thirty miles. The other was a short-wave tropical band radio, capable of a range of two to three hundred miles. Each set had a pole antenna, no piece longer than twenty-six inches in length and a coil of transmission line. A folder in each suitcase explained that these sets were introduced for use in Romania in the 1980's just before the collapse of the Communist regime. Thereafter they became staples of Christian missionary radio in nations with laws prohibiting Gospel witness.

Wide-eyed, Winston asked, "how did you come by this equipment, Dame Flora?" "I bought them from a Sergeant in the Royal North Surrey Regiment, who had confiscated them from a mission in Tel Aviv. He felt they were too valuable to destroy so he sold them to me for two hundred guineas." "Weren't you afraid he would turn you in?" "No, he hates serving in the European Union army. Besides I made him give me a receipt. He foolishly signed his name and gave me his service number."

"Sam, I've seen this equipment before. The FM antenna must be mounted on a pole or one or more circular polarized antennas, metal angles added like coat hangers to complete the suitcase equipment," Yarmolinsky explained. "In addition you need a 500 to 1,000-watt generator, a simple mixing board combining a microphone and CD or tape player. I will have all of that equipment ready for you. The AM short wave station requires two telescoping masts placed about one hundred feet apart and wired together. I will have the masts, too." Well, I've never used equipment like this, but I will learn," Winston said confidently. "I can see Hadassah broadcasting on the FM band in Hebrew and I will reach the army of the Antichrist with the short wave equipment. This is a godsend for these last days!" Bruce looked over Winston's copy of **How to Recognize the Messiah** and promised 10,000 copies in ten days. The three unlikely witnesses for Christ knelt together and prayed, none more passionately than the great lady from Edinburgh. She prayed for the courage of Christian martyrs, the wisdom of Knox and Calvin and the faithfulness of the missionaries that had gone before them. Winston dabbed at his eyes, wet with tears.

The days spent in Dame Flora's home were a welcome change from the Winstons' spartan existence in the Druze village. Hadassah, usually buoyant, was troubled. Tova Rudnick, her friend at the Technion's description of life under the occupation was a metaphor for life in Israel as a whole. The university was officially closed. The students, male and female, were conscripted for support for the army of occupation. Much of Roy's command and staff were quartered on the campus. "Sam, Tova said she has never seen our people so divided. Israelis who might want to fight against Roy must be careful what they say. Every day friends betray friends to the military police. If an EU officer arrests a Jew he is never seen again."

It was time to leave. The Mukhtar sent a truck usually employed in carrying camel dung to the farms and orchards of Carmel. Winston climbed into a hot, miserable box under the animal waste. The effluvium was something to endure. Hadassah in Druze costume, rode with the driver. Somewhere on board were the suitcases. Yarmolinsky promised to deliver the rest of the equipment over the next couple of weeks. The generator and the other parts would pass through many hands before they reached Deir Hakim.

# Chapter Twenty-two
*Fugitives*

Maurice Dupin studied the tract carefully. He sat back in his chair and tapped the leaflet against his knee. That morning, a waiter in a sidewalk cafe in Tel Aviv found **How to Recognize the Messiah** in English. A Hebrew edition was turned over to the military police in Petah Tikvah on Thursday. Dupin rolled his eyes. Copies were everywhere. Somehow, Colonel Winston was involved in producing and distributing **How to Recognize the Messiah**. How and where?

General Roy was screaming for action. The cold, unflappable Dupin had taken the blame again for the escape of Colonel Winston. Roy seemed to forget it was the Foreign Legion that had lost the man Dupin brought in from the United States. In a thirty-minute tantrum, Roy spewed forth venom that Dupin had never heard before. "Find and kill Winston, slowly, very slowly, or your own life will be on the line. No! let him see his wife die before his very eyes," Roy screamed. Dupin was sure Roy had gone over the edge. Ever since that man Ten Sing had taken up residence with Roy in the Third Temple, the General had grown daily more irrational.

Dupin looked more closely at the quality of the paper in the tracts. It was high quality stock. The Israeli police lab, usually uncooperative, disliked the message of the tract so they worked overtime to find the source of the paper supply. They found a Jerusalem merchant who said a sizeable shipment of the paper was stolen from his warehouse. He had not reported the theft, which took place he said, over a month ago. Dupin was sure he was lying. The merchant and his wife were detained for questioning. They had not made statements, but they would. The couple was in the hands of a German Army unit with extra-police powers. They looked and swaggered like the SS of World War II. This group was already responsible for excesses against the Israeli population. The unit called their operation, *Judenaktionen,* action against the Jews. It was the same ominously suggestive term their grandfathers used in the systematic murder of Jews in eastern Europe between 1940 and 1945.

Since his escape from Akko, Winston was public enemy number one. Dupin summoned the provost marshal of the EU occupation forces, Colonel Leon Torrez of the Spanish Army. Dupin knew only one fact about the Spaniard. He was ruthless. In Spain, he had risen to the top of the military police by the arrest and torture of Basque separatists, but he had failed to contain Basque ETA terrorist activities. Dupin disliked the man intensely. "What areas have you covered in searching for Winston?" Dupin demanded. "We have covered the coastal cities and plain like a blanket. We worked through the Negev carefully. I can guarantee you he is not in Jerusalem. My guess is he is no longer in Israel," Torrez replied pompously. What a dolt this man is, Dupin thought. He couldn't find a marshmallow factory if it was on fire. Dupin strode to the wall-sized map of Israel. He considered each area. He picked up a marker and drew a circle around the Lake Huleh area, north of Galilee.

"Winston is in there somewhere. Find him!" Dupin demanded. Torrez shrugged and walked out of the office.

Winston was very pleased with Yarmolinsky's printing. Thousands of copies of **How to Recognize the Messiah** were in circulation. The Hebrew edition was Hadassah's translation. A couple of thousand copies of the English version were also being passed from hand to hand, a testimony to a country that simply does not litter. Winston's Gospel tracts for Gentiles were in circulation in Arabic, French, Spanish and German the translation work of Dr. Jamal Aziz. The ex-Muslim's best work was his own article, **"Is Jesus Merely a Prophet?"**

Distribution was a major problem. The country was an armed camp. Every vehicle was subject to inspection. Every truck was carefully examined for contraband hidden in secret compartments. Not one tract was intercepted by the authorities. In one novel distribution, Yarmolinsky hired an Arab taxi driver to drive the roads of the heartland with thousands of copies of the tracts lying loose on the back seat of his taxi. The wind did the rest. The driver was rewarded with a handsome financial reward courtesy of Dame Flora MacLeigh.

Druze camel drovers were worth their weight in gold. They got into the most ultra-orthodox communities in all of Israel. They dropped stacks of Hadassah's Hebrew translation in key spots. The hunger for printed material insured the message got into the proper hands.

Winston was eager to put the suitcase radios to work. The FM set, with a line-of-sight limit of eighteen miles range would be ideal for Hadassah's Hebrew broadcast. She worked and worked to present a smooth reading of **How to Recognize the Messiah**. "Thank God for Judah Ha-Levi," she remarked to Sam. "Imagine Sam, Judah Ha-Levi had to convince life-long Yiddish speakers to give up their native tongue and learn a new language. Our Army is charged with teaching Hebrew to every Jew who comes to Israel under the Law of the Return." Sam hung his head in shame. "Do you realize, my cornflower, that I have served in Europe and in Israel and I have yet to learn any language but English?" "Yes," Hadassah said gravely, "you Americans don't bother to learn other languages and you are not really masters of your own. Don't you realize that a people's language is the sum total of their culture? For example, if you do not know Hebrew, you do not really know the Israeli people." "Honey," Sam replied, raising his hand in solemn affirmation, "I will learn Hebrew in the Kingdom Reign, although I am sure English will be the Lord's official language." "Oh, no, it won't," Hadassah said in mock scorn. "God spoke to Adam and Eve in Hebrew. I can prove it by my Hebrew Bible. Hebrew is the language of heaven."

Sam felt confident that English would be effective on the short wave transmitter. The goal was to reach EU military personnel, many of whom were conversant in the world's most important language. Sam wrote a Gospel message for Gentiles. He read it over and over again for clarity of expression and emphasis. Now, how do you broadcast in an occupied country? Very, very carefully, was Winston's conclusion.

The first on-air presentation was from a point just west of Narane in Syrian territory. The Mukhtar took the Winstons over the border under cover of night. On an outcropping of modest height, Sam set up a long pole topped by the FM antenna. He added two circular polarized antennas. The generator was in place along with a mixing board combining a CD and tape recorder. Hadassah began the first known Gospel presentation on air in Israel in the Great Tribulation. Beamed at northern Galilee to the west, the weather was perfect and the equipment was up to expectations. The Gospel bombarded the most religious communities in all the land as well as the most secularized. In fifteen minutes, the equipment was packed up and the Winstons moved south a few miles to safety under a black Bedouin tent. They watched surveillance aircraft circling their broadcast area. Winston was shocked at the speed of the EU tracking capabilities. It would have to be speak and run in order to avoid the bombing and strafing that would follow their discovery. They committed their first broadcast to the Lord and slowly moved back to Deir Hakim.

Beit Guvrin, thirty-eight miles southwest of Jerusalem was selected for the first short-wave broadcast. Winston was exhilarated by the thought of reaching all of Israel with the Gospel. The Mukhtar sent Sam south by devious routes, a trip that took two full days. A desolate wilderness area was designated by Winston's Druze guides as the safest place for the transmission. Sam decided that eight in the evening was the right time. Military units would be on stand-down and radios would be turned on in every cantonment area. "This is the Voice of Prophecy," Winston began with a head-rush of excitement. "Soldiers of the European Union and all who hear my voice, you are slaves of a mad man. General Roy is the man that the world has feared for more than two thousand years. General Roy is the Antichrist! The Antichrist fruitlessly struggles against Jesus Christ and conspires to secure His throne. Of course, he can do neither. But you soldiers of the occupation: you are in great danger. The God of all glory delivered you from the northern confederacy. You front-line troops know that you did not have to raise a rifle against the hordes from the north. You were in your hull-down positions watching in terror as God rained fire upon your enemies. You cheered and danced for joy. But now, the great army from the east is poised to strike. You won't escape this battle, nor will General Roy. But I have a message of deliverance for you. Those of you who have not received the mark it is not too late to turn to God. Tell God you know that you are a miserable sinner. Tell him you repent of your sins. The good news is that Jesus Christ came into the world to save sinners and if you will cast yourself upon Him this very day He will save you. He is coming back soon. You will meet Him on the battlefield at Megiddo. But you won't like meeting Him there. For all but those of you who trust Him as Savior, will be destroyed by the sword that proceeds out of His mouth. Give your life to Jesus today and be saved!" With that Winston closed down the net, packed up and fled for his life. Winston was unceremoniously rolled in a carpet, like so much baggage, thrown on a camel's saddle and slowly led away. A "J Star" surveillance plane flew low out of the setting sun. It was followed by a pilotless Predator drone that sent video pictures and then bombed the broadcast site.

Dupin listened to a tape of the broadcast. It was Winston all right. Roy ranted and raved. He ordered all privately-owned radios in the EU occupation army confiscated. Two men of a Portuguese army unit, heeding Winston's warning, deserted to avoid the battle. Both were executed by firing squad without a court-martial.

The Jerusalem paper merchant was tortured and his wife murdered before his very eyes. The Germans were merciless in their treatment of the aged man. He confessed to selling the paper to a Jew, who traveled in the disguise of an Arab from up north somewhere. He did not know the man's name. The merchant died of his wounds.

Bruce and Dame Flora were delighted with the success of their printing campaign. Dame Flora's radios were reaching the occupation forces. The net was closing in around them. Dame Flora insisted Bruce make the shelter his home. He countered that if he was apprehended at his shop she might escape the fury of the Antichrist if there was no direct evidence of her involvement. Dame Flora was adamant. Reluctantly, Yarmolinsky closed his boot shop and lived in the bomb shelter. The presses rolled at times that seemed safest. Dr. Aziz's work in several languages kept the word going out to the Muslims.

Ben-Zion appeared at Dame Flora's home. He warned Bruce and Dame Flora that their press was the object of an intensive search. On the bright side, he reported that all over Israel surprising numbers of Jews, Muslims and people from many nations, military and civilian, were turning to the Messiah Jesus. He added that thrilling conversions were taking place throughout the world. The 144,000 Jews were winning individuals to faith in Christ in great numbers and God was using believers like the Winston - Yarmolinsky - MacLeigh team to present the good news of salvation to a world enslaved by Satan. The human cost was high. Ben-Zion said the Antichrist and his henchmen had a very efficient system for dealing with believers. They were beheaded as soon as they were identified as Christians. Ben-Zion left, but looked back several times, as though it would be the last time he visited with Bruce and Dame Flora.

Back in Deir Hakim, Sam held Hadassah so tightly she begged to be released but he clinged all the harder. Life seemed to be a moment-by-moment thing for them. He had to hold her as though it would be for the very last time. Hadassah looked him full in the face wondering if it could be possible for her to love him more. She kissed him tenderly and whispered in his ear. "Our baby Samuel in heaven is going to have a little brother or a little sister." Sam, wide-eyed, held her at arm's length and simply beamed. "Have you nothing to say, Daddy?" she asked. "I am so proud of you darling," Sam said, drawing her to him. Sam poured out his praise to God in prayer. "Loving Father, you have opened the womb again for the conception of another Jewish life to glorify your name. Thank you for this baby. For our part, we covenant together to raise this child to your glory, to see this little one serve you all of his or her days. Grant O Lord, that we may be the parents that you would have us to be. In the name of the Messiah Jesus and for His glory. *Omen and Omen.*

Winston had to plan for additional radio broadcasts. He had long serious talks with the Mukhtar as they scanned the map of Israel for possible transmission sites. A site had to be remote, easily reached and most of all, easy to flee. Army signals trucks with triangulation equipment were prowling all interior roads of Israel. Overhead, aircraft with even more sophisticated equipment could pinpoint a radio broadcast in minutes. Global positioning satellites roamed the skies. Jamming was also a problem. In a couple of minutes of air time, the message had to be delivered and the net closed down. Winston thanked the Mukhtar for the Druze who made the broadcasts possible and who risked their lives in a cause that was not their own. "But you are wrong, Friend Winston, it is our cause. This land groans under the heel of this oppressor Roy, the one you call the Antichrist. Your fight is our fight. More important, I now know that your Jesus is not merely the prophet, honored by Islam, but the very Son of God, come to save us from our sins."

Winston was wild with excitement. "Do you know Jesus as Savior, Excellency?" "Yes, I know Him," the Mukhtar said with conviction. "And many of our people now believe." Winston wept openly, embraced his Druze friend and offered thanks to God. In one day, Winston learned Hadassah was expecting a physical birth and in the same day learned of the Mukhtar's spiritual rebirth. What a day!

"I've got it," Winston said, snapping his fingers, "I'm going to take the radios into Lebanon. No one in Roy's army has crossed the hot zone from Nahariya to Quneitra since the Lord's defeat of the northern confederacy. "It might work," the Mukhtar cried, there are thousands of Druze there. I believe if you go east to Mishmar Hayarden, then north avoiding Banias, you could slip into Lebanon at Metula." "That's the last Israeli settlement." Hadassah added with alarm, "what about the radiation barrier?" "Honey, I believe much of the so-called hot zone has little radiation hazard. The confederacy' ineffective demonstration was with "dirty bombs," shells tipped with low-yield uranium, but remember they didn't do much shelling. The EU army would have automatically assumed there was a hazard and ordered the zone off limits. I believe the Lord will take me through it." "Where do you get that "me," big guy, Hadassah said tersely, "I'm with you." Winston shrugged in resignation.

It was a hot, uncomfortable day for three EU strike forces operating in northern Israel. A team of British Royal Marines moved on Haifa. They were tasked with finding the printing presses that were grinding out Gospel literature. The merchant who died under torture gave only the information that the paper was carried up north. Dupin reasoned that only a fairly populous center would have the equipment for producing tracts. Tel Aviv turned up nothing. Haifa was next. In a house-to-house search, Sergeant-Major Reggie Hook of His Majesty's Royal Marines, led a squad up the driveway, past flower-beds in a riot of colors and well-manicured lawns, to the front door of the MacLeigh home. A butler resisted their entry with a simple, "Madame is not at home." Hook pushed past the butler, as Dame Flora descended the stairs. Hook snapped to attention and saluted, when he saw the red sash and badge. "Pardon this intrusion, your ladyship, but I am on His Majesty's service and I must subject your home to a brief search." Dame Flora smiled reassuringly. "Sergeant-Major, the Royal Marines are always welcome in this home. Conduct your search." "Thank you, your ladyship," Hook replied and saluted once again.

Hook felt sure no Briton wearing Royal Honours would be guilty of printing illicit materials. Hook didn't care for the EU alliance, but he had long ago surrendered personal feelings to the service of the crown. He wasn't just a marine, like, say the Americans, he was a Royal Marine. Hook was troubled by reports of unrest in England over the tyrannical rule of General Roy and the high cost of the European Union. What did that terrorist on radio call the general? "the Antichrist?"

It was a very cursory search. Hook opened the door of the summer house, peeked around without entering and closed the door. On the garden walk, he slipped on some kind of black liquid. It looked like ink. Printer's ink? Hook used the land rover radio to call the task force commander. In no time, red-hat British army military policemen had verified that the liquid was printer's ink. They covered the grounds carefully until they found the bomb shelter, and Yarmolinsky's press. Bruce was gone, delivering Dr. Aziz's literature to an Arab contact. The military police took samples of literature and informed Dame Flora of her arrest. She went quietly, silent about any knowledge of printing and distributing tracts.

Colonel Leon Torrez was irritated with the hot weather and Dupin's insistence that Winston must be hiding in the Lake Huleh district, north of Galilee. Arab and Druze towns without number, many not shown on any map, were searched. Torrez was sure Winston was nowhere around. He had his men ransack homes looking for anything worth stealing. He personally humiliated two young Muslim women by tearing away their burkas and exposing their bodies to the lecherous cries of his men. Late in the day, he directed Major Pietro De Luca to lead a platoon of Italians to a spot on the map. "What's it called? oh yes, Deir Hakim. The main column will bivouac in Rosh Pina tonight. Report to me when you return."

De Luca led two truckloads of Bersaglieri to Deir Hakim. A bare ten miles north of Rosh Pina, Deir Hakim was dazzling in the sunlight off the white stone buildings. No one was in sight as the convoy rolled slowly into the town. De Luca ordered a house-by-house search. He casually smoked a cigarette, leaning on the door of his vehicle. There was a shout from Teniente Piro and De Luca ran to the sound. His men had guns trained on Colonel Winston and the woman De Luca remembered as an Israeli officer. "Well, mon coronello, we meet again, but not under the most pleasant circumstances. You are under arrest, charged with treason and sedition. The lady," he swept a Latin bow to Hadassah, "must accompany us as well." De Luca turned to go and found his unit completely surrounded by what he took to be armed Arabs. Menaced by numbers and firepower, De Luca shrugged and unbuckled his revolver belt. Without command, his men laid down their arms.

Winston thanked the Mukhtar and directed De Luca to load his men and go. "Buono fortuna," De Luca yelled as his column left Deir Hakim. "You must go, quickly, friend Winston," the Mukhtar said urgently. "They will send aircraft and ground units as soon as he reports. They will not expect you to head south. Follow the west bank of the Jordan past Rosh Pina. Stay on the west bank. Thirty kilometers south, cross the Jordan to Waqqas. Ask there for the home of Jabal Akim. Tell him the camel is about to foal. He will keep you safe. I will see to it your suitcase radios arrive safely in Waqqas."

Dressed as a Druze, Winston walked ahead, Hadassah a few meters behind, carrying all of their necessities. She complained loudly. Winston, mocking the Druze culture replied, "quiet woman, or I shall have to beat you twice this day." It was the end of mirth, for Winston spotted a formation of eight planes in a vee, diving to attack Deir Hakim. Rockets, bombs and napalm quickly put an end to the simple home and the people they had come to love. It was surprising to Winston the EU made no effort to interrogate the Druze in order to learn the Winstons escape plans. Probably, the army knew the Druze would never tell. Was the Mukhtar and his people now with the Lord?

It was tense passing Rosh Pina, the bivouac of Torrez's task force. No one suspected the Druze couple trudging slowly along the road south. In a passing truck, a soldier laughed at the Druze woman carrying all of the baggage as her man strolled ahead of her with nothing in his hand. Hadassah responded as a Druze woman would with an ugly expression and spitting through her teeth. Sam felt they were much more conspicuous walking south along the Jordan, but they made it without incident. They went on to a point east of Moledet. Hadassah yearned to go to Halutz, mere minutes away. They crossed the Jordan, now at low ebb, and found their way into Waqqas. The Druze, Jabal Akim, welcomed them and put his exhausted guests to bed on pallets of straw.

British EU expeditionary forces in Israel were not quite sure how to handle a capital prisoner who was a Dame of the British Empire. Captain Jeffrey Smollett of the British Military Police treated her cordially, saw to it that she had plenty of tea and even offered her his own quarters. The English were convinced Dame Flora would spend little or no time in confinement. Somehow they had to take her statement, but that could wait. Smollett telephoned his headquarters in Tel Aviv. They informed Dupin in Jerusalem of her arrest. At his end, Dupin had to quell a demand from the German military police, who demanded the right to interrogate the English woman.

"We will take it to General Roy," the Germans protested. Dupin quietly reminded them he was Roy's chief of security. "I will handle the matter," he said firmly.

Bruce Yarmolinsky was never a suspect, until an Arab informant for a few Israeli lirot, gave the authorities a description of a man who hired him to distribute tracts. From his description, two British military policemen forced entry into the closed boot shop and took Yarmolinsky into custody. He went cheerfully, the ink under his nails all the evidence they needed against him. He could see Dame Flora in the office of Captain Smollett. Two burly policemen shoved him into a small cell and began the interrogation. "Who did you work with? For whom did you produce this literature? they demanded. "I worked for the Lord and I produced the material for Him," Yarmolinsky announced proudly. That earned him a fist in an ear. "What part did Dame Flora play in the sedition?" they demanded. "All of the dames I ever knew were from the south side of Chicago," Bruce said with a laugh. They hit him hard for that one. "We've got enough to send you to the wall," the policemen said and with that they left Yarmolinsky to contemplate his fate.

Colonel Torrez, smarting under Dupin's correct guess that Winston was hiding in the Lake Huleh region and Major De Luca's retreat from Deir Hakim without arms, the Colonel determined to wreak vengeance on his secondary assignment, the apprehension of Hadassah Weizmann's Kfar Halutz family. He personally led a column into Halutz and then into Degania A and B. Lieutenant Colonel Desmond Endicott-Symes of the British Army, responsible to keep food flowing from Degania to the occupation forces, raised no objection to Torrez's search for the Weizmann's. Dov, Miriam and Hadassah's brother could not be found. Torrez called for all the kibbutzniks in the area to be assembled at the Degania Alef parking lot. The Israelis endured Torrez's venomous attack on them as Christ-killers, who deserved death as vermin unworthy of life. Torrez slapped a riding crop against his elegant cavalry boots. "Who will step forward and tell me where the arch-criminals Dov and Miriam Weizmann are hiding?" There was a stir, as though the men were tempted to rush the guards, but no one spoke. "All right, I tried to treat you like decent people, but of course no Jew is a decent person. I will pass among you and I will make a selection."

Torrez used his riding crop to tell off every fifth person, without regard to age or gender. In all forty people were selected. Seventeen men, twelve women and eleven children, some as young as five, were marched to the bank of the Jordan River. Some mothers pleaded to take the place of their children, but were driven off with curses and kicks. Colonel Endicott-Symes protested vehemently.   The prisoners, bravely singing HaTikvah, the Israeli national anthem, were  mowed down. Obviously enjoying the scene, Torrez gave the coup de grace to any that quivered. "Dump their bodies in the river. Perhaps the sight of dead Jews will serve as a warning to others of this cursed race. Praised be Santa Ysabel," he said,and crossed himself.

After a second interrogation, Yarmolinsky was brought into the office where Dame Flora patiently sipped a cup of cold tea. "Cheers, Bruce," she said, but Yarmolinsky determined to keep up the ruse, said, "my name is Baruch, Madame." One of the English officers, an Army judge advocate, looked up from his brief and said, "do you still maintain that you do not know this woman." "That's right, sir. I don't talk to shiksas, particularly old, ugly ones." "Watch your tongue," the prosecutor warned. "Why not give up the deception. You are co-conspirators. If convicted you will die together." Dame Flora broke the ice. "Bruce, they are determined to do for us. I'm grateful we fell into the hands of British soldiers, but it won't make any difference in the end. The Antichrist is determined to get us, so let's go out like Christians. What do you say old chum?" The prosecutor rose from his seat and admonished Dame Flora sternly that General Roy was not to be spoken of as the Antichrist. "How do you know I consider General Roy to be the Antichrist? I never linked their names together." The prosecutor sat down in embarrassment. Yarmolinsky broke into smiles and said, "you're far from old and ugly, Dame Flora, and you were never more beautiful than you are right now. A real berrieh!" "What's a berrieh, Bruce," she asked. "That's Yiddish, my dear, for a woman of competence, a lady who gets things done. That's you, partner." Turning to the prosecutor he said triumphantly, "we did it. We two turned out the literature that has flooded the country. There is truth blowing on every wind in Israel. People are being touched for Jesus the Messiah. Yes, we did it."

Alone in adjoining cells, the doughty Scot and the Chicago boot salesman anticipated their demise with a serenity only Christ could convey. It suddenly occurred to Bruce to ask, "Dame Flora, would you do me the honor of becoming my wife before we meet the Lord?" She thought for a moment and replied, "Mr. Yarmolinsky, I accept your troth with honor, sir. I would be proud to be your wife" Elated, Yarmolinsky called for the guard to summon a British officer. "Sir, my fiancee, Dame Flora MacLeigh, and I would like to be joined in holy matrimony. Would you please summon the chaplain of your regiment and ask him to perform the service?" "Uhh," the officer stammered, "there are no more chaplains in the EU army. Religious services, including marriage, are forbidden. I'm sorry."

The only question remaining about Yarmolinsky and MacLeigh was the method of their death. "Behead them," the Antichrist demanded. At great personal risk, the British Expeditionary Force commander refused. Dame Flora was a British citizen and Britain had no capital punishment. Yarmolinsky had dual citizenship, but was a resident of Israel which also has no capital punishment. Ten Sing, on behalf of his master, fumed and cursed, but the British were adamant. No decapitation. Nonetheless, the duo were not to be given any kind of trial. They were marched to a wall the next morning at 0500 hours. Sergeant Major Hook, under the most unpleasant order he had ever received, commanded a firing squad of sixteen marines. Hook requested Dame Flora to remove her sash and badge for it would be bad form for other ranks to fire on Royal Honours. Dame Flora refused. Yarmolinsky asked if they could join hands. Hook looked away to the officer on parade, Brigadier Owens, who silently nodded. The beaming couple joined hands and looked at one another. The marksmen were true. Baruch Yarmolinsky and Flora MacLeigh were in the presence of the Lord.

"And I heard a voice from heaven saying unto me, Write, Blessed are the dead which die in the Lord from henceforth: Yea, saith the Spirit,      that they may rest from their labors, and their works do follow them."

(Revelation 14:13)

# Chapter Twenty-three
## *The Desert*

The sun was well up when Hadassah rubbed her eyes. She rubbed them again to be sure it was really her parents who were peering down at her. She hugged them, wept happy tears and dashed off to find Sam to share the good new that her folks were safe. Two nights earlier, Ari Avigdor had crept into Halutz from the Jordan with a couple of his men. He easily avoided the British requisition unit and found his way to the Weizmann's home. Come with me," he urged, "Hadassah and Sam are hunted as traitors. You are certainly on a watch list. It is only a matter of time before General Roy has you arrested." Dov and Miriam looked at one another, packed a few personal effects and left their home. They would not have gone if they had known that within hours Colonel Torrez would slaughter loved ones and friends.

The Waqqas Druze were kind, hospitable people. Sam and Hadassah felt the safety they had known in Deir Hakim. With the senior Weizmanns safe and Captain Avigdor and his men for security, Winston was eager to resume broadcasts from Lebanon. Somehow, the Mukhtar of Deir Hakim had managed to dispatch a camel and driver with the suitcase radios, minutes before the aerial attack on the village. The driver simply shrugged when asked about the fate of the Deir Hakim Druze.

"I don't believe we can remain for long in Waqqas," Avigdor opined. "We are too close to eastern coalition forces. I have a base of operations farther south that should take us out of their probable area of operations. I have two Land Rovers and an old American LTV. It is 150 kilometers. We will travel at night." Sam thought of his cherished dreams for broadcasting from Lebanon. "You're in charge, Ari, we'll follow," Sam replied, "all I want is a place to resume radio broadcasts."

It rained for two days. Avigdor thought it was dangerous to start the drive south in bad weather. Traveling at night, the chances of getting lost or separated were too great. Sam felt it wise to use the time to handle the serious spiritual questions posed by Dov, Miriam and occasionally by Ari Avigdor. In Doctor Boyd's study in Crescent, Sam had asked himself the tough questions concerning the Jews and Jesus. Lingering over coffee, Sam related what he had learned about the age-old issues that have confronted the Jewish people.

Sam began modestly. "I don't have all of the answers," he confessed, "I don't even know all of the questions. Hadassah, please translate for me where necessary." "A few years ago at home in America, I attended an elementary school graduation. There was a sprinkling of Jewish children in the class. I'll call one of them Sammy Waldman. He walked off with the top honors, including a $500. prize for his science project. Amy Bronstein took the district spelling bee trophy. Oh," Sam paused, "you probably never heard of a 'spelling bee.' In the United States year after year students compete in spelling the most difficult words in our language."

"Students named Levine, Grossman and Shapiro were recognized for achieving the top one percent of all students in mathematics. It was a great day for great Jewish kids. But you know, I could not help thinking that fifty years earlier in Nazi-occupied Europe, bright Jewish youngsters with the same sounding names, were murdered simply because they were Jewish. This is the focus of our problem.

"I believe," Sam continued, "I will start with the responsibility of Christian churches for the blood-soaked history of our people. A Jewish philosopher, Dagobert Runes in his important book "The War Against the Jew," wrote, "For all the two thousand years there was no act of war against the Jews in which the church did not play an intrinsic part." He documented this statement by pointing out the systematic oppression, expulsion and periods of annihilation of the Jews of England, France, Spain, Portugal, Germany and later, Poland, Russia and the Baltic States. Cross-wearing, cross-bearing Christians, were usually the initiators of pogroms and the murder of Jews. To this day, the symbol of the cross evokes the bitterest of memories for our people. What these Christians did to us, was often the product of what the churches taught.

A Holocaust survivor, Jules Isaac, a French Jew, complained to Pope John XXIII that the centuries of Jewish misery were the fruits of New Testament teachings. The New Testament is the book of the Christians. Isaac pointed out thirty-two places in the Gospel of John that were, in his view, antisemitic statements. The human author, John, was a Jew. The pope gave Isaac a sympathetic hearing and promised to direct the Roman Catholic Church in a reexamination of their treatment of the Jews. He delivered on his promise on Good Friday, 1963. For centuries, the Good Friday mass closed with a curse on our people as Christ-killers. In that Good Friday mass, as the priest-celebrant prepared to curse the Jews Pope John interrupted and on his authority as head of the church, put an end to the curse forever. It was an important step. History reflects that throughout the centuries, the Catholic faithful, forced to fast all day on Good Friday would rush out of their churches to attack the Jews. Murder, rape, pillage, theft, followed all because the malevolent crowds were told the Jews were responsible for their fast day discomfort."

"Well," Sam said reflectively, "was Jules Isaac right? He was right about the churches teaching hatred of the Jews and inciting, sanctioning and condoning murder of our people. But was he right about the New Testament, an essential part of Christian faith, teaching hatred of the Chosen People? Let me say, that as a first consideration, the so-called Christian churches of Europe, notably the Roman Catholic, Eastern Orthodox, and the Anglican, did not base their faith on the New Testament at all. They all claimed the New Testament as their own. They even sought to prove their existence from its pages, but they were and are to this day a living denial of its truths. You can be a Roman Catholic, a Greek or Russian Orthodox communicant or an Anglican and never, never open the New Testament. The Lutherans were a special case. They broke with Romanism over the truths of the New Testament. Martin Luther charged the religion he was born to with departure from New Testament teaching and left the Roman church forever. But Luther was unreformed in his hatred of the Jews. In his tract Shem Hamphoresh, (1544), Luther referred to the Jews as ritual murderers and poisoners of wells. He demanded the burning of all their synagogues and talmuds. Luther's devotion to New Testament truth did not pass to succeeding generations, but his antisemitism did.

We answer Jules Isaac's charge that the Gospel of John is an antisemitic document with the rejoinder that every statement he finds objectionable was aimed at the religious authorities who were disloyal to the laws of Moses and who harshly opposed the person and work of Jesus. Jules Isaac needed to take greater note of the people whom Jesus loved and healed, His own Jewish people who received kindness at His hand. My friends, there were Europeans in the Middle Ages who loved Jesus and the Bible, who were hunted and murdered as ruthlessly as the Jews. The four great churches of Europe had no love for the Bible, the people who loved the Bible and the people of the Bible, the children of Israel. I believe that the man who loves Jesus, the Bible, yes, including the Gospel of John, could never be antisemitic.

Now, let's consider what the New Testament teaches about the responsibility for the death of Jesus. An early follower of Jesus, Peter a Jew of Galilee, has a statement in the New Testament. He said,

"For of a truth against thy holy child Jesus, whom thou hast anointed, both Herod, and Pontius Pilate, with the Gentiles, and the people of Israel, were gathered together, For to do whatsoever thy hand and thy counsel determined before to be done."

(Acts 4:27-28)

Herod was the puppet ruler of Israel. Pilate was the Roman occupation governor. Peter is charging them with complicity in the murder of Jesus. Guilt is also shared by the children of Israel who cried out for the crucifixion of Jesus. The Gentiles are also guilty for they ignorantly allowed the death of an innocent man. But Peter goes on to say that all of these guilty human beings were only able to carry out what God permitted. If Jesus were here today, man would slay Him if they could. But wonder of wonders, His death is the very means of our salvation. Like the lambs slain at Pesach, Jesus is the Lamb of God which takes away the sin of the world. It seems to me, friends, that no one is free of guilt of the death of Jesus, and no one should want to be acquitted of His death, for that would make salvation unattainable. Efforts to fix the charge of deicide, the theological term used for the death of God (Jesus), has been a consuming study for centuries. In recent times, apologists have sought to acquit the Jews of the charge. A follower of Jesus, Paul a former rabbi and a believer, had this to say,

"For ye, brethren, became followers of the churches of God which in Judea are in Christ Jesus: for ye also have suffered like things of your own countrymen, even as they have of the Jews: Who both killed the Lord Jesus, and their own prophets, and have persecuted us; and they please not God, and are contrary to all men."

(1 Thessalonians 2:14-15)

Does this seem to lay all the responsibility on the Jews? I think not. Note, that Paul says the slayers were the children of those who had slain the prophets of God in earlier times. Their children were persecuting the Jew Paul, and acting in ways at odds with the Torah and the good order of Jewish life. Sadly, some of Jesus' followers in the second Christian century overlooked Peter's wider indictment and poured out their venom on the Jews as Christ-killers. For this reason, antisemitism became ingrained in the religious teachings of churches that forgot Jesus was a Jew. This egregious sin was compounded by another error. The Roman Catholic church teaches that the communion wafer, under the consecration of the priest, becomes the actual, body, blood, soul and divinity of Jesus the Messiah. Mostly uneducated, the Catholics of the Middle Ages swallowed the ridiculous story that Jews at every opportunity stole the wafer and then pierced it with nails or cut it up to make Jesus bleed and die again!

A second widely held belief was that Jews plotted to kidnap and kill a Catholic child in order to mix their blood with the matzo of the Passover feast. Ignorant of the fact that our people abominate blood in any form, as recently as 1946 in Kielce, Poland, Catholics attacked the few pitiful survivors of the Holocaust on the strength of this rumor.

As Jews, we insist that our people have done nothing wrong, including implication in the death of Jesus, to deserve the hatred of the world.

"To continue our study," Winston went on, "I believe that our people somehow lost the way to God. I ask, did our forefathers depart from the faith of Abraham, Isaac and Jacob? In the few years Jesus walked among men, the most telling charge He ever leveled, was against the religious rulers of Israel. In the Gospel of Matthew, Chapter 22, verse 29, Jesus said:

"Ye do err, not knowing the scriptures, nor the power of God."

Notice the import of the charge. The people of the Book, more than that the divinely appointed teachers of the Book, no longer knew the Bible! Note also, Jesus said they did not know God's power. We were a nation of miracles, but we had lost the mystery of the miraculous. When the miracle-worker Jesus healed the sick and raised the dead, we refused His gracious invitation to follow Him. But some of our people did follow Him. A few days before His death, Jesus told His followers,

"And when ye shall see Jerusalem compassed with armies, then know that the desolation thereof is nigh. Then let them which are in Judah flee to the mountains; and let them which are in the midst of it depart out; and let not them that are in the countries enter thereinto."

(Luke 21:20-21)

My friends, Jesus' siege prophecy took place less than forty years later. As you know *Yerushalayim shel Zahav*, Jerusalem of Gold, was taken and destroyed by the Romans in 70 A.D. According to Margolis and Marx, Jewish historians, in their book "History of the Jewish People," writing of the siege, said, "The Nazarenes, that is those who accepted Jesus of Nazareth as the Messiah, indifferent to the national cause, sought safety in flight from Jerusalem. The small community settled in Pella beyond the Jordan." Winston turned to Captain Avigdor, "I believe, Captain, Pella is only about eighteen kilometers south of where we are right now." Avigdor nodded in agreement. "In my opinion," Winston offered, "the rejection of the Messiah Jesus and the destruction of the temple in 70 A.D. signified that Adonay was finished with the sacrifice of animals under the Mosaic code. God was only satisfied with the sacrifice of Jesus, the Lamb of God without spot or blemish, who made one sacrifice for sin forever by the offering of Himself. He was the kipporah for every man.

I further believe that our forefathers ratified the end of animal sacrifice, by instituting the bloodless Judaism practiced to this day. You may know the fascinating story of Rabbi Johannan Ben Zakkai. In the siege of Jerusalem, Ben Zakkai realized the temple would be destroyed. The legend says that he had his disciples place him in a coffin and carry him through the siege lines. Stunned, Jewish defenders and assaulting Romans, allowed the funeral cortege to pass unmolested. At the tent of the Roman general, Ben Zakkai jumped out of the coffin and prophesied the general would one day be the emperor. Flattered, the general gave permission for the establishment of a new Judaism at Jabneh, near the Mediterranean coast. Ben Zakkai took Hosea 6:6 as the authority for a bloodless faith.

"For I desired mercy, and not sacrifice; and the knowledge of God more than burnt offerings."

(Hosea 6:6)

"A single verse taken out of context, became the pretext for what is now the heart of Judaism. How sad our people did not choose verse three of that sixth chapter of Hosea:

"Then shall we know, if we follow on to know the Lord: his going forth is prepared as the morning; and he shall come unto us as the rain, as the latter and former rain unto the earth."

(Hosea 6:3)

"Following on to know the Lord," to understand Y'shuah was God come in the flesh could have established our people in the faith of Abraham.

The destruction of the commonwealth of Israel in 70 A.D. and again in 135 A.D. resulted in a glut of Jewish slaves on the slave markets of the Mediterranean basin. Jews were too smart to waste on salt mines. They wound up in homes and palaces as the highly intelligent, trusted servants that influenced European life and culture for centuries to come. The emerging city-states of Western Europe, the merchant class, the crafts, healing arts and civil service were ideal for the highly literate Jews. Tragically, bogus Christianity, that we have already discussed, had a Jew-hating core and so our people groaned under civil oppression and limitations imposed on no other people. Periodically, Jews were massacred. Philosopher Runes says three and one half million of our people died at the hands of church-inspired atrocities. The church had a problem it never resolved. Claiming to be the one, true church of Jesus Christ on earth, they felt the Chosen People should have recognized them as such. The Jews ignored the claims. This angered the prelacy, to whom it seemed just to exterminate the Jews. But the church knew that if they murdered all the Jews history would record the church could not win the Jews so it slew them. Jews were often challenged to answer charges of deicide and other sticky questions. Our people learned the technique of the non-answer. They learned to reply without directly answering the charges. It spared many Jewish communities.

Despite the pressures of life in a hostile culture, *HaTikvah*, the Hope, remained alive in the hearts of the people of the wandering foot. In ghettoes and shtetls, "next year in Jerusalem," was a cherished dream of a persecuted people. "My family," Winston observed, " began its known history in Germany. German Jews in the eighteenth, nineteenth and early twentieth century, systematically worked their way through, ACCOMMODATION, ASSIMILATION and ultimately, ANNIHILATION. My Grandfather never identified himself as a Jew to a Gentile circle of acquaintances. He was a "German of the Mosaic persuasion." Jews like my Grandfather, many entitled to wear the Iron Cross for heroism in the service of the Kaiser, died in Nazi prison camps along with the Orthodox and the most ardent of Zionists. The Holocaust opened up new questions for our people. At some point, every Jew asks, "where was God when the six million were slaughtered?" No answer is satifying. Years ago, I read the book "Pursued" by Holocaust survivor, Dr Vera Schlamm. A believer in the Messiah Jesus, Dr. Schlamm offered the suggestion that the words of Zechariah 1:15 may apply. God said:

"And I am very sore displeased with the heathen [Gentiles] that are at ease: for I was but a little displeased [with the Jews], and they [the Gentiles] helped forward [exceeded] the affliction."

(Zechariah 1:15)

Dr. Schlamm is saying that God had some form of discipline in mind for the Jews, but that He never sanctioned the inhumane excesses of the Holocaust.

Winston felt it was time to rest his case. He was astonished at the amount of material he had presented and felt more than a little sheepish about it. He turned to Hadassah and asked, "how much did they get, Honey?" She queried Dov, Miriam and Ari in Hebrew and turned to report that they understood ninety percent of what he had to say. Sam groaned. "The devil is always in the details or in the most important ten percent of a message." Dov was restive. "Samele, my son, why do the *goyim* hate me?" Dov said with emphasis. Sam weighed his answer carefully. "The Devil, the Antichrist and the antisemite cannot hurt God. They crucified Jesus, but he rose from the dead and is alive and out of their reach in heaven today. They have tried everything to stamp out the Word of God. They cannot do it. At the moment, they occupy Israel, but shortly their hold will be broken. The only way then that they can get back at God is to strike at the Jews, at you my father. I am thoroughly convinced every act against the Jew is an act against the God they cannot hurt. One day soon they will have to answer to God for their hatred of Him and their treatment of you. The good news is that the children of Israel will shortly come into the kingdom promised to our Fathers. Satan knows his time is short. He will do everything possible to seize the throne of God before it is too late. It cannot be done, but he will try."

Winston turned to his notes once again. "I would like to cover one more point before your eyes glaze over." "Eyes? Glaze over?" The circle of Israelis looked puzzled. Hadassah thought for a moment and then told them in Hebrew it was an American expression for putting someone to sleep with a boring message. They smiled knowingly.

"When you look at the history of the dreadful sufferings of our people, you find tribulation followed by blessing. Let me illustrate. When our people were freed from slavery in Egypt, in the succeeding generations our people received the Bible from God's hand. The remnant returned from the Babylonian Captivity and the next great event was the birth, the miracle-working life, the death and resurrection of the Messiah Jesus. Following the Holocaust, Israel was reborn. Now, when the Great Tribulation draws to a close, the Kingdom of the Messiah will be established here in *Eretz Yisroel.*

Ari Avigdor circled the room deep in thought. He turned suddenly and confronted Winston. "Colonel, Israel after five successful wars, is now an occupied country. Our people are being murdered and more will die. I am now a follower of the Messiah, but I find it hard to believe the Messiah will come any time soon to put an end to the rule of the Antichrist."

"Captain, I have felt the same uncertainty," Winston replied. "As a first consideration, all of the answers about these desperate days are contained in the Word of

God. I have seen so many prophecies fulfilled in the last six years, I now have no doubt that every prophecy of the Bible will be fulfilled to the letter. Let's begin with the question of who is in charge during these dark days. The book of Revelation tells us:

"And the kings of the earth, and the great men, and the rich men, and the chief captains, and the mighty men, and every bondman, and every free man, hid themselves in the dens and in the rocks of the mountains; And said to the mountains and rocks, 'Fall on us, and hide us from the face of him that sitteth on the throne, and from the wrath of the Lamb; For the great day of his wrath is come; and who shall be able to stand?'"

(Revelation 6:15-17)

A terrified world seems to be under Satanic attack at every hand. But notice there is agreement among the rulers of the world, rank unbelievers that the Lamb, the Messiah is in charge! The commercial interests, the armed forces and the working class realize that the Messiah Jesus is really the one to fear. They say, "the great day of His wrath is come." They add, "who can stand up to Him?" Captain, these are days of almost daily fulfillment of Bible prophecy. I'm going along with the assurance that God is working this out for His glory. I read the Bible now as a travel guide to the Kingdom. We are now months, not more than a year away, from the day the Messiah returns. I am glad you trusted the Messiah" Quietly turning to the Dov and Miriam, Sam asked "are you ready to meet Him?" Neither replied, but they were thinking.

Ari broke the silence. "Colonel, we cannot remain in Waqqas. Roy's patrols are active on the West Bank. If they suspect that you are here, they will cross the Jordan. We must move south tonight."

# Chapter Twenty-four
*Passover*

Hadassah was sick. Sam was ashamed that he had nearly forgotten that she was pregnant. The trip south was an ordeal neither would forget. They started out in the Humvee, but it was just too rough for an expectant mother. Transfer to a Land Rover was a modest improvement, but every bump in the ancient road, once traveled by Jesus and his followers, was too much for Mrs. Winston. Avigdor was at pains to get to his wilderness headquarters before dawn. That left little time for retching. Is Hadassah dying? Sam thought. Is she going to lose this baby? It was a good thing her mother, Miriam, was along. She understood these things. She reassured Sam that this was just part of bearing a child. Sam felt that Hadassah needed to eat something. He offered her an M.R.E. Meals Ready to Eat was a U.S. Defense Department blessing left over from the millions produced for the Gulf War, Afghanistan and Iraq. The U.S. forced the surplus MRE's on the Israelis in the military aid package. Avigdor had liberated a generous supply when he decided to continue the fight against the EU. Some of the MRE menu items were *treyf* for Jews, meats or dairy food in forbidden combinations. The fifty men in Avigdor's command ate them anyway. An MRE was the last thing Hadassah wanted. She couldn't even handle water. The very suggestion of food put her into another round of gut-wrenching spasms. For miles they rode with Sam holding her over the side of the Land Rover by her belt. They arrived at sunup, exhausted from the ride.

Avigdor's "hooch," a series of three bunkers in a semicircle, was twenty miles east of the southern tip of the Dead Sea. It was ancient Moab, the land of the Nabateans, at one time part of Arabia and most recently of the Hashemite Kingdom of Jordan. Ari's party lived "hull down," that is, below ground level. Each bunker was roomy, built to hold about twenty men. It was roofed with sandbags, covered with rock and vegetation to make it inconspicuous from the air. A parapet and a firing step all the way around the bunker, provided unrestricted fields of fire. "No one is permitted out of the bunkers during the day," Avigdor ordered. "It is certain satellites have been re-tasked to find us. I have counted five flights of reconnaissance aircraft since we arrived here. We must also be on the watch for hostile Bedouins. They would turn us in for a shekel or plunder us themselves. You civilians - he jabbed Winston in the ribs - follow the orders of my men and you will be quite safe."

Avigdor had good television equipment. They monitored EU transmissions, but the Antichrist closely rationed international news. There was extensive coverage of one story. Deep sadness passed over the bunker as news came through of the execution of Dame Flora MacLeigh and Baruch Yarmolinsky. The two were described as traitors and terrorists. That story segued into news of the reprisals taken against Halutz and the Degania collective farms. The report said forty members of the collective were executed for harboring the international terrorists, Samuel Winston and his wife and her criminal parents. Miriam broke into tears and Hadassah turned away.

Dov rang his hands in anguish, but said nothing. Colonel Leon Torrez of the Spanish unit of the European Union forces was commended by General Roy for his heroism at Degania and was named "Protector of Israel" as a reward. The EU announced Winston was still at large, but would be apprehended and tried shortly. The communiqué went on to say, a former member of Torrez's command, Major Pietro De Luca of the Italian army, was executed for "cowardice in the face of the enemy." Winston could think of no words to console his family. Ari understood and silently placed his arm on Sam's shoulder.

Winston turned to Ari and asked, "Ari, have you ever been to Yad Mordechai?" "Yes, I have Colonel. It is two miles from the old Gaza strip border south of Ashkelon." "I should have gone there when I was on duty at the Temple, but I didn't make it," Winston said with evident chagrin. "The year after I finished the Command and General Staff College course, I was sent to the U.S. Army War College at Carlisle, Pennsylvania to lecture on the Warsaw Ghetto uprising. Do you know the history, Ari?" "It is a required course for IDF officers, but I must confess I have lost a lot of the details." "I never will," Winston said with firmness. "I was so proud of our people. Imagine, ghetto prisoners, starved, dying of typhus, without arms or support from the Allies or even the Poles on the other side of the wall rose up in revolt. Mordechai Anielwicz, and some others formed the ZOB and whipped crack formations of the SS. "Ari, the awful truth of the death camp at the end of the railroad tracks came to light on July 22, 1942. Six days later the ZOB organized for action. They began operations less than a month later with the assassination of the ghetto police chief, a Catholic convert. They began with ten mostly defective revolvers smuggled in from the outside. Then in the Spring of 1943, I believe on *Erev Pesach*, the night before Passover, 19 April 1943, they opened up on an SS column that marched into the ZOB crossfire."

Warming to his subject. Winston exclaimed, "they gave it to 'em, Ari, they gave it to 'em! Then two ZOB groups interdicted the entrance to the ghetto and in a seven-hour firefight knocked out six medium panzer tanks. What an outfit, the ZOB!" Avigdor caught Winston's excitement. "Colonel, as I remember, the next fight was at the Brushmakers factory. In that action, five groups took on the Germans and whipped them." "That's right," Winston agreed. "Well, German flame-throwers and sappers forced resistance fighters off the rooftops and into the basement bunkers. Then the Germans flooded the bunkers. On May 8, the Germans captured the ZOB command bunker. Anilewicz committed suicide. The next day, those who could took the sewer system south from Francisckanska Street to Twarda. Quite a feat in a sewer sometimes only eighteen inches wide. They popped up out of a manhole. Some made it to the outside to carry on the struggle. Many did not and died with their people. Ari, it was the most heroic action by any people, at any time, anywhere. The *Haganah* learned from them and the IDF carries on the ZOB spirit today." Ari was so moved by Winston's stirring recital of the Warsaw Ghetto uprising, he could only weep and stroke Winston's arm.

Meir Bar-Giora, a Sergeant in Avigdor's unit, and the son of a rabbi, was designated to lead in the recitation of the Kaddish for the Halutz and Degania dead. Dov stood like a sentinel throughout. Miriam and Hadassah were stricken with grief. Sam was silent, recalling the brief conversation he had with Dame Flora and how blessed he was to know Bruce, the boot salesman. Sam bore the weight of these deaths because they were all connected to him in some way. Hadassah realized what Sam was going through and prayed for him. Bar-Giora concluded the service with the words, "May the Omnipotent comfort you together with all the mourners of Zion and Jerusalem." Afterward, the MRE was the *Seudat Havraah*, the meal of condolence.

Later that night, Sam and Hadassah strolled hand-in-hand around the perimeter. A million stars poured out their light over the wilderness in a magnificent display of God's creation. It was a wonderful night, chilly, but they ignored it lost in love for one another. Hadassah picked out a star, low over the eastern horizon. "That one is ours, Sam, and our new baby's too. And for the baby that is with the Lord already." Sam held her close, tears welling up in his eyes. Tears flowed at every mention of the baby they had given back to the Lord in prison. Sam didn't say it, but he marveled again at Hadassah's courage in the clutches of Krueger and his legionnaires. Studying the heavens, Sam remarked, "Honey, you will see some awesome things in those heavens very soon. The enemies of the Messiah have no idea what they are in for."

Sam spent a great deal of time studying the seven last judgments of Revelation Chapter Sixteen. Sam explained, "considering the fact that only a short time remains before the end of the Tribulation and the return of the Messiah, this passage of scripture describes sufferings for the followers of the Antichrist, on a scale never before seen." Winston read,

"And I heard a great voice out of the temple saying to the seven angels, Go your ways, and pour out the vials of the wrath of God upon the earth."

(Revelation 16:1)

"It is payback time," Winston opined. "I doubt the Antichrist will make public the fact that God is responsible for these trials."

The first intimation of widespread suffering in the occupation was not long in coming. There were hints on the news that some kind of painful skin infection was gripping the nation and probably the entire world. The EU-controlled Israeli news sources revealed that public health officers had ordered hospitals and clinics closed to anyone with what they called "Virus X." Only non-viral ailments and injuries would be treated at medical facilities. Health authorities recommended home treatment of the infection with ointments or a paste made of baking soda. At supper, Sam read to the group and Hadassah translated:

"And the first [angel] went, and poured out his vial upon the earth; and there fell a noisome and grievous sore upon the men which had the mark of the beast, and upon them which worshipped his image."

(Revelation 16:2)

An excited Winston said, "this must be a worldwide event! It truly is "payback time." But we must remember to pray for sustaining grace for those who refuse to take the mark. The best indications are that the order to take the mark has been obeyed only in part in Israel. Those who refuse probably get one opportunity to worship the Antichrist or die. Believe me, death is preferable to joining in Satan's revolt against the Lord."

Winston looked around the room at the fifty men in Avigdor's command and at Dov and Miriam. Every one had escaped death so far and no one had experienced the painful Virux X. None of the soldiers had been around to take the mark. But, Sam asked himself, do they realize that God has drawn a line in the sand, challenging men to follow Christ or the Antichrist? It is time for them to decide for the Messiah. Perhaps this is a good time to simply explain what is at stake for every human being. Winston invited everyone to a Bible study on God's plan of salvation. Avidgdor and all but eight of his men came to the study. All of the men were Orthodox Jews in varying degrees of loyalty to their faith.

"Adonay has a case against mankind," Winston began. "He created us, gave us everything we needed and we rebelled against Him. He gave us the law. The law spelled out what we should do and should not do. But as *Yeshaiah Ha-Novi*, Isaiah the prophet wrote of our people:

"The ox knoweth his owner, and the ass his master's crib: but Israel doth not know, my people doth not consider. Ah sinful nation, a people laden with iniquity, a seed of evildoers, children that are corrupters: they have forsaken the Lord, they have provoked the Holy One of Israel unto anger, they are gone away backward."

(Isaiah 1:3-4)

My friends, this is a ringing indictment of our nation. Remember Israel alone, had the knowledge of the Holy One. He gave us His laws. Our fathers vowed to follow His laws to the fullest. But we did not. A gracious God was faithful to His promises to bless the children of Israel. Note His gracious response to our sin:

"Come now, and let us reason together, saith the Lord: though your sins be as scarlet, they shall be as white as snow; though they be red like crimson, they shall be as wool."

(Isaiah 1:18)

God looks for the penitent heart, but many of us turn away from the truth. Some make their own rules about what will please God. This includes false religions of all kinds. Notice Isaiah's commentary on self-righteousness,

"But we are all as an unclean thing, and all our righteousnesses are as filthy rags; and we all do fade as a leaf; and our iniquities, like the wind, have taken us away. And there is none that calleth upon thy name, that stirreth himself up to take hold of thee: for thou hast hid thy face from us, and hast consumed us, because of our iniquities."

(Isaiah 64:6-7)

My friends, "iniquities," covers faults, errors, mischief, a whole range of things, but one idea is dominant, sin is common to every man. This is our nature and this is what we do by choice. I was a non-observant Jew. I looked down on you who were more *frum* than I chose to be. You may have done the very best you can, but you cannot change your basic nature, which is that of a sinner, running from God. Well, what answer is there for sin? God took the initiative to do what man cannot do for himself. Our friend Isaiah, has the answer. Sam read Isaiah 53:1-5 and then carefully emphasized verse number six:

"All we like sheep have gone astray; we have turned every one to his own way; and the Lord hath laid on him the iniquity of us all."

(Isaiah 53:6)

"Ah, friends, there is God's answer to the problem of iniquity. He sent Y'shuah HaMushiach, Jesus the Messiah, His sinless Son, to be the satisfaction, the kipporah, for our iniquities. All you need do is ask Him to save you from your sins. Will you do it today? I'm praying for you and I will help you with anything you do not understand about this marvelous gift of salvation." Winston prayed. He was sure he had botched the opportunity. When alone he poured out his heart to God for his failure. That night he tossed and turned in his sleeping bag. He was roused with a soft nudge, to find Dov kneeling beside him. "Samele, Miriam and I are ready to meet your Y'shuah. We could wait until morning, but we need you to go over this salvation once more." Delighted, Sam slipped out of the hooch with his Bible. He wakened Hadassah to share in the joy of the moment. By the light of the moon he led Dov and Miriam to faith in Jesus the Messiah. The four, united in Christ, praised God until morning.

Over the next week, twelve men sought out Winston to learn more about Y'shuah and biblical salvation. Nine made decisions for the Savior-Messiah. The other three wrestled with the strong tug of loyalty to the faith of their fathers. "Faith of your fathers," Winston explained, "probably means loyalty to the bloodless Judaism of two thousand years, or the false sacrificial Judaism in the Third Temple. As you know so well, that has turned out to be a ghastly experience for Jews. Neither brand of Judaism is the genuine "faith of the fathers." You have heard the words of Isaiah. Do you believe for a moment he would join in any system today that denies man's sin and denies the blood of a sinless Lamb of God? Friends, "faith of the fathers," can only mean the faith that is of Y'shuah Ha-Mushiach. Within a few days, the three hesitant Jews came to Winston and poured out their hearts to God for salvation.

Ari Avigdor's Messianic faith posed an unusual problem for him. He came to Christ soon after Winston's decision. Bar-Giora and some of the men were holdouts. Captain Avigdor was fearful that his men might make salvation decisions because they wanted to please their saved commanding officer. The men who followed Bar-Giora's example and resisted the Gospel, stopped short of commitment because they were troubled by the question "what will my family say?" Some family members had taken the mark. Winston prayed for the young soldiers, deep in the valley of decision.

Bar-Giora reminded Avigdor that Pesach, Passover, was fast approaching. Winston was elated at the prospect of celebrating the feast. Miriam reminisced about how her mother taught her how to kasher the home. "We removed all grain-base ingredients from the home. The special Pesach dinnerware was brought out and thoroughly scrubbed. We took the cutlery out and plunged them into the earth. The counter and the kitchen table were scrubbed with a stone and hot water. When all was in readiness, mother carefully sprinkled a few crumbs of bread near windows and doors. My father lit a candle looking for the *hometz*. With a feather and a spoon he swept them up."

The clear choice to officiate at the *Seder* was Sergeant Bar-Giora, the rabbi's son. But he was not willing. Messianic Jews were not in his frame of reference, Hadassah concluded. He was willing to take the boy's customary part of reciting the Four Questions. There was no Passover *Hagaddah*, the book that describes and illustrates the two and a half hour home Seder observance. Bar-Giora could virtually recite it from memory, but said nothing. Winston felt they could have a good Messianic Seder without the book.

Bar-Giora intoned *"Mah nishtanah halighla ha zey, mi'hol ha ligh los?"* "How does this night different from all other nights?" the first of the Four Questions. With promptings from Dov, Winston was able to recount the story of the deliverance of the Jewish slaves from Egypt. In his own commentary, Sam pointed out that there was no lamb on the table. "If our Jewish brothers and sisters are able to observe Pesach this year, there will be no lamb on their tables. I grieve that the very heart of this memorial celebration has been missing for centuries. In the first Passover, the blood of an innocent lamb was shed and its blood placed on the lintels and doorposts of their home. This signified the death of the innocent for those in need of a covering before God. Then that lamb was roasted and eaten. Thus, our people with no lamb on the table illustrate that they have no covering today and are as open to the death angel as the Egyptians were. I most firmly believe that God provided a Lamb without spot or blemish. He read,

"...Behold the Lamb of God, which taketh away the sin of the world."

(John 1:29)

Winston picked up bread from the table and asked, do you know why the matzo is baked in stripes? Because the Messiah endured stripes.

"But he was wounded for our transgressions, he was bruised for our iniquities: the chastisement of our peace was upon him; and with his stripes we are healed."

(Isaiah 53:5)

The matzo must also have holes,

"...and they shall look upon me whom they have pierced."

(Zechariah 12:10)

Sam asked, "should Messianic Jews do away with the Passover Seder?" There was a chorus of "no." Indeed, a Rabbi named Paul had this to say about leaven, sin in the life of a believer,

"Your glorying is not good. Know ye not that a little leaven leaveneth the whole lump? Purge out therefore the old leaven, that ye may be a new lump, as ye are unleavened. For even Christ our Passover is sacrificed for us: Therefore let us keep the feast, not with old leaven, neither with the leaven of malice and wickedness; but with the unleavened bread of sincerity and truth."

(1 Corinthians 5:6-8)

We need the Seder to remind us of the great deliverance we have from slavery to sin and to Satan and to remind us to keep ourselves clean of sin for the rest of our lives.

The table guests had no wine. Water would have to do. Sam reminded the worshippers of the words of Jesus,

"But I say unto you, I will not drink henceforth of this fruit of the vine, until that day when I drink it new with you in my Father's kingdom."

(Matthew 26:29)

"Friends," Sam said solemnly, "that day is very near!"

Sam expected a backlash from Bar-Gore over the messianic emphasis in the Seder, but the sergeant said nothing.

The bunker family had no security problems. They remained inside during daylight hours. Avigdor had patrols out day and night. The Bedouins knew they were there, Avigdor guessed, but wisely considered the position too strong to be worth a frontal assault. Ari's men were growing restive. Ari conferred with Winston about it. "Their morale will evaporate in this wilderness heat if I do not do something soon to bring them back to the razor sharp unit they have been up to now." Ari explained. "We are short of water and provisions. We are going back to Degania. I would like to meet those men who murdered the kibbutzniks. I think we will leave tonight. Colonel, I realize that I am leaving you in danger of a Bedouin raid. I have four men who are too ill to take part in a firefight. I will leave them with you. You may have weapons and ammunition for your own defense." "Thanks, Ari," Winston said with a smile, "we are trusting in the living God to protect us if it is His will. If you feel you must go, we will be with you in prayer." Late that night, Avigdor, forty-six men and three vehicles slipped out of the bunker complex.

Every day more and more refugees streamed southward to Petra. Most followed the eastern shoreline of the Dead Sea, bringing them very close to the bunker complex, but no one seemed to see the camouflaged strong points. Winston felt they should do something to reach them with water, food and the Gospel, but Hadassah wisely pointed out that it was doubtful terrified people would stop or be willing to listen.

No one expected a straggler from the south, but one afternoon a lone figure, more dead than alive, weaved his way toward the complex. He was barefoot and delirious. He struggled toward them and fell, unable to rise. Winston rushed out to help him. From his ragged uniform Winston knew he was an American sailor. The man took a mouthful of water and threw it up. Allowed to rest, he slowly came around and explained that he was a coxswain in the U.S. Seventh fleet. On shore duty, in the Gulf of Aqaba, he had watched his ship, an "L" Class destroyer, go down with all hands on board. "It was the most dreadful thing I have ever seen." The man began to whimper like a baby. A cup of coffee helped to calm him and he resumed his story. "I was ashore. I looked out to sea about the time the second watch would have gone on duty. Suddenly there was this great wind that nearly blew everything away and, and - I know you won't believe me, but the sea had turned to blood." Wide-eyed he cried, "blood, can you imagine? Blood! I looked for my ship and it was gone. Vanished! Just like that, into those bloody waters. I didn't know what to do so I ran for it, Mister, I ran. I ran until I could not run another step. I had been planning to desert for a long time. This was my chance. I knew there were cities and towns up north, but I did not realize how far I would have to walk to find them. I bought food and water from Bedouins along the way. One insisted on taking my wristwatch, but no one really bothered me. By the way, I'm Josh Cleary. I'm from Denver, Colorado." "You are safe here, Josh," Winston said. "You just rest for a while. We will get some hot food into you and then we will talk some more."

Outside the hooch, Hadassah asked, "did you notice anything different about him, Sam?" "Hmm, no, I don't think so." "He doesn't have the mark," Hadassah observed. "Yeah, you're right. There must be a story there." Hadassah quickly turned to what was troubling her. "Sam, do you buy this story of a sea of blood, a sea so overwhelming it takes a destroyer to the bottom of the Gulf of Aqaba? Could it be Josh's delirium?" Without a word, Sam took out his pocket New Testament and read Revelation 16:3:

"And the second angel poured out his vial upon the sea; and it became as the blood of a dead man: and every living soul died in the sea."

"Josh's story is an exact fulfillment of the second bowl judgment. I'm surprised it took a ship down, but we're dealing with God's judgment."

Josh, thanks to a young healthy body, speedily recovered from his long walk through the desert. Asked about the mark of the beast, he explained that he was assigned to a work detail in Eilat when orders came down for the crew to assemble on the fantail for the tattoo. Josh related that he had a Pentecostal grandmother who made him promise the day he went off to Boot Camp that he would never get any kind of tattoo. Grandma said, "God forbids any cutting in the flesh, Joshua, and don't you forget it." "I'm the only cox'un in the United States Navy that has never had a tattoo of any kind. Anyway, I just wasn't around when the crew was ordered to take the mark. A Yeoman's mate kept hounding me to get it done, but I managed to be in the wrong place at the right time."

Sam spent a great deal of time explaining to Josh that the blood in the sea was but one of God's judgments. "I don't know anything about God's hand in these things" Josh responded," but I have experienced some of these scary things. Our ship was in fleet maneuvers off Diego Garcia in the Indian Ocean when a great ball of fire, a meteor perhaps – whatever - fell into the ocean. A tsunami miles and miles wide engulfed the fleet anchorage and at least one-third of our fleet went down." "That squares with scripture, Josh."

"and the third part of the ships were destroyed."

(Revelation 8:9)

"Then recently," Josh continued, "everyone on our ship and I guess everyone in the fleet, fell sick with the most painful skin infection you ever saw. The medics couldn't do anything for it. No one was allowed to go to sick bay on orders of fleet headquarters. The Officer of the Deck was forbidden to put it in the log. But you know what? I didn't get it, the infection I mean." "That squares with scripture, too, Josh," Winston said with a smile, "according to Revelation 16:2, only those who have the mark get the infection."

"Josh," Sam said gravely, "I was a U.S. Army colonel. I'm not in the Army now. What I am is a fugitive from General Roy and the EU army. They want to kill me because I am a witness for Jesus Christ. General Roy is the Antichrist, that is, he is the agent of the Devil in a last-ditch attempt to steal the throne of Jesus. But in a few months, Jesus is coming back to earth and the Antichrist and his army will be destroyed. Your fleet will be destroyed with them. Josh, I would say, it is the grace of God that brought you through the desert to this place of relative safety." Josh scratched hid head. "My Pentecostal grandma must be in heaven. She was lookin' for the Lord's return, longer than I have been alive." Soberly, Sam asked, "but what about you? What does the return of Christ mean to you?" "My grandma told me that one day I would have to decide for Christ or decide for the devil. I want to decide for Jesus, Colonel, but I don't know what to do." "I can help you with that, Josh," Sam exclaimed. Sam pointed out a handful of Gospel verses, invited Josh to read them for himself and then asked if he was ready to make a decision. Josh was ready. He went to his knees with Winston and from his heart asked Jesus to save him. "Josh, I must warn you that if you are taken with us you would have a hard time escaping our end." "Colonel, I'm a deserter in a war zone. I will be executed before you are."

Avigdor's convoy returned from Degania just before dawn. Ari was on a stretcher covering the rear seat of the Humvee. He had taken RPG fragments in the chest and stomach. He had bled a great deal. It was a marvel he was still alive. The Army medics looked at Winston and shook their heads. Ari faded in and out. In a lucid moment, Ari pulled a scrap of paper out of the breast pocket of his battle dress uniform. It was in Hebrew. "Read it, read it," Ari urged. Sam gave it to Hadassah. "This is my verse," Ari explained. Hadassah read aloud,

"And this is life eternal that they might know thee, the only true God and Jesus Christ whom thou has sent."

(John 17:3)

224

With a smile, Ari Avigdor passed to his eternal reward.

Sergeant Bar-Giora, now senior in rank in the unit, related how they successfully entered Degania and disarmed the small EU requisition team. Colonel Endicott-Symes told them Torrez was to return within hours. They did not have long to wait. Standing tall in his command vehicle, Torrez rode in to Degania with orders to execute all of the inhabitants and to destroy Degania A and B. Torrez and his aides went up in a fearful explosion, the result of Claymore mines planted in the road leading in to the compound. The ambush was successful. Avigdor's men cut down three truckloads of Spanish troops. Few escaped. The kibbutzniks cheered. Then it happened. A badly wounded Spaniard rose and fired an RPG. Ari went down, urging the kibbutzniks to flee to Petra. The drive south was slow in order to spare Avigdor as much pain as possible. Four other men had minor wounds.

European Union aircraft kept the skies hot over the East bank of the Jordan. Bar-Giora was sure that ground reconnaissance units would soon discover the bunker complex. "I don't think so, Sergeant," Winston opined, "because the book of Daniel says "these shall escape out of his hand," that's the Antichrist, "even Edom, and Moab, and chief of the children of Ammon." That's Daniel 11:41. For some reason, the area east of the Jordan and the Dead Sea is out of bounds for him." Bar-Giora turned away, displeased with a biblical answer to his professional opinion. It was a symptom of a growing rupture in what had been a very comfortable arrangement for the bunker family.

Winston was anxious to resume broadcasting. The petulant Bar-Giora was unwilling to use his men for an evangelistic broadcast. Winston offered to drive into the wilderness alone. "I don't need your men, Sergeant," Winston explained. "Just lend me a vehicle and I will do the rest." Hands on his hips, Bar-Giora stared him down. "We are soldiers, Mr. Winston, not missionaries. I know Captain Avigdor was willing to aid you in your propaganda campaign, but things have changed. We are dangerously close to being discovered. I think it is time to move the unit. We must fight, run away and live to fight another day. There will be no broadcast, now or ever, while I am in charge. Is that clear ex-Colonel Winston?"

Early the next morning, Bar-Giora's patrol returned from a reconnaissance to the north end of the Dead Sea. Grimly shaken, they reported that the Dead Sea and the Jordan flowing into it were blood red! "You were seeing things!" Bar-Giora insisted. He had laughed at Josh Cleary's report of the bloody Gulf of Aqaba. "Sergeant," the patrol leader reported, "you selected us for this reconnaissance because you knew we would bring back factual information. Well, I am telling you the Dead Sea and the Jordan have turned to blood. Each of us dipped a hand in the stuff and it was blood in appearance, blood in consistency and, I went a step further, it tasted like blood. I got sick for my trouble, but I had to make sure." "All right, all right," get some food and get some rest," the Sergeant ordered with a wave of his hand.

Winston was ready. Without an invitation, he read:

"And the third angel poured out his vial upon the rivers and fountains of waters; and they became blood. And I heard the angel of the waters say, Thou art righteous, O Lord, which art, and wast, and shalt be, because thou hast judged thus. For they have shed the blood of saints and prophets, and thou hast given them blood to drink, for they are worthy."

(Revelation 16:4-6)

The marvel of the bloody waters was quickly forgotten in the sudden scorching heat that assailed the wilderness. Days before, Sam had found a passage in Isaiah 30:26 that told of a day when the heat of one day would equal the heat of seven. This was another judgment Winston was sure, from the reading of Revelation 16:8 and 9. No one dared leave the bunker complex, but to remain inside was no treat either. The heat was debilitating, but the suns rays were deadly. One soldier ignored the warnings, touched one of the vehicles and was burned severely. As the bunker company sweltered, they were amazed to hear from Radio Jerusalem that the capital was plunged into a darkness so severe General Roy's staff had suspended operations. The government spokesman went on to say General Roy was unable to officiate at the Temple. In a related news item, Roy's City of Babylon operations were suspended for the same reason, preternatural darkness. "That is the fulfillment of Revelation 16:10 and 11," Winston pointed out. Bar-Giora turned away in disgust.

Reading on in Revelation 16, Winston informed everyone that the next events would be so cataclysmic that all would do well to continue to remain in the bunker complex for safety. Winston read Revelation 16:12, the prophecy of the drying up of the Tigris and Euphrates Rivers to facilitate the movement of the mammoth eastern military coalition. "No doubt," Winston speculated, "this will mean the end of the Antichrist's Babylon adventure. Millions of men are in that great army, heading for a showdown at Megiddo. The Antichrist with only a fraction that number will be there with every thermo-nuclear weapon, every nerve gas component, every ray gun, for he is certain he can win. But before that great battle, there will be a major earthquake followed by a hail-storm. Earthquakes on the order of 7.5 on the Richter scale are devastating. This will be much more intense than anything the world has ever seen. The hail stones, of a talent in weight, say one hundred pounds each, will rain down on the whole earth. This will reduce cities to ruins and these tragedies will be the major cause of death for one-fourth of earth's inhabitants and two-thirds of Israelis. That's the summation of Revelation 16:17-21."

Three hours later, Winston heard the three military vehicles hum to life. Bar-Giora ordered his men to pack up and prepare to move. Winston appealed to the Sergeant to remain, but Bar-Giora was determined to go. "What is your mission, Sergeant?" Winston inquired. "We're going back into Jerusalem," the Sergeant replied. "With all the action up north, no one will notice a small unit passing through the city. Then...well, I don't know what we will do."

Alarmed, Winston placed his hand upon the sergeant's sleeve and begged him not to go. If you should survive the earthquake and the hail-storm, you will be swept up in the greatest battle of all time. And let me tell you, friend, only those who belong to Jesus the Messiah will live through the next few weeks." Woodenly impassive, Bar-Giora swept his hand in a circle and the convoy moved off.

# Chapter Twenty-five
*The beginning of woes*

How do you sleep when the world as you know it is about to be changed forever? As Sam strolled around the bunker complex and savored the cool breeze from the north, it was a welcome relief from the incredible heat they had suffered. A billion stars lighted the night sky, a sky tranquil yet disturbed by occasional bursts of light over the eastern horizon. Were the lights a precursor of the coming battle? For a couple of days a hum born on desert winds suggested to Winston the eastern confederacy was heading for Megiddo.

Hadassah slept fitfully. She was just far enough along to make it difficult to sleep on any side. Sleeping on the ground didn't help. Miriam slept on a time-table, one eye always on Hadassah. Winston wondered did Miriam know how Hadassah lost their first child? Dov was never in REM sleep which made him a valuable watchman. Josh Cleary slept like a sailor on calm seas.

Then no one slept. In a never-to-be-forgotten atmospheric display, thunder and lightning out of nowhere crashed around the complex. That terror was followed by the ground rolling and rumbling in spasms from the very core of the earth. For a full fourteen minutes the world underwent the worst earthquake in history. "The world is swirling around the drain," Winston said with a laugh, while reaching out to cover Hadassah. The supports of the hooch groaned under the tension of the ground above and below. A sand storm blew in over the parapets. Somewhere nearby, a chasm opened up, spelling the end of two of Avigdor's bunkers. Dov absently tried to rise and was tossed against the wall like a rag doll. Winston crawled to him only to be reassured that the hardy kibbutznik was all right. Hadassah was unharmed, but grimaced as she tried to shift her weight on a floor with eight inches of loose sand. Everyone blew sand out of nostrils, ears and eyes. Socks, shoes, and waist-bands had to be purged. But it was good to be alive! Then all was quiet.

Winston rubbed his eyes. It was time to think about their situation. Food was running short. Soon they would have to find water. It was not wise to move for the hail-storm judgment would be soon. Itching to get the Gospel out for what would probably be the last time, Winton concluded, the Lord knows what He is doing. I believe He will give the warring nations one more chance to turn to Him.

Black clouds swirled out of the north, and the wind picked up. Could this be an even more devastating judgment?" Winston struggled to get back into the hooch. Everyone was there, but Josh. Winston yelled for Cleary, but his voice was lost on the wind. He circled the hooch one more time and then took cover. He urged everyone to lie down in the center of the room and pray. It was the big one as huge boulders bombarded the roof of the bunker. Boulders rolled in through the doorway, narrowly missing legs and feet. "Where is Cleary?" an anxious Dov cried. The supports shivered and shook, but remained firm. It was over in what seemed like an hour, actually barely fifteen minutes. When Winston thought it safe to venture outside, they found the hooch was in a miniature valley surrounded by immense stones. The two bunkers seriously damaged in the earthquake were literally erased from the landscape. A very shaken Cleary emerged from a cavern he had found some distance from the complex. "Our kitten has used up two of his nine lives, Hadassah," Winston said with relief as he hugged his young friend.

Winston shivered at the thought of earthquake and hail damage in the rest of the world. My city of Saint Louis is no more. Chicago is gone. Revelation 16:19 said that the "cities of the nations fell." But what of Jerusalem? The same verse says the great city was divided into three parts. That statement was hard to figure out. Winston felt it probably indicated Jerusalem was spared, the earthquake's devastation, but was somehow changed. The passage goes on to say,

"...and great Babylon came in remembrance before God, to give unto her the cup of the wine of the fierceness of his wrath."

(Revelation 16:19)

Winston took that to mean the Vatican's trillion dollar investment in the Antichrist's commercial empire in Iraq fell victim to the earthquake. What remains, would be looted by the advancing eastern army. Winston read again Revelation 18, the complete record of the brief rise and mind-blowing demise of the greatest financial venture ever attempted.

Winston reviewed the history of Babylonianism for the group. "When the complete biblical record on Babylon is examined, it weaves an incredible story of satanic perfidy in the attempt to forge a one-world government, one-world religion and one-world economic order. It begins in Genesis Chapters 10 and 11, with the sinister figure of Nimrod, a city-builder and a charismatic military genius. Nimrod means "rebel." His rebellion began with defiance of the God-given order to scatter and multiply the earth. Nimrod countered,

"And they said, Go to, let us build us a city and a tower, whose top may reach unto heaven; and let us make us a name, lest we be scattered abroad upon the face of the whole earth."

(Genesis 11:4)

"Secular historians believed," Winston said, quoting Doctor Boyd's reference materials, "that Nimrod was a slave trader, using men to build the cities and to man an army which swept all the way to the Mediterranean. Some scholars suggest Cush, the grandson of Noah was the evil genius behind these acts of rebellion against God. Interestingly, the Greeks knew Cush by the name Chaos. This was Satan's first attempt at one-world government.

229

Revisiting Genesis 11:4, Winston discussed the tower that Nimrod built. "It was not to reach heaven, but rather to portray the heavens on the vault of the tower roof. The starry heavens were portrayed there for this is the first mention of astrology, the prediction of the future by the stars. The tower held more. Historians tell of Nimrod's wife, Semiramis, the chief priestess and the object of worship in the tower-temple. One ancient historian told of the temple trinity. Semiramis, under the name Rhea, was the center of three god-like figures. Jove, evidently a counterfeit of our Jehovah was on one side and Juno, carrying a dove, a biblical symbol of the Holy Spirit, stood on the other side. This was one-world religion in full blossom.

God was concerned enough about the tower to confound the builders' language. The city, called *Bab-El*, in Sumerian "the gate of God," became "babble," a place of unintelligible voices, when God confounded the language (Genesis 11:9). Two verses, Genesis 11:8 and 9, indicate that the confusion of tongues led to a worldwide dispersion. Apparently the idolaters of Bab-El took their idols with them for cultic figures from crude images in clay to immense works of art, are found the world around. A favorite theme was one of the mother and child. Paul found Athens, "a city wholly given to idolatry" (Acts 17:16). Later, Paul dealt with the followers of the colossal figure of Diana of the Ephesians (Acts 19:35). Idolatry found in every culture, is a besetting sin of man.

Roman Catholicism, the skeleton and sinew of the Universal Church the Antichrist recently destroyed was the quintessential example of Babylonianism. The Book of Revelation symbolizes false religion as Mystery Babylon the Great, the Mother of Harlots and Abominations of the Earth (Revelation 17:5). Winston reflected on the history of the Roman church, the scarlet mother. It was one blood-soaked chapter after another, particularly for the Jews and for the true followers of Jesus Christ. History nails its ninety-five theses to the door of the Vatican. She was responsible for the Crusades, the Inquisition, pogroms and ultimately bears responsibility for much of the Holocaust. In his 1933 concordat with the Vatican, Hitler said he was simply" continuing the policy of the Catholic Church in the containment of the Jews." It was the truest statement he ever made. Incidentally, Hitler, Mussolini and their sometime henchman, Francisco Franco, were all nominal Catholics."

"But didn't the Roman Church loosen up after Pope John XXIII initiated the Second Vatican Council reforms" asked Hadassah? Sam shook his head. "There were cosmetic changes that led many of the faithful to believe changes were imminent, but Romanism did not undergo a heart transplant. It couldn't. Sold out to Satan's Babylonianism, it was doomed to repeat its worst errors. Corrupt at its core, beyond the pomp and circumstance, robes and candles, the real Romanism showed itself from time to time. For example, in recent history, Bishop Paul Marcinkus, one-time president of the Vatican Bank was involved in some underworld machinations including charges of money laundering through the Bank of the Holy Spirit. A rogues-gallery of Mafia figures were involved. A shadowy Masonic group known as P-2, said to include highly placed Vatican officials, was implicated. The scandal filled the pages of newspapers the world over. The papacy pleaded ignorance of financial manipulation, but protected Bishop Marcinkus.

The ink was barely dry on the Vatican money revelations when the world awakened to the facts of widespread pedophilia within the priesthood. The first sensational case broke in Louisiana. The victims and their families ignored the traditional code of silence regarding priestly excesses and informed on their tormentors. Some even sued. The time-honored hierarchical ploy to urge the victims families not to embarrass Holy Mother Church did not work. The church was tampering with disillusioned and deeply wounded people. The seemy-sided beginnings of this sordid story is contained in a book by a Roman Catholic, Jason Berry, entitled "Lead Us Not Into Temptation," published by Doubleday in October 1992. In 2004, a Catholic board of inquiry reported more than 4,000 priests accused of molesting more than 10,000 children, 80% were boys.

The pedophile scandal was only the beginning. All over the United States and Canada rectories and monasteries were scrutinized as the sacred places in which the moral laws of God and church were ignored in the sexual abuse of children. Reports of a wide range of wrong-doing surfaced. An Irish bishop resigned after his mistress revealed his paternity in a long-standing relationship. A convent of Dublin nuns was exposed for enslavement and physical abuse of children in a for-profit laundry operation.

A prize-winning journalist in Kansas City checked the death records of priests over a period of years and learned that priests had died of AIDS at a rate faster than the general public. This was page-one news in the Kansas City Star for January 30, 2000. A Notre Dame theologian lecturing his students said that he had no problem with the gay life style, but the growing number of gay priests in the Church had resulted in a gay sub-culture that was undermining the faith.

The nadir of clergy morals was seen in the news out of Africa. Africa in 2001 was ravaged by AIDS. The National Catholic Reporter for March 16, 2001, revealed that African priests were reported to be pressuring nuns for sex. The nuns, victims of their confessors, represented "safe sex" for the clergy.

This was the situation in the billion-member Catholic Church when the one-world religion came to full flower in the Universal Church. Perhaps the most cherished goal in the long history of Romanism, the Universal Church may have been born out of the secret protocols in the Antichrist's covenant with Israel. Satan was willing to sponsor religion in order to bring the Antichrist to power. When that goal was accomplished he looted the church and destroyed her (Revelation 17:16-17)."

"How successful was Satan's one-world economic order? Winston related that Cormac O'Brien had informed him that the bill for rebuilding Babylon as a world trade center was nearly a trillion dollar investment for the Roman Catholic Church.

Where did they get that kind of money? Visitors to the Vatican are wide-eyed at the enormous wealth of the church in jewels, paintings and objet d'art. But these treasures are worthless in terms of the income needed to fuel a world-wide system. The church could not sell their treasures and no one could afford to buy them. That means the money must be generated in the religious custom of donations, never easy for the Catholics, and the capitalist's custom of buying, selling and trading.

The Catholic Church was a cash-strapped operation until Bishop Bernardino Nogara took over the purse-strings in 1929. Nogara, a shrewd businessman saw that World War I had closed Europe as the primary financial plantation for the church. He looked to America as the future for Roman financial development. But that took time. Nogara began with an important agreement with the rising Catholic-atheist dictator of Italy, Benito Mussolini. Mussolini for political reasons was willing to shake hands with the pope to consolidate his hold on the electorate. The pope for his part received the promise that the church's revenues would never be taxed, including money made on investments. Mussolini forked over considerable cash and in time, most of the Italian utilities and construction industry wound up in Vatican ownership.

Investment in America followed. Investment in blue-chip companies traded on the New York Stock Exchange generate cash for the Vatican investments. Rome does not publish a financial statement, but the best guess is that capital investments net them about ninety billion per year in the United States. Some locally-funded religious orders and shrines do well financially, particularly ones involved in Marian devotion. Some religious orders experience financial difficulties. For example, the Benedictines of Chicago, had to adapt their monastery to a bed-and-breakfast in order to pay the bills. A great deal of real estate money changed hands in the 1970's and 1980's as religious orders, dogged by diminished numbers of vocations, were forced to sell their properties. The humorous side of Roman Catholic finance, Winston learned, was the fact that Roman Catholics are not big givers. Tithing campaigns usually end in failure.

"Scripture says the commercial empire centered in the rebuilt Babylon, is doomed due to catastrophic events. The evaporation of the Tigris and Euphrates Rivers, the earthquake and the rain of hail stones will leave it in ruins. The eastern confederation, like scavengers, will pick Babylon's bones."

Winston turned to Revelation Chapter 18 for an overview of Babylon's brief success and her demise. Winston marveled at the grace of the Lord in warning,

"...Come out of her, my people, that ye be not partakers of her sins, and that ye receive not of her plagues."

(Revelation 18:4)

Could that mean Jewish people caught up in technical and commercial occupations were in God's mind for a special warning? Winston quickly prayed that Jews would heed this message from heaven, for the word to Babylon was,

"...in one hour is thy judgment come"

(Revelation 18:10)

It was certain to be a serious blow to the Antichrist's investors and speculators. The text reads,

"And the merchants of the earth shall weep and mourn over her; for no man buyeth their merchandise any more."

(Revelation 18:11)

Winston found that Revelation 18 has a great deal to say about the types of commercial enterprise in Babylon. There were all kinds of luxury items, construction materials, foodstuffs and agricultural staples. The most ominous trade item was in "slaves and souls of men." Dr. Boyd had written a note in the margin of his Bible, a quotation from Henry M. Morris' "The Revelation Record," Institute for Creation Research, Pg 365, that this refers to "white slavery," the sale of women and men for sexual purposes." Winston shook his head in disgust, but remembered there was no restraining ministry of the Holy Spirit. Babylon, Satan's one-world economic order was doomed from the start. Winston read that an angel would announce, "Babylon the great is fallen, is fallen." Then another angel will say,

"Thus with violence shall that great city Babylon be thrown down, and shall be found no more at all."

(Revelation 18:21)

Pregnant Hadassah was miserable. But she was as cheerful as if they were on a picnic. It was the impending birth and the anticipation of the close of the Tribulation, Winston guessed. Her next question proved he was right. "Sam, what is the schedule of events in the wind-up of these grim days?" "Ah, glad you asked, honey," he said with evident delight. "I've got it down, point by point. First of all, the Messiah will meet the armies of the Antichrist and the invaders from the east in a very dramatic confrontation. But early on that day a frightful darkness will cover the land. The prophet Joel tells us:

"Blow ye the trumpet in Zion, and sound an alarm in my holy mountain: let all the inhabitants of the land tremble: for the day of the Lord cometh, for it is nigh at hand; A day of darkness and of gloominess, a day of clouds and of      thick darkness, as the morning spread upon the mountains..."

(Joel 2:1-2a)

"The day of the Lord, in scripture, is not simply one twenty-four hour period. The day of the Lord covers all of the end-time, but it seems to me that Joel's prophecy is of the morning of the day of the Lord's return to end the career of the Antichrist. The succeeding events of that day are a good deal clearer. The Gospel of Matthew tells us:

"And then shall appear the sign of the Son of man in heaven: and then shall all the tribes of the earth mourn, and they shall see the Son of man coming in the clouds of heaven with power and great glory."

(Matthew 24:30)

Josh murmured approvingly. Winston continued, "the nature of His coming seems to be the primary focus of prophecy. Revelation tells us:

"And I saw heaven opened, and behold a white horse; and he that sat upon him was called Faithful and True, and in righteousness he doth judge and make war."

(Revelation 19:11)

The passage goes on to say

"And out of his mouth goeth a sharp sword, that with it he should smite the nations: and he shall rule them with a rod of iron: and he treadeth the winepress of the fierceness and wrath of Almighty God."

(Revelation 19:15)

"The stage is set for the battle," Sam explained. "A few verses further on we read:"

"And I saw the beast, and the kings of the earth, and their armies, gathered together to make war against him that sat on the horse, and against his army."

(Revelation 19:19)

The imagery prompted Winston to whistle. "Look," he said with excitement, "the beast, the Antichrist, his army and the armies from the east realize that Jesus the Messiah is really their enemy and so both will fight against the Lord and the saints who ride with Him.

As to the location of the Lord's return, Isaiah tells us about the Messiah's appearance on a battlefield about eighty miles east of Megiddo. Isaiah 63:1a asks:

"Who is this that cometh from Edom, with dyed garments from Bozrah?"

The passage goes on to describe One, who could only be the Messiah,

"I have trodden the winepress alone; and of the people there was none with me: for I will tread them in mine anger, and trample them in my fury; and their blood shall be sprinkled upon my garments, and I will stain all my raiment."

(Isaiah 63:3)

"Well, that ends the war, but it is now time for the judgment of the people of the Great Tribulation. The purpose of the Great Tribulation is the purification of the Jews and the purging of the Gentiles. Matthew Chapter 25, relates the purging, the judgment of the Gentiles. The basis of judgment is "how did you treat the Lord's brethren, the Jewish people, during the Tribulation?" Some mistakenly interpret that to mean that it is exclusively a judgment based on works, but the works are really a proof of saving faith. When I look back over the last seven years, "Winston said reflectively, "it was those who did something for the Jews, and refused the mark of the beast and refused to worship him, that believed the message of salvation."

Our people, the Jews, have a date with judgment, too, Winston continued. Ezekiel tells us:

"And I will bring you out from the people, and will gather you out of the countries wherein ye are scattered, with a mighty hand, and with a stretched out arm, and with fury poured out. And I will bring you into the wilderness of the people, and there will plead with you face to face. Like as I pleaded with your fathers in the wilderness of the land of Egypt, so will I plead with you, saith the Lord God. And I will cause you to pass under the rod, and I will bring you into the bond of the covenant; And I will purge out from among you the rebels, and them that transgress against me: I will bring them forth out of the country where they sojourn, and they shall not enter into the land of Israel: and ye shall know that I am the Lord."

(Ezekiel 20:34-38)

"Some scholars believe the judgment will take place in the wilderness" Sam explained, "in Kadesh Barnea, where the murmuring and the rebellion of our people angered the Lord. Elements of that rebellion remain to this day and the Lord will deal with it. But just like the observation we made on the Gentiles, the primary purpose in the judgment of the Jews will be the question: "what did you do with the offer of the Messiah Jesus as Savior and Lord? Only the saved get into the Kingdom reign of the Messiah."

General Roy seemed less concerned about the imminent fall of Babylon than he was about apprehending the fugitive Winstons. For three hours, he railed at Maurice

Dupin for his failure to bring in the man Roy blamed for just about everything. The usually unflappable Dupin was shocked at his leader's slide over the edge of insanity. By turns, Roy sobbed uncontrollably, struck out angrily, slobbered like a child, at times lapsing into incoherence. Roy quaffed down great drafts of what he called "medicine," in order to be understood.

"Excellency, we will find Winston," Dupin reassured him. "We found his printing plant and destroyed it. Winston hardly dares broadcast for our "J Star" and "Predator" drones are on target in seconds of his radio transmission. Deir Hakim, the Druze village that sheltered him, is no more. It is only a matter of time before Winston is killed or captured."

"Dupin, you do not reassure me," Roy exclaimed. Turning to an aide, "get Lord Ten Sing on the internet. In seconds, Ten Sing in the Temple at Jerusalem reported, "I am at your service, Excellency." "Ten Sing, I am surrounded by incompetent people. Send your spirit guides to find Winston." Ten Sing was silent momentarily, fishing for an answer. "Excellency, I have probed the unseen world for his location, but so far we have not been able to pin it down." Petulantly, Roy responded, "our Master is the prince of the power of the air. He can do anything. Have you asked him to tell us where Winston is hiding?" "I have your Excellency, but the Master says he simply does not know the traitor's location. Our leader once had access to the dwelling place of That One. He could ask permission to afflict the followers, but that opportunity ended when our Master, uhh, decided to leave. For some reason, That One is protecting this Winston and his gang."

Dupin couldn't leave Roy's field command headquarters fast enough. A weary Roy had quietly asked him to redouble his efforts to bring in the Winstons. Feeling partially vindicated, Dupin knew what to do. Winston, Dupin guessed, was hiding east of the Dead Sea. Roy had never permitted a ground reconnaissance of the area. Arabs would have to bring in the Winstons.

Driving alone to the Gaza Strip, Dupin moved cautiously through souks and bazaars, sickened by the sights, sounds and smells. The Palestinians had suffered for decades, held captive by their own hatred and bitterness. No oil-rich Arabs came here; none cared. The bitter fruits of poverty and illiteracy were reflected in children who could make explosives and field strip Kalashnikov rifles, but could not write. It took a great deal of baksheesh, greasing many palms for false leads, lies, and vague promises in order to find a Hamas bounty hunter who would take on the task of bringing in Winston, dead or alive.

Winston was on a quest of his own. Scrutinizing a map of the Galilee-Syria region, he longed for a remote area for more broadcasts to the EU forces. Hadassah had given up hope of dissuading him. She suggested the kibbutz village of Ma'ayan Baruch, near the Syrian border. "South African and American Jews settled the area. You might find a friendly face there. You will need me Sam. You cannot pose as

Druze up there. "No darling," he responded, "this is my show. You stay put and I'll be back as soon as I can. Let's see, I can manage the AM suitcase. I'll pray for some poles when I get there."

# Chapter Twenty-six
*Captives*

The hooch family went to ground at the low growl of a military vehicle bouncing toward them. The lone occupant was in uniform. "It's Bar-Giora," exclaimed Josh. The sergeant pulled to a stop and slumped over the steering wheel. "We had a brush with the enemy at the river crossing. I lost three men and most of our equipment. Two men were wounded and captured. The rest of my men melted into the countryside." Eyes narrowed, Winston said, "I'm surprised you came back Sergeant." "I'm sorry we left, Colonel. I won't pretend to understand everything you stand for, but I know you are a soldier of Israel in a different army. Colonel, if you would like to resume your broadcasts, I'm your man." Winston bowed his head and softly offered a prayer of thanksgiving.

Abdul Razuli adjusted his field glasses one more time to take in the bunker he estimated to be about 800 meters north of his hill position. He counted only two figures outside the bunker. They were unarmed. Razuli's commando was specially trained in hostage taking. He would deploy his men in two columns. One element, line abreast, would assault the bunker directly. A second element would swing around in a right-hook operation to cover any possibility of escape. The trap would be sprung. The infidel could not run and he was unarmed. Signaling a cautious advance just after dawn, Razuli carefully moved his men forward in a textbook maneuver. Weapons leveled, they crept to within a few meters undetected. "Hands up," Razuli demanded, in Hebrew and in English. Hadassah and Josh complied immediately. Dov and Miriam emerged from the bunker and raised their arms.

It was too easy, but there was no Winston. "Where is your man? Razuli demanded. "Gone, thank God," she replied. "Gone where?" Razuli cried holding Hadassah's face firmly in his left hand. Josh reached out to defend her and was battered to the ground. "You find him," she shouted through clenched teeth. Noting the chain around her neck, Razuli tore it away and examined it. It was her military dog tags. "What have we here? So you are an Israeli soldier." "A captain in the reserves," she snapped. Razuli tore her blouse open. "You are with child Mrs. Winston. I could use you for my own pleasure, then rip you up and present your dead body to the French infidel. He will pay for you dead or alive, but you are worth more to me alive. Tell me where your man is hiding."

With a nod from Razuli, Hadassah was thrown to the ground. Her boots and socks were torn off. A commando handed Razuli a Malacca cane. He tested it with a few tentative swipes at the air. "Hold her," he ordered. Hadassah swallowed hard. It was a Turkish bastinado, a torture that lacerated the bottom of the feet. She closed her eyes determined to choke back a scream.

Hadassah didn't break. Razuli did not molest her. A woman that close to child-bearing was not fit for a warrior, he reasoned. Dragged into the back of a truck, Hadassah and a groggy Josh Cleary were forced to the floor. Dov and Miriam were left unbound and allowed to sit on the pull-down bench. The vehicles took a route around the south end of the Dead Sea. It was slow, rough going. The earthquake had changed the land dramatically. It was a moonscape. The Wadi el Arabah was hardly recognizable. The angel had erased centuries-old roads and caravan tracks in a moment of time. Devastating hail damage was evident on every side. The drivers sweated and strained to avoid the boulders. They slowly passed on the right what had once been ancient Arad and headed north for Jerusalem.

The trucks wound their way through the boulder-strewn streets of Jerusalem. They pulled up at the Temple and the prisoners were turned over to a squad of German gendarmes. They were forced to sit on the ground on the east side of the edifice. Forbidden to speak, Hadassah in constant pain, took time to pray. Unterscharfuhrer Schimmel, flushed with a sense of victory, smiled at the captives and prodded Hadassah with his toe. "I pity you Jew, when General Roy gets hold of you." "I welcome the meeting, Lieutenant," she replied, "for I could very well be the last person to see the Antichrist alive!" Infuriated, Schimmel slammed the barrel of his luger into Hadassah's forehead. "Antichrist? I am Antichrist," the German screamed. Blood trickling down her face, Hadassah looked squarely at Schimmel. "You're right, Lieutenant. The Bible says,

"Little children, it is the last time: and as ye have heard that antichrist shall come, even now are there many antichrists; whereby we know that it is the last time."

(1 John 2:18)

"It is the last time for you Lieutenant!"

Guttural orders were passed. Dov, Miriam and Josh Cleary were prodded into a line against the Temple wall. Hadassah cried, "no! no!" The Weizmanns clasped hands. Miriam offered a hand to Josh. Hadassah couldn't bear to watch. Schimmel cried, "Der Fuhrer lives! Feuer!" Hadassah moaned and sobbed," Oh, Lord," she said plaintively, "first our baby Samuel, now my parents. Where will it end?" "It will end very, very soon," a voice within seemed to say.

"And when he had opened the fifth seal, I saw under the altar the souls of them that were slain for the word of God, and for the testimony which they held: And they cried with a loud voice saying, How long, O Lord, holy and true, dost thou not judge and avenge our blood on them that dwell on the earth? And white robes were given unto every one of them; and it was said unto them, that they should rest yet for a little season, until their fellow-servants also and their brethren, that should be killed as they were, should be fulfilled."

(Revelation 6:9-11)

**239**

Hadassah was dragged into the Temple. She was shocked to see how the house of worship had been desecrated. Satanic pentagrams, the inverted five-pointed stars, were everywhere. Hideous he-goats with extended tongues were poised over vile sexual perversions. A black statue of Beelzebul, the Lord of the Flies, towered over the entryway. The Third Temple was not in God's plans like the first two, but it was dedicated to Yahweh in the Antichrist's mock ceremony. God takes what men give Him, she thought, regardless of the intent. In symbolically measuring the temple (Revelation 11:1), Hadassah recalled Sam's teaching, God considered the sanctuary His property. He gave the outer court and the city to Gentile control, for one half of the Tribulation period or forty-two months. The sanctuary was God's. For men to make it a center of hellish idolatry would certainly bring down the wrath of God upon them.

Taken into a Temple room in the west wing, Hadassah found a chamber designed for the robing of the priests. It was dimly lit with the same chill vapors they had experienced in Roy's Belgian headquarters. She was forced to kneel before an altar. Hadassah gasped. A woman, nude except for a diaphanous white robe, was prostrate on the altar. A golden chalice was balanced on her navel. "A black mass!" Hadassah shuddered. The woman moaned, fighting off a stupefying drug.

Ten Sing, the spokesman for General Roy, and the man Winston considered to be the False Prophet of Revelation 13, entered the room, accompanied by two men in what Hadassah guessed was Tibetan dress. The attendants intoned a low, repetitive "aum." In a flowing red robe, emblazoned with a golden dragon, Ten Sing was in a trance-like state. He drank from the chalice. The beverage was blood. He cried, "Lucifer, our Master, receive us today. Grant victory to your servant, Key-Ky-Sigma, **666**." Hadassah prayed. Everyone else in the room was prostrate on the floor. From his robe, Ten Sing drew out a long, silver dagger. With one, swift motion he plunged it into the nude's throat. Blood flew. The woman gurgled once and her body went limp. "Die for Lucifer," Ten Sing cried.

"What did you think of that Mrs. Winston?" Ten Sing said with a sneer. Hadassah, choked with anger replied, "The Bible said your Master was a murderer from the beginning. Jesus gives life, but Lucifer, the Antichrist and you, can only give death." Ten Sing, furious, shot back, "the next sacrifice to Lucifer will be yours and your unborn child unless you tell us the whereabouts of that traitorous Jew, your husband."

From behind Ten Sing, curtains opened and a man's head moved and spoke. It was virtual reality, an audio-animatronics device, perhaps a smaller edition of the image of the beast in the holy of holies. "Welcome, Mrs. Winston, I've waited patiently for this moment." The voice was low and artificial. "Your husband was my friend. I gave him favored status in my organization and you two deserted me for That One." Hadassah replied sharply, "That One is Jesus Christ the Righteous." The image recoiled as if struck. "You'll pay dearly for that Mrs. Winston. This is my hour. I will lead my army against the colossus from the east. We will find your husband and handle you both with exquisite pain." "You are finished, Roy," Hadassah replied in triumph. "It is the hour of judgment for you." The head recoiled again. "Shackle the prisoner" Roy screamed, "bring her to me. Ten Sing, summon the entire garrison and report to me at Megiddo this afternoon." With that, the screen went to black. The curtain closed.

Rough hands dragged Hadassah off to another Temple room. It was a star chamber, a place of torture for anyone that failed to worship the image of the beast or to take the mark. All the grim instruments of a medieval inquisition were on display. The room smelled of blood and wreaked of death. The Iron Mistress, beds of nails, the rack, whips of all sorts, pincers for tearing out nails and knives for cropping ears and noses, axes for maiming limbs, showed considerable use. A blacksmith's forge kept an assortment of pokers red hot. There was only one other prisoner in the room. Hadassah was chained to the wall next to the frail, sagging body of a man of great age. The guards left, locking the heavy door behind them.

The frail prisoner seemed to waken. He turned sightless eyes toward Hadassah. The man wore a ragged brown nightshirt that floated over an emaciated frame. Spindly legs, covered with sores, descended to bare feet, bruised and bloody, blue with cold. His wrists were ringed with dried blood from the manacles that cut deeply into the flesh. His hair was long and matted and covered what should have been his eyes. Raising his head the better to be seen, the black holes were visible that had once been his windows on the world. "I am Hayim Lefkovitz, a believer in the Messiah Jesus," he said in Hebrew and then broke into English. "What brings you to this outpost of hell, my friend?" he asked. "I am Hadassah Winston, my brother, like you a believer in Y'shuah HaMushiach. Roy is looking for my husband for we are charged with a whole range of crimes, especially treason against the Antichrist."

The man brightened, "I came to faith in the Messiah Jesus through the preaching of the two witnesses at the door of this Temple. When they were slain, I went into hiding. We made it for three years, but a neighbor turned us in. I was marked for the headsman's ax on three counts. I would not worship the image of the beast and I do not have the mark. My great crime they told me was for being a Christian and a Jew. They brought me to the Temple for a public execution. They had so many to kill it was postponed. I kept reciting scripture and telling them "thus saith the Lord." They got so angry they said I would never read scripture again. They burned my eyes out. It was no great loss. It keeps me from seeing what vile creatures are arrayed against our Lord. I am ready to die and I know I shall see my Savior soon." Lefkovitz hung his head as he related that guards had told him his daughter had surrendered to the authorities pleading to be allowed to care for her father. "I don't know what they have done with her," he said plaintively. Hadassah said nothing, concluding the sacrificial victim was probably Hayim's daughter.

Hadassah looked at her bloody footprints. Standing for a long period of time produced pain in the abdomen and the lower back. She wouldn't allow herself to think she might lose another baby. Minutes seemed like hours. Hadassah's suffering mounted. Schimmel returned and bound the two with piano wire. It took three men to put her in the truck. Hadassah's spirits soared with every mile of the drive north to Megiddo. "We're going to meet the Messiah," she cried in glee. It earned her a jackboot in the small of the back. "Very soon," Hadassah whispered to Hayim, "we will welcome loved ones, American and Israeli believers and some we have not met in this life." Hadassah pictured baby Samuel and her parents. Hayim thought of his daughter. Hadassah had memorized John's triumphant prophecy,

"Beloved, now are we the sons [children] of God, and it doth not yet appear what we shall be: but we know that, when He shall appear, we shall be like him; for we shall see him as he is."

(1 John 3:2)

"Just think of it, Hayim," Hadassah said with excitement, "our people are going to be important figures in the Kingdom! The prophet Zechariah says ten men will take hold of a Jew, to sort of use him as a ticket for a close view of the Messiah at the Temple in Jerusalem. For two thousand years, any time ten Gentiles took hold of the skirt of a Jew it was to rob him, kill him or put him out of his land."

Schimmel's convoy picked its way through roads clogged with military traffic. The largest allied army since World War II was marshaled on the plain of Megiddo. Napoleon had pronounced it the most ideal battlefield he had ever seen. Roy's headquarters were in the largest tent among acres of canvass units aligned with military precision.

The captives were bound to ridgepoles in Roy's tent. Wrists and ankles were wet with blood from the piano wire bindings. They were left alone for hours. Except for the guards nearby, the hustle and bustle of big brass, aides and messengers, the prisoners were ignored. With a shout, heels clicked, and Roy strode into the tent, followed by Ten Sing. "The Antichrist and the False Prophet are here," Hadassah said softly, grimacing in pain. Allowing herself to be heard, she said, "this is too good." "Silence, you traitor!" Roy cried. Every inch a general, Roy was resplendent in French horizon blue with the marshal's insignia on the sleeves. Ten Sing was dressed in the same red robe he wore at the Temple. Their attire seemed out of place among soldiers in camouflage gear and kevlar helmets.

"Well, Mrs. Winston here you are and your husband will join us shortly, if he is not already dead." Looking Hayim up and down Roy demanded, "who is this wretched creature?" "Another Jewish follower of That One," the oriental replied. Effecting a pontifical look at Hadassah, Roy began, "you know I must punish you Mrs. Winston, but I want to be merciful to you and your husband. If you will fall down before me and take the mark, you will die decently. I will have you shot. Refuse and it is the sword for you." "Worship you?" Hadassah sneered venomously, "take your mark? Never! We belong to Jesus Christ. You can kill the body, but not the soul and spirit. We belong to Christ." "Silence," Roy screamed. "Leave them to me, Excellency," Ten Sing said with a fiendish smile.

Patrols kept Sam and Bar-Giora away from the collective farms Hadassah guessed might help with broadcasts. They were able to find the poles they would need for the transmission. Bar-Giora suggested they try the two wadis on the Syrian side of the border that converged like the edges of a cut of pie. The wadis offered cover and the possibility of a hasty exit. They explored the dry, forbidding land carefully. The duo quickly assembled the equipment, got off quick broadcasts and fled from one wadi to another.

Bar-Giora had a sixth sense for danger. The sergeant searched the sky for aircraft and the horizon for ground patrols. The EU patrols were out there and maybe Eastern forces as well, Bar-Giora was certain, but both sides were probably reluctant to move into Syrian territory. Winston got off three, hard-hitting broadcasts to the EU army. Strangely, the broadcast sites were never rocketed when Winston signed off. "They want you alive, Colonel," Bar Giora guessed.

The Syrian town of Der'a lay exactly in the middle of the wadis. More out of curiosity than anything, Winston wanted to enter the town. Against his better judgment, Bar Giora-turned west out of Wadi el Zedi. They made ten of the eighteen miles when it hit. A rocket propelled grenade hit the windshield of the vehicle. Bar-Giora was dead before he hit the ground. Winston flew out of the passenger side. He would have shared Bar Giora's fate, but he had bent over to tie his shoe a second before the rocket struck the vehicle. Winston was unconscious. For how long? Coming around, he dragged himself away from the still-burning wreck. Certain Bar-Giora was dead and his radio equipment smashed, Winston lowered his head and wept.

A booted foot turned him over. Flickering, late afternoon shadows played tricks with his eyes. He found himself in a circle of heavily armed men, who spoke a kind of guttural Arabic. Were they al Qaeda? Taliban? Winston couldn't tell. The circle parted to admit a tall, swarthy man, perhaps a Caucasian. He wore jackboots, a crisp, caped army uniform, a gleaming black pistol belt and a kaffieyeh headdress. "Who are you," the officer demanded, "Are you EU? Your driver was uniformed, but you are not. CIA? What do you have to say for yourself, before my men slit your gullet and feed your entrails to the buzzards."

"I came here to preach the good news of Jesus Christ to the army of General Roy. You can find what remains of my radio equipment in the vehicle." "A preacher?" the officer laughed. "We found the radio, but why should I believe such a ridiculous story? I choose to believe you were transmitting intelligence information about our troop movements." "Believe what you want," Sir, but I really did broadcast the Gospel to the EU army. Once upon a time, I was a U.S. army officer on Roy's staff, before he invaded Israel. When I realized he was satan's agent, I got out of uniform and enlisted in God's army,"

The officer waved to a guard. "Truss up this pig and bring him along. We'll examine him later." His arms lashed behind him and a noose loosely tied around his neck, Winston was dragged behind an LTV for what seemed like an eternity. In a widely dispersed cantonment area, Winston was tied to a quarter ton truck wheel while his captors dug what he assumed was his grave. It gave Winston time to pray. A serenity came over him he had never known before. Life or death in this situation wouldn't matter. It would be only a matter of minutes or hours before the Lord returns.

Winston was thrown into the pit and buried up to his neck. The ache in his body seemed to evaporate in the cooling sand, but the pain behind his eyeballs and the dull throbbing in his head was excruciating. Left there all night, wind-whipped sands stung the face and the bitter night chill made him yearn for the day. The ache in his lower extremities crept back with every hour in the pit. Somehow, he nodded off.

He wakened to find the officer sitting on a campstool, studying Winston closely. He slapped a leather quirt against a boot. "Tell me again who you are," the officer demanded. "I don't like to kill men without knowing their identity." "I am Sam Winston. As I told you, I was a one-time U S Army officer, but now I am a civilian. I am a believer in Jesus the Messiah, a Zionist and an opponent of Roy and if you are an officer in the eastern army, I am an opponent of yours as well," Winston replied through swollen lips. The officer brightened fiendishly, "you are a dirty Jew! You have come to the right place Jew Winston. We know how to take care of Jews." Without a word, a soldier nearby, drew a gleaming scimitar from its richly studded scabbard.

"Actually, we know all about you ex-Colonel Winston. We have monitored EU radio transmissions. They are scouring the country for you." "Ex-Colonel, is right. I am a civilian and under the rules of the Geneva Convention, I am a non-combatant." The officer laughed. "My men will whet their blades in your blood. But how rude of me, Jew-Winston. I should introduce myself. I am Rudiger Meyer of the SS." "SS?" an incredulous Winston replied. "Aren't you several generations removed from the days of the black and silver?" "Ja, hein." Meyer braced to attention. "I am third generation SS. My grandfather, Major Kurt Meyer was a hero of the Fatherland." Winston looked away contemptuously. This guy is another Rolf Krueger of the Foreign Legion, Winston thought to himself. Meyer, his knuckles white on the quirt, swung the riding crop and creased Winston's forehead. Blood in his eyes, forced Sam to blink in order to focus on Meyer. "My father served on the eastern front battling the Bolshevik-Jewish menace." Come on, Meyer, your father fought no one but innocent, sick, half-starved Jewish men, women and children; defenseless and alone. Let me guess," Winston continued, "your grandfather was a concentration camp commandant. Did you say he was a major? He was probably in charge of selections for the gas chamber. The *brausebad*, the phony showers that dispensed Zyklon B. The crystals vaporized and your father's victims clawed at the walls and the floors until suffocated. Then the *sonderkommando*, another poor Jew, entered the chamber, removed the bodies and burned them."

Meyer, livid with rage, thrashed the air with his quirt. "I told you Jew Winston, my grandfather was a war hero. He had nothing to do with gassing women and children. As the world now knows, no such crimes actually took place." Like a hunter closing in for the kill, Winston asked, "whom did your grandfather serve under?" "Colonel Franz Stangl said my grandfather was the finest soldier in his army." Winston smiled wanly. "So I was right. Franz Stangl was the commandant of Treblinka. Treblinka had only one function, the mass murder of innocent Jews."

Meyer kicked sand into Winston's face. Grains stuck to the blood trickling from his forehead. Winston wouldn't let up. "At the close of the war, I bet your grandfather like Stangl, joined a river of displaced persons clogging the roads of eastern and central Europe, heading for Italy to escape justice. He got some help from the mysterious ODESSA movement, the organization of former SS men. He got a great deal of help from Nazi sympathizers in key places. Am I right?" Winston asked.

Meyer ignored the question, but he was clearly impressed with Winston's knowledge of the successful plot that allowed Nazi war criminals to escape justice. "What do you know about ODESSA?" Meyer asked. Drawing on his memory of a course at the Army War College, Winston said, "the war crimes trials of major Nazi figures, made it clear to the perpetrators of genocide that in time the wheels of justice would get around to dealing with the second and third level of their accomplices in the murder of six million Jews and millions of Russians and Poles. It was time to clear out. The gold and jewels stolen from living Jews and the gold teeth of dead victims, financed the escapes. ODESSA was real enough, but novelists have given it more life than it really had. The big story is the help your grandfather and other killers received from the most powerful organization in Europe and even from the Allies that had won the war."

"And what do you know of the SS refugees in Italy?" continued Meyer. Winston thought for a moment, reconstructing the history. "The archives reflect that in the early days of the Nazi exodus, the war criminals were hidden in monasteries in Genoa, Milan and in other northern Italian cities. The head of the German Catholic community in Rome - let me think," Winston said, "what was his name? Oh yes, Bishop Alois Hudal. Hudal secured blank passports from the International Red Cross. Funding came directly from the Vatican. Archbishop Montini, later Pope Paul the Sixth, was on the Vatican staff and knew of the plot and was directly involved." "Why would the Catholic Church do that for German refugees?" Meyer interjected. Winston responded, "the refugees as you call them, were thought to be an indispensable part of the defense against the spread of the international Communist menace. The United States, Britain and France, shared the Vatican's views on the matter."

Meyer took up the story. "ODESSA informed my grandfather about Bishop Hudal and his services to war heroes, but the patriotic prelate was compromised before my grandfather reached Villach on the Austrian-Yugoslav border." Winston took up the thread of the story. "Probably your grandfather went directly to Rome and hid out in the Monastery of San Girolamo until a Croatian priest, whose name escapes me, was able to obtain phony travel documents and Vatican money to get your grandfather out of Europe." "Brilliant," cried Meyer. "You have the story correct in every particular. The Croatian priest was Franciscan Father Krunoslav Draganovich, himself a hero of the struggle against the bolshevists and the Jews. Draganovich performed valuable services to the survivors of the Fatherland."

"Your grandfather then took what was known as "the Vatican ratlines," the sea transports that smuggled SS men into Canada, the United States, Australia and South America." "My father could have gone to Canada traveling as a Catholic priest, but he was determined to carry on the struggle. He took a tramp steamer, buses and donkey carts to Syria. He became a general in the Syrian army training Arabs for the destruction of the Zionist State of Israel." "It didn't work, did it," Winston said with satisfaction. "American-Jewish money kept the Zionists alive," Meyer responded angrily. "My father got my mother, Kunagonde out of Austria in 1949. My father, Ernst Meyer, was born in Damascus in 1951. He too could have vanished into the West, but he carried on my grandfather's crusade. He was an advisor to Sheik Muhammad Hussein Fadlallah, the spiritual leader of the Hezbollah in Lebanon. He married a Lebanese girl, my mother. My father, only thirty years of age, was killed in the Bekaa Valley, a victim of Zionist aggression."

"What about you, Meyer, are you an SS army of one?" "Jawohl," Meyer replied proudly. "My lightning SS tattoo with my blood group is under my left arm. I received my grandfather's SS dagger with the heroic legend, *Blut und Ehre*, Blood and Honor on the blade. I am a Captain in the Syrian army assigned to the guerrilla forces of the great Eastern Confederation. I trained Pashtuns in Waziristan, Uzbeks, Tajiks, Georgians, Taliban and al Qaeda. I am treated with honor and respect. They call it "milmastia," the courtesy shown a warrior, even if they do not share his views."

Winston began to think, "I owe it to this slime-bag to tell him about the Messiah Jesus. "Captain, do you understand what you are up against in the battle you are facing?" "Yes, yes, I do Winston," Meyer said with glee, "I will slay Jews and the soldiers of the West, grandchildren of the armies that fought against the Third Reich. Your grandfathers should have joined in the battle against the real Zionist-Bolshevik menace. And I will fight right in the land of the Jews. It will be glorious." "No, that is not whom you will face at Megiddo. You must face the Lord Jesus Christ and a heavenly army that will destroy you, the Eastern Confederacy, Roy and all his army, in a moment of time. What you need to know is that God loves sinners, yes, sinners like you and me. He sent His Son to die for sinners and God invites you today to receive Him as your Savior. There is no other way out, Captain. Do it now!"

"Rubbish," cried Meyer, "I have no need of the Jew Jesus. He has done nothing for you Winston. You are entombed in sand up to your neck and you are about to die horribly. I am captain of my own destiny and I will yet build the thousand-year Reich my family died for." Meyer strode away to his tent.

Left alone, Sam prayed for the poor, misguided Nazi. Winston became conscious of the sun that burned deeply into his bloody, sand-encrusted visage. Pain pounded at his temples. "If they could only see me now at the Infantry School," he said with a chuckle.

Marcel Dupin in the dispersal hut of the former Mossad anti-terrorist training center at Kfar Sirkin, studied the intelligence report for the fourth or fifth time. The aerial photos clearly showed the twisted, burned-out wreckage of a military vehicle. The unidentified nude body a few meters from the crash site could be Winston. Dupin theorized it was the vehicle driver, naked, after Bedouins had stripped the body. Tire impressions and the footprints of many feet, some booted, suggested a large party had been on the scene and then moved off north, northeast. Radio intercepts had identified at least five Middle Eastern dialects in a suspected force of hostiles a few kilometers from Der'a. The exact composition of the patrol was not known. "That's our target," Dupin said with conviction, "if Winston is yet alive, he is in that compound. We have to take him out tonight."

Major Cedric Cooke of Twelve Group of the crack, British Special Air Service, the SAS, studied the photos and pinpointed the enemy force in grease pencil on his situation map. "We must get off by 2300, Inspector," Cooke said to the tired and drawn Dupin, "ETA 2345. I plan on an LZ about four kilometers west of Der'a. That is rather closer to the village than I like, but well, that's it. If there is nothing more, we'll be off." Cedric tossed a careless salute. Dupin mused, the SAS is the best commando unit in the world. If Winston is held by an eastern army patrol Cooke will get him.

Three Blackhawk helicopters followed the Wadi el Zedi, at fifty feet above the ground. It was the route Winston and Bar Giora had traversed. A faint yellow moon played tag with soft clouds as they sped through the night. On signal from Cooke they turned north. The dim lights of Der'a were on their left. Touchdown was at 2344, Sgt. Knobby Clark noted in his log. Twenty-four men dropped to the ground. One section of six men quickly established a perimeter defense around the choppers. Three sections moved the four kilometers to the camp. "About thirty in the patrol," I judge, said Cooke adjusting his night vision equipment. "Right. Take your positions. Burns, dispatch the sentries. On my signal lads, in five."

It was over quickly. Reeling from a grenade that burst his eardrums, Meyer was cut down outside his tent by a short burst from the only Jew in Cooke's Twelve Group, Lance Corporal Arnold Perlstein of Birmingham. Corporal Herby Latham tripped over Winston in the dark. The Lancashireman was stunned to find a man buried to his neck. "All right sir?" he asked. "Frightfully sorry, old boy, I just didn't see you there." "Tsokay," Winston replied, "tsokay." "Latham, you're a bleeding' shower, you are," a disgusted Sergeant Major crowed. The commandos dug Winston out of his sand prison, plunged a syringe into his arm and four commandos carried him back to the waiting helicopters. The code word "Samaritan" was flashed to headquarters and Winston was in Dupin's custody at 0250 zulu. Roy was informed of Winston's capture at a Canadian officers mess. He was ecstatic.

Winston slowly emerged from the blue fog he had floundered in since the SAS medic emptied the syringe in his arm. He seemed to be on a sawdust floor. Dim figures danced before his eyes, but none reached out to him. "Wouldn't they help me to my feet?" One figure stood motionless. The other seemed to be a weaving, heaving abdomen, but without a voice.

Kicked awake by a soldier, Winston was pulled to his feet and lashed to a ridgepole. Slumping against the ropes, Winston fought to clear his head. "Darling, darling," someone cried nearby. He blinked to focus. Could it be? It was. It was Hadassah. "Oh Sam," she cried, "you're alive. Praise God. They told me you were dead." "No, honey, it just feels like it." Winston brightened, "we got three broadcasts in, but it cost Bar Giora his life. We were ambushed by an Eastern Confederacy patrol. I was the prisoner of a late-day SS officer who planned to kill me. Then everything exploded. I was kicked in the head by a clumsy English commando and then I was whisked away on a magic carpet. Unceremoniously dumped on the ground, the first person I saw was this fat lady." "Fat lady? Why you wife deserter, wait until I get my hands on you. Sam, this is my fellow prisoner, Hayim Lefkovitz, a Messianic Jew." "*Baruch Ha-Shem*," blessed be the Name," Sam greeted him. "*Todah rabbah*, many thanks Brother Shmuel. I am sightless awaiting the sighting of the Messiah. It is good to have you here, but not to be chained before the Antichrist." "Yes Sam," Hadassah added, "we are the guests of the Man of Sin, Field Marshall Roy."

Roy strolled into the tent, savoring the moment. "Well, well, Sam, you naughty boy. You've caused me a great deal of trouble, not that your nonsense broadcasts accomplished anything. No, you have caused me trouble in your defiance of my authority." Roy's appearance changed before the captives eyes. A wide-eyed, haunted look came over him. He screamed," The world is mine. You can't spoil my hour on the stage of history. I am the only world ruler who ever lived. Alexander, the Caesars, Napoleon, Hitler, all failed. I succeeded." Winston said softly, "Roy, you are mad. The Messiah is coming back to reclaim the world from your hands and the hands of your infernal master. It is over for you."

An officer, obviously shaken, burst into the tent crying, "Excellency! there is something in the sky!" Roy and Ten Sing rushed out. Ten Sing could be heard crying, "it's Him, Excellency, it is That One." "Nonsense," Roy barked, "that's an optical illusion." Winston turned to Hadassah excitedly, "Honey, I believe they just saw the sign of the coming of the Son of man. We'll be free very soon, my darling." Winston turned to Hayim, "hang on dear brother, it is the beginning of the end for the Antichrist and a new beginning for us." The sunlight faded and an unusual darkness covered the plain of Megiddo. For what seemed like hours, really mere minutes, a low-pitched sound stopped the ears like a Texas tornado. Knees buckled under a strange weight. A magnetic field, Winston guessed. An ear-splitting bugle call was followed by a fierce wind that threatened to take the tent. "Here comes the Messiah," Winston cried in triumph. "I believe Roy's army and the Eastern confederacy just felt the edge of the sword of the Lord."

Then all was quiet. The captives wept and cried. There was a furtive step behind them. Ben Zion appeared. "You are free, my friends." He loosed their bonds. "The Messiah has come! The Antichrist and the False Prophet were cast into a lake of fire." Hadassah slumped to the floor muttering, "it's the time Sam."

Winston carried his wife to a chamber at the rear of the tent. It was Roy's bedroom, sheltered by floor to ceiling drapery. Laying Hadassah on the beautifully brocaded couch, Sam said to himself, "what do I know about delivering a baby? Lord, you will have to help me." Sam washed his hands in water and a bottle of Roy's whiskey. It was the time. He assisted Hadassah as the baby passed through the birth canal. It was an easy birth. A boy! A slick, squalling, pink thing, with a shock of black hair, wound up in Sam's arms. Through the drape, Ben-Zion handed him a knife to cut the cord. Sam tenderly washed him up. It was somehow fitting, Winston thought, to use Roy's monogrammed towels to wrap the infant.

"Ben-Zion, would you take the baby while I tend to Hadassah?" He handed the baby back through the drape to waiting hands. "What a beautiful boy. This is the first baby born in My Father's Kingdom," a deep, regal voice announced. Winston drew back the drape in shock. It had to be the Messiah, holding baby Aaron! Winston fell on his face. Ben-Zion and Hayim knelt in worship. "Stand up, my brothers," the Messiah ordered, "and see this remarkable child." Hadassah rose slowly and walked to the door of the chamber. She smiled at the Messiah tenderly holding her baby. In her joy she recited,

**"And it shall be said in that day, Lo, this is our God; we have waited for Him, and He will save us; this is the Lord; we have waited for Him, we will be glad and rejoice in His salvation."**

**(Isaiah 25:9)**

# A MESSAGE FOR THE JEWISH PEOPLE

This is a novel about a Jewish couple, Sam, from an American Jewish home and Hadassah, a *sabra* from an imaginary kibbutz just south of Galilee. The novel is set in a time of great peril for the children of Israel in the land and in the diaspora. The prophet Jeremiah calls the period "the time of Jacob's trouble" (Jeremiah 30:6-7). We will say more about Jeremiah's prophecy in due course.

But let me tell you about myself. I am a Gentile Christian. My faith journey began with the Bible. You gave the world that precious book and I cannot thank you enough for it. The faith of your people revealed in scripture has civilized me and other Gentiles. My ancestors painted themselves blue and drank hot blood at the time the great Temple of Solomon was one of the wonders of the world. In the grace of G-d and through the Jewish people we have come a long way.

We have a debt to pay to you. We believe the Bible has a message for all men, and a particular message for the children of Israel. This novel is constructed on the premise that the Bible is the inerrant Word of God. We quote it here 126 times. We are biblical literalists, that means that when the words we read in scripture make sense we look for no other sense.

Three times in the Book of Jeremiah, the prophet warns that the citizens of Jerusalem will know "fear on every side." Jeremiah spoke of the fear born of the Babylonian siege of the city. But he looked beyond his own day to a future time more terrifying than that suffered at the hand of Nebuchadnezzar. Many believers in the Messiah are convinced that Jeremiah's prophetic day is near at hand. Jeremiah called it "the time of Jacob's trouble." In another place the Bible calls it the Great Tribulation.

Your people have been sore-pressed by violence through a long blood-soaked history. In my lifetime, six million Jews were murdered for no crime. I believe every pogrom, every act of genocide against your people is part of a plot to usurp G-d's throne. It cannot be done, but they wreak vengeance on His Chosen People.

It is not a pleasant task to remind you of the bloody trial that lies ahead for your people. Some will even suggest that writing about it may invite another Pharaoh, a Haman or a Hitler to undertake a deadly campaign against the Jews. All I can say in response it that knowing what the prophetic scriptures have to say shall shortly come to pass, I feel I must warn the Jewish people and provide them with evidence from the Bible to show that the danger is imminent and real. The novel includes a way of dealing with the long-term effects of the period.

The Bible gives accurate information on the extent of human misery in that period of time. One-quarter of the earth's inhabitants will be slain in that seven-year period. That would include 25% of the Jewish people in the diaspora. In Israel itself, the prophet Zechariah tells us two-thirds of Israeli Jews will perish. Is it *narish* to believe these things? I believe it is *narish* not to give the Bible a fair reading and then make your assessment and take a position. I pray that this novel will move you to make that kind of fair-minded investigation.

If it would add urgency to the message, I would gladly proclaim this warning from the rooftops. I have chosen the medium of a fictionalized account of the people in the Tribulation, with the fervent prayer that you will read it and heed it's message. The Jews are endowed with an amazing capacity to find the best in the worst of situations. This phenomenon has kept your people optimistic through many dark periods in your history. It is not in my heart to spoil anyone's golden days with grim forecasts of desperate days ahead. Nevertheless, I am a prisoner of the sacred scriptures which hold a large body of teaching on The Time of Jacob's Trouble.

Bible prophecy ends with the hopeful news, "but he [the Jewish people] shall be saved out of it." That is when the long-awaited Messiah will return. The Jewish people will be the head and not the tail; no longer a hissing and a by-word, for those will be the days of the great Kingdom Reign of the Messiah. To be a Jew in those days will be a time of blessing beyond anyone's wildest dreams. Until that great and glorious day, it is our duty to stand as watchmen on the walls, to warn the Jewish people to carefully read the prophetic scriptures of the Jews and the Christians and to heed the warnings of the wrath to come. Making the scriptures known is the best way I can discharge my sacred obligation to a people to whom I owe so much.

Shalom, Shalom.

Lyle Murphy,

# TERMS USED IN THIS BOOK

**Antichrist** – The mortal who becomes the tool of Satan in the end-time plot to seize the throne of God and subvert the anticipated Kingdom reign of the Messiah. "Anti," means against. It also means to take the place of. Both prepositions apply in the case of Satan's masterpiece. During the Seven-Year Great Tribulation, the Antichrist will present a program that includes a one-world religion, one-world government and one-world economic order. See also Beast, Man of Sin.

**Antisemitism** – Hatred of the Jews. Manifest in history in calumny, restrictive measures and finally in annihilation.

**Armageddon (Megiddo)** – Biblical location in northwest Israel. Site of the final battle in the Great Tribulation (Revelation 16:16). Armageddon is a transliteration of Har Megiddo, the mount of Megiddo. Napoleon called it the greatest natural battlefield in the world.

**Babylon** – Ancient city-state, southwest of Baghdad. Originally built by Nimrod (Gen. 10:10). In Nebuchadnezzar's day, it was a large fortress city marked by beautiful hanging gardens. Also the name of the nation to which Judah was carried captive in 586 B.C.E. Some scholars believe it will be the center of the antigod program of Satan (Revelation 17:3-7; Revelation 18).

**Beast** – The Apostle John's name for the Antichrist in the book of Revelation.

**Bible** – This novel assumes that the sixty-six books of the Hebrew Old Testament and the twenty-seven books of the Christian New Testament together comprise The Holy Bible. The King James Bible is quoted throughout as the version most likely to be available to the Jewish people.

**"blood libel," etc.** – Two monstrous lies about the Jewish people dating from the Middle Ages. In Catholic countries rumors spread almost on an annual basis that the Jews abduct Gentile children in order to mix their blood with the matzo, the unleavened bread of Passover. At other times, the Jews were accused of stealing communion wafers in order to stab and cut the host. The lie holds the Jews crucify Christ anew. The basis of the lie was the Catholic teaching that the wafer becomes the actual body, blood, soul and divinity of Christ when the priest consecrates the communion wafer.

**Casualties of the Great Tribulation** – Zechariah 13:8-9) relates that two-thirds of Israelis will be slain in the Seven-Year Great Tribulation. In the same period, Revelation 6:8 foretells of one-fourth of earth's inhabitants who are casualties of war, pestilence, famine and wild animals.

## Terms, Contd.

**Demons -** Followers of Satan, probably fallen angels. They carry out the will of their master. Ephesians 6:12 describes divisions of demons and the areas of their employment to aid in the conspiracy to seized the throne of God. *Dybbuks -* demon-like creatures in Yiddish literature who may be demons. They seem to share the same malevolent character as demons.

**European Union** – A consortium of nations, principally of Western Europe that share common background with the historic Roman Empire. The book of Daniel focuses the end-time prophecy on the revival of that Empire. In the novel, the EU and the revived Roman Empire are identical.

**False Prophet** – Revelation 13:11-18. Miracle-working tool of Satan who promotes the worship of Antichrist and promotes the taking of his mark (See mark of the beast).

*Frum* – Yiddish term meaning one who is religious.

**Good News** – Rendering of the word Gospel, Old English for any good news. In the New Testament it is exclusively news of the death, burial and resurrection of Jesus Christ (1 Corinthians 15:1-8).

**Great Tribulation** – Jesus' own title for the Seven-Year period of political, natural, and spiritual distress upon the earth. Unlike any other tribulation known to man, Jesus explained, "For then shall be great tribulation, such as was not since the beginning of the world to this time, no, nor ever shall be" (Matthew 14:21). Jeremiah called it the "time of Jacob's trouble" Jeremiah 30:6-7.

**Jews for Jesus** – Movement begun in early 1970's and led by Martin Meyer Rosen, a Messianic Jew active in Jewish evangelization in New York City. With a small number of volunteers, Rosen opened up in the Haight-Ashbury district of San Francisco in an effort to reach young Jewish people in the "flower children" counter-culture. Using confrontation, humorous literature and music "Moishe" Rosen led the group to a successful ministry. Now numbering almost three hundred missionaries, they operate throughout the world.

**Judgments** – A number of divine judgments are prophesied in the Bible. Two notable judgments are in view in this novel. Matthew 24:31-46 describes the judgment of the Gentile nations at the close of the Great Tribulation. The basis of judgment is "what did you do with or for the Jewish people?" Ezekiel 20:34-44 relates the judgment of the children of Israel at the close of the Tribulation, perhaps in the wilderness at Kadesh Barnea. The basis of judgment will be their response to the Gospel.

**Kingdom Reign of Messiah** – A thousand-year, world-wide rule by the Messiah centering on Jerusalem and a Fourth Temple (Ezekiel 40-48). This reign immediately follows the Great Tribulation and the time mark is set by Revelation 19:1-3. A large number of passages in the Old Testament prophets describe the blessings of life in that Kingdom.

**Terms, Contd.**

**Kings of the South, North and East** – Antichrist's principal military opposition in the last half of the Great Tribulation. The King of the South represents a coalition of North African nations (Daniel 10:44). The King of the North is a coalition of Muslim nations to the north of Israel. The King of the East seems to be a very large gathering of east Asian peoples (Daniel 10:44).

**Man of Sin** – The Apostle Paul's name for the Antichrist (2 Thessalonians 2:3-4).

*Mamzer* – The illegitimate one. Pejorative name some Jews gave to Jesus.

**Mark of the Beast** – Some type of tattoo to identify the worshippers and followers of the Antichrist, taken in the right hand or the forehead Revelation 13:16-18.

**Messiah, Christ** – Title given to Jesus as the Son of God, the heir and ruler of all things.

**144,000 Witnesses** – Jewish followers of the Messiah drawn from all twelve tribes of Israel for service as missionaries to the world during the Great Tribulation (Revelation 7:1-8). There is the suggestion that the witnesses are protected from physical harm and appear with the Messiah at the close of the Tribulation (Revelation 14:1-5).

**Rapture** – Term not found in the New Testament referring to the imminent, soon return of Jesus to take out His born again believers from the present age, before the Great Tribulation. (1 Thessalonians 4:13-18; 1 Corinthians 15:51). See novel Chapter 8.

**Revelation, Book of** – The Apostle John's account of events in the prophetic program. Written just before 100 C.E.

**Revived Roman Empire** – See European Union, above.

## Terms, Contd.

**Roman Catholic Church** – Skeleton and sinew of the one-world religion or Universal Church during the Great Tribulation. The Antichrist will loot the church and then destroy it (Revelation 17:16). For an extended treatment of the history of the Roman Catholic Church and the Jewish people see novel Chapter 25.

**Saved, born again** – Biblical terms used to describe the personal, new-birth experience of those who have trusted Jesus the Savior/ Messiah for salvation. The Apostle Paul used the term "saved." He wrote, "for by grace are ye saved through faith; and that not of yourselves: it is the gift of God: not of works, lest any man should boast" (Ephesians 2:8,9). Jesus and the Apostle Peter used the term "born again," to describe the same experience. Jesus said to the Pharisee Nicodemus, "ye must be born again" (John 3:3,7). Peter wrote, "being born again, not of corruptible seed, but of incorruptible, by the Word of God, which liveth and abideth for ever" (1 Peter 1:23).

**Signs of the coming Great Tribulation** – On the occasion of the re-dedication of Herod's Temple, Jesus prophesied the destruction of the Temple that took place in 70 A.D. He also added prophecies about the coming Great Tribulation, still future to the

time of this writing. He gave five signs to warn of the coming of that Seven-Year period. First, there would be many who will say, "I am the Messiah; and shall deceive many" (Matthew 24:5). Secondly, (vs. 6) "wars and rumors of wars. The list ends with, "famines, pestilences, and earthquakes in divers places " (vs. 7).

**Temple, Third and Fourth -** Solomon built and dedicated the first Temple (2 Chronicles 5-7), on Mount Moriah where Abraham had prepared to offer Isaac in sacrifice (Genesis 22:2, 13). The second Temple was erected late in the sixth century B.C.E., by a remnant returning from the captivity in Babylon. This temple was refurbished by the Herods in a program of over four decades.

The Third Temple will be built just after the beginning of the Seven-Year Great Tribulation by the Antichrist. It is not clear how access to the Temple Mount will be accomplished, now in the hands of Muslim authorities. After centuries of Jewish sorrow over the destruction of the Temple, to give the opening of Jewish sacrifices once more a false veneer of divine approval, it is dedicated to Jehovah, the God of Israel. God accepts what is given to Him (Revelation 11:1,2). After 3 ½ years, the Antichrist breaks his covenant allowing the Jewish sacrifices and makes himself the object of worship (Daniel 9:27; Matthew 24:15-21; 2 Thessalonians 2:3-4). Much of this novel deals with the significance of the building of the Third Temple.

The Fourth Temple will be built soon after the return of the Messiah at the end of the Great Tribulation, on a Jerusalem-area landscape vastly different from the present topography.

***"That One"*** - This novel places these words in the mouths of the Antichrist and his henchman in order for them to avoid mentioning the Messiah by name. This artifice seems consistent with the fact that demon forces know their end as the enemies of Jehovah.

***Treyf, Treyfah*** - Foods forbidden to Jews through Leviticus 11 and the glosses on those regulations added over the centuries.

**The Time of Jacob's Trouble** - Jeremiah 30:6-7. Jeremiah's title for the Great Tribulation, (above).

**Universal Church** – Our name to describe the unification of the antigod, antibible, antichrist elements that coalesce around the skeleton and sinew of the Roman Catholic Church in the Great Tribulation. We assume from the covenant that Antichrist will make with the Jews to permit the Temple to be rebuilt and sacrifices to resume will have a hidden accord giving worship in the rest of the world to ungodly cults and world religions united. This one-world religion will be destroyed in the middle of the Tribulation when the Temple sacrifices are proscribed.

|  |  |
|---|---|
| **Questions?** | **Grace Bible Mission**<br>**P O Box 1414, Lee's Summit MO 64063-7414** |

# How to be a follower of the Messiah
## Saved, certain, bound for Heaven

You must agree with God about your sin *nature*. Your sinful acts are the expression of what you are by nature. This nature must be replaced with a new nature. A religious leader in Jesus' day, came to the Messiah by night. He had flowery things to say about Jesus, but Jesus saw his real need: a new nature. Jesus said, "ye must be born again" (John 3:3,7). Listen to the Prophet Isaiah: "But we are all as an unclean thing, and all our righteousnesses are as filthy rags; and we all do fade as a leaf; and our iniquities, like the wind, have taken us away" (Isaiah 64:6).

A righteous God must judge the sinner. Ezekiel testified:
"Therefore I will judge you, O house of Israel, every one according to his ways, saith the Lord God. Repent, and turn yourselves from all your transgressions, so iniquity shall not be your ruin. Cast away from you all your transgressions. whereby ye have transgressed; and make you a new heart and a new spirit: for why will ye die, O house of Israel? For I have no pleasure in the death of him that dieth, saith the Lord God: wherefore turn yourselves, and live ye" (Ezekiel 18:30-32). The Gentiles face the same decisions about sin; the same certain judgment!

God saw our need. He had no interest in the burnt offerings of Israel as a lasting sacrifice for sins (see Hosea 6:6). He had a lamb for sacrifice, God's own Son. Isaiah described his sufferings: "He is despised and rejected of men; a man of sorrows, and acquainted with grief: and we his as it were our faces from him; he was despised, an we esteemed him not. Surely he hath borne our griefs, and carried our sorrows: yet we did esteem him stricken, smitten of God, and afflicted. But he was wounded for our transgressions, he was bruised for our iniquities: the chastisement of our peace was upon him; and with his stripes we are healed. All we like sheep have gone astray; we have turned every one to his own way; and the Lord hath laid on him the iniquity of us all" (Isaiah 53:3-6).

Now the decision is yours. You are a sinner. God will judge sin and sinners. The way of escape is to invite Jesus the Messiah, here and now, to save you. In your own way, ask Jesus right now to save you from your sins. He will. Jesus said: "My sheep hear my voice, and I know them, and they follow me: and I give unto them eternal life and they shall never perish, neither shall any man pluck them out of my hand" John 10:27-28).

(See the closing portion of Chapter Six for a dialogue presentation of these truths).